Attention all CIERP certification students: Please read the Introduction for important updated information on the CIERP certification program.

ERP: A-Z Implementer's Guide For Success

ERP: A-Z Implementer's Guide For Success

Travis Anderegg, CFPIM, CIRM, CIERP

Resource Publishing
Eau Claire, WI

ISBN 0-9700352-1-7

Library of Congress Card Number: xx-xxxxxx

Printed and bound by Resource Publishing.
Build 1.0.164

This book is dedicated to the ERP forces-users, project managers, consultants, team leaders, programmers, technicians, venders, service providers, executives- and all others that entered the war rooms to unravel the mysteries behind the ERP fables, in recognition of the small children that tried to understand their parent's problems wondering when they were going to come home, and to my comrades, that had to bear notions of how everything was going to be ok and witty humor of the author.

Special thanks to the following CIBRES associates that have contributed greatly to this publication and the general body of knowledge for ERP systems.

Janice Knox, CIERP
Research Associate
CIBRES Organization

Dr. Rhonda Hensley, CIERP
Educational Developer
North Carolina A&T State University

Dr. Joanne Sulek, CIERP
Educational Developer
North Carolina A&T State University

Beth DePopus
Educational Programs
CIBRES Organization

Ronnie Bishop, CPIM, CPA, CIERP
Internal Consultant
Titan Wheel International Corporation

Leif DuVall, CIERP
Corp Process Systems Mgr
Kay Chemical Co, div of Ecolab, Inc

Introduction

The purpose of this book is to make ERP (Enterprise Resource Planning) successful. It is amazing that after four decades of effort in trying to make ERP and its predecessors successful, 60 to 80 percent of all ERP systems will either fail or not meet expectations. Reviewing the material that I collected over the years leading up to this publication, I found the usefulness of the material falling into three basic categories: helpful, of no help, and poison. Most of the material discussed the meaning of ERP and the components of a good system. Only a small portion specifically addressed *how* to be successful in the implementation and use of an ERP system. Many of the books and articles were much too general and did not consider the delicate intricacies of today's complex ERP systems.

With this book all levels of ERP practitioners and students can develop foundation knowledge required for implementing successful ERP systems. Successful ERP systems do not happen by chance. They start with people like you, looking to understand through education and research, what makes these complex systems click. After reading this book, you will understand that ERP systems work closely with people in the functional modules of the business in creating the successful ERM (Enterprise Resource Management) system. All too often management will blame ERP systems for their resource management problems not knowing the difference between the two. Through the use of this publication you'll have the opportunity to discover what the *real* problem is.

ERP is a very popular theme that has received much interest in recent years. A barrage of articles, presentations, books, advertising and software demos have created shell shock for the professional communities in an attempt to glorify its goodness. Many of these efforts have been more fallacy than delivery of good content. All of these combined efforts have not achieved one simple goal: to increase the success rate of ERP. This book reviews the overall perspective of ERP and its relationship in helping companies achieve the long-term competitive advantage in the marketplace needed to put this methodology in perspective for the common practitioner.

The creation of the CIERP certification program has brought a historical new standard to the ERP industry. CIERP stands for Certified Implementer of Enterprise Resource Planning. The certification ensures that the basic skill sets necessary to successfully implement and maintain an ERP system are present. Upon successfully passing the certification the participant will be legally certified by the CIBRES organization to use CIERP after their name and will receive their certification papers by mail.

The CIERP is a professional certification that recognizes individuals for their level of expertise and knowledge in ERP (Enterprise Resource Planning) systems. It has been developed for the purpose of advancing professionals and companies who use and implement ERP systems.

A wide variety of people will find CIERP a valuable certification for career advancement and company growth. Some positions include:

- Project Managers
- Consultants
- ERP Team Members
- End Users
- Senior Management
- Functional Managers
- Students
- Implementers

- Help Desk Support

Now companies and practitioners have a standard to gauge their knowledge. Those successfully passing the CIERP certification exam will be recognized throughout the world as having mastered the basic knowledge for making ERP systems successful. The certification exam is available in 1000s of cities across the United States and many foreign countries. To check for testing opportunities in your area visit CIBRES on the web at www.cibres.com.

Individuals may choose to prepare for the certification exam by attending seminars, classes, or through self-study techniques. The CIBRES website at www.cibres.com offers much information on the CIERP certification program including:

- Educational materials
- Seminars and educational classcs
- Testing dates and locations
- Listing of CIERP certified professionals
- Press releases
- Program reviews
- E-mail subscription services
- Learning tools
- Articles and news

The certification exam may be taken through a variety of outlets. The test consists of multiple choice questions. It covers all the fundamental aspects of an ERP system. No information, specific to an ERP vendor, will be tested. The objective of the test is to ensure that the practitioner contains the knowledge that is common to all ERP systems for their implementation and successful use. No preparation should be done without using the latest educational materials from the CIBRES organization. The content of the certification exam and educational materials changes frequently to reflect trends in technology that effect the ERP industry.

About 67% of the exam is based upon this textbook ("*ERP: A-Z Implementer's Guide For Success*"). The remaining content of the exam comes from the general body of knowledge that includes other related publications from the CIBRES organization and publications from other sources.

A study strategy for any CIERP student should include the study of the basic concepts found in the CIERP certification textbook ("*ERP: A-Z Implementer's Guide For Success*"). The chapter on *Diagnostic and Measurement Systems* needs special attention for CIERP preparation canidates. Students should understand how the Scorecard system works, but will not be tested on specific questions found in the subchapters (18.x).

All of us at the CIBRES organization look forward to your success with your ERP system and the CIERP certification program.

Contents

When I first heard the term ERP used at our company I thought it was a new kind of early retirement program.

1

Introduction to Enterprise Resource Planning

ERP stands for Enterprise Resource Planning. It is the software system that keeps today's businesses running. Most companies that have multiple business functions have an ERP system. The majority of companies struggle in achieving the full benefits of an ERP system. This is related in part to the complexity of ERP systems and management not understanding fundamental principles of ERP systems. For ERP systems to function properly they must work in harmony with the functional day to day activities of the business. The process of combining ERP systems with the functional activities of the business makes up ERM (Enterprise Resource Management). Very few companies can survive without a functional ERM system.

ERP systems are an evolutionary product. The predecessors to modern day ERP systems have gone by a number of different acronyms. Some of the acronyms that have caused some confusion over the years include: MRP, MRP II, ERP, and more recently: ERM. A graphical depiction of the evolution of modern-day ERP systems is shown in Figure 1-1. Previous research in MRP (Material Requirements Planning) and related topics focused on four fundamental areas. These areas included: economic order quantity (EOQ), safety stock, bill of materials processing (BOMP), and work order management. They served as the cornerstones for emerging MRP systems to follow in the mid 1960s. These cornerstones had been in practice throughout industry long prior to the advent of MRP. What was the turning point in the mid 1960s that enabled the integration of these four areas into a single system called MRP?

The answer: the computer. How the computer changed everything! The computer began the journey into modern-day planning systems.

The four acronyms used that include or are related to ERP systems include:

MRP:	Material Requirements Planning
MRP II:	Manufacturing Resource Planning
ERP:	Enterprise Resource Planning
ERM:	Enterprise Resource Management

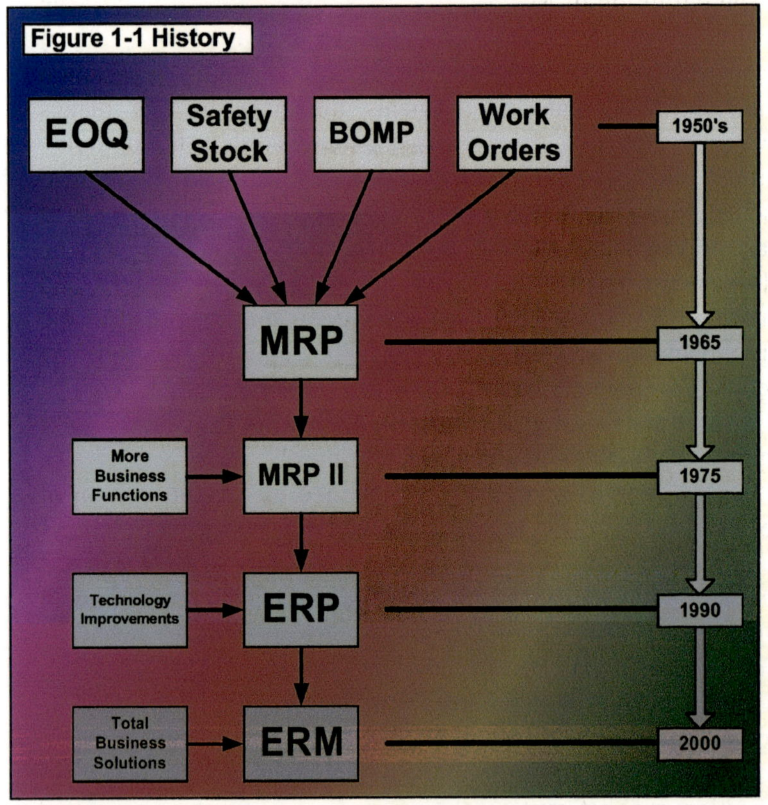

Figure 1-1 History

By 1975 enough MRP systems had been installed to begin the formation of MRP II systems. Confusion between MRP II and MRP began shortly after the introduction of MRP II. The problem with confusing terminology began with education and the generic definitions of MRP and MRP II. When students, consultants, practitioners, and educators started using the term MRP, it was unclear whether the discussion was about MRP or MRP II.

The APICS organization, an educational society of resource management, has actively followed the history of MRP systems through numerous conferences, seminars, and publications since its origin.

The definition of MRP as explained by the 9th edition of the APICS dictionary is: "A set of techniques that uses bill of material data, inventory data, and the master production schedule to calculate requirements for materials. It makes recommendations to release replenishment orders for material. Further, because it is time phased, it makes recommendations to reschedule open orders when due dates and need dates are not in phase. Time phased MRP begins with the items listed on the MPS and determines (1) the quantity of all components and materials required to fabricate those items and (2) the date the components and materials are required. Time phased MRP is accomplished by exploding the bill of material, adjusting for inventory quantities on hand or on order, and offsetting the net requirements by the appropriate lead times."

The definition of MRP II as explained by the 9th edition of the APICS dictionary is: "A method for the effective planning of all resources of a manufacturing company. Ideally, it addresses operational planning in units, financial planning in dollars, and has a simulation capability to answer "what if" questions. It is made up of a variety of functions, each linked together: business planning, sales and operations planning, production planning, master production scheduling, material requirements planning, capacity requirements planning, and the execution support systems for capacity and material. Output from these systems is integrated with financial reports such as the business plan, purchase commitment report, shipping budget, and inventory projection in dollars. Manufacturing resource planning is a direct outgrowth and extension of closed loop MRP."

The definitions of MRP and MRP II are generally well accepted by students, consultants, practitioners, and educators. Lack of education was, and still is, the only real reason for confusing MRP with MRP II.

Remember BRP? It stands for: Business Resource Planning. Use of BRP was an attempt at renaming MRP II systems. It is the same thing as an ERP system. The use of the word "business" in BRP recognized that an MRP II system was more than a tool for manufacturing companies. The term recognized that the functionality found in an MRP II system applied equally well to many other types of businesses. Some of these functions include accounting, sales, purchasing, and inventory.

BRP fit nicely with business process reengineering. BRP did not last long. At about the same time, ERP (Enterprise Resource Planning) came to age. Practitioners actively working with planning systems and keeping abreast of the changes, saw ERP as exactly the same as MRP II. The only difference was that the name had changed.

Within a few years after the introduction of ERP, it became apparent that not all professionals agreed upon the definition of an ERP system. Some sources had defined ERP systems as: An accounting oriented information system that uses new technologies such as graphical user interfaces, relational databases, fourth generation languages, computer-aided software engineering tools, and client/server architecture.

Some practitioners found this definition of an ERP system a little confusing. MRP II or ERP may or may not include capabilities such as fourth generation languages or relational databases. Technology is important, but it should not dominate the definition of an ERP system. A definition of an ERP system should include the functional areas needed to operate most businesses. Some of these business functions include:

accounting, manufacturing, distribution, purchasing, sales, inventory, quality, etc.

An ERP system is more accurately defined as: ERP, standing for Enterprise Resource Planning, a complete enterprise wide business software solution. The ERP system consists of software support modules such as: marketing and sales, field service, product design and development, production and inventory control, procurement, distribution, industrial facilities management, process design and development, manufacturing, quality, human resources, finance and accounting, and information services. Integration of the modules is accomplished without the duplication of information. ERP systems are an outgrowth of MRP II systems and a supporting function of ERM using available technology.

What is ERM? At the time of this writing, it has not been well defined by many sources. Many different definitions have emerged, many of them conflicting with each other.

Despite all the different definitions that have emerged for ERM, one common concept exists for them all: characteristics of ERP are part of ERM. Does ERM have the same relation to ERP as ERP had to MRP II? The answer is no.

Some of the definitions that have emerged directly define ERM as being a software system. ERM stands for Enterprise Resource Management; the key words Resource and Management can be stressed. Management and software are not the same! Software is a tool to aid in management, not replace it! Enterprise Resource Management can be thought of as the tools and techniques for managing the resources of an enterprise. ERP is only one of the many resources to be found in any enterprise.

In Figure 1-2 we see that ERP + Functions (business functions) = ERM. In support of the ERM definition the two fundamental building blocks that make up an ERP system are integration and functional software modules. The ERM equation can also be stated as: integration + functional software modules + business functions = ERM.

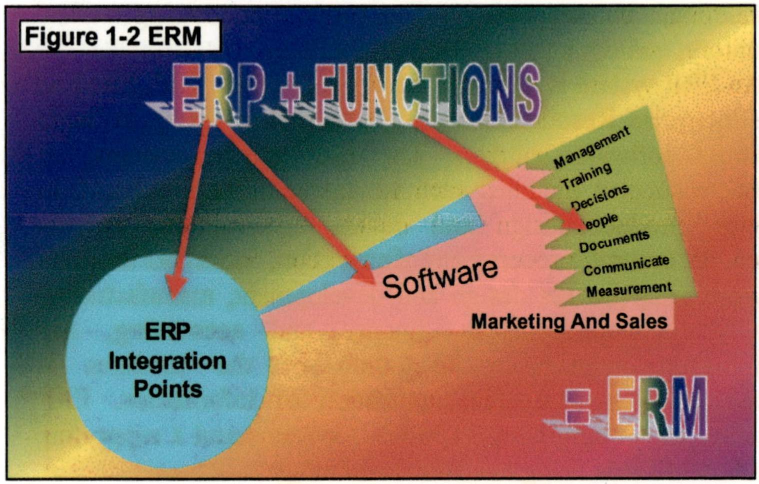

The functional part of an ERP system provides for commonly understood business process flows. Some common functions include: payroll, human resources, accounts payable, general ledger, accounts receivable, purchasing, inventory, material requirements planning, shop floor control, sales orders, forecasting and more. It's not uncommon for some ERP systems to contain 75 or more of these business functions.

The integration part of an ERP system provides for the connectivity between the functional business process flows. Integration can be thought of as the communication technique. Often technology plays a significant role in integration and communication. Some common ways that communication takes place through the use of integration in ERP systems include: source code, local area networks, wide area networks, Internet, email, protocols and databases.

ERP systems use these functions and integration to synchronize and coordinate the operations of the business. Few companies excel in successfully integrating their ERP systems with operational management. The process of integrating and synchronizing a company's business functions is known as Enterprise Resource Management (ERM). Companies become more demanding in how well their ERM system works as they learn more about their troubles with ERP.

Understanding the difference between ERP and ERM is essential for the successful use of an ERP system. A large portion of companies that struggle with ERP systems fail because of a lack of understanding between ERP and ERM. In cases like these, the functional parts of a module, such as management, documentation, training, etc., are not performed properly.

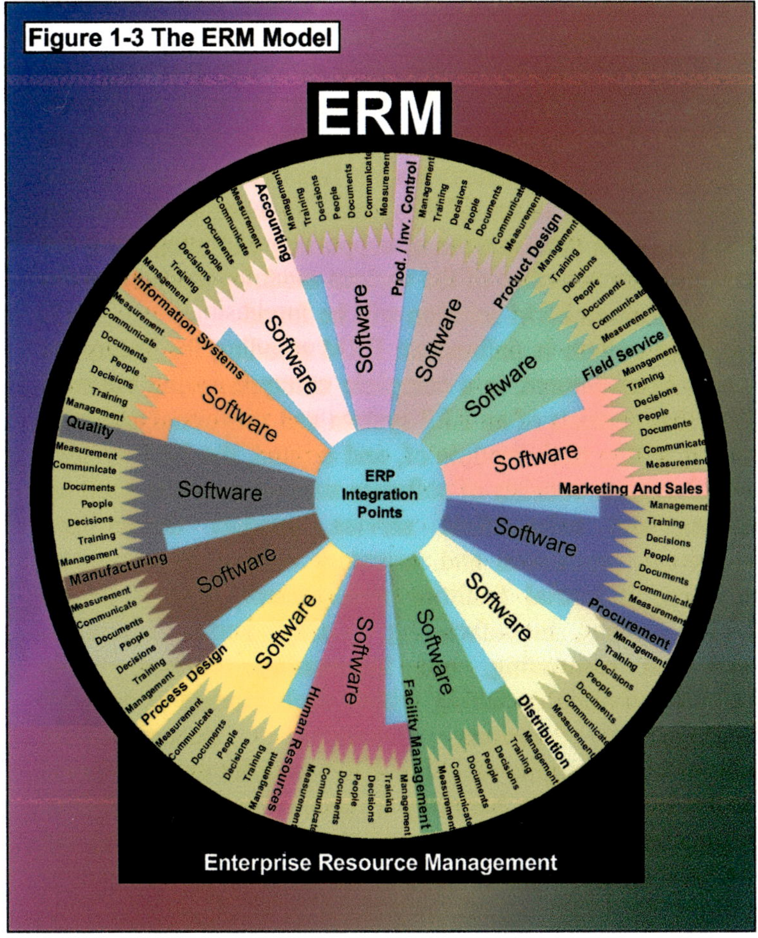

Figure 1-3 The ERM Model

Figure 1-3 defines the ERM model. Towards the center of the circle is the traditional ERP model consisting of all the various support functions of an ERP system and their related integration. Moving towards the outer edges of the circle is the integration with the software for the various activities that occur inside that function.

The activities that occur inside each function include: management, decisions, training, people, documentation etc. This process of combining the ERP system with functional activities of each module makes up the ERM model.

How does a company's use of a software planning tool determine if it is ERM or ERP? If a company uses a software package for the purpose of replacing a legacy system without concern of how it will integrate with functional activities, then the software works as an ERP system. If a company uses an ERP system with the intention of supporting and integrating the system with the activities of the various modules throughout the enterprise, then an ERM solution will be found.

An ERM system is defined as: ERM standing for Enterprise Resource Management, is a complete enterprise wide business solution that consists of an ERP system and functional activities occurring within each module of, and around, the ERP system. The ERP system consists of software support modules such as: marketing and sales, field service, product design and development, production and inventory control, procurement, distribution, industrial facilities management, process design and development, manufacturing, quality, human resources, finance and accounting, and information services. The functional activities occurring within each module consist of: management, decisions, training, documentation, communication, people, etc. The ERP modules and functional activities must exist in harmony to become an ERM solution. The integration/interface points of the ERP system bind the entire ERM solution together.

The ERM model is not a passing fad. The ERM model has existed since the mid 1970's, and was clearly recognized, but never received a formal definition. As long as there are companies that use ERP systems and perform activities within functional modules, the ERM model will exist. Whether the term ERM will become another fatality like BRP is yet to be seen. With proper education and nurturing, practitioners and educators will be able to avoid the confusion that occurred with MRP and the confusing definitions of ERP systems.

The success of an ERM system is dependent upon people. Too many companies have taken the approach that competitive market advantage can be programmed into an ERP system as a substitute for an ERM system. The success of an ERP system works closely with how people use and integrate their functional business activities with the ERP system. Figure 1-4 shows the old way of using ERP systems compared to the new way.

Today's ERP industry has evolved into a multi-billion dollar industry. Unlike the automotive industry, where a few giants dominate, allowing consumers only a few choices, there are over 1000 ERP vendors and solutions to from which to choose. However, most of them are very small and escape the detection of companies looking for new ERP systems. At any given time between 60 and 70 percent of the market will be occupied by 8 to 12 ERP vendors.

ERP systems do not have to be purchased. Many are developed in house as a complete custom solution. The "home grown" systems are often designed for maximum streamlined efficiency and provide very close or perfect matches for business process flows. Just as with commercial ERP systems, these home grown systems have various degrees of success. More companies migrate from home grown systems to commercial ERP solutions than vice versa. Often companies find the incredible complexity of developing and maintaining an ERP system in house to be beyond the developmental and support capability of their organization.

Figure 1-4 ERP systems

Old Way	New Way
Sue the ERP vendor for bad software	Build long term strategic relationships with the ERP vendor
Treat ERP as a software system	Treat ERP as a people system
Massive cost overruns	Cost as expected
Lack of top management support	Top management provides support and nourishment
Expect quick easy implementations	Realistic expectations
Install software and use it	Carefully prototype and test software before using it
ERP system is obsolete before implementation is complete	Finish implementation before obsolescence
React to massive problems	Dynamic control of the system
Deal with ERP problems	Prevent ERP problems through education
ERP system used for data collection, processing, and output	ERP system integrated with long term strategic and tactical planning
Lack of ownership	ERP users embrace their systems
Lots of software packages	One or few software packages
Reward non-participants	Reward implementers
Implement and forget	Continuous ongoing improvement
Few ERP users	Lots of ERP users
ERP operates independently of the organization	ERP system integrates functions tightly as a part of ERM
Outside consultants implement software	Company employees implement software, consultants work as consultants
Electronic communication conducted in-house	Electronic communication is conducted with outside world
Communication through chaos	Communication through integration
Limited data access	Bountiful data access

Case Study
Beta Site - Lesson Learned the Hard Way

In July of 1999, a Californian based high tensile steel cable manufacture discovered that its commercial ERP system was not compliant with year 2000. The company looked at several different solutions ranging from a new commercial ERP system to custom developed solutions.

After talking with several different commercial ERP vendors they discovered that it would be unlikely that they could install an ERP system by the year 2000. Consultants were too busy helping other companies at the time and the solutions were just too complex for rapid implementation.

Looking for simpler solutions, they turned to an outside subcontractor programmer that they had relied on for many years. After talking with him, they discovered that his company had developed an ERP solution for a thread manufacturer. He felt that there were many similarities and it would not be too difficult to "adjust" the code to their needs.

After discussions with the programmer's company, it was agreed that the cable manufacturer would become a beta test site and receive the software for free, provided they pay for all programming services.

This took a great psychological load off of the company, for now they did not have to worry about selecting software, finding financial resources to support it, and consultants to implement it. Everything could be programmed in from a trusted source.

This allowed the managers of the company to return to their responsibilities while their trusted programmer started with the process of programming.

The proposed solution was a distributed computing solution that ran on a local area network, much different from the centralized solution that they were using. The management believed that being a beta test site was not that big of a deal. The idea of the low cost and not needing to purchase additional hardware, created a temptation that they could not refuse.

It turned out that very little code was transferable from the thread company. Most of the code had to be reprogrammed.

Everything went along well with a management team that was disconnected from the process until the first week of December 1999. Some how, all the critical day-to-day data had to be transferred over to the new system. No conversion programs were written and not enough time was left to create them.

Power users came to the rescue performing data entry tasks for critical files. Superhuman efforts with people working around the clock prepared the go live date on January 1st, 2000. On December 31st they were ready, or so they thought.

The next week an unbelievable number of problems occurred. Programs started crashing, transactions were mysteriously disappearing, miscalculations were occurring in cost and price files, sections of the database were going corrupt and the wrong information was appearing on videos. The company quickly shifted its focus from operations management and customer service to maintaining and supporting the new ERP system.

The new ERP system consumed a huge amount of company resources. Each and every step had to be carefully checked and rechecked manually. Almost all the ERP users' workloads increased to 70+ hours per week.

Case Study

Beta Site - Lesson Learned the Hard Way (cont)

Operations management and customer service had suffered severely. Customers were being billed the wrong amounts, receiving other customer's products, not getting refunds, and a host of other problems. They had gone from best in the industry to worst in a period of just three months.

Realizing the graveness of the situation, the functional managers called a meeting to decide what to do. They were in too deep at this point and they could not turn back to the legacy system because of year 2000 issues. The primary issue was one of support. There were not enough people to support the system. Between them all, each functional manager agreed to give up their best computer users to spend 100% of their time troubleshooting and supporting the system.

As dedicated employees having ownership in the company, they jumped to the challenge, blasting away at system problems, working many 21 hour days.

The functional areas of the business started hiring clerical workers to support a paper based backup system and quality checkers to manually check everything for errors that came out of the system.

The programmer worked steadily to help solve programming and technical problems in the system. Some managers greatly feared his withdrawal because he was the only person alive that understood the technical side of the system. Relations had been badly stressed.

Slowly they made progress in stabilizing the system. By February it looked like they were going to survive, although not well. Customer service still suffered badly and operations management struggled. Looking at a very long recovery period with a deteriorating customer base, the company decided to call in an outside consultant agency that specialized in ERP systems to audit the situation.

The consulting company came in and did a thorough review of the entire system and interviewed all the critical stakeholders.

Upon completion of the audit, the consultant company documented its findings and explained to the management what it had found.

The consultant company felt that the company was in a vulnerable situation using a completely proprietary ERP system that only one person knew how to program. There was going to be no quick solution to the problem. A new commercial ERP system, with access to support services, was going to have to be purchased and installed, requiring the company to dedicate another team above and beyond the one that was supporting the current system.

The company continued to focus their efforts on stabilizing the system while beginning a search for a commercial ERP system.

The IS manager stated: "We did not really understand what it meant to be a beta test site. Had we known then what we know now we would have done things much differently".

The company will continue to struggle with their current system for some time to come as well as another ERP implementation that could take them into the year 2003. A lot of unnecessary money had been spent and their business threatened because fundamental concepts of ERP systems had been overlooked.

Some companies have much less need for a computerized ERP system than others. Business environments that tend to have stable process flows, like high volume repetitive manufacturing in Japan, can get by with minimal to no computerized ERP systems. But larger organizations that undergo changes in business process flows need some type of computer system capable of collecting, storing, and processing information.

As we move into the future we continue to learn from our mistakes. What we expect from ERP systems, how we use them, and the benefits we receive from them are slowly changing as we become better trained and educated in these complex systems.

Questions--

1. What does ERP stand for?
2. What does ERM stand for?
3. What two things make up an ERM system?
4. What is a "home grown" system?
5. What did ERP evolve out of?
6. What are the two fundamental components that make up an ERP system?
7. Why do businesses need ERP systems?
8. Why do many companies struggle in their use and implementation of ERP systems?
9. Why is the role of people so important for the success of an ERP or an ERM system?
10. What are 10 examples of business functions?
11. What is a software module?
12. What are 5 examples of functional parts of a module?

We found that our ERP system communicated through its integration, and achieved its integration through its communication.

2

Basic ERP Concepts and Design

This chapter reviews basic concepts and designs found in most modern ERP systems. Modern computer technology has tremendously increased in capability over the last four decades. Despite these increases, the basic concepts of an ERP system and how it works have changed very little in this time period.

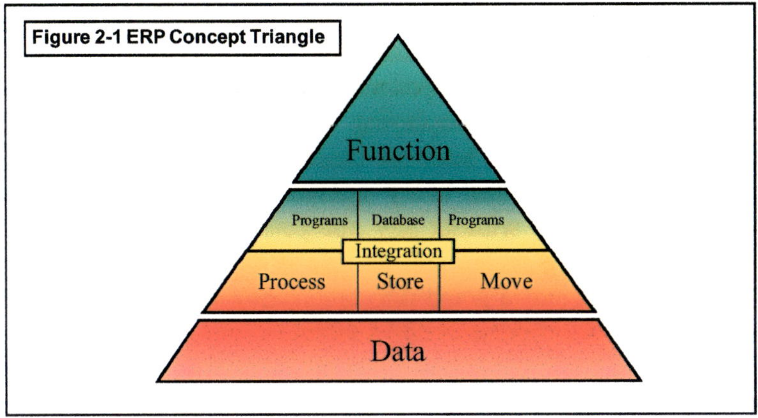

Figure 2-1 ERP Concept Triangle

Figure 2-1 shows the basic components of an ERP system. All ERP systems contain at least these basic components. At the base of the triangle the foundation takes its form as data. Data is the information needed to run a business. It takes the form of account numbers, sales orders, inventory, etc. All businesses need to handle data in three different ways. They need to process the data, such as performing some calculation. They need to store information in a secure place such as the database. And they need to move data between databases, collection devices, programs, and output devices. Through integration, programs interact with databases as they process, store and display/collect (move) data. The process of programs interacting with databases for the purpose of processing, storing and displaying/collecting data represents function. Functionality represents the highest point of an ERP system and can only be achieved through the solid foundations created at the lower levels.

People play a most important role in all the components shown in Figure 2-1. Many leading ERP articles and books have stressed an ERP system as a people system. This is a very interesting observation when considering ERP systems before the introduction of the computer. According to today's viewpoint, an ERP system is some type of computer-based system. While today's ERP systems are represented by some type of computer-based system, computer-based systems are not required in achieving the components shown in figure 2-1. The process of storing data, displaying it, and processing it to achieve a certain type of business function began in the early 1800's. Some businesses today operate a system with the functionality of ERP without any computer-based system. A small number of businesses still do this as a matter of routine while others do it out of some dire emergency such as a failed or struggling ERP implementation attempt.

Data creates the foundation of any ERP system. A database is a centralized repository for storing and organizing data. With today's technology it usually exists in some type of electronically accessible system on some physical medium. The number of databases used by ERP vendors is small compared to the total number of available ERP solutions on the marketplace. With over 1000 ERP solutions available, almost all of them will resort to one of 20 commercial database solutions. Some ERP vendors choose to completely develop their own databases with varying degrees of success. An even smaller number seek truly exotic solutions as they merge databases directly with source code used in operating their programs. There have been few recorded success stories using this strategy.

Databases can be broken down into several basic components including: files, records, and data fields. Databases usually contain many of each.

Files, sometimes called tables, can be thought of as "mini databases". Modern ERP systems usually contain at least one file for each of the major functional modules of an ERP system. Inventory management contains its own dedicated file along with sales, purchasing, accounts payable, etc. Some ERP systems combine all files into one "super file" marking each record as belonging to some specific functional module. But the majority will use configuration as shown in Figure 2-2.

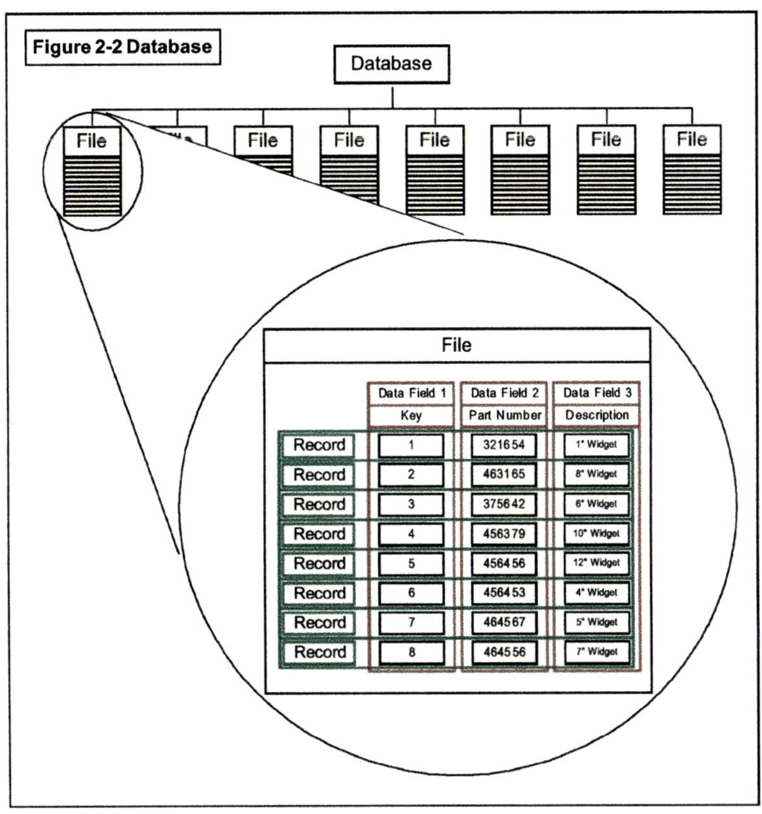

Figure 2-2 Database

Records are a grouping of related information specific to some functional need. Information is seldom duplicated inside a record. Almost all the information found within a record is unique compared to the other information also found in that same record.

A data element, also called a data field, represents a piece of information in a database. Data elements are usually predefined to receive some characteristic type of information shown in Figure 2-2 such as telephone number, name, part number, sales order number, a description, etc. Some databases and ERP vendors allow the addition of data elements or leave some data elements blank in the database for some type of future need.

The concept of a city resembles that of a database. At the highest level, the city is the equivalent of a database. Moving down to the next level, a section of the town, such as eastside or westside, can be thought of as a file. A particular street within that section of town can be thought of as a record and the houses along the street are the equivalent of data elements.

The concept of the key is important in understanding relational databases. The purpose of the key is to create a unique identity for each and every record within a file that will help it relate to information and other files. By use of keys, databases can significantly reduce the amount of data they have to store while still providing the same amount of information.

Figure 2-3 Without Key / One File

Data Element 1	Data Element 2	Data Element 3	4......99	Data Element 100	Data Element 1	Data Element 2
32151	Widget	Red	......	591	A-10	54
32151	Widget	Red	......	591	B-5	89
32151	Widget	Red	......	591	G-9	52
32151	Widget	Red	......	591	C-1	1325
32151	Widget	Red	......	591	G-3	21
100 Records x 102 Data Elements = 10,200						

Figure 2-4 With Key / Two Files

File 1						File 2		
Data Element 1	Data Element 2	Data Element 3	......	Data Element 100	Key		Data Element 1	Data Element 2
32151	Widget	Red	......	591	1	1	A-10	54
						1	B-5	89
						1	G-9	52
						1	C-1	1325
						1	G-3	21

(1 Record x 101 Data Elements) + (100 Records x 3 Data Elements) = 401

Figure 2-3 and figure 2-4 show the powerful ability of using keys in reducing database size. In figure 2-3 we see a file structure containing basic item information, the area in gray, and location and quantity information to the right, the area in yellow. The basic item information contains 100 data elements, all of which are identical. Variable information is found on the right hand side shaded in yellow. These are inventory locations and on hand quantities. In this example there are 100 records in the file with 102 data elements creating columns across the top. The 100 records times 102 data elements equals 10,200 pieces of information.

Figure 2-4 demonstrates the concept of using a key. The single file that existed in figure 2-4 is now broken into two separate files. In file 1 the total number of records now becomes just one. Another data element is added to both file 1 and file 2, which is the key. File 2 still contains 100 records. File 2 contains 100 records because each and every record is different or a unique. Through the use of the key, the computer can take the first record from file 1 and connect to the 100 different records found in file 2. The computer takes this information from two different files, combines them in memory, and then sends the output to reports or video monitors for further processing. For the end user of an ERP system, the file structure of figure 2-4 looks no different than figure 2-3. As shown in the calculation in figure 2-4 ERP systems are capable of storing the same exact information with only 401 pieces of information, approximately four percent of the 10,200 shown in figure 2-3. The larger the database, the greater the savings.

Programs serve as the link between databases and functionality. The functionality of an ERP system is achieved through the process of programs interacting with databases. Programs provide many important functions including:

- Collecting data
- Temporarily storing data
- Processing data
- Exporting data
- Transferring data

Programs collect information from a variety of sources as shown in figure 2-5. Programs collect information from people through a variety of input devices including keyboards, mouses, bar-code scanners, and radio frequency terminals. Databases serve as another important source of information previously collected by other programs. The channels between programs and databases are usually well developed in most ERP systems. Interfaces continually become more important as technology further develops, making communication between computer programs and operating systems easier. Interfaces provide a wide range of input sources including: Internet, EDI, machines, and other software programs.

The Internet has had a major impact on ERP systems and how ERP vendors are marketing to companies. As of the time of this publication, every ERP vendor with more than one-percent market share has adopted some type of Internet strategy. These Internet strategies vary considerably based on the amount of functionality that they choose to provide by use of Internet technology. Almost all provide some type of e-business solutions.

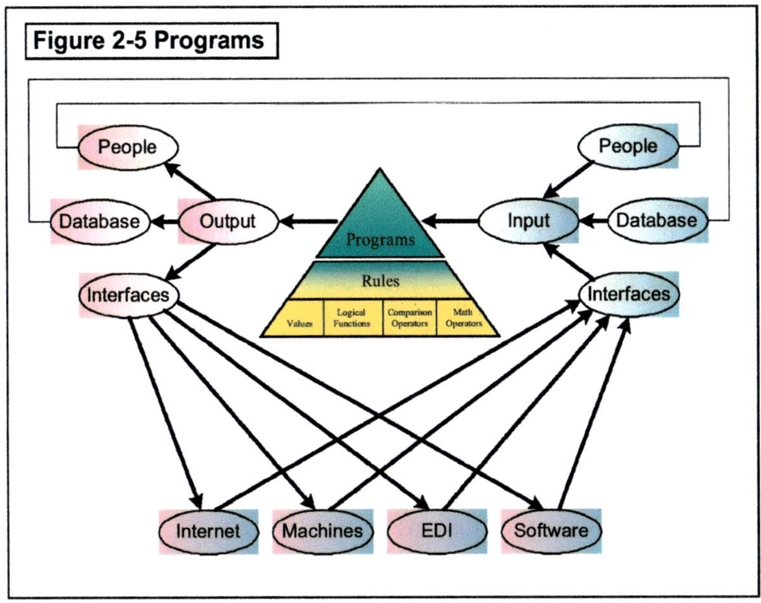

Figure 2-5 Programs

EDI (electronic data interchange) is an electronic communication standard for trading documents. It is generally used for purchase orders and sales orders that use a standardized document format such as X-12. EDI can send shipment authorizations, advance shipping notices, and invoices.

Some companies choose to interface their ERP systems directly with their manufacturing machinery. Some interfaces are so sophisticated that the machines will start automatically according to instructions from the ERP system, and report production quantities as they occur in real time. ERP vendors seldom provide standard interfaces for manufacturing equipment. These interfaces are usually custom developed.

Once the program has collected the information, it can begin processing it. All programs are based on rules. These rules are programmed by developers, and reside directly in the source code of the program.

These rules consist of a series of "if-then" logical functions, comparison operators, mathematical operators, and values.

ERP systems are usually developed through the use of CASE tools. CASE tools are another type of software program that computer programmers type logical functions and comparison operators into. CASE stands for computer-aided software engineering. Its purpose is to provide a method for consistent source code development.

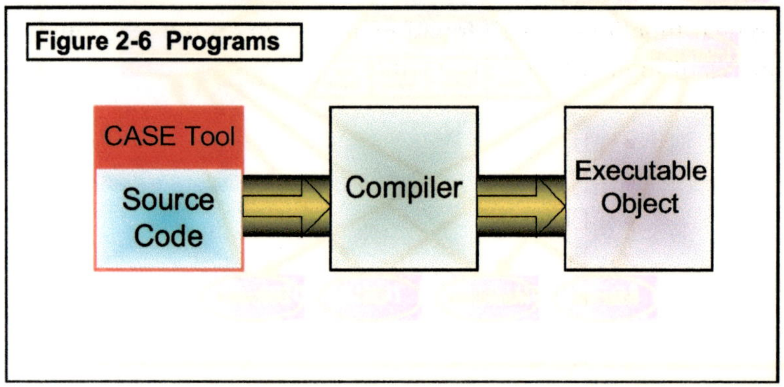

Figure 2-6 Programs

There are two main types of case tools: source code and entire ERP systems. Case tools used for source code have little capability to create consistent source code for ERP systems. Their primary purpose is to develop source code and to provide edit checking to prevent software errors and allow the proper compilation to occur in creating an executable object. An example of an executable object is a program.

Case tools for ERP systems are usually software vendor specific. Case tools for ERP systems allow the consistent stable development of software for all the functional areas of an ERP system. They allow developers to create consistent code that can be understood much easier. By use of case tools for ERP systems, teams of developers and programmers can create an ERP system that looks and feels consistent to anyone. Through the use of CASE tools vendors are able to maintain consistent standards and functionality such as: F1 for help.

After its development, source code is usually submitted to a compiler. A compiler translates the source code into computer optimized execution code. This optimized code takes up less space and can be executed faster than the original source code. Computer optimized execution code is what makes up computer programs. After the compiler is completed, for most ERP systems, an object is created which represents the program. This object can then be attached to menus so users may execute the program upon demand.

Logical functions can be found in almost any program. Some examples of logical functions include:

- If
- Not
- Else
- For
- Next
- Loop
- Do
- While
- Until
- Goto
- Or

Logical functions allow the evaluation of data and a decision making process. Branching instructions can be merged into the evaluation process so the program based upon the data it is evaluating can perform an appropriate response.

Logical functions work closely with comparison operators. Some examples of comparison operators include:

- Equal to
- Greater than
- Less than
- Not equal to

Comparison operators work closely with logical functions and allow programs to compare data to some known standard. The combination of logical functions and comparison operators logic provide an almost infinite number of solutions capable of meeting some of the most demanding requirements to be found in business process flows.

Mathematical operators allow programs to perform calculations in a controlled predetermined way. Some examples of mathematical operators include:

- + Add
- - Subtract
- * Multiply
- / Divide
- ABS Absolute Value
- SQR Square Root

Values are the standard for comparison. The values can be directly hard coded within the source code of program or they can be imported from a variety of sources. The values fall into two broad categories: alpha and numeric. Alpha values are values that contain alpha characters such as letter A, letter B, letter C, etc. Numeric values are values such as No. 1 or No. 315643. Data fields within files are often predefined as being either numeric or alpha.

The term hard coded refers to a program that is fixed in functionality. In other words, it has no flexibility in adapting to the desired change. It can be thought of as the opposite of soft coded.

Figure 2-7 Source Code

```
If Right$(temp$, 2) = "PM" Or Right$(temp$, 2) = "AM" Then
    Col = Col + 1
    If rowtemp < Row Then rowtemp = Row
    Row = 0
End If
```

Figure 2-7 is a simple example of source code showing all four components that make up rules for programs. "If" in the first line is an example of a logical function. "PM" in line one and "Col" in line two are examples of values. "<" in line three is the sign for "less than" which is an example of a comparison operator. The "+" sign in line two is an example of a mathematical operator. Programming, at the source code level, is considered to be one of the most capable methods of achieving functionality in ERP systems. Programs provide great capability for functionality. Once the source code is set and compiled it can be difficult to change because of the deep integration found in ERP systems.

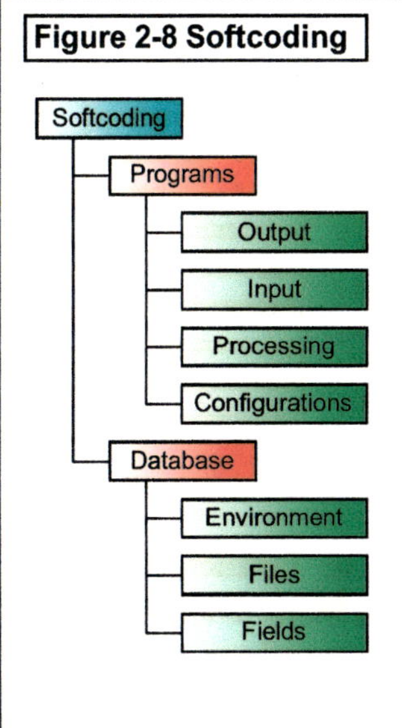

Figure 2-8 Softcoding

Soft coding in programs is important in achieving the desired functionality in any ERP system. Soft coding applies to the output, input, and the processing of data. Configuration version saving has importance because it allows users of ERP systems to operate the same program a variety of ways. Each configuration can be saved to the system's memory and can be recalled in the future for a specific situation. This concept is most helpful when installing a new ERP system during the prototype and development phase.

Soft coding the output of programs occurs in three areas: videos, files, and reports. The soft coding concept for output works equally well for all three.

Videos represent the most interactive way of obtaining information. Videos can be soft coded in a variety of ways to provide flexibility in function. Some different ways of soft coding videos include: data fields, text description, data sort, data selection, and data totaling. Historically speaking, video displays for ERP systems have been limited in their capability to display information. Figure 2-9 shows a video configuration with relatively limited flexibility consistent with what ERP vendors have historically provided. This type of display is capable of showing one record at a time. Soft coding can allow the text description, such as "Part Number", to be changed to "Our Part Number". Soft coding can also allow various fields to be displayed or not displayed given various dependencies.

Figure 2-9 Video Display

Part Number:		Description:	
Type:		Lot Control:	
Location:		Cost:	
Quantity:		Price:	
Planner:		Code 1:	
Buyer:		Code 2:	
Supplier:		Code 3:	
Lead Time:		Code 4:	
Planning Code:		Code 5:	
Order Quantity:		Code 6:	

A dependency is nothing more than an instruction to do something based on some predefined condition. Dependencies work closely with the concept of soft coding and are often used in setting up the security of an ERP system. The number of dependencies in an ERP system varies by vendor, and ranges from zero to ten or more.

A good example is the Cost field in figure 2-9. This information may be very helpful to a cost accountant but may be unnecessary for other functional areas depending upon company policy. Using a dependency combined with soft coding the Cost field will be displayed for the cost accountant, but not for any other user on the system.

Figure 2-10 Video Display

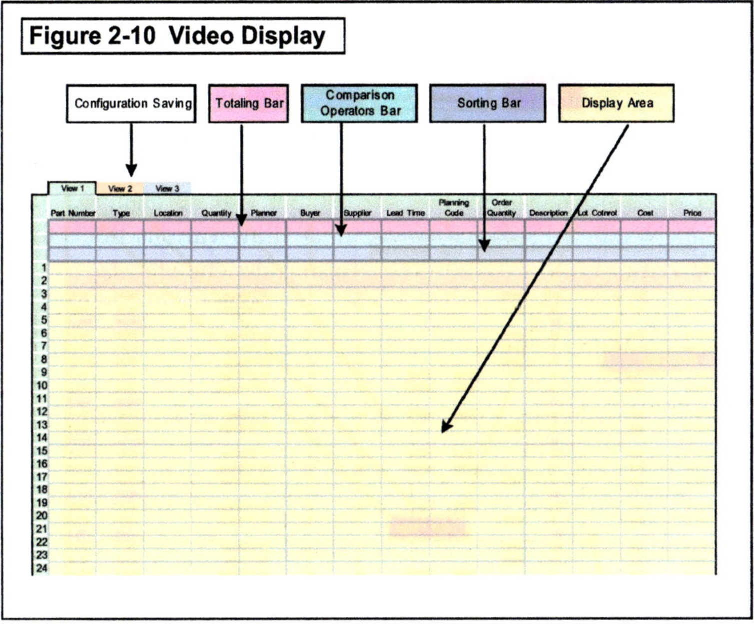

Advancements in computer technology and programming have allowed some ERP vendors to create sophisticated interactive feature rich displays like the one shown in figure 2-10. Its design is much more efficient because it allows the custom display of multiple records at the same time. The comparison operator bar allows almost infinite methods of inquiring on data. The totaling bar allows for the summation of numeric values for numeric data fields based on a different field that is either numeric or alpha based. The sorting of information allows it to be displayed in the most efficient sequence. The configuration saving allows different views to be saved. Each view has a different combination of totaling, comparison operators, and sorting. ERP vendors have historically used report writers to provide totaling, comparison operators, and sorting capabilities. Figure 2-11 shows the concept of totaling, comparison operators, and sorting, all working together to provide a specific display output.

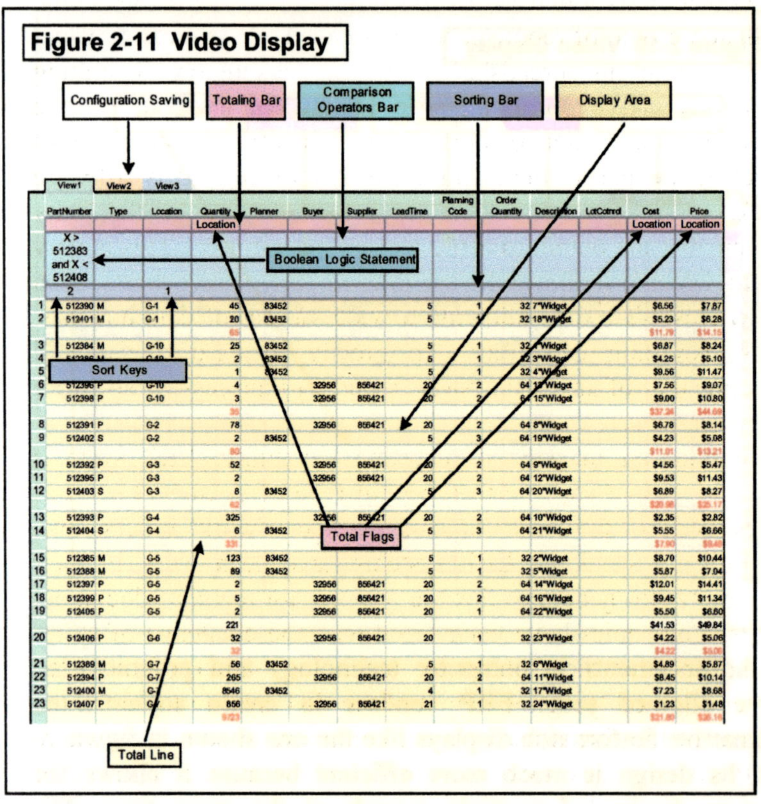

Figure 2-11 Video Display

The comparison operator bar provides the function of data selection. Data totaling works on the principal of sorted data with record changes. The data is first sorted by the Location field, as indicated by sort key number one. Because the Cost,

Quantity, and Price fields are set to total based on the Location field, totals are provided for each one whenever the Location field changes in value. Although figure 2-11 is feature rich compared to figure 2-9, such feature rich capabilities do not necessarily make an ERP system more successful. Simplistic designs as shown in figure 2-9 can perform well if their designs match the business process flows of a company.

The concept of paper-based reports works very similar to the functionality as found in figure 2-11. Most ERP systems come with some type of report generating capability that can create a report output in spreadsheet format. This report generating capability can be program specific, created and run from a general report writer, or created and run from a general report writer that is part of the operating system or third party software package. Some programs and report writers have the capability to generate the output to a file instead of a printer. This is very useful because it allows the use of third party spreadsheets, such as Microsoft's Excel, allowing a wide variety of data analysis. This exporting capability can greatly increase the overall functionality of an ERP system, avoiding unnecessary software modifications.

In addition to general reporting capability, ERP systems generate output specific to a certain type of document such as sales orders, purchase orders, invoices, work orders, etc. Historically speaking, ERP systems have been weak in their capability to generate flexible output for certain document types. Companies have been faced with the challenge of either changing over their forms to match the output of the ERP system or modifying the output of the ERP system to match the format of the forms used by the company. In situations where ERP systems lack flexibility in form output, the industry or business needs dictate a specific output and the form output is usually modified, often at the source code level. Other times ERP systems contain or use a third party form design aid to create flexible form output. These custom output packages often contain graphical capability (for the placement of a company logo), free form text, and calculation capability between fields. The functionality of soft coding for input is needed for the integrity checking of data. Programs use saved configuration settings and UDT (user defined tables) to achieve this effect.

UDTs are considered a form of soft coding for the database. UDTs are tables that consist of a series of codes and text descriptions that are supplied by the ERP vendor or custom created for a specific business environment. The flexibility of an ERP system is greatly extended through the use of UDTs. UDTs are usually attached to a data entry field of a program. In figure 2-12 we see that a UDT is attached to the country field for one billing address. Since the program validates the information against the user-defined table, only CAN, MEX, and USA can be entered. If another country must be used then it must be added to the table. Programs working with user-defined tables ensure consistent stable data that can later ease data processing.

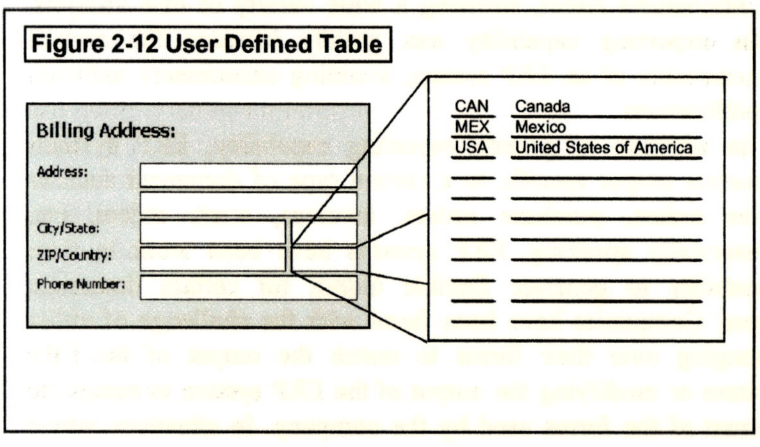

Figure 2-12 User Defined Table

Saved configuration settings do not provide near the flexibility as using the user defined table approach. This, however, does not present a significant disadvantage when only a few options or choices are required that do not require the use of tables. A good example is the country code used in figure 2-

12. A configuration setting could be used to generate a soft error, which would still allow the data entry of an invalid country code. If the switch is turned off, the program generates a hard error, prohibiting data entry until the country code is fixed.

Soft coding for the processing of data by programs is needed in almost every functional module of an ERP system. Soft coding for the processing of data works closely with the soft coding for the output of a program. Sometimes these are so similar to each other they cannot be distinguished from each other. A series of instructions instruct the program how to process the information. These instructions range in complexity from a simple yes/no switch to files or tables containing hundreds of thousands of instructional records.

A good example of soft coding for the processing of data by programs is configuration management. Configuration management works closely with sales order processing in defining the configuration of products for specific customers. Configuration management is highly rules driven, consisting of logical functions and comparison operators. Companies that sell large capital equipment, such as industrial machinery, often use configurators to help configure their products for their customers. Through the use of soft coding, these rules are programmed in through the configurator and stored in files or tables for future use. Because of these rules, the configurator knows how to process the initial information it receives, providing instructions on how to build the capital equipment.

Soft coding is helpful in the files and data elements of the database. Soft coding for databases allows companies to override the default text descriptions and replace it with a company's specific text descriptions. This in turn reduces the learning curve for the new ERP users. This concept applies most strongly to data elements. Some ERP systems allow vocabulary overrides to occur for one particular field throughout the database and programs. These same systems may also allow changes within just programs or the database.

This way the program may contain company specific text description, while the database remains unchanged.

Environments (sometimes called a libraries) represent a database file structure dedicated for one specific task. These specific tasks include: holding the go live data, testing area, post live production area, and conference room pilot. The use of environments greatly increases an ERP systems capability to test and prototype business process flows within the software.

Figure 2-13 Environments

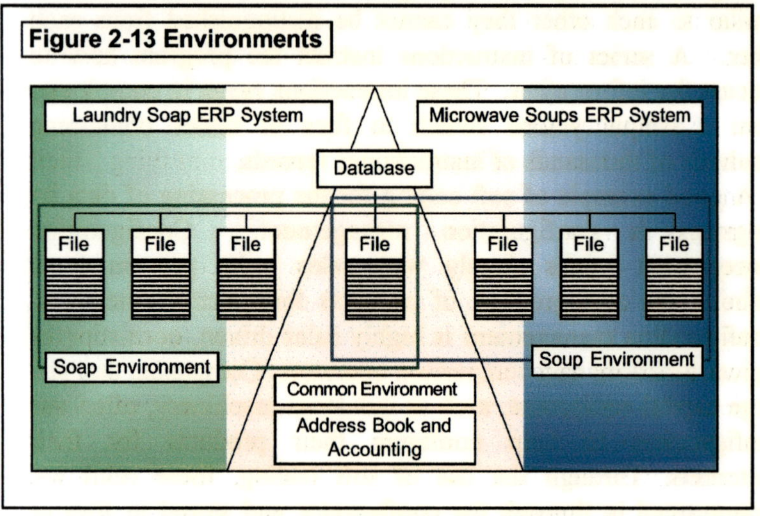

The need for environments is proportional to the length and complexity of an ERP implementation. Companies that use environments in the early stages of an ERP implementation often continue to use them long after they go live. Environments are needed when a company contains several different business units with different process flows that are implementing the same ERP system. These different business units will often be separated geographically and contain their own management groups. The concept of environments can be used at the computer system operating level, databases, and files.

Figure 2-13 shows how the concept of environments can be used to extend out the functionality of an ERP system for two different business environments at the same corporation. On the left-hand side we have a soap manufacturing division and on the right-hand side we have a division that manufactures microwave soups. The center defines an area of commonality. Both divisions have the same customers since both product lines are distributed by common grocery chain stores. By creating a common environment, one that is accessible to both divisions, the two divisions can share address book and accounting functions with each other. This lowers the overall cost of operation by avoiding the duplication of function and data. Advantages for the customer exist too. Customers can receive consolidated billing statements, simplifying their payment processes.

Process flows are similar to what are known as workflows. Process flows are simply the flow of a particular functional process, such as processing a sales order, through thc ERP system. Workflow is the functional capability to set up the software to manage a business process flow found in a particular functional area. There are two types of workflow: application-specific and cross-functional. Traditionally, ERP systems have been based on application specific workflows. Only recently have cross-functional workflows become available. They both work with status codes or sequences that position each step or action to another.

Workflows have two different meanings in ERP systems. In all ERP systems workflow represents how the business activities are sequenced and managed in and around the ERP system. In addition, for its second meaning, some ERP systems contain a functional module that is used to set up and manage customized workflows.

Figure 2-14 shows the concept of workflow for application-specific and cross-functional workflows and compares them to each other. On the left side is the traditional application specific workflow used by most ERP systems for a sales order process flow. This concept shown on the left side of figure 2-14 has been used most heavily for documents such as sales orders, purchase orders, and work orders.

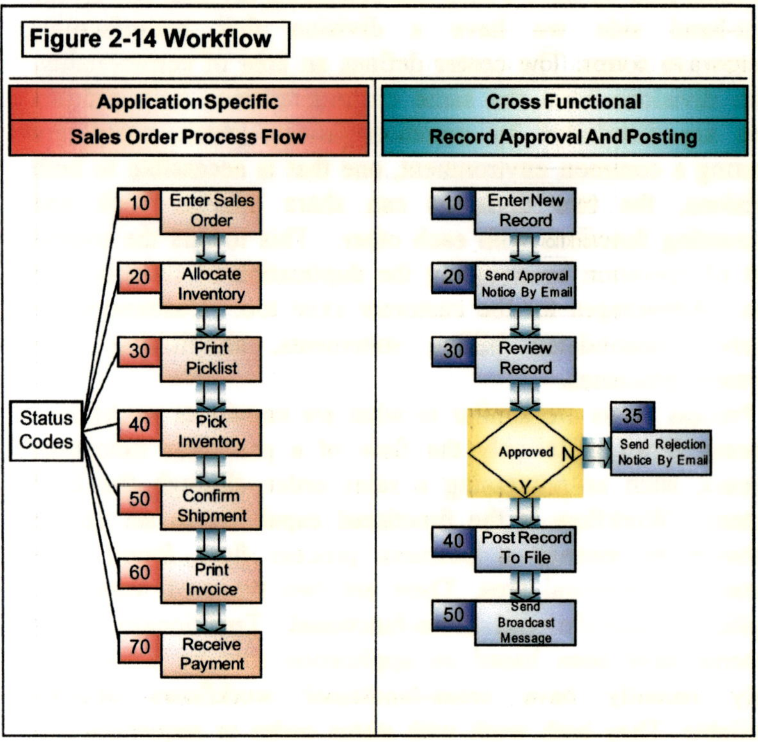

The flexibility of workflows allows the workflow to be modified specifically to match business process flows. Some companies may not need to allocate inventory at status code 20, so that step may be removed to match the process flow. Some systems allow the addition of new steps unique to an industry. Different ERP vendors take different approaches in how they set up workflows on their system. Some use tables that programs read and others will use configuration settings tied directly to the program. Some systems have decision logic built in that allows two different outcomes based on the input.

Workflows have built in flexibility to allow for change. Workflows can also be used to bind together functions from several different functional modules in an ERP system as shown in figure 2-15.

Figure 2-15 Workflow Integration

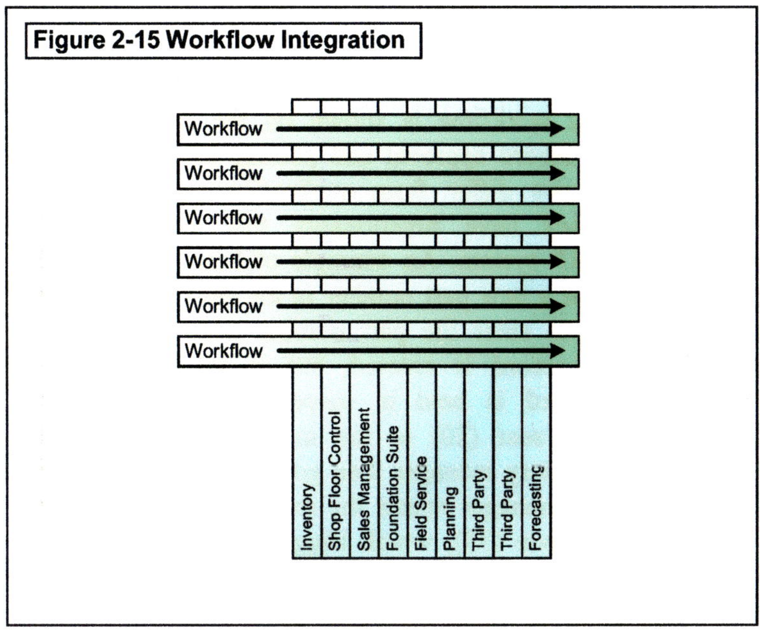

Workflow is a form of programming that does not need to be compiled. This makes it different from traditional forms of programming that require advanced skill sets and knowledge in programming language. Usually, traditional programming languages such as COBOL, BASIC and RPG can perform the same functions of workflow. The primary difference comes in flexibility; workflow is more flexible. Some components that make up workflow include:

- Status codes
- Sequences
- Events

- Activities
- Relationships
- Routes
- Decision logic
- Approvals
- Filters

Cross-functional workflow is shown on the right side of figure 2-14 for a record approval and posting process. Cross-functional workflows differ from application specific work flows in that they have functionality that allows usage throughout the ERP system. An example of how this may be used is the entry of a new part number in the item master. The first step (10) is to enter the part number with all relevant information. The record is entered, but is not sent to the database. The record is held in suspense. After entry an approval notice is sent (20) to the inventory manager for approval. The inventory manager then goes in and reviews the record (30). If the manager rejects the record, the system then sends it to status code (35), which triggers a rejection notice back to the person who entered the record. If the inventory manager approves the record then the system posts (40) the record to the file making it accessible to the necessary parties. After completing that, it then sends out a broadcast message (50) by email alerting all concerning parties that a new part number has been added to the item master. This same process flow can work for sales orders, purchase orders, a new account added to the chart of accounts in accounting, work orders and more. Cross-functional workflows allow the capability to be flexible by having the ability to add or subtract steps and logic for the specific need. Cross-functional workflow tends to be more complex having more logical functions, comparison operators, and interfacing capability to programs usually found in application specific workflows.

Because the concept of workflow applies well to email programs as a method of communicating status and notices, ERP vendors raced to incorporate Internet functionality in their ERP systems by the turn of the century. Internet email programs have become a rapidly growing method for viewing system activity and receiving notices. A good example is customers who receive shipping acknowledgements from vendors by Internet email to let them know that their products have been shipped.

Figure 2-16 Documents

Types	Regular, Credit, Return	Regular, Outside, Return	Manufacturing, Maintenance, Field Service	Manufacturing, Field Service	Adjustments, Transfers
Header	Sales Order	Purchase Order	Work Order	ECO	Inventory Transactions
Detail	1	1	2	2+	1

All ERP systems use documents. Some general characteristics of documents are shown in figure 2-16. Documents are the paper or electronic output, input, or storage of an ERP system specific to certain functions such as sales orders, purchase orders, invoices, shipping acknowledgements, work orders, etc. Documents usually represent a record in a database. Three components make up a document:

- Header
- Detail
- Types

The header information of a document provides a centralized connection point for all supporting detailed records that make up a document. The header section of a document contains information that generally applies to all detail lines of that same document.

The detail of a document allows ERP users to enter a large number of different records that relate to the header document record. A good example is in sales order entry. The sales order consists of one header document, which will contain common information such as customer, payment terms, and billing address. The detail records will consist of all the different line items that are going to be sold to the customer. Generally, the detail records of a document are unlimited, or can contain a very large number of records. Some documents, such as work orders, have more than one type of detail. In the case of work orders they have both a parts list and routing information. When a document has more than one type of detail, each kind of detail is usually based upon its own file. So if a document has two different types of detail, it will usually have two supporting files that tie to the header of that document.

The type of document refers to how that document is used. An example would be in sales orders. Many different types of sales orders usually exist within one organization. They may be broken apart by function, or product line, or both. Different types of sales orders include a regular sales order, credits, and customer returns. Companies classify documents into different types because they have different process flows. By classifying documents into different types, companies can benefit by applying custom workflow patterns to each type. In many ERP systems this can be done through using soft coding.

The integration part of an ERP system provides for the connectivity between the functional business process flows. Integration can be thought of as the communication technique. Often technology plays a significant role in the integration and communication. Some common ways that communication takes place through the use of integration in ERP systems include: source code, local area networks, wide area networks, Internet, email, workflow, automatic configuration tools, protocols and databases. Communication is achieved by integration and integration is achieved by communication.

The functional part of an ERP system provides for commonly understood business process flows. Some common business functions include: payroll, human resources, accounts payable, general ledger, accounts receivable, purchasing, inventory, material requirements planning, shop floor control, sales orders, forecasting, and more. It's not uncommon for some ERP systems to contain 30 or more functions.

Functions also exist common to all business functions such as: email, menu navigation, overrides, data sorting, data sequencing, data selection, and more.

ERP systems use these functions and integration to synchronize and coordinate the operations of the business. Few companies excel in successfully integrating their ERP systems with operational management. Companies become more demanding in how well their ERM system works as they learn more about their troubles with ERP.

Questions--

1. What are the three things that happen to data?
2. What are functions based on?
3. What is the role of integration?
4. What is integration most similar to?
5. How can all the components of figure 2-1 occur without a computer system?
6. What is the foundation strength of an ERP system?
7. What is the ratio of commercial databases to ERP software systems?
8. Is an electronic database required for an ERP system?
9. Describe the difference between a database, file, record, and data element.
10. What is a key?
11. How does a concept of a key reduce the database size?
12. The benefit of a key is directly related to what?
13. What is soft coding?
14. What is a program?
15. What are four functions of a program?
16. Where do programs obtain data?
17. What are programs based upon?
18. What are rules based upon?
19. How would you describe the difference between a comparative and mathematical operator?
20. What are logical functions?
21. Give an example of how an ERP program uses a logical function.
22. Give an example of how an ERP program uses comparison operators.
23. Give an example of how an ERP program uses math operators.
24. What are some ways that the output of a program is similar to the input of a program?
25. What are some ways that the output of a program is different to the input of a program?

26. What is the difference between an interface program and a conversion program?
27. What is EDI?
28. Where do the rules of a program come from?
29. What does CASE stand for?
30. What are values and where do they come from?
31. What does hard coded mean?
32. What does soft coded mean?
33. What is configuration saving?
34. What is an override?
35. What is a dependency?
36. What are the four "channels" of soft coding for programs?
37. What is an environment?
38. Why is having environment capability so important?
39. What is a UDT?
40. Where do UDTs come from?
41. What are some of the advantages of having and using UDTs?
42. What is a vocabulary override?
43. What are some commonly used environments?
44. What is a process flow?
45. What is workflow?
46. What is the difference between process flow and workflow?
47. What are the two different types of workflows? Give examples of each.
48. What is the role of the Internet and email in workflow?
49. What is integration?
50. What is communication?
51. What are the three parts of a document?

Our ERP system can do a lot, but not like we originally thought.

3

ERP Functional Modules

This chapter reviews the different ERP functional capabilities most commonly offered by ERP vendors. Generally, these functional capabilities are broken down into modules. In other cases the functional capabilities can be spread across several different modules. The number of modules needed for any particular business depends upon the need of that business.

ERP vendors often group functional modules into suites. Some common suites include financials, manufacturing, and distribution. For example, a financial suite usually consists of an accounts payable, accounts receivable, and general ledger.

In many cases ERP vendors use terminology specific to their own product in describing a particular ERP functional module. For this reason we find variation in terminology between two different ERP vendors even though functional characteristics of the module in discussion are almost identical. Be careful in comparing ERP systems based on terminology, for it is better to compare them based on functional capabilities.

Address Book

The address book contains basic contact information and names of customers, vendors, employees, or anybody with an address. It is highly interfaced with any ERP module in need of an address identification number or address information.

Accounts Payable

Accounts payable tracks the payments due to vendors for services and materials. This module integrates tightly with purchase order management, purchase order receiving, and the general ledger.

Accounts Receivable

This module tracks the short-term monetary assets that arise from sales on credit to customers at either the wholesale or retail level. Accounts receivable integrates tightly with sales order processing and the general ledger.

General Ledger

The general ledger is where all of a company's accounts, arranged as the chart of accounts, are stored and managed. The chart of accounts is a key component of the general ledger. The chart of accounts consists of a numbering scheme that assigns a unique number to each account to facilitate location of that account in the general ledger. The chart of accounts tracks how much money the company has in each different account.

Payroll

Payroll issues payments and tracks the amount of money owed to each employee of the company. It will do standard deductions for federal, state and local taxes as well as specialized deductions. Some systems also accumulate and track vacation and sick pay. Payroll integrates with the general ledger.

Human Resources

Human resources helps manage human resource administration, benefits administration, employee development, recruitment, and training. Human Resources often interfaces with payroll.

Fixed Assets

Fixed assets track the long-term assets of the company. These assets have a useful life of more than one year, are acquired for use in operation of the business, and are not intended for resale to customers. Fixed assets often include items such as large specialized equipment or office furniture. The fixed assets will track the value of the assets and depreciate it using one of a number of different depreciation methods. Fixed assets integrate with the general ledger.

Forecasting

Forecasting integrates with sales order history and the master production schedule (MPS) and/or material requirements planning. Forecasting is used to predict what customers will want based on past demand. The forecasting module does this by using a number of different mathematical formulas that are usually chosen by the company that uses the ERP system. Forecasting modules can consist of two parts: detail and aggregate. Detail forecasting predicts customer demand for a particular part number. Aggregate forecasting does forecasting in groups or families through the use of hierarchy pyramid structures.

Master Production Schedule (MPS)

Master production schedule plans and schedules the finished good items that are sold to the customer. It will make a recommendation to make the finished good item for manufacturing environments based on simple rules and demand for the finished good item. The master production schedule is most commonly found in the manufacturing environment. It interfaces between sales orders, forecasts, and material requirements planning.

Finite Scheduling

Finite scheduling is a rules-based optimization technique designed to provide functionality above and beyond the master production schedule working with capacity requirements planning. If then and boolean logic combined with sequencing are often used in the creation of rules to drive the finite scheduler.

Material Requirements Planning (MRP)

Material requirements planning plans for materials and when they will be needed. Generally, this is for manufacturing environments. This module will look at the master production schedule, or customer requirements if a master production schedule is not used, to determine how much material to order for purchasing. It takes the demand and consolidates it into buckets, which usually consist of days, weeks, months or some combination of them. MRP can consolidate demand into single a order and does so based upon programmed rules provided by the ERP user.

Distribution Requirements Planning (DRP)

Distribution requirements planning handles supply and demand between warehouses and facilities such as manufacturing plants. It often integrates with purchase orders and sales orders. Distribution requirements planning recognizes the demand in one plant, and based upon predefined rules, sends a signal to another plant to fulfill the demand. Distribution requirements planning is based upon inventory managed items.

Capacity Requirements Planning (CRP)

Capacity requirements planning plans projected capacity loads for, most commonly but not limited to, manufacturing work centers. Capacity requirements planning looks at the Master Production Schedule and product routings to determine the load for work centers. Based on these loading requirements, management can make decisions on how to shift loads and/or prepare work centers.

Bills of Material

Bills of material is the material list that defines what parts go into a product. This function is often associated with manufacturing. Sometimes it is used in field maintenance and re-manufacturing environments. Bills of material is used for finished goods that are sold to the customer and for sub-assemblies that are created in manufacturing environments. Bills of material is also used for planing families of parts and for establishing relationships for creating non-manufactured kits in sales and purchase orders. Several functions interface with bills of material including: master production schedule, material requirements planning, and work order management.

Product Routings

Product routings define how a manufactured product flows through work centers. Product routings are considered the standard for how long it will take a person or a machine to perform an operation on the product that is flowing through the work center. This module provides the source data in capacity requirements planning.

Project Management

Project management provides functionality specific to projects such as costs, orders, approval routings, approval transactions, change management, billing, contract management, scheduling, evaluation, budgeting, and work order management. Project management often uses functional modules from other areas of an ERP system.

Inventory Management

Inventory management provides for the basic tracking and record keeping for inventory items. It is widely interfaced with many different modules. Some common functionality found in inventory management includes: simple transactions, on hand quantities, inventory analysis, item master, transaction history and location management.

Warehouse Management

Warehouse management provides functionality above and beyond the functionality found in inventory management. Common types of functions found in warehouse management include pick optimizations, put away requests, material storage compatibility logic, consolidation planning, and warehouse space utilization.

Bar Coding

Bar coding (a series of vertical lines) is a system for tracking inventory or other objects that can be bar coded. Bar coding systems consist of hardware and software that speed the transactions and reduce keypunch errors by reading bar codes. Barcoding systems are usually not part of ERP systems and come from third party providers.

Customer Service Management

Customer service management consists of customer service oriented functionality such as sales order taking, tracking and expediting. This module interfaces with many other modules including: forecasting, inventory management, supplier management, accounts receivable, and more. Special pricing functionality is often found nested into this module. This pricing can define specific prices or discounts for specific customers.

Configuration Management

Configuration Management is the process of specifying compatible features and options for customer orders. It works based on the principals of 'if then' logic, sequencing, and boolean logic. Configuration management is often used for complex engineered to order products for specific applications. It interfaces with customer service management, bills of material, and work order management. Configuration management may configure pricing, costs, routings, and bills of material.

Supplier Management

Supplier management provides the purchasing function needed to place purchase order, track, expedite, etc. Additional functionality, such as blanket ordering, supplier scheduling, pricing rules, receiving inspection and supplier analysis can often be found. This module interfaces with others including inventory management, accounts payable, and material requirements planning.

Work Order Management

Work order management is the tracking tool for work orders. Work orders are most commonly used in manufacturing environments but are also used in maintenance and service situations. Work orders allow companies to prioritize through the use of sequencing. Work orders usually represent unique jobs that the company must complete. Work order management interfaces with inventory management, material requirements planning, general ledger, and master production scheduling.

Engineering Change Management

Engineering change management provides functionality for handling changes to base data structures such as bills of material or routings. It provides an integrated change management process to help facilitate the change in an efficient method. It often contains functionality such as approval processing, workflow, and implementation of the changes. Engineering change management is a document management system or the documents serve as a central collection point for all related activities.

Preventative Maintenance

Preventative maintenance provides for the maintenance of equipment. This module can generate maintenance schedules that specify when a particular piece of equipment should receive maintenance based on either predefined cycles or time intervals. After reaching the maintenance time, it can launch a preventative maintenance work order containing instructions on how to perform the maintenance and what materials to use. This module interfaces with inventory management and general ledger.

Transportation Management

Transportation management helps to manage the effective use of transportation resources. Functions such as route scheduling, carrier consolidations, capacity limitations, and preferred service carriers can be found in this module.

Field Service

Field service provides functionality specific to the management of maintaining and servicing products in the field. The functionality in this module closely relates to the combination of customer service management, work order management, and preventive maintenance. Through the use of this functionality companies can plan for field service requirements and record activity. This module interfaces with inventory management and general ledger.

Industry Specific Solutions

Industry specific solutions provide for specific functionality that is found specifically for a particular industry. Some examples of industry specific functionality include: banking, automotive, health-care, insurance, public utilities, and transportation.

Report Generator

Report generators provide custom report generation for all functional modules based upon the database of the ERP system. The report writers usually have functionality that allows for data selection, data sequencing, totaling, and modification of the data fields. They allow ERP users to generate custom reports specific for the needs of a particular module or modules.

Questions---

1. What financial module integrates tightly with Supplier Management?
2. What financial module integrates tightly with Customer Service Management?
3. What two modules use 'if then' logic and sequencing?
4. What module provides additional Inventory Management functionality?
5. What module is used to predict customer demand?
6. What modules do not involve a person's input?
7. What does CRP stand for?
8. What two modules does Finite Scheduling supplement?
9. Which module often contains quality inspection procedures?
10. What are two main components of a forecasting module?

I figured it would take about seven years to fully install all parts of our ERP system. I never planned on it being obsolete in five.

4

Life Cycles and Sequences

The purpose of this chapter is to explain all the individual events that make up the life-cycle of an ERP system from conception to death, and how those events may be sequenced. Tremendous fluctuation occurs from company to company and from implementation to implementation in the installation of ERP systems. It is important for the student, practitioner, senior management, consultants, programmer, or others to have a good understanding of the large-scale conceptual picture of an ERP project. Without the capability to understand the big picture, ERP practitioners can become lost. It is important to have a solid foundation for understanding the big picture so that the practitioners can understand the detail of what they deal with on a day-to-day basis and how it relates to the rest of the project.

There are two basic characteristics common to all ERP projects: objectives and events. Objectives are the major high-level characteristics that can have a great impact upon the success of an ERP project. These objectives include characteristics such as:

- Speed
- Scope
- Resources
- Risk
- Complexity
- Benefit

The speed of a project is directly related to the amount of time that a company has before some critical deadline or the amount of time that the company would like to take. The speed of the project in the context of this chapter is how much time the company would like to take implementing the system. The amount of time that the company actually takes may be dramatically different. The amount of time that the company would like to take should be the figure that is used when developing a project plan.

The scope of the project includes all of the functional and technical characteristics that the company wants to implement. A company installing 15 different functional modules would have a much greater scope than a company installing just three functional modules.

Resources are everything that is needed to support the project. This includes people, hardware systems, software systems, technical support and consultants. All the different resources of an implementation usually have one thing in common: money.

The risk of a project is a factor that impacts the overall success of an implementation. Success is measured by factors such as overall user acceptance, return on investment, and time to implement. High-risk situations are less likely to possess these characteristics.

Complexity is the degree of difficulty of implementing and maintaining the software. Companies of different sizes and business environments have different levels of complexity. A multi-billion dollar corporation that has multi-language, multi-currency and a variety of business manufacturing plants with different process flows is generally much more complex than a small company with 50 employees occupying one geographical location.

Benefits are the amount to which the company will utilize functionality of the software working with their people systems. Companies utilizing the functionality of inventory cycle counting programs for improving inventory accuracy benefit far more than companies who use the software as a database storage tool. Using the inventory cycle counting program allows for better customer service, which leads to an increase in market share and profits.

Each of these objectives can be rated on a scale from low to high. Interrelationships exist between the objectives. For example, companies that attempt to install an ERP system with low resources, high complexity, at high-speed would place themselves at high risk. Readjusting risk to a low value would cause other objectives to change their value based on other factors such as complexity.

Figure 4-1 Objective Dependencies

If these are high then...

	Benefits	Resources	Risk	Complex	Speed	Scope
Benefits		+	O	O	O	+
Resources			O	+	O	+
Risk				+	+	+
Complex					-	+
Speed						-
Scope						

Key
+ = Positive correlation
O = Neutral correlation
- = Negative correlation

Figure 4-1 shows the general dependencies between objectives in installing an ERP system. The subject of implementation time tends to be of interest for companies interested in purchasing ERP systems. Examining the speed column, we can find relationships with five other objectives. An ERP system that is installed rapidly may or may not yield good benefits to the company, so it is labeled as a neutral correlation. A rapid ERP implementation may or may not require a high degree of resources. This is because the amount of resources is dependent upon the complexity of the project. The dependencies between complexity and resources create a neutral correlation between resources and speed. Quickly implemented ERP systems tend to be at higher risk than those implemented at a slower pace, taking the necessary precautions. It should be carefully noted that objective dependencies are not necessarily constant in their relationships with each other. Objective dependencies can vary from company to company and are affected by such things as technical skill sets of the IS department.

Figure 4-2 Objectives

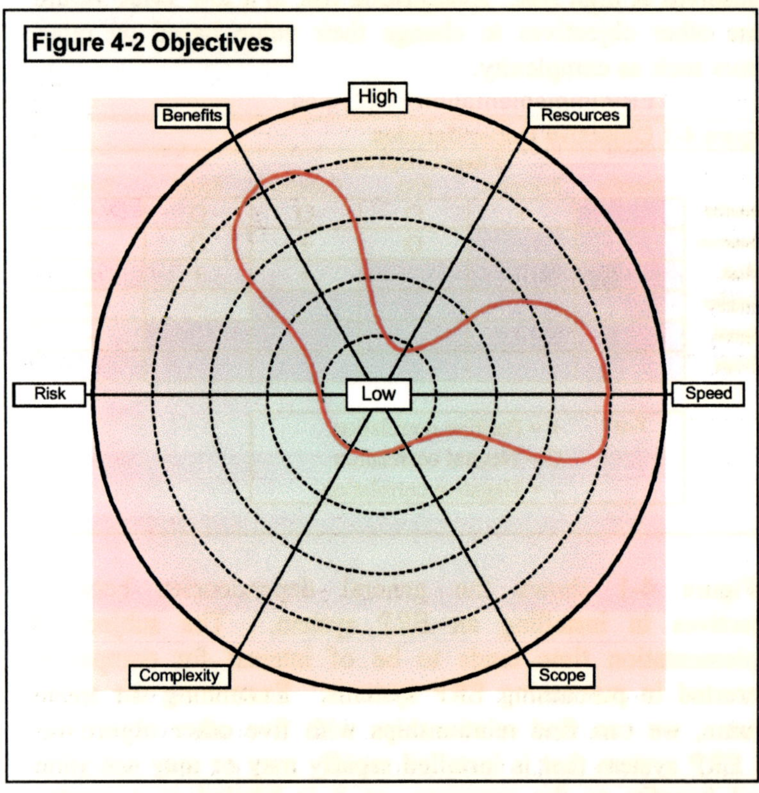

A good example is the dependencies between complexity and risk. A company with a really strong IS department containing strong technical skill sets may be much more apt to deal with technical issues in a complex ERP implementation. The relationship for such a company may be closer to a neutral correlation than the positive correlation as shown in figure 4-1.

The objective dependencies in figure 4-1 can be plotted against a spider diagram as shown in figure 4-2. The spider diagram gives us the capability to graphically interpret the objective dependencies for any given ERP project following the rules set up in figure 4-1. The correlations for objective dependencies should be determined first, for the company that will implement the ERP system, before spider diagrams are plotted.

Figure 4-3 ERP Implementation Strategies

10 = High, 0 = Low, P = Perceived, A = Actual

Name	Speed	Resources	Benefits	Risk	Complex	Scope
Breakneck	10P	2P	8P	2P	2P	5P
Breakneck	3A	8A	2A	8A	7A	5A
Star	6P	10P	6P	6P	5P	5P
Star	8A	10A	8A	4A	5A	7A
Turnkey	6P	7P	8P	2P	5P	4P
Turnkey	2A	10A	2A	9A	5A	7A
In-house	5P	3P	8P	2P	5P	6P
In-house	7A	8A	3A	6A	6A	6A
Budget	4P	1P	6P	2P	3P	3P
Budget	1A	2A	2A	10A	3A	3A
Partner	7P	6P	8P	4P	7P	6P
Partner	4A	8A	7A	6A	7A	8A
Low Risk	3P	9P	8P	1P	2P	2P
Low Risk	2A	10A	8A	2A	3A	3A

Various combinations of objective dependencies can create standard ERP implementation strategies. Looking at figure 4-3 we find several standard configurations of ERP implementation strategies. Each one has its own combination of objectives. By using the spider diagram technique, we can get a graphical interpretation of using the breakneck strategy as shown in figure 4-4.

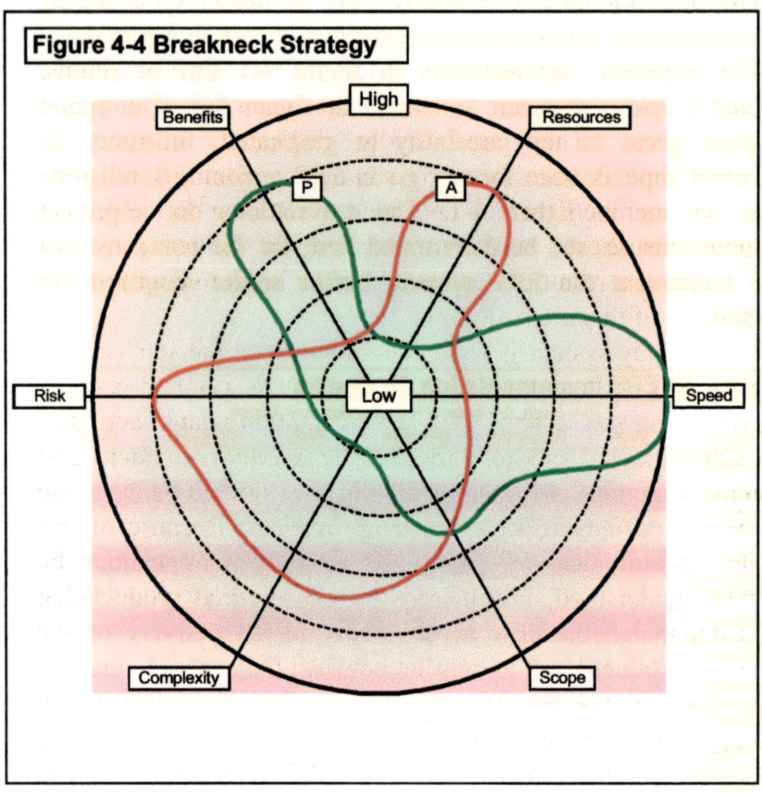

The breakneck strategy is a common methodology for many companies. The idea is to find and implement a solution as quickly and cheaply as possible. ERP vendors will market their software using strategies such as: "rapid implementation", "can be installed in 60 days". This strategy seeks to eliminate as many steps as possible in the attempt to create a quick implementation. In some cases, companies purchase ERP software without seeing the software, a demo, or checking references. The results are sometimes catastrophic for companies, as this strategy tends to be high-risk.

The star strategy is one that few companies take despite its significant advantages. Its primary focus is on doing things the right way, which often results in faster and cheaper installations. Placing senior managers in the core team is a common characteristic. They are usually dedicated full-time, or whatever time is necessary. The company commits full-time ERP team members that are dedicated to working on the project to help ensure its success. Creating a higher sense of ownership, as a result of dedicated people, helps to contribute to the success of this methodology.

The turnkey system is in striking contrast to the star system. The turnkey system takes a complete hands off approach to implementing the system. All implementation related activities are subcontracted out to various ERP service providers and system integrators. Communication is most limited between the company and outside ERP service providers. Because of this limited communication, functional specifications cannot be properly understood, which leads to a configured product that does not match business needs. The missed delivery of the expected product leads to conflict between the company and the ERP service providers. Many companies think that this is a low risk approach, feeling that they are contracting out the project to professionals who know what they are doing. With a complete lack of internal ownership, it places the project at high-risk with low probability for success. The resulting benefits can be much less than expected.

The in-house approach strategy uses internal resources to fulfill all needs of the ERP system as much as possible. This approach is often driven by the need for saving money and building internal ownership of the systems. This approach can be troublesome in the early phases of an ERP project. Because of the steep learning curves and the unfamiliarity of the software, a significant amount of time and money can be spent implementing the solution. This approach completely ignores time saving outside expertise that can be found with consulting companies and service providers. Companies have trouble obtaining the full benefits of the system. The risk tends to be considerably higher than expected because of the difficulty of installing the product without outside expertise.

The budget approach has a complete focus on cost management. The goal is to eliminate as much of the cost as possible. Companies do this by eliminating consultants, reducing the scope of the project, and resulting in limiting the benefits to be achieved from the implementation. The budget approach can drag on forever as senior executives are unwilling to finance any future expenditure to get the project moving. This general lack of support by senior management filters down to the rest of the organization. ERP users identify the senior managers of the company as having little interest in the success of the project. Without the buy-in of senior management, lower level ERP users place little faith in the success of the project and withdraw their support. Companies using this approach do not spend a whole lot more than what they initially planned, simply because they are reluctant to spend anything at all. A project using this strategy is considered to have a very high-risk of failure. Without the backing of senior management and financial resources, probability of success remains low.

The partner approach seeks to implement software by using a combination of internal and external resources. The partner approach is quite common and these companies turn to outside sources, such as consulting agencies and ERP service providers, to help them implement the solutions. Companies taking this approach usually spend more money and take more time than originally planned for implementing their software. The partner approach fits its name in terms of how responsibility is dedicated and shared in the implementation of the ERP system. Both the external sources and the company share a certain amount of responsibility for the successful use and implementation of the system. The star approach may have just as much outside assistance as the partner approach, but what makes it different is that the responsibility for success of the project is placed within internal sources of the company.

Because of the shared responsibility, conflict often erupts between the service providers and the company when outstanding issues develop. This conflict drains the perpetual energy out of the ERP implementation effort, creating higher levels of risk and probabilities for failure.

A low risk approach commits a high-level of resources with low complexity and scope combined with forgiving milestones to create a project with a high probability of success. The strategy contains the highest number of sequential and parallel events that are connected together using 'if then' conditional logic. 'If then' conditional logic is used to verify milestones as being completed or not. Without the completion of a critical milestone, the project will either be halted or recycled to complete the previous events. In this strategy, the process would be halted if an ERP vendor could not provide suitable references for the successful use of implementation of their software. Other strategies would continue without the verification of references. The low risk strategy is similar to the star strategy in many ways. The primary difference comes with the focus on implementation speed. The star strategy focuses on implementing quickly while the low-risk strategy takes more time for the same results. By keeping the scope and complexity very low and the dedicated resources high, risk is eliminated through careful analysis and painstaking research of the company. Each and every step is attended to carefully and methodically. This is the most complicated way of installing an ERP system because it contains the highest number of events.

Different ERP implementation strategies, driven by different objectives, will require different combinations of events. ERP implementations are subject to much confusion and misunderstanding. This is because a lack of understanding often exists concerning the proper content and structure of events to support a certain combination of objectives. Even further confusion can result when the interdependencies of objectives are not properly understood. For example, a senior manager uneducated in ERP fundamentals may not realize that installing an ERP system with a large scope, high-speed, high complexity, at low cost would not be very practical. Understanding the interrelationships and interdependencies of objectives and events are keys for successful understanding of ERP life cycles and sequences.

Events are all the characteristics that make up a project. A project is all the events that take place from conception to end. Almost all events in an ERP implementation usually involve people. Examples of events include:

- First cut education
- Forming project teams
- Needs analysis
- Business integration planning session
- Vision / Mission statements
- Project team education
- RFIs and general research
- ROI analysis
- RFPs
- Reference site surveys
- Hardware sizing
- ERP vendor site surveys
- Demo scripts
- Software demo
- Early planning session
- Decision selection process
- Contract negotiations
- Installation
- Project planning session
- Detail project plans
- War Room
- ERP education
- Answer configuration questions
- Policy formations

- Report equivalents
- Functional mapping
- Testing and prototyping
- Software modifications
- Database conversion
- Contingency planning
- Documentation
- End user training
- Audits
- Performance measurements
- Go live
- Post implementation support
- Ongoing education and maintenance

First cut education is the educational process that precedes all other events and activities in an ERP project. Traditionally, it has been focused on the senior management, but should also include all critical stakeholders regardless of their position in the organization. The purpose of first cut education is to educate the critical stakeholders on two things: foundation ERP knowledge and technology factors.

Foundation ERP knowledge includes knowledge that is common to all ERP systems. It is not software specific training or education. It is education for understanding how ERP systems work, how they can be implemented, the risks involved, and elements for successful use and implementation. The CIBRES CIERP certification is an excellent educational process for teaching critical stakeholders ERP foundation knowledge.

Technology factors include all the characteristics and elements that affect ERP systems in their business environments. With computer technology becoming obsolete every two years, it is important that the critical stakeholders of an ERP project understand the capabilities and limitations of modern-day ERP systems. Understanding what ERP systems are capable of helps the organization to ask the right questions in the later stages of an ERP implementation.

Formation of project teams should be done in the earliest stages possible following the first cut education. The content and structure of the team should be formulated based upon the needs of the organization and what was learned in the first cut education. It is important to form the project team early so that the critical mass of support can be built for the successful implementation and usage of an ERP system. Without early involvement, ERP team members may reject, or not support, ERP implementation strategies that were formed in the early stages of the project. The ERP project team is not necessarily the implementation team. The ERP project team should consist of all critical stakeholders of the organization capable of making a contribution. The number of ERP team members varies significantly from company to company and from situation to situation. The number of ERP team members should be such that it will help ensure thc success of the project.

The needs analysis is the process of determining what an organization needs in an ERP system. It is a high level draft that addresses all the major functional characteristics needed to support the company's long-term business needs. The needs analysis can not be conducted without careful examination of the company's future business direction and growth potential. With the first cut education in place, the critical stakeholders know what they can reasonably expect from modern-day ERP systems for the formulation of the organization's needs.

Many consulting agencies and educational institutes place the needs analysis before the first cut education. There are several disadvantages to doing this. One problem with placing the needs analysis before the first cut education is that the needs analysis is often done improperly because the people were not educated on how to do it. An ERP project is something like NASA's inter-planetary space probe, Voyager. It was launched from earth and visited several planets on its endless journey out of the solar system. An ERP project starts with a clear starting point and no definitive end. Once the project is launched, it is difficult to change certain mission objectives or the scope of the project. It is best to start the journey with education and training, for if that is done correctly, all other steps of the project will fall into place with a much higher chance of success for fulfilling the mission objectives.

The business integration planning session takes the information from the needs analysis and merges it with the operational (both current and future) characteristics needed to support the company's business strategies. The ERP project team comes together to decide what the software is going to do and how it's going to do it (in a general sense). For example, the company has decided to make their products more available to their customers through the use of Internet sales. The company wants the capability to sell their products over the Internet and seeks a totally integrated solution between the Internet sales function and the ERP system. Another functional area may decide that thcy need to increase their inventory accuracy to 95 percent, to better support customer service, through the use of integrated cycle counting programs.

Vision and mission statements provide the foundation and origins for changing both management and the organization implementing the ERP system. The vision statement is a continuous ongoing statement of how the company foresees their ERP system interacting with their business functions. An example of a vision statement for a company could be: "To provide number one customer service by the effective use and implementation of an ERP system working with effective operations management." Missions have more definitive statements with attached expiration dates. The reason that missions must have an attached expiration date is that if they do not, the lack of an expiration date makes them continuous and on going, which makes them no different than a vision statement. Mission statements directly support the vision statements. An example of a mission statement for a company could be: "To implement a fully integrated ERP system covering all functional aspects of the business by January of 2003." Vision and mission statements are formed from the output obtained in the needs analysis and the business integration planning session.

Project team education focuses on educating ERP team members on basic ERP concepts. It is similar to the first cut education, but more expanded. Project team education covers detailed critical success factors in an ERP implementation. It educates the ERP team members on the entire ERP life cycle. It covers things like how to interact with ERP vendors during the site survey, purposes of references, the role of documentation, data integrity, database conversions, and creating a detailed project plan. Having the proper foundations of an ERP project helps to prepare the organization for the successful implementation and use of an ERP system.

RFIs (request for information) is a high level documented request for general information from the ERP vendor. They seek to answer very general questions like: What are all of the functional modules offered? How much does the base product cost? Are there specific user licenses to consider? What is the ERP vendor's market share? RFIs combined with general market research help to provide the basic cost range with which the company may be faced for the implementation of the ERP system. It also provides an initial starting list from which to select ERP vendors. Sometimes this is called the long list. RFIs may be cemented electronically or in paper format to potential ERP vendors or they may be filled out directly over the phone or through person to person interviews.

ROI (Return on Investment) analysis provides the financial justification to pursue the expensive project of purchasing and implementing an ERP system. Through the business integration planning session and the collection of RFIs, qualitative justification is transferred into quantitative numbers capable of satisfying financial planners' needs. ROI analysis helps to provide a sanity check for the rationale of the new ERP system. Many situations exist where a company must still choose to purchase and implement a new ERP system even though previous ROI calculations did not meet company expectations. This happened to many companies that were faced with non-compliant year 2000 source code of legacy ERP systems.

RFPs (request for proposal) is a series of questions given to a sales function representing an ERP system. The questions are designed to determine if the ERP system contains the necessary business functionality desired by the company that submitted the RFP to the ERP vendor or party representing the ERP vendor. RFPs often go by the name of RFQ (request for quotation). After receiving RFPs, the list of potential ERP vendors may be narrowed down and further contact made with each one of them. RFPs should be formed based upon the needs of the business. They should accurately reflect in greater detail what came out of the original needs analysis.

The power of the Internet should not be overlooked when requesting RFPs from ERP vendors. As of the time of this publication, the technology had developed to a point where it was just as easy to format RFP questions capable of being displayed through Web browsers over the Internet. The most significant advantage of using RFPs over the Internet is that all of the results from different ERP vendors can be electronically collected back to one centralized source. This allows the effective comparison of different ERP vendors without the labor-intensive process of manually typing thousands of different responses into spreadsheets.

References help to narrow the list further by validating the capabilities of the software and service providers in real-life conditions. References can be supplied by ERP vendors or they can come from other sources such as trade associations or professional development societies. When ERP vendors supply references, there is always the opportunity for misrepresentation. ERP vendors will generally contact a reference in advance to explain who will be contacting them and what to say. In some cases, the references will receive a kickback if the sale is made, which presents significant problems for the integrity of the ERP vendor and the reference. Independent references operate completely outside the scope and control of an ERP vendor and provide the best opportunity for obtaining true unbiased information.

Hardware sizing can be a painstakingly difficult process to go through, but a very important one. Hardware sizing involves the process of estimating the amount of computer hardware resources needed to support the business and its future business plans. Sometimes the ERP vendor provides the prospect with a questionnaire that contains anywhere from less than 100 to several thousand questions related to transaction, storage, and processing needs of the organization. Examples of questions include: How many sales order detail lines are entered per day? How many pages of reports are generated each day? How many users use the system concurrently? How many years of history must be kept online? Most companies purchasing computer hardware for their ERP system usually purchase computer systems that are undersized for the company's needs. This happens for two reasons: the company is trying to save money, and ERP vendors tend to quote undersized computers in their proposals in order to make their systems less expensive than their competitors, allowing them better chances to win the sale. It is extremely rare to find ERP users or IS managers who claim that their computer system is just too big for their needs.

ERP vendor site surveys provide an opportunity for perspective ERP vendors to come into the company to learn more about what the company does. Generally, ERP vendors do this as an information-gathering act to provide specific future demonstrable solutions to help win the software sale. Some ERP vendors come with a carefully prepared list of interview questions while others generate impromptu questions. The company at this point should be prepared to submit a document package containing reports, screen captures, sample data, electronic documentation, and other specifics originally developed in the needs analysis. The ERP vendor will sometimes take this information and enter it into their own system to help prepare for a future demonstration that will show how their system can be used to satisfy the company's business needs.

Demo scripts are a formally documented demonstration method for the ERP vendor to follow. The sophistication of demo scripts can vary significantly. Some are nothing more than a schedule of who will be present in something and what they will present. Others go into an unbelievable degree of detail specifically describing each function that must be performed and how it must be performed down to individual keystrokes. The best demo scripts focus on the business needs of the organization as originally developed in the needs analysis. Sometimes ERP vendors provide their own demo scripts and less organized projects. More organized projects often require that all ERP vendors use the same demo scripts for the sake of fair comparisons.

Software demos provide an opportunity for critical stakeholders to view the system, ask questions, and interact with representatives from the ERP vendor. The software demo is often a major input into the decision-making process of selecting software. Software demonstrations are often held at the company site. They may also be held at the ERP vendor site or even through the Internet. The length may range from a few hours for a simple company, to several weeks for large complex organizations. Software demonstrations do not necessarily represent the quality or functionality of an ERP system. What is seen in the software demo, what is interpreted by a critical stakeholder, and what the ERP system can actually do, can be drastically different. Software demonstrations are subject to much error. Some ERP vendors provide a canned demo, which only shows the features and functions of the software in a general sense. Other ERP vendors provide customized demos with preloaded company data and setups that show specifically how the software system can satisfy the company's business needs. Software demos, many times for the wrong reasons, are often used to narrow down the list of ERP vendors.

Early planning sessions help to provide the company more detailed information on the scope, time, and resources needed to implement the solution from one particular ERP vendor. Ideally, it is a joint planning session that occurs between the company and an ERP vendor and possibly, a third party outside consulting service. The planning session determines what functional modules will be implemented, how much time is available, and the resources to implement them. The resources may come from internal or external sources. Estimates are made regarding how many resources will come from internal sources and how many will come from external sources either from the ERP service provider or other sources. This will give a more detailed estimate, than what was originally calculated in the ROI, of the total costs involved for implementing the proposed solution. This detailed estimate, when collected from all the different ERP vendors, provides for a more detailed comparison between them.

The decision-making process should consist of all the critical stakeholders and information that has been collected to date. In many cases the decision will be clear and a relative consensus will already exist for the selected solution. In other more competitive situations, the ERP team will be split between one or more ERP solutions. ERP solutions should be evaluated on their capability to satisfy the overall needs of the organization, not necessarily what was shown in the software demo, for these can be very different, depending upon the skill sets of the person performing the demonstration and the style of demo. The outcome of the decision-making process should not be complete until all critical stakeholders obtain a consensus. A consensus does not mean that all critical stakeholders have voted for the same solution, it means that they will support the solution even though they may have had a different choice.

Be very wary of teams that make a unanimous decision for one particular ERP vendor. Without one or two team members casting a negative vote the ERP team may not exhibit critical thinking in their decision making process. Having a unanimous decision in no way assures the successful implementation of an ERP project. Countless large-scale ERP projects have been observed as troublesome or failing completely after a core team had made a unanimous decision on one ERP system.

Figure 4-5

The ERP decision-making process, for many companies, resembles the decision-making process that was used in the ill-fated Jan. 28, 1986 Challenger space shuttle disaster. Leading up to the decision to launch the space vehicle, a series of ambiguous situations, eagerness for launch, and peer pressure, lead to the decision to launch, creating an irreversible catastrophic situation.

A viable option for many companies is to not purchase any ERP system and remain with their legacy system. Some companies, very wisely, pause the process at the decision-making step while waiting for additional information. The length of the pause can range anywhere from a few days to years.

The decision-making process is a critical point in the life cycle of an ERP system. Once committed, it can be very awkward to stop the process and reverse the cycle. For these reasons, the final decision should be made most carefully.

Contract negotiations are a documented formal agreement between the company purchasing the software and the ERP vendor and/or service provider. Sometimes the contracts will be split up to include a contract for software, hardware, and services. In other cases they will all be included together under one contract. Most ERP vendors begin with a standard boilerplate contract. It is very common for the terms and conditions to be changed before the signing of the contracts. This is usually done during a negotiation and bargaining process with the prospective client. Certain terms and conditions may be given up by the ERP vendor in order to obtain the sale. Different companies take different approaches in how thoroughly they review the contract. Some companies simply review and sign the contract the same day that they receive it. Other companies spend weeks analyzing it with lawyers and senior management. The process of contract negotiations can often be frustrating, time-consuming, and unproductive. The signing by both parties initiates the formal agreement to implement the new ERP system.

After the signing of the contract, there usually is a big rush to get the software installed and ready for implementation. It is a small goal that gives a little lift to the project. People are usually eager to see something for their money. Installation varies widely depending upon company size, operating systems, and type of ERP systems chosen. Generally, centralized solutions install quicker with less problems. Decentralized solutions that must be installed on several different computers and networking systems, can sometimes take several weeks to several months to install.

There are some situations where installations do not take place. Some companies buy into an existing system using a part ownership strategy. This strategy is not uncommon in very large corporate environments, which often contain more than one ERP system. A smaller subdivision may discard their old system and buy into their new corporate system using their already pre-established communication lines and hardware systems. Internet technology has increased the possibility of doing this, making it much more practical for smaller companies. ERP software companies, as of the time of this writing, were rapidly adapting their systems to Internet technology. Partnership strategies can often suffer from conflicting technical or database requirements. This is especially common when very diverse business environments use the same operating system, database, and software system. Sometimes there is no other way to resolve problems other than to split the system by using a different software system, database, or operating system.

The project planning session is a workshop that plans the implementation of the new system. It brings together all the critical stakeholders of a project to unify them under common vision and mission statements, and to develop an execution strategy for the implementation. It is an expansion of the previous early planning session. It also serves as a method of re-evaluating the output of the original early planning session. The project planning session provides the company an opportunity to obtain the latest information regarding the availability of resources. The project planning session usually lasts at least one day and can go as long as one week. All of the information collected in the project planning session serves as input in developing the detailed project plan.

The detailed project plan is a formal documented timeline showing the implementation strategy with critical due dates. This detailed project plan includes the functional modules that will be installed and the sequence for the installation. The decision must be made regarding the amount and combination of parallel, process, and phasing to exist within the project.

Once consensus has been reached on the high-level plan for the modules to be implemented and the sequence of doing so, specific tasks can be assigned to core team members. Some of these tasks include training, testing, data conversion, prototyping, implementing, documenting, and issue resolution.

After completion of all the elements of the detailed project plan, it can be documented electronically in a number of popular project-planning software packages. It is often graphically displayed as a Gantt chart. The entire detailed project plan should be circulated to all critical stakeholders of the organization.

A war room is a dedicated room for the purpose of installing an ERP system. War rooms serve as a centralized location that can be used for holding meetings, computer terminals, projection devices, visual aids, and small training classes. Some companies move their war rooms to an off-site location to allow the full concentrated efforts of the ERP core team members. While this can increase the concentrated effort, it also does reduce functional communications and provide technical issues for connection to remote locations. A healthy war room has a tremendous amount of activity in it. For some people, war rooms become their temporary home away from home. It's not uncommon to find leftover drinks and pizza crumbs on the tables.

ERP education classes are focused on the functionality of the ERP system and should be directed at the core ERP team. Additional team members, such as an executive sponsor or critical stakeholder, may also attend for their own benefit. Early ERP education classes should not be directed at the end users. The purpose of early ERP education classes is to understand the "know why" of an ERP system. Educational classes help the core team members fully understand the complete functional capabilities and limitations of the ERP system. These classes should not be custom developed specifically for the company. Canned ERP educational classes can be effective as they present the complete functionality of the system and an objective nonbiased method. Observing all of the functionality of the system allows the ERP core team to determine in detail how the ERP system will specifically interact with the company's business functions.

Configuration questions are questions that are asked by the ERP service provider for the purposes of better understanding the company and how to best configure the software. Configuration questions are administered by using one of three approaches: manual, semi-automated, and automated.

In the manual approach, the ERP vendor sits down and interviews the customer, asking a variety of questions that relate to the functionality of the software. In more organized efforts, each question correlates specifically with a software feature or function, or more specifically, a configuration setting in the software. Consultants then make manual adjustments throughout the software based upon how the questions were answered.

The semi-automated approach goes through the same process as the manual approach except that the ERP consultants load the results into a computer system or Internet enabled tools for purposes of electronic configuration of the software. This is usually done before the software is delivered to the end customer. Upon delivery, the software is fully configured and ready for testing.

The automated approach takes advantage of full electronic automation. Using this approach, the ERP system displays a series of intuitive question and answer sessions. Working with ERP consultants, or sometimes by themselves, ERP users answer all of the questions. Upon completion, the ERP system automatically updates its electronic configuration settings based upon how the ERP users answered the configuration questions.

Although these electronic configuration tools may seem very attractive for helping companies achieve low-cost rapid implementations, they seldom perform that function. In many cases the default settings of the ERP system perform just as well as in the electronic configuration process. This is due to several reasons. In the early stages of ERP implementation, ERP users cannot fully understand the complete functional capabilities of the software. Not understanding capabilities of the software tends to create situations in which answers cannot be provided with complete accuracy. As ERP core team members spend more time learning the software to generate new and innovative ideas, they help to streamline business process flows and gain additional functionality. Inaccuracy of answers to early questions and innovative solutions tend to cause a significant number of changes to the configuration of the ERP system before it goes live. Electronic configuration tools and interviewing techniques help the consulting agency to gain a better understanding of the organization and vice versa, but it does not ensure the success of an ERP system. A good portion of questions covered will be examined in detail several times over before the go live date.

Policy formation serves to establish the ground rules for implementing and making changes to the ERP system. An issue resolution policy is a formal documented procedure for dealing with issues beyond the immediate control of an ERP team member. Escalation phases are common in issue resolution policies. Using escalation techniques, non-resolvable problems and issues are passed to higher levels of management until a decision is made. There is an effort to resolve as many issues as possible at the lowest level. Only those critical issues beyond the control of the immediate core team pass up to the senior management.

A software modification policy is a formal documented process that explains procedures for making software modifications. The process may require several key stakeholders to sign off and review cost/benefit justifications related to the software modification.

Reporting equivalents represent the connection between reports that appeared on the legacy system and reports that will appear in the new ERP system. Most legacy systems contain an entire series of various reports for almost every functional module. These reports will be driven by three primary factors: data selection, data sorting, and data display. Provided that there is no business process reengineering, the same functional reports will need to appear in the new ERP system. Because of the enhanced functionality of the new ERP system, reports that are in paper based format may not be necessary. There may be many cases where the equivalent report can be found on an online video containing workbench functions or a highly interactive video interface containing query and spreadsheet like display capabilities. Should business process reengineering take place, then different types of reports may be needed from the ones originally used in the legacy ERP system.

Functional mapping is a process in which people work together to document and understand business process flows and how they may interact with the software. The ERP team first starts with the original needs analysis and business integration planning session and then fine tunes them to work within the capabilities and limitations of the software. Functional mapping is most effective when a complete body of knowledge is represented. This knowledge includes all the functional capabilities and limitations of the system, organizational specific knowledge, industry specific knowledge, and the people skills of the organization. Usually this must be a team effort that requires the participation of ERP core team members working with outside consultants who have an intimate understanding of software capabilities. When the team works together to perform functional mapping, the process becomes a highly interactive cross-functional communication style that uses graphical icons. Chalkboard and white boards work well for mapping out the business process flows because you can use them to make quick changes to reflect the current discussion. Functional mapping may be done as one huge session or as several individual sessions. It is better to do functional mapping as several individual sessions specific to the subject at hand and the module being implemented. ERP team core members can spend less time reviewing information that they forgot and more time focusing on the implementation of the software.

Testing and prototyping takes results from the functional mapping and proves or disproves the capability of the software configuration to meet the business functional needs. During the testing and prototyping phase, ERP team members working with consultants configure the software, enter sample data, perform transactions, review output, and determine if the process performs as expected. The process can be performed for one business process flow anywhere from one to several hundred times. Each time the process is repeated, an adjustment is made and results are evaluated again. When a process meets expectations, the configuration settings are saved and documented. Testing and prototyping starts small and becomes large. Individual components of business process flows are first developed, tested, and proved. Proven process flows are continuously put together to form larger business process flows. Each one of those larger business process flows are tested and adjusted based on the components that make it up. Eventually enough business process flows are built and assembled to represent an entire enterprise. An entire enterprise test is sometimes called a conference room pilot. The need for testing and prototyping varies from organization to organization. Organizations that have highly proprietary business process flows will probably have a higher need for testing and prototyping than organizations that have industry standard or common process flows. In many cases, organizations are unaware of how unique their business process flows really are. In such cases it is a good idea to test the software ahead of time.

Performing software modifications allows a company to extend the functional capabilities of the software beyond what is normally provided by the ERP vendor. It is an intricate part of prototyping and testing. Software modifications are defined as anything that restricts the capability to adapt technology and upgrade to future software versions. Software modifications should only be performed after the combination of functional mapping and prototyping has proven that the software will not and cannot perform the needed function. In addition to this, each software modification should go through a cost/benefit analysis to determine if it is truly more economical to perform the modification than it is to use other alternatives such as clerical assistants. Many companies that come from home-grown legacy systems perform software modifications with relatively little thought. In these types of organizations the culture understands functionality as coming from technical resources performing software modifications. Many companies do not realize that additional functionality can come from a thorough prototyping and testing. It is easy for consultants to identify such organizations. Statements like: "We will have to make a modification to that so it works right." from an ERP team member before the prototyping and testing phase, is indicative that the culture of the company relates functionality to technical programming vs. careful prototyping and testing. It is undesirable to perform unnecessary software modifications because of the many hidden costs and complexity of maintaining them.

Database conversions are the process of converting data from the legacy system to the new ERP system. Database conversions can be done manually through human intervention or by using one of several different electronic methods. ERP team members and others can thoroughly test the software and learn a great deal while providing opportunities to clean up data integrity problems by performing data conversions manually. The files of the legacy system and the new ERP system must both be carefully considered when mapping out database conversions. Another advantage of using manual conversion strategies is that the software will often perform integrity checking of the data through its normal program logic. This data integrity checking process is usually bypassed when using electronic methods. Database conversion utilities are programs that usually have to be developed for many types of information that changes rapidly, such as account balances, or on hand inventory. Other methods must be used in many cases because there is not enough time to manually convert data from the legacy system to the new ERP system during the time that it will go live. All database conversion utilities and programs should be thoroughly tested for quality and reliability. A mishap in a database conversion utility program just before the go live date can create havoc in the ERP database for months or even years afterwards.

Contingency planning is a process of creating contingency plans in case something goes wrong. Contingency plans can be thought of as 'what if' situations like: What if the database goes corrupt two days after we go live? How do we recover from the resignation of the critical stakeholders? What happens if we experience non-resolvable technical issues during the prototyping and testing phase? How do we dissolve the project if top management loses interest and withdraws all financial resources?

There are literally hundreds of different areas in an ERP project to which contingency plans can apply and be beneficial. One of the most critical points is during the go live phase. Few companies are formal enough to create a documented strategy in case something goes wrong during or shortly after the go live. Few companies even consider contingency plans at all. Companies installing an ERP system generally do not like to think about the worst things that can happen, so when they *do* happen, the companies are generally unprepared! It is good practice to ask your consultants about all the things that can and have gone wrong in the projects that they have worked on or heard about. Not only will this will alert you for possible areas to create contingency plans, it will also give you much better insights on potential limitations of the software.

Documentation serves as an important communication tool in an ERP implementation. Documentation exists on several different levels. It is needed for software modifications, business process flows, issue resolution, ERP configuration settings, training, audits, education, cost/benefit analysis, and for general communications. Documentation helps slow the rapid pace of an implementation by forcing ERP users to think clearly when generating documentation. Some ERP systems provide document management capability. Document management capability that is built into the ERP system can have great advantages. With some systems, capability exists to drill down into the documentation from the source for which it was designed. For example, some systems can attach documentation to a menu option. Attaching documentation at the source can simplify and organize document management strategy.

End user training provides training for the final users of the ERP system as well as ERP team core members. End user training programs are developed specifically for the company. The training provides the end users the knowledge of what to do and when to do it. It shows users what menus they will use and how to execute functionality of the applications that are related to their functional area. Training manuals that were previously created through documentation efforts facilitate the process and serve as future reference guides that end users can take with them. Instructors can come from a variety of sources within the company as well as external sources such as consulting companies. While consultants may show some success in these areas, it is better for the internal members of the company to conduct the training for end-users. In some cases, it may be necessary to provide those people with additional training on how to train people.

Audits can apply to almost every step of the ERP project. Audits help to insure that the project is meeting expectations by staying on time and within budget. ERP vendors and external consultant agencies can be of great assistance in providing pre-documented audits. Many ERP vendors can provide checklists for all the important configuration settings in an ERP system. The company and the ERP project team are responsible for making sure that the necessary audits are performed on time. ERP vendors and outside consultant agencies rarely provide any kind of guarantee that they will effectively perform audits. Critical points for performing audits include pre-implementation, implementation, and post implementation. One of the most critical points during the implementation is just before the go live.

Electronic auditing tools such as the CIBRES Scorecard System can provide cross-functional auditing and diagnostic functions. The CIBRES Scorecard System provides direct scorecard results along with three levels of comparison: overall average, industry average, and software average. By combining scorecard and comparison information, companies can get a relative understanding of how well their ERP systems are performing from several different viewpoints. The scorecard tool can be used directly over the Internet through the CIBRES website with results sent back in electronic format by email.

Performance measurements focus on characteristic critical information related to the functional modules of an ERP system and operational activities related to those modules. Many companies overlook the tremendous measurement capability that can be found in the ERP systems. Bundles of electronic files combined with automated reporting tools create a bountiful harvest of performance measurements. Some commonly overlooked performance measurements include: negative on hand inventory, on-time customer shipments, on-time manufacturing work orders, on-time vendor delivery performance, action messages for MPS/DRP/MRP, customer returns, and vendor returns. Other performance measurements, often requiring more work, but still very important, include: inventory accuracy, bill of material accuracy, routing accuracy, orders shipped complete, and internal operations variances.

Post implementation support serves to provide all of the support activities necessary after the go live date of the system. Most companies find that their ERP systems require a high degree of support for considerable lengths of time after the go live. As users become more familiar with the system the need for post implementation support declines. Post implementation support can become severe or chronic if a significant malfunction occurs, such as an electronic conversion program not performing properly. Many times these mistakes are not caught until several days or weeks after the go live date. By this time recovery options become more expensive than the cost of remaining on the new system. For these reasons severe demands can be placed upon external consulting sources, ERP service providers, and ERP core team members. The best way to prevent these severe demands for post implementation support is to make sure that the previous steps in the ERP project, such as prototyping and testing, are performed carefully and thoroughly. Through careful preparation, surprises can be minimized, but no matter how careful the preparation, a company should always be prepared to provide high post implementation support.

Ongoing education and maintenance serves to provide investment protection for the ERP system. Internal education should continue for new people that are hired into the company and for job rotation and cross training. External education provides insight into the latest software, management, and computer technology to keep management and ERP users up-to-date. ERP user groups, specific to ERP packages, are a great way for ERP users to learn new tips and tricks and to keep up-to-date on the latest events of their software. ERP user groups often function as nonprofit organizations for the successful use and advancement of a particular ERP system. Local chapters are scattered throughout the world for major ERP systems. Professional development societies, trade magazines, and the Internet all provide additional ways for ERP users to keep in touch with what is going on. Ongoing maintenance provides continuous post implementation support. Help desk support is often thought of as an ongoing maintenance function. Help desks support the ERP users with a variety of needs related to ERP systems. Help desks can be set up internally, specifically for a company, or they can be provided through the ERP vendor or service provider.

How are elements arranged in supporting the objectives recognizing the dependencies between them? Each major ERP implementation strategy as shown in figure 4-3 will have a certain combination of elements to support that strategy. Each combination of elements makes up an ERP implementation strategy.

Figure 4-6 illustrates the graphical timeline of the breakneck strategy showing the basic elements and their sequence as perceived by companies as an easy, low-cost, rapid methodology for implementing an ERP system. In order to cut costs and save time, many important steps are eliminated. Very little time is spent researching ERP vendors and asking questions. The decision to purchase usually rests with a few or one senior manager. Contract negotiations occur swiftly without much talk or thought. There is usually a big rush to install the software as quickly as possible so that the company can be live on the new software soon. Database conversions are usually done manually by clerical personnel and company employees loading the information. Electronic database conversions are usually not used simply because there is not enough time to develop them. Breakneck strategies use very little to zero amount of phasing, which results in a big bang strategy for the go live.

Figure 4-6 Breakneck Strategy

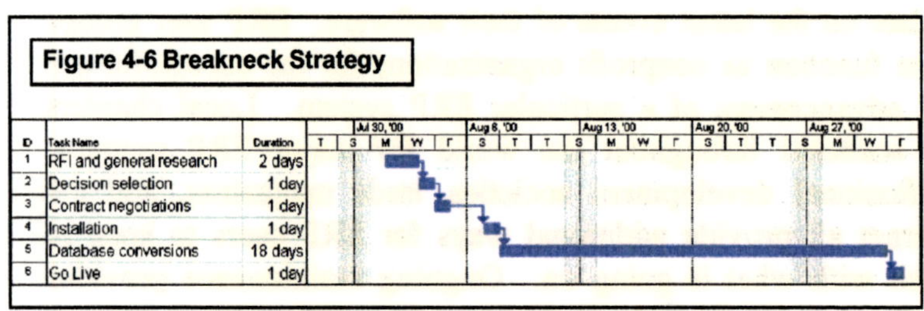

Because the breakneck strategy eliminates most of the necessary steps to help ensure success, it is considered a high-risk strategy. Some advantages to the breakneck strategy include:

- Simple
- Fast
- Requires little planning
- No politics
- Low initial cost

Some disadvantages of the breakneck strategy include:

- High risk
- Tremendous amount of rework

- Organizational rejection
- Performance problems
- Functional problems
- Low benefits

Figure 4-7 Low Risk

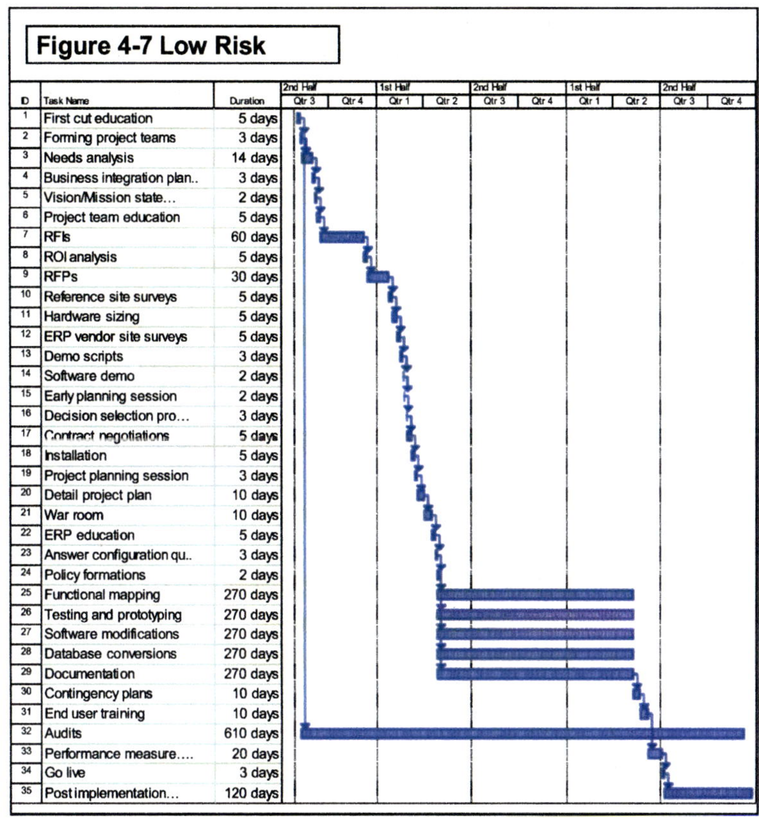

ID	Task Name	Duration
1	First cut education	5 days
2	Forming project teams	3 days
3	Needs analysis	14 days
4	Business integration plan..	3 days
5	Vision/Mission state...	2 days
6	Project team education	5 days
7	RFIs	60 days
8	ROI analysis	5 days
9	RFPs	30 days
10	Reference site surveys	5 days
11	Hardware sizing	5 days
12	ERP vendor site surveys	5 days
13	Demo scripts	3 days
14	Software demo	2 days
15	Early planning session	2 days
16	Decision selection pro...	3 days
17	Contract negotiations	5 days
18	Installation	5 days
19	Project planning session	3 days
20	Detail project plan	10 days
21	War room	10 days
22	ERP education	5 days
23	Answer configuration qu..	3 days
24	Policy formations	2 days
25	Functional mapping	270 days
26	Testing and prototyping	270 days
27	Software modifications	270 days
28	Database conversions	270 days
29	Documentation	270 days
30	Contingency plans	10 days
31	End user training	10 days
32	Audits	610 days
33	Performance measure....	20 days
34	Go live	3 days
35	Post implementation...	120 days

Figure 4-7 shows a timeline for the low risk strategy. The number of steps and its complexity is in striking contrast to the breakneck strategy. We also notice that the duration for implementation goes up considerably, about two years. It contains almost every single step that the ERP project can have. Upon reviewing figure 4-7 the student should keep in mind that the number of days are not necessarily the number of days it takes to perform that activity. Instead, think of it as that activity occurring over the number of days specified. Two interesting highlights to the timeline in figure 4-7 is the auditing process that takes place from beginning to end and the large number of parallel activities that occur from the functional mapping to the documentation. All of the activities within the range, including audits, can occur at the same time. That entire section can be broken down into much greater detail as a detailed project plan. Few companies pre-plan their activities in such great detail as shown here and the low risk strategy. Many companies wander blindly through performing many of the same tasks, perhaps only by chance, on their journey to implement an ERP system. The star, turnkey, and partner strategies can also have similar configurations as the low risk strategy. The sequence from one strategy can support several different strategies with differences coming in scope, complexity, speed, risk, and resources.

Some advantages to the low risk strategy include:

- More predictable outcomes
- Low scope creep
- Better conformance to budget
- Less disruptive to business
- Maximum benefits achieved
- Few major surprises

Some disadvantages of the low risk strategy include:

- Lengthy implementations
- Conceptually difficult to learn
- Requires top management support
- Requires dedicated resources
- Expensive

Figure 4-8 Budget Strategy

ID	Task Name	Duration
1	RFIs	60 days
2	ROI analysis	5 days
3	Reference site surveys	5 days
4	ERP vendor site surveys	5 days
5	Software demo	2 days
6	Decision selection pro...	3 days
7	Contract negotiations	5 days
8	Installation	5 days
9	Answer configuration qu..	3 days
10	Database conversions	270 days
11	Go live	3 days

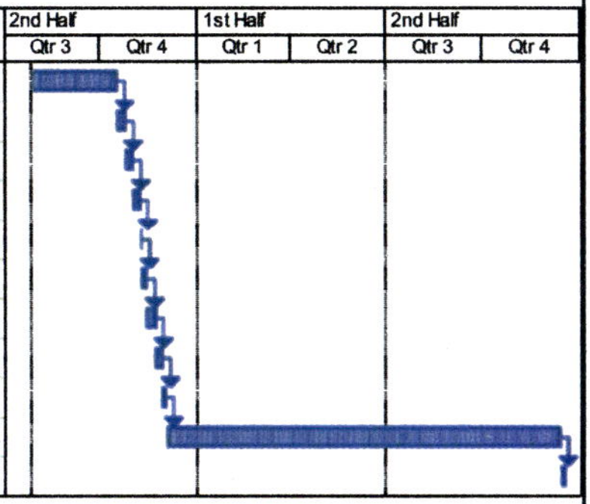

Figure 4-8 shows the events and the sequences for the budget strategy. The budget strategy is similar in many ways to the breakneck strategy in that there are relatively few numbers of steps that take place. Its primary focus is to implement the software with the least amount of money. Most of the steps that can be found above and beyond the breakneck strategy are those that add more value and do not cost any money. A difference between the low-budget strategy in the breakneck strategy is speed. The low-budget approach is willing to sacrifice the speed of the implementation in order to save money. Companies using this approach usually find it a frustrating experience when they find out that they have software that does not work as expected and they have to pay a consultant to help them figure out how to use it.

Some advantages to the budget strategy include:

- Simple
- Requires little planning
- No politics
- Low initial cost

Some disadvantages of the budget strategy include:

- High risk
- Very long implementations
- Tremendous amount of rework
- Organizational rejection
- Performance problems
- Functional problems
- Low benefits

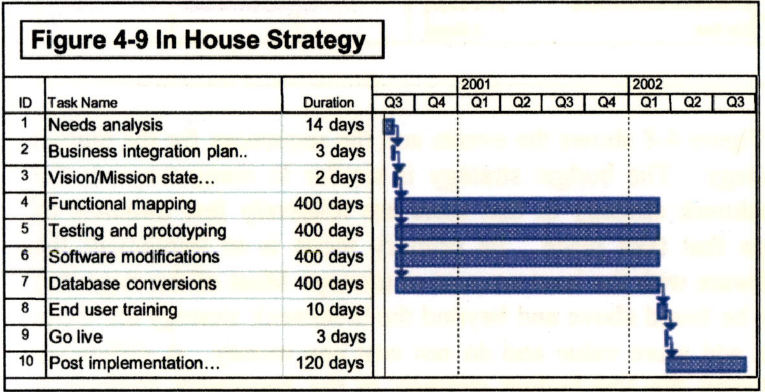

Figure 4-9 In House Strategy

ID	Task Name	Duration
1	Needs analysis	14 days
2	Business integration plan..	3 days
3	Vision/Mission state...	2 days
4	Functional mapping	400 days
5	Testing and prototyping	400 days
6	Software modifications	400 days
7	Database conversions	400 days
8	End user training	10 days
9	Go live	3 days
10	Post implementation...	120 days

Figure 4-9 shows the sequence and configuration of the in-house strategy. It uses a series of in-house programmers to develop the solution at the source code level. Like the breakneck and the budget approach, it has a relatively few number of steps. One thing that makes the in-house strategy significantly different from the breakneck and budget strategy is that it contains core ERP implementation elements such as functional mapping, testing and prototyping, and software modifications. Because of the nature of in-house strategy, the process of functional mapping and prototyping must take place in order to develop the solution. We also notice that the needs analysis begins the process. The needs analysis and business integration planning session must take place or it would be impossible to program a solution. In-house development strategies can take a very long time to develop and debug in the post implementation support. Many companies struggle with the in-house strategy because of its high maintenance needs and complexity to troubleshoot. Tight integration often suffers.

Some advantages to the in house strategy include:

- Requires the use of core ERP implementation elements
- Builds strong technical resources
- Matches business process flows closely
- Source code is usually more compact requiring less computer resources
- Forces cross communication

Some disadvantages of the in house strategy include:

- High risk
- High post implementation support
- Vulnerable to employee turnover
- Inflexible
- Adapts to technology slowly
- No knowledgeable external support
- Lacks integration

While the star strategy may have similar events and sequences as the low risk strategy, the emphasis on objectives make it very different in terms of its advantages and disadvantages.

Some advantages of the strategy include:

- Low risk
- High benefits

- Predictable outcome
- Builds strong knowledge base
- High user ownership
- Strong integration

Some disadvantages of the star strategy include:

- Expensive
- Can severely stress organizational resources
- Psychologically stressful

The turnkey strategy has similar structure and sequences as the low risk strategy. Its primary difference comes in who provides most of the events and planning for the ERP project. Turnkey ERP implementations always use outside resources to plan and implement the solutions. Ownership can make it significantly different than the other types of implementation strategies.

Some advantages of the turnkey include:

- No or very little internal resources required

Some disadvantages of the turnkey strategy include:

- High risk
- Expensive
- Lack of ownership
- Rework / missing functionally
- Adversarial relationships
- Vulnerable to vendor turnover

The partner strategy has as much structure and sequences as the low risk strategy. It is different from the other implementation strategies in that the responsibilities for implementing the ERP solution are jointly shared by external and internal resources.

Some advantages of the partner strategy include:

- Good access to functional and technical knowledge
- Lowers demand on organizational resources

Some disadvantages of the partner strategy include:

- Moderate risk
- Expensive
- Ownership problems
- Adversarial relationships
- Vulnerable to vendor turnover

Because of the complex nature of ERP implementations, few will be exactly the same. Many will closely resemble the events and sequences as outlined in this chapter. Some will be similar, showing a few differences, and still others will be so different that it will be difficult to classify them according to any presented here.

Questions--

1. What is an objective?
2. What is an event?
3. What is scope?
4. What is an objective dependency?
5. List five objective dependencies that have a positive correlation. Negative correlation.
6. What is a spider diagram?
7. Plot a spider diagram for your company with what you believe is real and what is perceived.
8. Is your company ready to implement a new ERP system?
9. List 7 implementation strategies.
10. How is an implementation strategy different from a conversion strategy?
11. Which implementation strategy takes a hands off approach?
12. What is the difference between a ROI and a RFP?
13. What is the purpose of the business integration planning session?
14. How do companies verify the quality of ERP systems?
15. Which strategy has the most steps?

We did not give our project team much consideration when we first started, and it showed.

5

ERP Project Teams

The way a company organizes its ERP project team can greatly influence the successful outcome of an ERP implementation. ERP project teams are formed not just for implementing ERP software but also for the ongoing maintenance required of an ERP system.

Companies typically do not give much thought as to how the ERP teams should be structured. The successful formation of an ERP team, more often than not, happens out of blind chance rather than education and careful thought. ERP vendors often stress the need for an ERP team but seldom explain how teams should be formed and what the pros and cons are for different types of team structures. In other cases, subcontractors, ERP consulting agencies, service providers, and ERP vendors recommend the wrong type of structure in order to obtain work for themselves. Team structures vary tremendously from company to company and situation to situation.

In this chapter we discuss the different ERP team positions and how they can be used in forming several different ERP teams. Different types of situations influence the optimal type of team to be used. The pros and cons of each strategy are considered.

The participation of people in an implementation can fall into several different positions: steering committee, executive sponsor, project manager, functional manager, team leader, team member, functional participant, consultant, service representative, and end user.

Basic skill sets that are important to any ERP team position include communication skills, computer literacy, maturity, conceptual skills, and organizational knowledge.

The steering committee (also called steering counsel) usually consists of two or more company officials. The steering committee tends to contain members of the senior management as well as mid level management. Their purpose is to establish the overall high-level strategy of the ERP system in relationship to their company and to establish visions and missions for the ERP system. The visions are perpetual while missions have a specific objective tied to a due date. The steering committee communications are generally very limited with other ERP team positions.

The responsibility of an executive sponsor usually belongs to a senior manager. This person fulfills a role similar to the steering committee when there is only one executive sponsor. Executive sponsors do not represent any one particular functional area. They serve as a source of motivational, inspirational, and sometimes financial support for the overall ERP project. When there is more than one executive sponsor, the distinction between executive sponsor and steering committee becomes more clear as the communication channels become split between the executive sponsors. If the executive sponsors communicate with each other, coordinating and creating consistent uniform messages to the other team positions, then they are a steering committee. If the executive sponsors do not communicate with each other, or are very limited in their communication with each other, then they function as independent executive sponsors for the same ERP project.

Executive sponsors or steering committees that provide no direction, missions, and visions can be considered phantom executive sponsors or phantom steering committees. Although they may receive recognition, they either choose or do not have the capability to exercise leadership. Phantom executive sponsors are quite common in ERP implementations. They usually rely on their chain of command to supply them information about the progress of the implementation.

Project managers' responsibilities vary widely depending upon how the ERP team is formed. All project managers are involved with communication and coordination of resources. Communications and coordination may include taking ERP team meeting notes, issue resolution, developing budgets and time lines, performing updates for executive sponsors and steering committees, and documentation.

Project managers are selected based on a variety of criteria including: availability, technical expertise, product knowledge, organizational knowledge, political power, software knowledge, technology knowledge, cost, authority, availability, vendor agreements, communication skills, maturity, computer literacy, and organizational respect.

Companies often do a poor job in selecting project managers from either internal or external sources. All too often companies select people based upon their availability without considering critical characteristics such as communication skills and computer literacy. Project managers are usually a full time dedicated resource in all except small implementations.

Good project managers have an adequate blend of management and leadership skills. Too often companies look to project managers to perform basic management functions, such as scheduling and tracking issues related to an ERP project without providing the necessary leadership skills. Because ERP projects integrate deeply with business process flows overlapping onto functional managers' areas of responsibility, companies will choose a weak project manager to prevent confrontational situations with functional managers. While this may protect political strongholds, it often leads to fierce confrontation with the ERP team.

A strong project manager exercises authority and power over the people and resources in and around the project. Project managers use their authority and power in persuading others to enthusiastically pursue the visions and missions related to the

ERP project. This is how a good ERP project manager carries out the function of leadership. A combination of education, technical expertise and business knowledge allows the ERP project manager to carry out the function of management related to the project. These skill sets allow the ERP project manager to be more effective. Figure 5-1 shows characteristics that distinguish between leadership and management in an ERP project.

Figure 5-1

Leadership	Management
Builds goodwill	Copes with complexity
Promotes business changes	Maintains oversight
Builds support systems	Designs and executes
Establishes project direction	Monitors efficiency
Motivates ERP team	Communicates aggressively
Watches for problems	Controls resources
Does what is best for all	Monitors ERP team
People have faith in	Enforces communication
Commands political support	Develops individuals
Concerned with effectiveness	Develops teams
	Does things correctly
	Makes few mistakes

Figure 5-2 shows characteristics common in identifying the difference between a good project manager and a poor one.

Functional managers are a pre-existing position that does not need to be fulfilled. Functional managers oversee the day-to-day operations of their respective functional areas. Ideally, they should have strong conceptual skills in understanding the overall ERP project and how it relates to the business. The amount of time they spend on the ERP implementation is usually minimal. They play a significant role in the success of an ERP team in certain conditions.

Figure 5-2

Good Project Manager	Poor Project Manager
Stresses teamwork	Lacks communication skills
Recognizes individuals	Is not people oriented
Gives trust	Places blame on others
Communicates vision	Listens poorly
Technical expertise	Focused on self-promotion
Computer skills	Rejects creative thought
Recognized leader	Rejects input
Positive attitude	Cannot translate vision
Interested in personal wellness	No technical expertise
Excellent role model	Uses title to direct people
Foresees the future	Does not try to understand
Accepts blame	Does not ask for help
Knows how to get there	Does not do the right thing
Listens to subordinates	Does not do things right
Develops harmony	Argumentative
Asks for input	Gives out incorrect information
Does not place blame	Overreacts
Works the front-line	Lacks organization acceptance
Organizational knowledge	Reacts without thought
Strong communication skills	Lacks experience
	Weak computer skills
	No organizational knowledge
	Unpredictable

In situations where ERP team members serve both as implementation team members and functional participants, support is needed from their functional managers in the allocation of resources. Often, when team members' time is split between implementing the ERP system and carrying out functional duties, the majority of their time is spent carrying out the functional activities of their respective area rather than implementing the ERP system. Without education and training, functional managers are more supportive of carrying out the functional activities of the business rather than implementing ERP systems.

Team leaders carry out widely varied roles in terms of scope and the amount of time spent on the project. They serve as coordinators and communicators for their respective area. They are usually involved with training and documentation. They work closely with application consultants in understanding how software features and functions can be used for business process flows of the company. They help configure the software and serve as ongoing support for the rest of the functional area.

Team leaders need to be able to dedicate 60 to 100 percent of their time to the ERP project. Team leaders who dedicate less than 60% of their time become redundant because of the high learning curves required for new ERP systems.

Team members have roles similar to team leaders except they focus more on matching the business process flows with the capabilities of the software and spend less time communicating with project managers, other team leaders, executive sponsors, and steering committees. They are more involved with documentation and working with consultants. Team members generally continue participating in the functional area that they represent during the implementation. They attend ERP team meetings and have common knowledge of what is going on with the project. Team members generally return to their functional area full-time upon the completion of the implementation of the ERP system. The amount of time they dedicate is usually equal to or less than the team leaders.

Functional participants have a limited role in the implementation of the project. Most of their time is spent carrying out the day-to-day activities of the functional area. Functional participants answer questions, review training programs, and review business process flows proposed in the new software. Through the feedback of the functional participant, other members of the ERP team can get a basic feel of how well the new ERP system may work.

Functional participants usually have a significant amount of organizational and product knowledge. After the implementation of the ERP system, they become end-users.

Consultants provide a wide variety of functions often filling in the gaps. Positions consultants can fill include project manager, team leader, team member, service representative, and end-user. A consultant's success depends upon a number of factors including computer literacy, conceptual skills, software knowledge, industry knowledge, maturity, problem solving capability, communication skills, and organizational skills.

The success of any particular consultant can vary tremendously from company to company and from situation to situation. Surprisingly, (to some) a consultant's industry and software knowledge does not correlate strongly with his or her success or capability to help a company. Case after case has identified consultants lacking in software and industry knowledge who were able to consistently out perform other consultants considered thc most knowledgeable in software and industry. These consultants showed strong interpersonal communication skills, were self-starters requiring little or no training, had good computer literacy, problem solving capability, and conceptual skills.

Consultants provide three general categories of services: management, application, and technical. The service provider will divide consultants into these three general categories. Some consultants can perform two of these categories, but it is rare to find consultants who can perform all three.

Management consultants focus primarily on the function of management as it relates to the organization of resources and business process flows. Management consultants often participate in project management and will provide high-level direction for the overall successful implementation and use of an ERP system.

Application consultants focus on the process of communicating, teaching, demonstrating, and configuring software for the business process flows. A management consultant may consult on how to perform a business process flow where an application consultant would show the company how to perform the business process flow in the new software.

Technical consultants deal with technical issues such as database conversions, source code modifications, communication protocols, operating systems, software installation, hardware systems, and integration programs. Technical consultants work closely with application and management consultants.

It can be difficult to estimate the proper ratio of management, application, and technical consultants required for a particular ERP project. Even slight changes in the ERP implementation strategy can affect the ratios. The ratios fluctuate between the beginning and the end of an implementation.

The service representative is the primary coordinating resource of the service provider for the ERP system. This person schedules consultants for the company installing the ERP system. This person sometimes steps in to resolve issues that cannot be solved by the rest of the ERP team implementation members.

One of the primary responsibilities placed on a service representative is to keep the consultants busy. In order to satisfy this objective, service representatives often recommend consultants based on availability, and overlook the skill sets of the consultants and how well they match with the company requesting the consultant. Because of this, consultants are often badly mismatched for the assignment. Because the ERP system is so new to the company, this is often overlooked until deep into the implementation when it is too late.

End-users, who represent the largest group, are the general mass of people who will use the new ERP system. Tremendous variation in skill sets can be found among this group. They have the least control over the outcome of the ERP project. Documentation and training programs are often prepared specifically for this group of people. High end-user acceptance of the new ERP system is required for its success.

There are several million different ways of organizing ERP teams. With such a high number, it becomes impossible to test all of the possible combinations for optimal performance in a given company. Fortunately, these millions of combinations can be broken down into four general categories. Each one of these categories has unique characteristics and relatively predictable performance.

Figure 5-3 ERP Teams

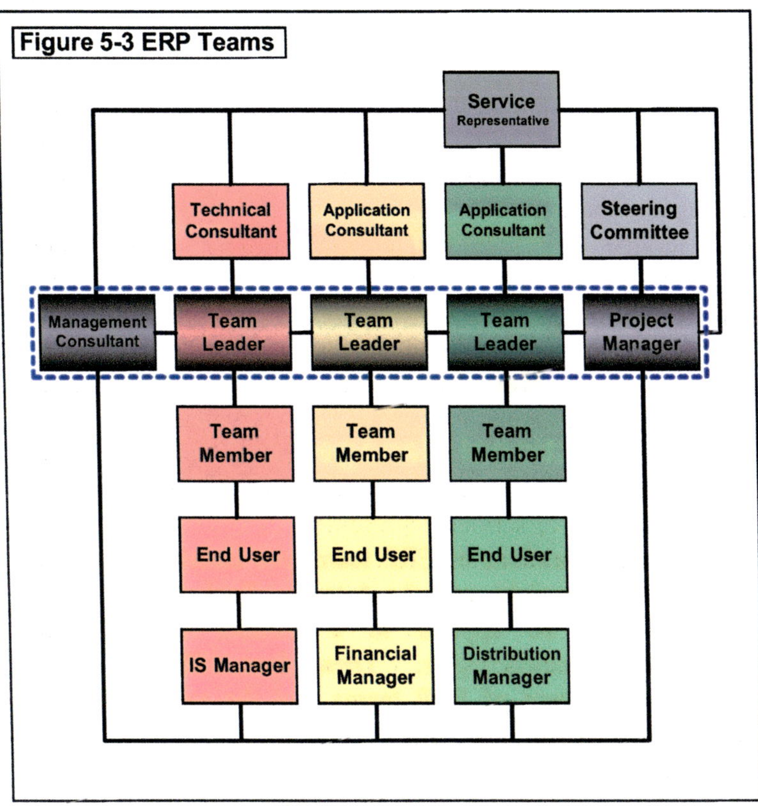

Figure 5-3 illustrates a sample configuration of an ERP team. The core ERP team is outlined by the blue dotted line. The core ERP team can be defined as the team leaders for the functional areas with the project managers. If the application consultants serve the ERP project as a dedicated resource they may be considered part of the core team as well. Communication will be most intensive inside the core team with inputs and outputs to the other team positions. Communication from any team position to another is usually unrestricted and occurs as needed. ERP teams are in a constant state of flux; positions appear or disappear, communication channels change, and responsibilities change.

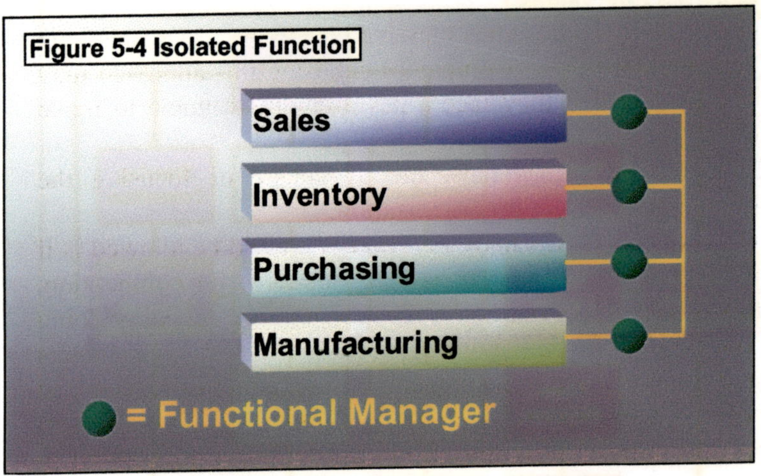

Figure 5-4 Isolated Function

The four classifications of ERP teams are isolated function, lightweight, heavyweight, and the A-team. Each one of these ERP teams can be applied to a number of different implementation methodologies. These four different styles represent the structure of ERP teams, not the way the ERP software is installed, for that is different. These four approaches represent the formation of the core ERP team. Other positions outside the core ERP team such as: steering committee, management consultant, technical consultant, and application consultant, can be applied and arranged to support any one of these four strategies.

The isolated function approach, as shown in figure 5-4 consists of the various functional parts of the business overseen by the respected functional manager. Participants from each functional area are responsible for their own implementation and use of the software. The functional managers' primary concern is for their own functional area.

Communication between the functional modules is limited with only occasional meetings to discuss issues and concerns between the modules. There is no centralized resource for coordinating and synchronizing the activities of implementing an ERP system.

This technique consumes massive resources and creates long implementation times. Companies choosing this approach may eventually feel that they face a never-ending struggle to make their ERP system work.

This approach does have the advantage of focusing the functional resources of an organization.

The only situation where this strategy should be allowed is if companies dominate market position or have no competition. In this type of situation, companies are not threatened by doing a poor job of implementing their ERP system. Customers cannot go elsewhere to receive the same product or service and the company can recover their costs of implementing the system simply by raising their prices. Few companies can afford to adopt such strategy.

The lightweight strategy, shown in figure 5-5, is a much more popular method of organizing teams for ERP systems. This configuration consists of functional managers, lead persons, and a lightweight project manager. In many cases the lead person and the functional manager are the same person. This is particularly true in smaller companies. In larger more complex projects, the lead person and the functional manager are usually different people. The lead person from the respective functional area would then report to the functional manager and communicate with the lightweight project manager. If the functional manager takes the responsibility of acting as the lead person, then that functional manager participates in the implementation and continues to manage the day-to-day situations for the respective functional area.

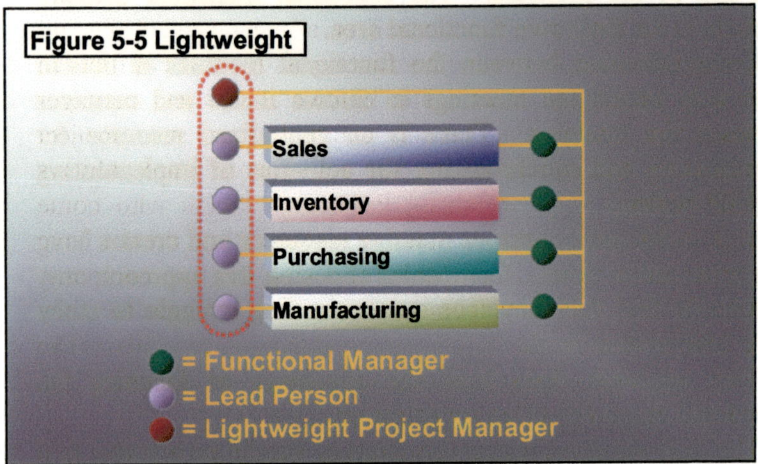

Communication is greatly improved over the isolated function. Meetings are usually held on a regular schedule and as needed during the project, with all concerned parties invited. Cross-functional communication takes place through the team members and project manager. The project manager carries the responsibility of communication between the functional areas and from outside sources. Despite the improvements over the isolated functional approach, conflicts are common. Endless meetings and red tape are used in an attempt to resolve issues and problems. Signature cycles are typical. A signature cycle is where several key people, such as lead persons or functional managers, must sign off before the issue can be resolved.

Team members often receive conflicting messages from the lightweight project manager and the respective functional managers concerning the allocation of resources and methodologies. Ideally, the project manager communicates with the functional managers in creating uniform visions and missions that will appear consistent to the team leaders through both the lightweight project manager and the functional managers. But this can become a daunting to impossible task if communications are blocked or if the functional managers have non-resolvable issues between them relating to the ERP project.

A lightweight project manager is a person who has no authority or power to resolve conflicting issues and conflicts in the allocation of resources. The lightweight project manager comes from either internal or external sources. Project managers who come from external sources are always considered to be lightweights. Project managers who come from internal sources are only lightweights if they do not have authority or power over team members of the company. Lightweight project managers are often chosen because they have available time or they have good computer skills. The project managers' responsibilities include communication, coordination, and distribution of information.

The lightweight approach is highly dependent upon the skill sets of the project manager. The project manager must have exceptionally good skills in communication, computer literacy, industry knowledge, software product, and conflict resolution for this strategy to work. The project manager must also be well respected. Extensive amounts of rework combined with cost overruns are commonplace. The lightweight strategy does have the advantage of freeing up critical senior management resources that would otherwise be used filling the position of project manager.

Some companies adopt a multi-layered lightweight strategy. The multi-layered lightweight strategy is similar to the lightweight except two or more lightweight project managers are involved. A multi-layered lightweight strategy is common to large ERP installations. Companies containing several manufacturing plants with different process flows and management groups may use a multi-layered lightweight strategy. Another example, single geographic facilities may use an internal lightweight project manager combined with an external lightweight project manager provided by the ERP service provider. A multi-layered lightweight strategy becomes increasingly dysfunctional as the team members receive conflicting messages by different lightweight project managers.

Environments using lightweight project managers often have power struggles between the functional managers. Like inter-city gangs, they look to protect their turf. Without higher management to resolve issues among the functional managers, impossible deadlocks occur, driving dysfunction into the ERP project. In addition to these deadlocks, team members receive different vision and mission statements for the ERP project from the project manager and functional managers. These conflicting vision and mission statements lead to confusion for the team members. When companies do not comprehend the problems associated with this strategy, they often start blaming ERP vendors and service providers, leading to stressed relationships. Despite all the problems of the lightweight strategy, it is one of the most popular techniques to use. Few companies understand the long-term implications of using this strategy when they are forming their ERP teams and selecting a project manager.

The heavyweight approach, shown in figure 5-6 is a significant departure in integration and conflict resolution over the isolated function and lightweight approaches. In this strategy a strong internal senior manager leads the core ERP team as a heavyweight project manager. This senior manager has direct authority and control over the ERP core team. He or she will communicate with the functional managers in resolving conflicts. The heavyweight project manager is at a higher managerial level than the functional managers. The functional participant's participation changes dynamically depending upon the situation. At any moment the functional participant can become a team member or a team leader. Functional participants bring strong functional knowledge from their respective areas.

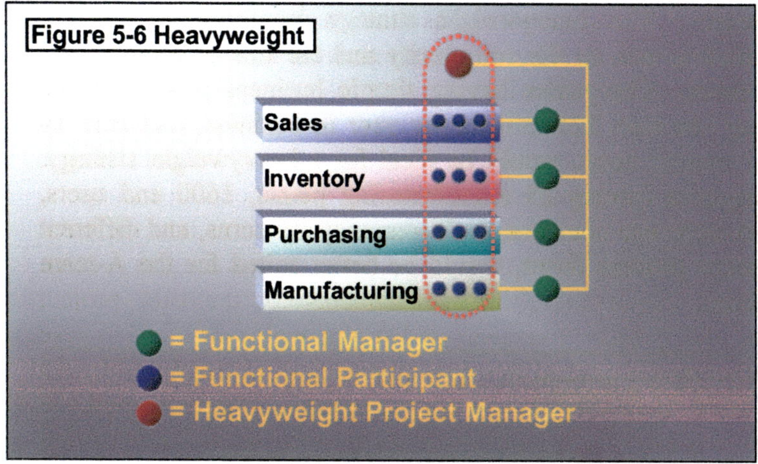

Figure 5-6 Heavyweight

Communication and sense of direction become almost crystal clear. Because the senior manager has authority and power over the ERP core team and functional managers, clear vision and mission statements can be developed and integrated into the company's overall business strategy. With clear vision and mission statements, the ERP core team knows what needs to be done, how it's going to happen, who is responsible for it, and when it's going to be done.

Interestingly, in a strong heavyweight profile, ERP team meetings are relatively rare because ERP team leaders and members spend more time focusing on the task and less time engaged in politics and red tape. Communication still takes place as needed between the functional areas. The heavy weight project manager is equipped to step in as soon as a conflict or potential conflict arises. There are no signature cycles and no red tape.

The heavyweight works well for small companies seeking rapid installations of their ERP systems. It is streamlined for efficiency because full-time dedicated team members are not required. A functional participant's responsibilities can shrink or grow depending upon the requirements of the ERP project. Some of the best success stories have used the heavyweight strategy. The heavyweight strategy becomes increasingly difficult to use, as the complexity and the size of ERP project increases. Companies having simple business process flows, doing less than $25 million per year in business, and only 10 ERP system users, would be ideal for a heavyweight strategy. Companies having 25 manufacturing plants, 1600 end users, multi-language concerns, multi-currency concerns, and different business process flows, would be better suited for the A-team strategy.

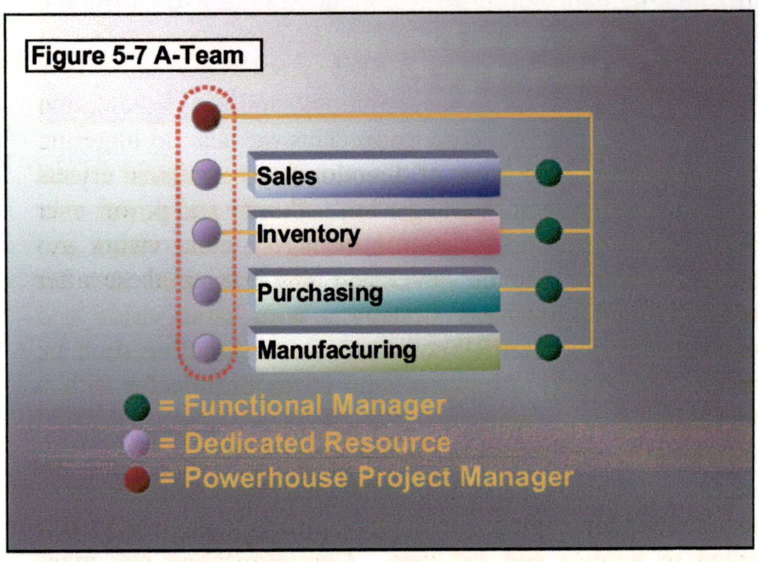

Figure 5-7 A-Team

The A-team approach (figure 5-7) contains a heavyweight powerhouse project manager with all the same characteristics found in the heavyweight approach. What makes this approach different from the heavyweight approach is that functional participants are transformed into full-time dedicated team leaders. Each team leader's objective is to make the ERP system successful. The ERP team still consists of ERP members and fluctuating functional participants whose roles change as the situation and heavyweight project manager dictate.

Communication becomes much more intensified within the ERP core team. Communication inputs and outputs to other team members decrease proportionally. The number of meetings and bureaucratic red tape is limited.

The A-team sometimes suffers from user ownership issues and organizational rejection. This is because the installation and development efforts become intensified inside the core team with communication and participation decreasing from the other team members. Functional participants and end-users develop anxiety over the coming ERP system. End-users may not understand or accept the solutions and implementation strategy developed by the core team. This can lead to lingering after effects in the ERP implementation. These after effects include concerns such as additional training, lack of user ownership, organizational rejection, user rejection, rework, re-implementation and more. With careful planning these after effects can be minimized.

The A-team formation is used for difficult situations such as: large and complex implementations, companies faced with a short amount of time with an unmovable installation date, and environments highly resistant to change. Companies failing three consecutive times in installing an ERP system may choose to use the A-team to help ensure their success. The success of ERP projects correlates strongly with dedicated resources. Companies dedicating resources are much more likely to succeed in implementing their ERP system.

There are two physical arrangements in how team members interact with software through the use of computers or other devices: war rooms and distributed approach. A war room is a multifunctional dedicated area where team members can come to train, hold meetings, perform testing, and develop solutions. War rooms are generally isolated from the other functional areas of the business. War rooms are ideal because of their flexibility and ability to allow team members to concentrate their resources.

The distributed approach takes advantage of existing computer hardware and infrastructure. It is a low-cost alternative to the war room but usually provides only limited flexibility. Sometimes in very small companies all the computers and functional areas exist within the same office room without physical barriers. In cases like these, slight adjustments can create an adequate war room. In other cases, computer systems and meeting rooms will be spread through out the company.

The need for a war room increases proportionally to the complexity of the project, the number of team members, and the speed in which the system will be installed. Extremely rapid and small installations generally go without a war room. Large and complex installations almost always have a war room.

Questions---

1. What is the function of the steering committee?
2. How is a lightweight project manager defined?
3. How is a heavyweight project manager defined?
4. What is the difference between a team leader and a team member?
5. What is an advantage to using the isolated functional approach?
6. What team structure approach is most commonly used?
7. What is the function of a management consultant?
8. What is the function of a technical consultant?
9. What is a war room?
10. List some common reasons for using war rooms.
11. How is a functional participant defined?
12. What types of ERP team structures often contain political struggles?
13. What types of ERP team structures have clear vision and mission statements?
14. What types of ERP team structures are most likely to have conflicting communications from different sources?
15. Why do companies put little effort into determining the best ERP team formation for their ERP implementation?
16. What type of ERP team formation has the most meetings?
17. What is one of the primary goals of the ERP service representative?
18. What are some of the most important skill sets an ERP team core member should have?
19. What role does the executive sponsor play for an ERP project?
20. What are some characteristics of good project managers?
21. What is the difference between leadership and management for an ERP project manager?

I did not realize that there was more than one choice. If we had known what we know today we would have done things much differently.

6

ERP Transition Strategies

An ERP transition implementation strategy determines how the ERP system will be installed. This chapter covers several basic ERP transition implementation strategies including: big bang, phased, parallel, process line, and hybrid. These techniques focus on the strategy of how to make the transition from a legacy system to a new ERP system. ERP implementations all begin with the simple question: how do we make the transition from our legacy ERP system to the new ERP system? The process of implementing ERP for most companies quickly becomes complex, making it difficult for newcomers to learn.

Figure 6-1 The Question

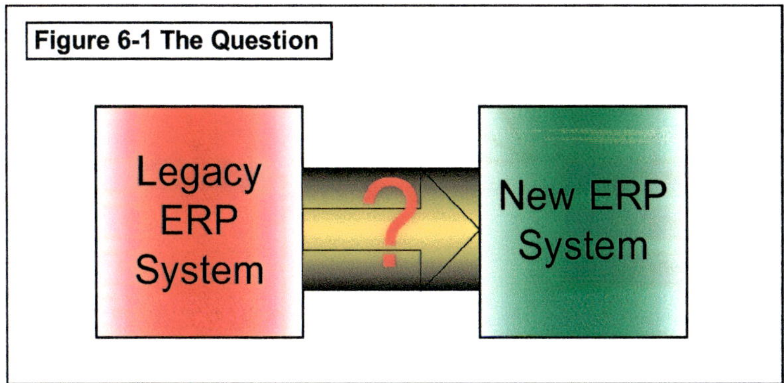

Fortunately, most ERP implementation strategies can be classified into a handful of categories. ERP implementation strategies appear relatively simple initially. But as more details are revealed, delicate intricacies come up that often lead to lengthy discussion among ERP team members. The subject of

ERP implementation strategies is a hotly debated issue among leading ERP professionals, increasing the confusion for companies and implementers searching for answers. ERP professionals often favor one strategy over another based on their experience, and often their experience is lacking! Because of the long implementation times of ERP, and the number of different techniques available to implement, it could take more than a 100 years to understand all of them based on experience.

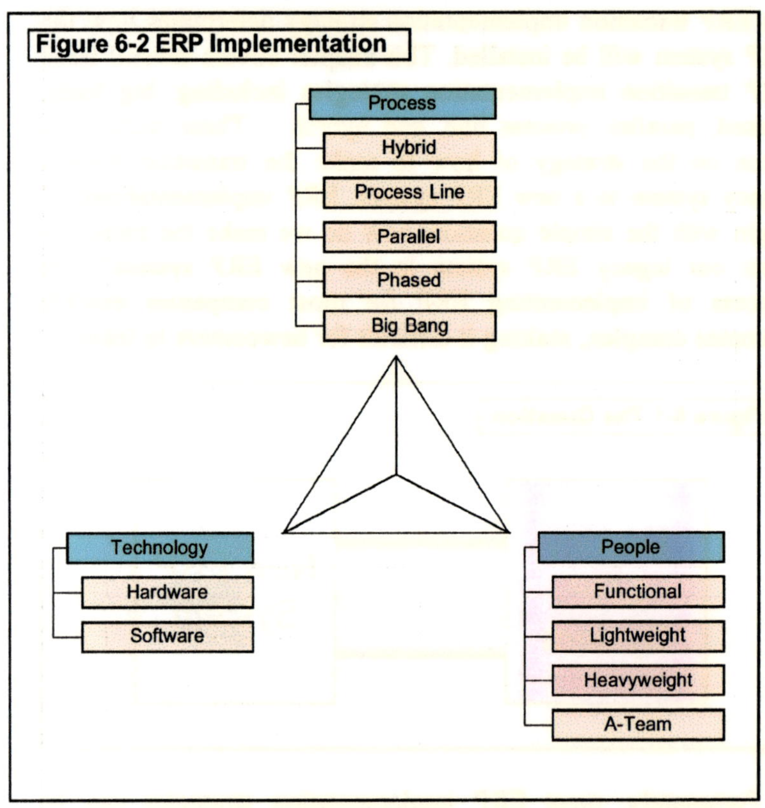

Any ERP implementation is supported by a three-leg stool. The three legs, as shown in figure 6-2, include process, people and technology. Failure to use one of these legs can cause an ERP project to quickly tumble. Understanding the relationships between the process, people and technology will assist the ERP implementers to better understanding what type or combination of types of ERP transition strategy is best.

The big bang strategy, also called cold turkey, converts from the legacy system to the new ERP system at some predetermined point in time. All of the business functions performed in the legacy system across the entire enterprise are simultaneously transferred to the new legacy system during a period of one day or a weekend.

Figure 6-3 Big Bang

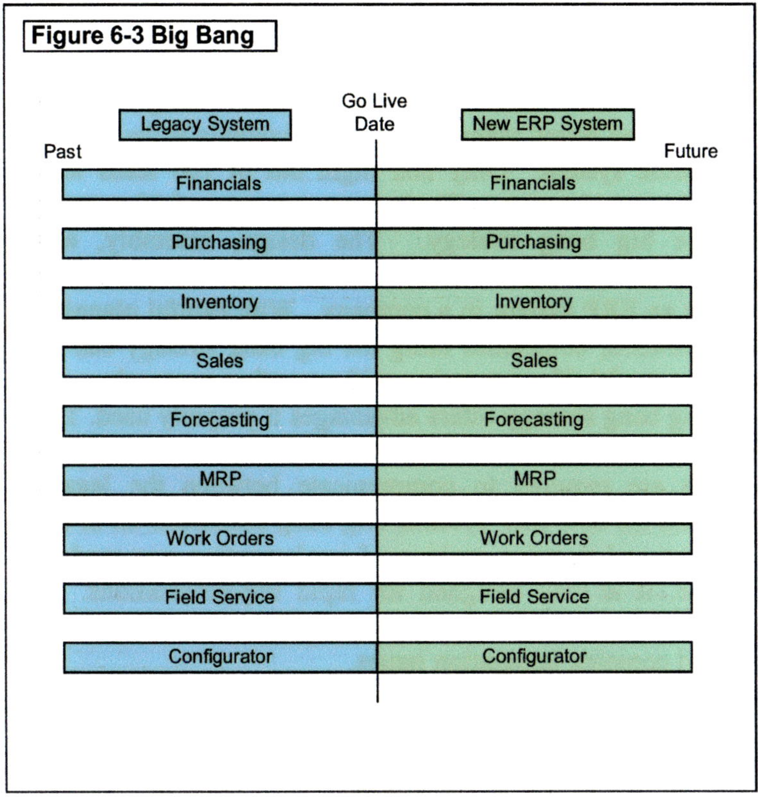

The big bang strategy is seldom used and often not recommended by ERP vendors, systems integrators, and service providers. Many companies struggle in deciding whether the big bang approach is the right choice for their company. One of the reasons given for not using the big bang approach is that it consumes too many resources to support the go live of the ERP system. Without question, high failure rates have been found using the big bang approach, but high failure rates have also been found using other strategies! Success in using the big bang strategy comes with careful preparation and planning prior to using big bang. It is not a question of whether the big bang is a good approach for ERP systems. The success of the big bang strategy depends on how well an organization plans and prepares prior to implementation.

Large-scale scientific and technical projects requiring mass coordination are often successful when using careful preparation and sound planning. A good example is the NASA space shuttle system. Only one flight out of 100 leads to a catastrophic malfunction. That's a success rate of 99 percent using the big bang strategy. The design, assembly, and launching of the space shuttle is far more complex than installing an ERP system in a company. With careful planning and preparation, companies using the big bang strategy can be just as successful (if not more) as with any other approach.

The big bang strategy offers advantages if properly used. The overall cost of implementation is less because no interface programs are required to communicate between the legacy system and the new ERP system. Big bang eliminates all of the sequencing and decision making of implementing one module at a time. It is well designed for rapid implementations. It creates a strong central focus for all the ERP team members. It can avoid complex integration issues.

Some of the disadvantages of the big bang include the time and cost of careful planning and preparation for the go live, bottleneck of critical resources, lack of professionals experienced in the big bang technique, and difficult recovery options.

Big bang has application for several situations. It can be used in situations where an immediate ERP solution is needed. For example, companies who need to go to the new ERP system immediately because their legacy ERP system has suffered a catastrophic malfunction such as physical destruction or database corruption. In general, the big bang approach seems to be better suited for smaller companies where all the critical resources of the project can fall within the immediate control of a project manager. The big bang strategy applies to any situation where a limited amount of time is available combined with an immovable go live date. This was the situation faced by many companies just prior to the year 2000 as they raced to implement new ERP systems to replace their systems that were year 2000 non-compliant.

Figure 6-4 Mini Big Bang

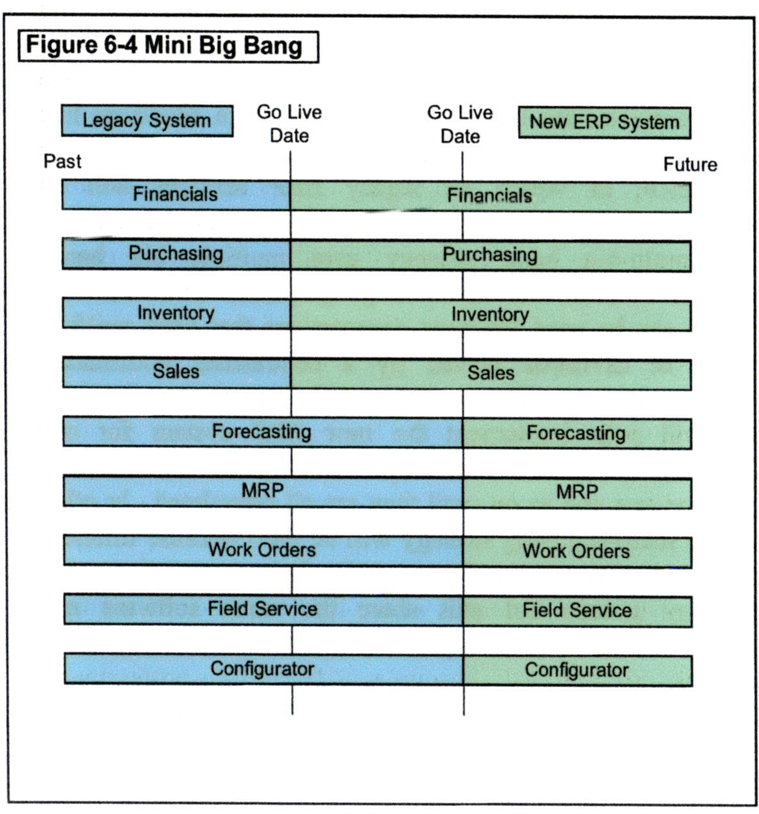

There are several variants of the big bang strategy. The mini big bang strategy takes a single big bang approach and breaks it into two or more sections. Each section consists of several software modules. Common sections, sometimes called suites, for a mini big bang strategy include financials, distribution, and manufacturing. For example the distribution section would include purchasing, inventory, and sales. The mini big bang strategy contains some phasing but still is not considered a pure phased implementation. ERP providers, system integrators, and service providers often refer to the mini big bang strategy as a phased implementation. The mini big bang strategy tends to be quite popular with varying degrees of success.

The mega-big bang strategy refers to a large company, with multiple sites, all going live at the same time using the big bang strategy. Some corporations have taken this approach as a "do or die" motivator for lingering ERP projects. In situations like this the senior management will issue a termination date for the legacy ERP, in which all legacy ERP services will be terminated, regardless of the readiness of any functional unit.

The multi-big bang strategy uses multiple big bangs sequenced in order for different geographical facilities. This approach can be used for large corporations that have multiple facilities or divisions served by a centralized information technology group. The centralized information technology group will help implement the new ERP system for one geographical location. After completion they will then move on to the next one and so on until they are all completed. In other cases the multi-big bang strategy will be used because different divisions of the corporation contain their own information technology groups but still share the same software and hardware resources.

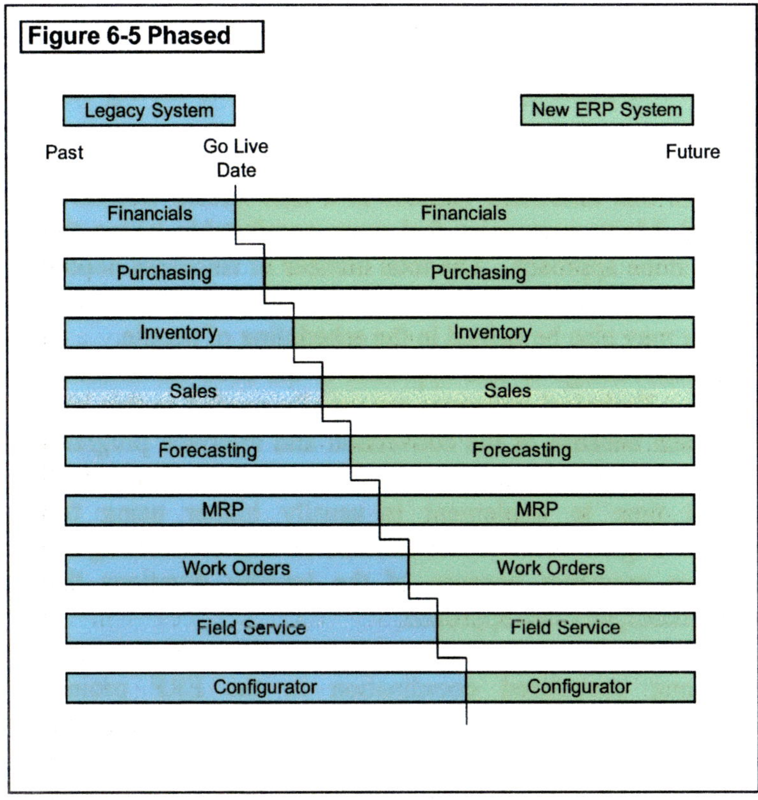

Figure 6-5 Phased

The phased approach, shown in figure 6-5, implements one functional module at a time in sequential order. The phased approach also goes by the names of modular, functional, and sequential. Interface programs are common in their use for the phased approach, or any situation that contains phasing. These interface programs are required to bridge the gap between the legacy ERP system and the new ERP system until the new ERP system becomes fully functional. A good example is where the financial modules go live on the new ERP software while the inventory module still remains active on the legacy ERP system. Through the use of interface and conversion programs, the financial activity that occurs in the inventory modules is exported to the new financial system in a format that can be understood by the new ERP system. Financial functions are usually implemented before distribution and manufacturing functions. The phase approach is closely related to the big bang technique.

The advantage is that this approach allows companies to implement one functional module at a time before another is attempted. Many companies feel more comfortable taking this stepping stone approach. The total number of resources needed at any one given point in time may be less. Additional flexibility may also be gained in the scheduling of people.

The disadvantage to this approach is the need for technical resources. Technical resources are usually needed in this kind of approach because of the conversion and interface programs that are required between the two ERP systems. The overall cost and time to implement is usually higher using this approach. Higher turnover rate can also be expected among key ERP team members because of the lengthy durations that usually accompany this approach.

The highly phased approach is often used in situations that lack strong centralized coordination in the ERP project. Without strong leadership and coordination in a project, the functional managers or assigned team leaders tend to take over the direction for their particular functional area. Because no one functional manager has more power than another, each is allowed to determine his or her own deadlines. The phased approach fits in well for this particular strategy; however, it does not necessarily generate higher success rates because of the good fit. Implementations that last a long time, greater than 18 months, usually use the phased approach.

A variant of the phased approach includes the mini big bang. As, previously discussed, with the mini big bang, two or more functional modules are combined into one sub-implementation for one single go live date.

The parallel approach keeps both the legacy system and the new ERP system active simultaneously for a length of time. The amount of time the systems are both in operation ranges from one day to several months. As shown in figure 6-6, portions of the same functional business areas (including software), such as purchasing, inventory, forecasting, etc., are operating at the same time for each of the ERP systems. The parallel approach can be thought of as another dimension to an ERP implementation strategy.

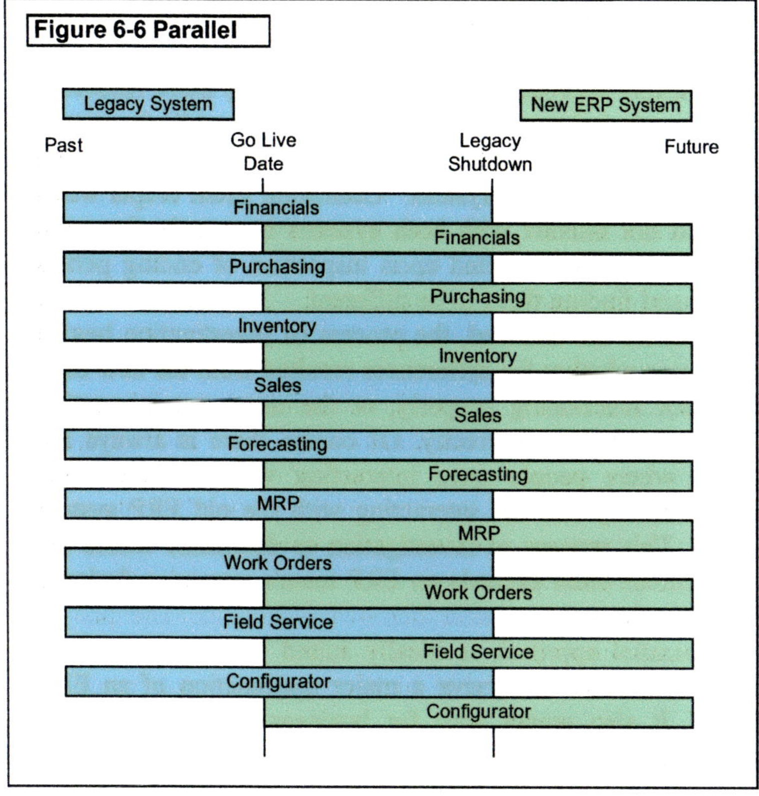

Figure 6-6 Parallel

An advantage to the parallel approach is that it has good recovery options in case something goes wrong. Because both the legacy ERP system and the new ERP system are in operation at the same time for a particular module, the company's business processes will not be interrupted if the new ERP system malfunctions.

For any company a new ERP system represents a gigantic variable. Because of the high failure rates of ERP systems the concept of running parallel to protect against implementation malfunction can provide a significant psychological cushion for the organization. The parallel approach also provides the most realistic number-to-number comparisons to validate that the new ERP system is performing the necessary business process flows. The parallel approach provides an exact number comparison in real world conditions.

The parallel approach consumes considerably more resources than other techniques during the transition. All functional interaction with the legacy system must also be duplicated exactly in the new ERP system. Confusion often erupts when people do not interact with both systems in exactly the same way. This is often detected upon inspection of ending period balances and finding them to be different.

Once errors are detected, the process of investigation begins to determine whether the differences resulted from the new ERP system not functioning properly, or the users not interacting with the new system correctly. Of course there is always the situation where people were interacting with the new ERP system correctly and not interacting with the old ERP system properly. This process of investigation to determine where the error occurred often exceeds an ERP team's resources during a go live situation.

The parallel approach is ideally suited for mission critical situations that cannot survive a major malfunction of an ERP system. It also works well for business environments that require the utmost in stability of an ERP system such as pharmaceutical or medical companies.

The parallel approach does not work well in situations where the legacy system has an expiration limitation that is within the needed amount of time for the system to operate in parallel mode. A classic example of this was the year 2000 situation. Because many legacy ERP systems had fatal year 2000 programming flaws, they could not continue beyond December

31st 1999, their expiration date. It would, of course, be impossible to run in parallel mode beyond this date.

A variant of the parallel mode is the paper parallel. This is an ingenious way to obtain the benefits of parallel implementation strategy while avoiding the high resources and confusion associated with using the parallel. The concept works the same, but how team members and end users interact with the legacy system makes it different.

Figure 6-7 Paper Parallel

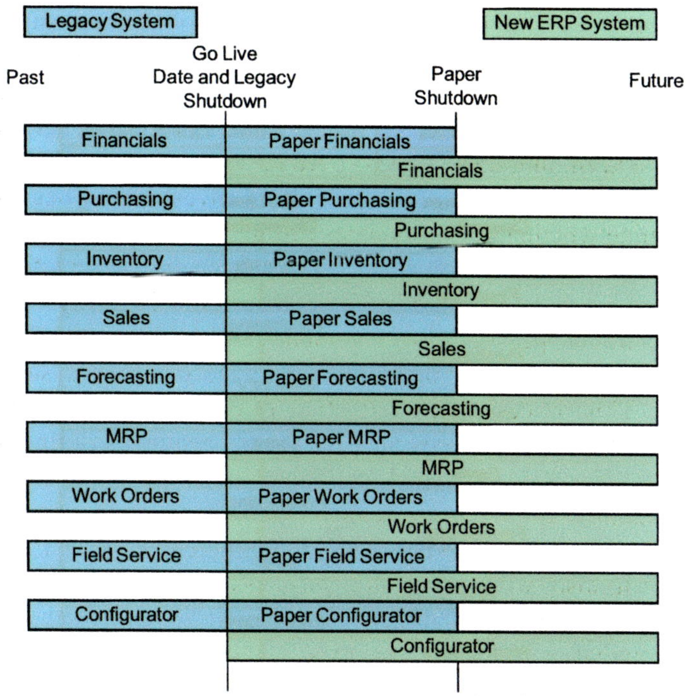

Instead of interacting directly with the legacy system, they record all transaction activity on paper. They accumulate the paper for the period of time in which the system runs parallel.

After confidence has been gained in the new ERP system, the accumulation of paper representing transactions of the legacy system then comes to a stop.

If a catastrophic malfunction does occur with the new ERP system, then people can use their paperwork to enter in all transaction activity that occurred during the parallel period into the old legacy system bringing all the balances up to the correct quantities. For many organizations, the process of recording all transaction activity on paper during the parallel period represents no disadvantage since most transaction activity is recorded anyway in some type of paper format.

Figure 6-8 Process Line

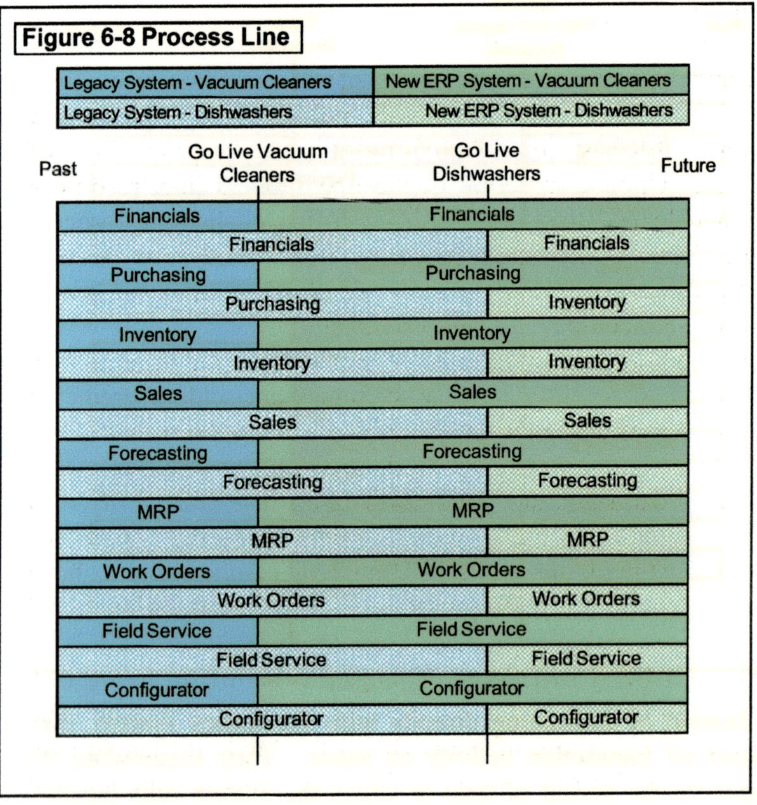

The process line strategy is conceptually similar to the mini big bang; however, it breaks the implementation strategy to manage parallel business process flows or product lines. An example includes an appliance manufacture that makes both vacuum cleaners and dishwashers within the same manufacturing plant. Few resources are shared between the vacuum cleaner and manufacturing departments. Using the process line strategy, the vacuum cleaner product line and all related resources goes first in making the transition from the legacy ERP system to the new ERP system.

After the vacuum cleaner product line successfully makes the transition, the dishwasher product line begins the transition from the legacy ERP system to the new one. When using the process line strategy, the smaller process lines, which pose less risk and have a higher probability of success, usually go first. This initial success victory helps to build organizational trust in the new ERP system, increasing its overall probability of success. Upon completion of the first process line, resources are then loaned to the more difficult and challenging process lines. This same concept can be applied for service organizations except that it would be implemented along focused service lines instead of product lines.

The hybrid strategy is some combination of the process line, phasing, and parallel. Hybrid strategies are seldom predicted precisely at the beginning of an ERP implementation. They tend to evolve into the needed configuration as ERP team members learn and analyze information. The complexity of a hybrid strategy varies tremendously depending upon the situation. Small single site ERP implementations tend to have simpler hybrid strategies than those used by large multinational corporations with many different geographical locations.

The CIBRES ERP hybrid triangle, as shown in figure 6-9, consists of three fundamental dimensions: process, phasing, and parallel. The purpose of the CIBRES ERP hybrid triangle is to demonstrate the relationship of how the process, parallel, and phasing techniques can merge together for a single implementation strategy.

Figure 6-9 *CIBRES* ERP Hybrid Triangle

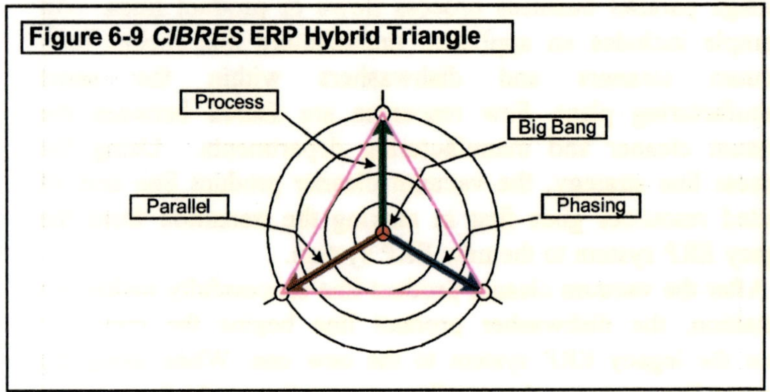

At the end of each arrow is a small white circle. This small white circle represents the amount of characteristic that exists for the particular dimension. By moving each one of the small white circles for its respected dimension, we can generate an infinite number of combinations of hybrid strategies. Figure 6-9 shows the graphical interpretation represented by the configuration shown in figure 6-10. Figure 6-10 represents the most complex implementation strategy.

The concept of a hybrid strategy is not necessarily fixed over the implementation of an ERP system. It can, and often does, change (the circles move) as people learn more about the software and project scope changes.

For example, for the phasing dimension, if the small circle is all the way out to the outer circle it represents a completely phased or modular implementation strategy. If the small circle is located all the way into the center of the circle, then it represents a complete big bang implementation strategy.

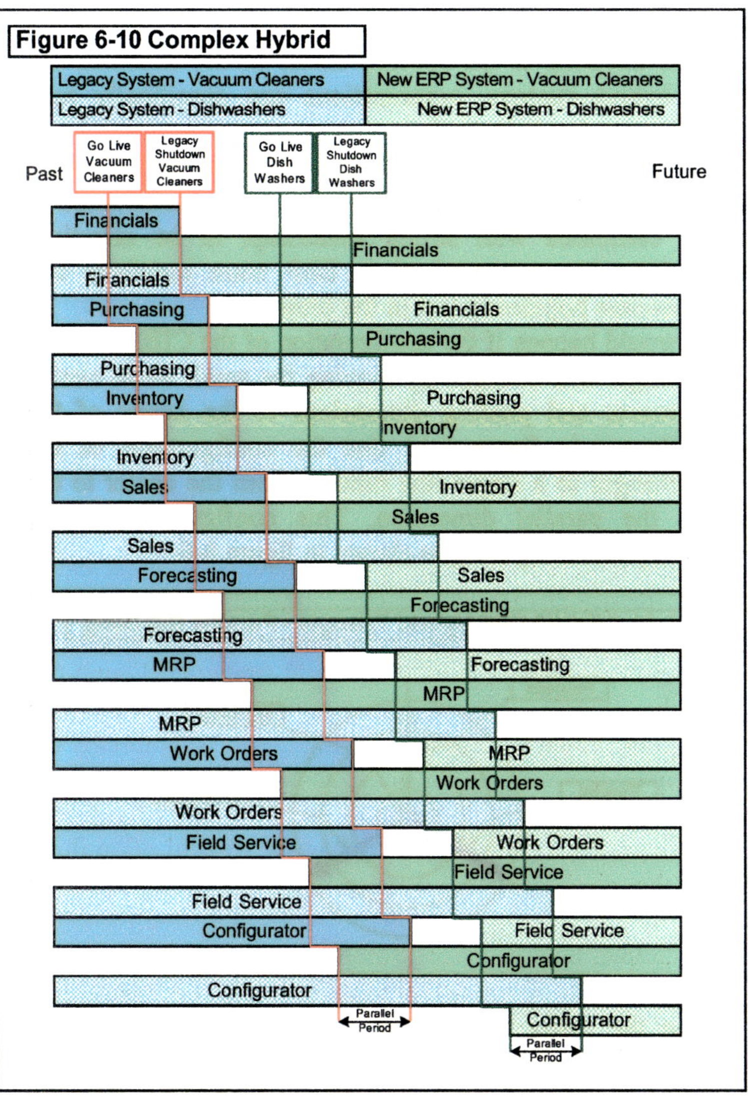
Figure 6-10 Complex Hybrid
Legacy System - Vacuum Cleaners
New ERP System - Vacuum Cleaners
Legacy System - Dishwashers
New ERP System - Dishwashers
Past
Go Live Vacuum Cleaners
Legacy Shutdown Vacuum Cleaners
Go Live Dish Washers
Legacy Shutdown Dish Washers
Future
Financials
Financials
Financials
Purchasing
Financials
Purchasing
Purchasing
Inventory
Purchasing
Inventory
Inventory
Sales
Inventory
Sales
Sales
Forecasting
Sales
Forecasting
Forecasting
MRP
Forecasting
MRP
MRP
Work Orders
MRP
Work Orders
Work Orders
Field Service
Work Orders
Field Service
Field Service
Configurator
Field Service
Configurator
Configurator
Configurator
Parallel Period
Parallel Period

Many implementations use hybrid strategies because they are flexible in adapting to the specific needs of the situation. By using a hybrid strategy, organizations can specifically tune implementation for their needs.

Hybrid implementations often become difficult for ERP team members to learn to adjust. A great deal of communication is required, combined with strong leadership, to be effective. Without intensive communication, ERP team members can quickly become hopelessly lost in the project.

What would happen if the configuration of the CIBRES ERP hybrid triangle was changed by moving the small white circles of the process and phasing dimensions to the center of the circle? We see in figure 6-11 that the configuration of the triangle changes to a single line running from the center to the edge on the parallel dimension. This configuration would represent a parallel big bang as shown in figure 6-6.

Figure 6-11 *CIBRES* ERP Hybrid Triangle - Parallel Big Bang

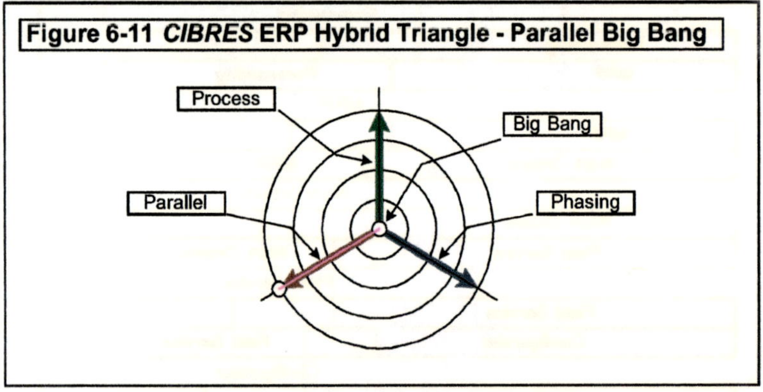

Among the many factors that could cause a company to choose one ERP strategy over another are: technical resource availability, number of users, consultant availability, structure of ERP team, deadlines, reliability and hardware resources.

Data conversions (the process of transitioning data over from the legacy ERP system to the new ERP system) play an important role as well. Data conversion strategies can lead to lengthy discussions in an ERP implementation and is included in this publication as another chapter.

Questions--

1. What are the three dimensions of the CIBRES ERP triangle?
2. What dimension represents the sequencing of individual modules?
3. What dimension represents the same module operating at the same time for two different ERP systems?
4. What dimension represents implementation by process or service line?
5. What are the four main types of ERP transition techniques?
6. Which of the four main types of ERP transition techniques exist along the same dimension?
7. What type of ERP transition technique can represent the most complex approach?
8. An isolated functional ERP team would most likely use what type of ERP transition technique?
9. What ERP transition technique is well suited for rapid implementations?
10. Interfaces would be a concern for which type of ERP transition technique(s)?
11. What is the paper parallel?
12. What is the mega-big bang?
13. What is the mini big bang?
14. Draw a graphical interpretation of figure 6-12 showing five different functional modules and their transition points.
15. Draw a graphical interpretation of figure 6-13 showing five different functional modules and their transition points.
16. Draw a graphical interpretation of figure 6-14 showing five different functional modules and their transition points.
17. What type of ERP transition technique could be used where there was a high concern for reliability?
18. What are two reasons that would make it impossible to use a parallel strategy?
19. Which ERP transition technique does not require the use of interfaces?
20. Which ERP transition techniques require data conversions?

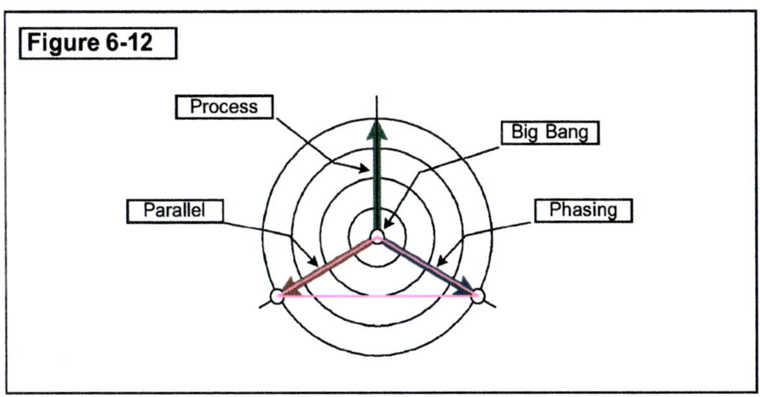

Figure 6-12

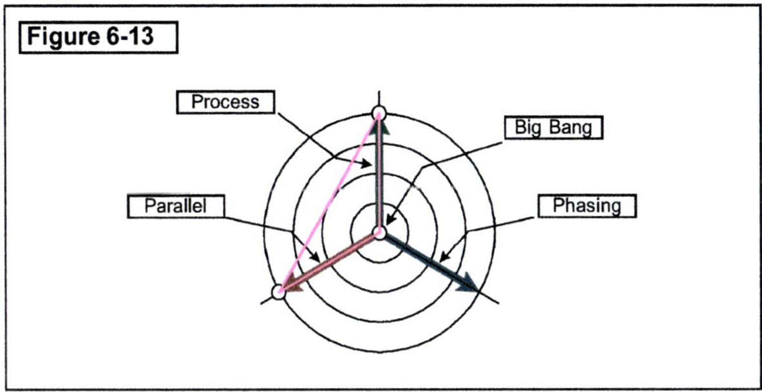

Figure 6-13

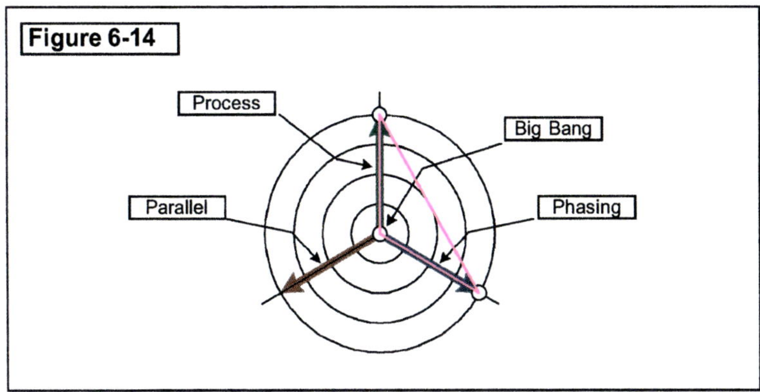

Figure 6-14

After running the data conversion programs just before the go live I notice a 15-cent variance in the extended inventory balance. Not thinking that to be a big amount we decide to go live. How I wished we had not gone live that day!

7

Data Conversions

The question of how to convert data from a legacy computer system to a new ERP system comes up in any installation of a new planning system as shown in figure 7-1.

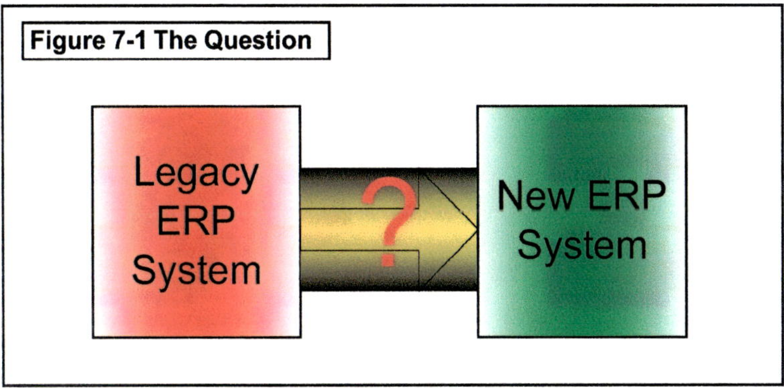

Figure 7-1 The Question

Two primary methods used include manual or an electronic method. In the electronic method, some type of database conversion process is used. This process can range anywhere from true source code development to complex copy utilities. The manual approach does not seek to use an electronic method, but instead involves human intervention. The manual approach will use a non-technical human resource to examine the data on the legacy system and decide how to enter in the information to the new ERP system.

Some of the factors to go into determining whether to use one approach or the other include: availability of technical resources, quality of legacy data, nature of operating systems and platforms, availability of human resources, database size, time constraints, budgets, user friendliness, and tradition. The process of choosing one approach over the other is seldom straightforward. Often the wrong choice is made. There is no universal rule in choosing one over the other; it depends on the situation. We will first examine the manual and electronic approaches and their major components.

Figure 7-2

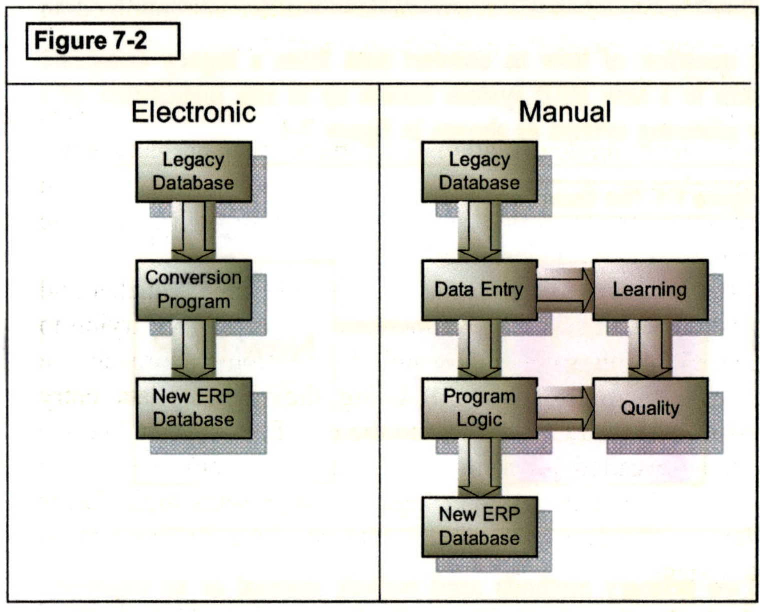

Figure 7-2 displays the major steps of electronic and manual approaches used in database conversions. On the left-hand side, we have the electronic approach. We first start with raw data in a legacy system such as an inventory item master file. Using technical resources, we come up with a conversion strategy to export data to the new ERP system. In some cases a conversion is relatively straightforward, with almost all relevant data coming from one file going to another. In other cases the situation becomes much more complex. Sometimes the information will come from one file and it will split into several different files in the new ERP system. Often special logic has to be applied to the process. A good example is when the legacy system uses an alpha field for part numbers and the new ERP system uses a numeric part number field. Special logic must be applied to convert from alpha to numeric. In this approach implementation team members generally are not involved in the technical solution from getting the data from one system to another. Implementation team members often get involved in data review to check the quality to see that it came through OK at a later time.

On the right hand side we find the manual approach. This strategy uses implementation team members and data entry personnel to convert data. The number of people involved can range anywhere from one to dozens. The size of the database often plays a key role in using this strategy.

If the database is very small it can often be much quicker and less expensive to simply enter the data in manually vs. trying to find an electronic solution. As with the electronic approach, we start with the legacy system. Using the manual data entry approach, the data is entered in to the new ERP system. We see a box here called program logic that we do not see on the electronic side. This program logic box represents logic that is applied to the data to verify the integrity by a program in an ERP system.

A good example is: someone attempts to enter a numeric value into an alpha field. The program halts the process, warning the user of invalid data. This type of logic must often be specially planned in the electronic approach. The final end results are the same. Data ends up in the new ERP database.

We notice that two secondary side benefits occur on the manual side, which include learning and quality. As the data entry was being performed, implementation team members learn more about the software and how to use it. Quality also comes as a secondary benefit. Quality, however, in this strategy can be somewhat elusive. Sometimes the benefits of quality are not achieved because the particular software does not contain integrity checking of the data before it allows it to pass to the database. The benefits of quality depend upon the software and situation.

Some software vendors attempt to compensate for missing program logic in the electronic solution. Electronic filters are often placed between the conversion program and the new ERP database. Varying degrees of success have been seen using this approach. The probability of success with electronic filters declines as the complexity of the conversion increases. Electronic filters attempt to fulfill the same role as program logic does using the manual approach.

The process of prototyping and testing in an ERP system is much more critical when using electronic conversion process then a manual process. This is because the special program logic found in the manual approach is often missing in the electronic process. Figure 7-3 shows various situations and probable outcomes.

Figure 7-3

	Testing		
	Low	Med	High
Electronic	Disaster	Trouble	Ok to Good
Manual	Trouble	OK	Good

We see that the need for testing becomes more demanding using electronic methods vs. manual. This can be attributed to the missing program logic used to validate data that can usually be found in manual methods. Failure to thoroughly test and review the data using either electronic or manual methods can, and often does, lead to catastrophic results.

There is often a misconception that an electronic approach will be a substitute for a manual one. In many cases a manual editing cleanup process must take place after an electronic conversion. This is especially true when the quality of the data is very poor. Sometimes programmers and technical resources can use special logic to help clean up the database. In other cases only direct human manual intervention can determine the proper coding for the database.

It's not uncommon, between the beginning of an implementation up to the go live phase, to make four or five manual revision sweeps of the database to clean up data integrity problems. Implementation team members will find that as they learn more about the software they find new and innovative ways to code the database to provide more functional capabilities in the ERP database. These discoveries often come several months after an electronic conversion has been performed.

Conversions, whether they are electronic or manual, usually begin in the early to mid phases of the ERP implementation. There are several reasons why companies choose to perform database conversions early in the process. Some of the reasons include:

- Prototyping
- Testing
- Training
- Documentation

What are some of the reasons for choosing one approach over the other? Availability of time is one. The time consideration can be broken into two different types of time: long-term and short-term. Long-term time is defined as the time between the beginning of the implementation and the go live of the ERP project or particular module. Short-term time is defined as a short period of time that exists between the closure of the legacy system and the go live of the new ERP system. Typically, this time can range anywhere from an hour to several weeks. A weekend is often the choice to go live on a new ERP system.

In the long-term time situation either manual or electronic may be used. The probability of an electronic solution being used increases as the availability of time between the beginning of the implementation process and the go live date decreases and the size of the database increases. A very large database and a very short period of time lends itself to an electronic solution. A very small database and large amount of time lends itself well to a manual solution.

In the short-term time situation either manual or electronic may be used. Some cases clearly dictate that an electronic solution must be the choice. An example includes the conversion of inventory on hand quantities of 2,000,000 items over the period of a weekend. Although it may be theoretically possible to perform this process manually using teams of data entry clerks, it is not necessarily recommended. Human mistakes are often used as an excuse to not use manual methods. Electronic methods are hardly fool proof as well. Even after painstaking prototyping and testing of an electronic conversion process, catastrophic mistakes can still occur and go undetected until long after the go live date.

The cultural viewpoint of ERP ownership can play a role. Companies that view the ERP system as a computer system to be set up and implemented via information system specialists will be much more likely to use an electronic solution. In other companies that choose to have ownership instilled at the user level will be more likely to use a manual approach. A manual approach is most advantageous because it provides extensive training and learned information of the new ERP system. Large volumes of manual data entry can also serve to thoroughly test the new ERP system. Extraordinary differences in performance, regarding ERP and human interaction, have been seen in manual approaches over electronic. One case has been observed where an ERP system with 12 million lines of code went live on all manufacturing and distribution functions in a period of about one month using purely manual conversion methods.

There are several major categories of data to be considered in conversions. Some of these major categories include:

- Setup information
- Day-to-day dynamic data
- Day-to-day static data
- Sequencing information
- Historical data

An example of setup information could include how often MRP should run. Software systems do this through switches or special processing options. Setup information is most commonly converted manually. Day-to-day dynamic data can be defined as data that changes often such as inventory quantities. Day-to-day static data can be defined as data that is more stable in nature such as part numbers. Sequencing information determines how information will be displayed on the new ERP system. This can be in the form of reports or online inquiries. Sequencing information is often converted manually or provided as defaults from the software vendor. Historical data includes information that is not needed on the day-to-day basis. This can include sales orders and purchase orders from several years back.

Many factors go into the decision of whether to use an electronic or manual conversion process. Because situations are so dynamic, generalizations and past experiences can be unreliable. Often the wrong choice is made. The two general strategies used include electronic and manual. Quality and learned information are important considerations in choosing one approach over the other. Tradition and cultural viewpoints of ERP systems also play significant roles. Several different classes of data exist to be considered for conversion in an ERP system. Manual processes often yield higher quality and instill greater ownership of an ERP system to the end-users.

Questions--

1. What are the two methods of performing data conversion?
2. What is an electronic filter?
3. What is a database conversion?
4. What approach to a database conversion is most likely to yield the highest user ownership?
5. Give an example where an electronic database conversion must be use instead of a manual approach?
6. Why do manual methods often create a higher quality ERP database?
7. What are the two secondary benefits of using a manual approach?
8. What are three disadvantages of using an electronic approach?
9. What are some disadvantages of using a manual approach?
10. Give two reasons why data conversions are performed early in the ERP implementation process?
11. What are the two different types of time considerations?
12. What are five major categories of data?
13. What is the difference between dynamic and static data?

We have to test the software? I thought that's what the ERP vendor does...

8

Prototyping and Testing

Prototyping and testing is an important part of any ERP implementation. The purpose of this chapter is to stress its importance and provide a methodology for implementers to use to help ensure that the functionality of the software will perform as expected upon the go live date of an ERP system or module. All too often companies in a dire rush to implement their ERP systems overlooked this important step, which often brings about irreversible damage to the culture of an organization and the successful use of an ERP system. One of the most disruptive things that an organization can face is an ERP system that does not perform as expected. The prototyping and testing phase will help bring the capabilities of the software and the expectations of the organization to a common meeting point, a point in which few surprises occur. The further apart the capabilities of the software and the expectations of the ERP users, the greater the disruption to the organization and frustration of ERP users.

Prototyping and testing should be conducted in the relatively early phases of an ERP implementation. Generally, this phase will not take place until after the software sales cycle has been completed. For many companies, prototyping and testing does not take place until a situation develops that seriously threatens the welfare of the company. The situation often develops after a company has gone live on the software and realizes that it is not performing as expected. After the go live date is a poor time to begin the prototyping and testing process. This process, however, must be performed for the resolution of many issues.

There are several important reasons why prototyping and testing should take place in the early phases of the project.

Prototyping and testing provides one of the highest forms of learning that ERP team participants can receive. Its effective use can greatly reduce the amount of required education and training as well as consultation support. Effective use of prototyping and testing can easily pay for itself many times over by eliminating future consultation services and costly mismatches between software capabilities in business process flows.

Prototyping and testing generates a high degree of user ownership in a project. Because significant thought processes are required to perform the prototyping and testing process, it brings ERP team members closer to the software, allowing them to see more functionality and better solutions, bringing about better understanding and user ownership. As the ERP team develops a better sense of ownership in the new ERP system, so will the rest of the organization, further increasing successful use in implementation of the ERP system.

Prototyping and testing is often the only way to find answers for complex questions. Although consultants and software demos can be helpful in gaining better understanding of software process flows, they do not provide the same quality of answer that can be provided through prototyping and testing. A consultant may say, "Yes; the software can do that." However, prototyping and testing provides a more definitive answer while providing how it can or cannot do something. It provides the opportunity to help reduce miscommunication between the consultants and ERP team members.

Prototyping and testing provides opportunity to reduce barriers between functional silos of an organization. Because the prototyping and testing process can be conducted by participation of several different functional silos related to one business process flow, it provides the opportunity for many different people from different functional silos of the organization to communicate with each other. This provides a great opportunity for cross communication that would otherwise not be available in the normal day-to-day routines of the company. This provides much deeper insight on the needs and process flows within functional silos for the ERP team members.

Prototyping and testing provides a key opportunity for business process reengineering. Business process reengineering is the process of rethinking, finding new solutions, and implementing better and more efficient business process flows. In short, it can be thought of as blowing up the old and using something better. During the prototyping and testing phase, the ease of change is at its highest point of any time in the ERP project. During the later steps, change can become increasingly difficult. The combination of ERP team members from several different functional areas, consultants, and new software provides right opportunity for change.

Prototyping and testing builds integrity and quality into the final delivered business process flow. Higher quality business process flows prevent costly rework after the go live date of the ERP system. A variety of quality management tools can be applied to the prototyping and testing phase, and should be. Prototyping and testing helps to ensure that the delivered process flow will be statistically stable. Stable ERP systems provide the foundation and framework for strategic and tactical management in business environments. The effective use of strategic and tactical management in an ERP system can provide one of the highest forms of return on investment in an ERP system.

Prototyping and testing is the process of creating ERP process flows that match the business process flows of the company. Many modern-day ERP systems come with a tremendous amount of flexibility; they can be used in an almost infinite number of ways. With so much capability comes the question of how, or what would be the best way? Prototyping and testing provides these answers. In prototyping and testing the ERP software is modified through the use of soft coding to match the business process flows. After the adjustments are made, the software is then tested to see that the results are as expected. If the results are not as expected, then further adjustments will be made until the ERP software flow matches the desired business process flows. Should the software be incapable of performing the necessary functions, custom modification of the software may be sought, or the business process flows may be changed.

ERP team members and consultants are the primary people involved in the prototyping and testing process. ERP team members will provide the business process flows and the consultants will provide the functional capabilities of the software. Working together they often find common ground for a solution. Employees from other functional areas of the business may attend sessions to review output developed in the prototyping and testing sessions. Technical programmers may become involved should the desired solutions exceed the software capabilities.

Highly experienced consultants are not required for the prototyping and testing phase, although their presence may be helpful. By its very nature, prototyping and testing, is designed to perform well outside the presence of a strong software knowledge base normally provided by a consultant. This is the purpose of prototyping and testing. The quality of the consultants can be very difficult to determine in the early phases of an ERP implementation. Companies entrust their ERP vendors and service providers to send qualified consultants. All too often, ERP vendors and service providers will take advantage of this by sending unprepared consultants out into the field in order to obtain billable hours. Entrusting the future of a business to an unqualified consultant can have long-term repercussions. Prototyping and testing may not eliminate unqualified consultants, but it can prevent unnecessary damage to the company. Wise consultants that are uncertain of the situation will proactively recommend prototyping and testing sessions to validate functional software capabilities and business process flows.

Prototyping and testing is done at the software level and business process flow level. ERP vendors will test their software extensively, although often it is not enough, to help ensure that the software will perform as expected. The business process flows may be tested as well, although generally they are generic in nature, not specific to any business.

Really good matches with the ERP process flows and business process flows can only come from prototyping and testing being conducted at the site where the ERP software has been installed. Prototyping and testing is most successful on site because that is where the highest knowledge base can be obtained. In fact, many ERP software vendors will prototype and test their software at a customer's site. Customers will often allow this in exchange for free software or services. These sites are often called beta sites and usually experience an abnormal amount of problems because of the newness of the software.

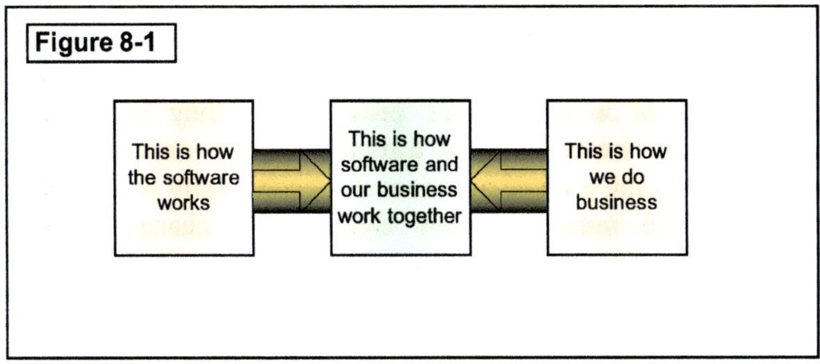

In its most fundamental sense, prototyping and testing seeks to answer the question of how. Figure 8-1 shows a desirable combination after performing prototyping and testing. Figure 8-2 shows the common question for many companies as they enter the prototyping and testing stage. Many companies will understand how they do business but are unaware of how the software works and how the business and software will work together to provide a common uniform solution.

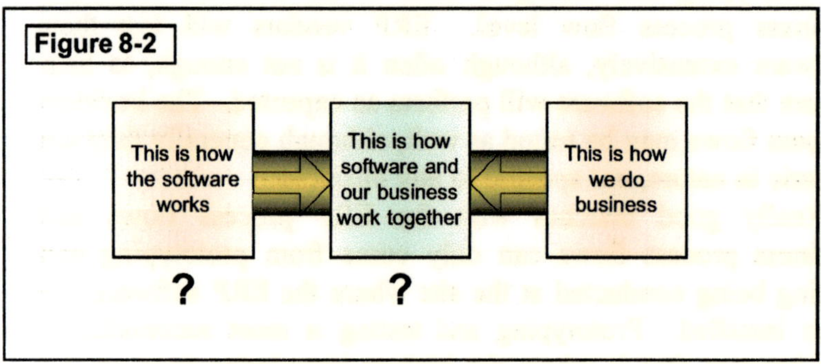

Figure 8-3 shows another common situation where all three components are in question. Surprisingly, the question of how a company does business is quite common. Many consultants, ERP vendors, and ERP service providers will often provide documents called 'client questions'. Client questions consist of a series of organized questions to help consultants, and their clients, understand how the business process flows of the company are taking place. The questions may be answered independently of a consultant's presence or they may be answered in an interview type format. Highly experienced consultants may ask a lot of questions during the early phases of prototyping and testing. They dynamically change their questions based upon the last answers received, guided by an internal 'if then' conditional process.

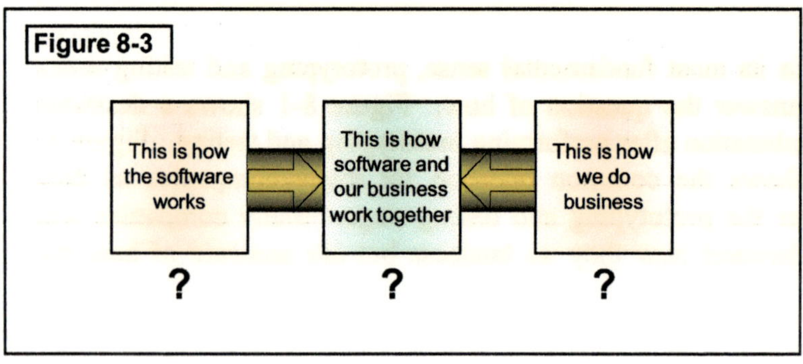

Figure 8-4 Prototyping and Testing Steps

Step	Task	Skill	People
Conception	Planning and Integration	Multi-functional	ERP team members
Functional Mapping	Interviewing	Communication, creativity	ERP team members, consultants
Specification	Systems development	Documentation and engineering	ERP team members
Research	Finding answers and performing proof of concepts	Design and evaluation	ERP team members, consultants
Options	Presenting solutions	Communication	ERP team members
Approval	Selecting options	Decision making	Managers, critical stakeholders
Construction	Building prototype	Building solutions	ERP team members
Testing	Validating prototype	Quality	ERP team members, consultants
Documentation	Recording configuration settings	Record keeping	ERP team members
Approval	Final system review	Management	Managers, critical stakeholders
Implementation	Installation	Project	Project manager, ERP team members

Figure 8-5 Prototyping and testing process flow

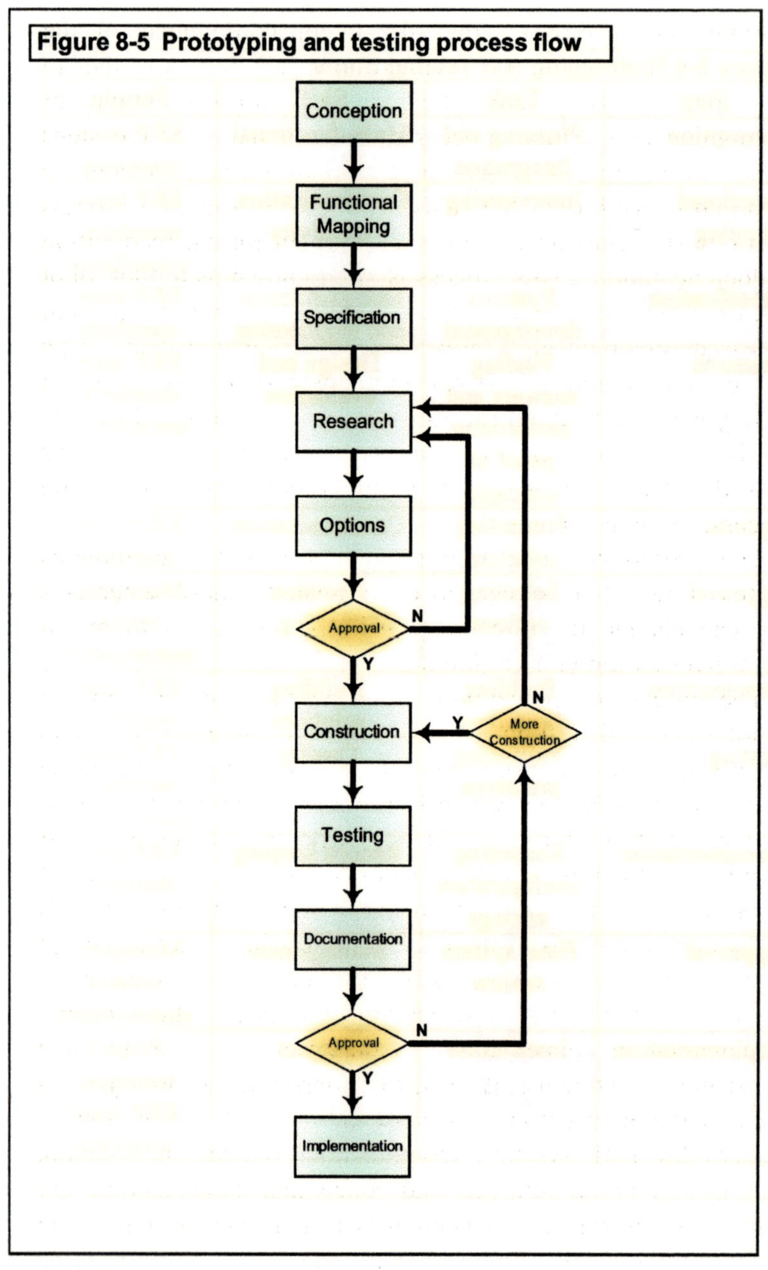

Figure 8-4 and 8-5 shows the major components of the prototyping and testing process and how they work together to develop a process flow. Most companies will use some type of prototyping and testing process containing many of the steps shown in figure 8-4. Companies seldom formally recognize each and every one of the steps; it's more of a natural process with one step flowing into the next without formal recognition or documentation. This process is often known as a pilot, pilot test, or conference room pilot. Some pilot tests will use a small cross-section of business process flows using live data. This can be considered a process implementation. It is not a prototyping and testing process. A pilot test that uses live data for the purpose of performing day-to-day business transactions goes directly to the last step in the prototyping and testing process: implementation.

The prototyping and testing process is not a continuous process flow. It is subject to conditional 'if then' statements that can change the direction causing certain steps to repeat themselves as shown in figure 8-5.

The process of conception occurs at the beginning of the prototyping and testing phase or before. It integrates and directly supports the visions and missions of the project and the company. It covers the system from a very broad perspective as well as from a narrow focused viewpoint. It applies most specifically to a particular functional module, such as sales order entry or forecast management. In addition, conception is based upon the needs of the organization, which may come out of the original business needs analysis conducted in the early phases of the ERP justification process. For people participating in conception, it is important for them to have broad multifunctional skill sets, to understand the organization from global perspective. Because of the high integration of modern-day ERP systems, few functions operate in isolation. This is why broad skill sets and conceptual understanding are helpful in this stage. Conception is usually performed by the ERP team members during the ERP implementation for specific functional activities. Higher, more general types of conception often come from other sources such as senior management or the steering committee.

Functional mapping is an important part of the prototyping and testing phase. Functional mapping is the process of interviewing and working together as a team in understanding and documenting business process flows. Functional maps are often created on a visual aid, such as a white board or projector, so groups of people can interact, creating the best possible business process flow that matches the capabilities of the ERP software. ERP team functional members and outside consultants are active participants.

Functional mapping is an extension of the conception stage. It converts conceptual ideas, supported by vision, mission, and business needs, into process flow patterns that can be interpreted by the participants creating it. Often a facilitator will lead a group that has strong business knowledge of the company and its process flows. They discuss how those business process flows take place, or could be better, what is really needed, and capabilities of the software. In some cases they split a white board up the middle. The left-hand side shows the old business process flow as it is currently being used and on the right-hand side shows the desired business process flow. Working together with consultants, business process flows on the right hand side may be modified based upon the capabilities and limitations of the software. The functional mapping eventually becomes the specification for future research.

During the research phase, ERP team members and consultants may work together to identify one or more ways of using the software to provide the necessary business process flows. The purpose of the research is to find the 'how' of the software. This phase contains many different types of activities. It may involve the exploration of software manuals, making telephone calls to the ERP vendor, discussing with consultants, performing proof of concepts, and more. Proof of concepts involves the testing of an idea to prove or disprove the application for a given type of business process flow. ERP team members and consultants may go into the new ERP software to perform the basic setup necessary to perform the test. The number of people involved for a proof of concept model is very small, usually between two and four. Several different proof of concepts may be conducted to help determine which ones are feasible. The length of time of the research step may range anywhere from a few minutes to several weeks. The goal of the research step is to determine the validity of available options. Once the validity of the option has been established, no further research will be required on that option.

Using the research output, formal documentation may be created that specifies the option and the option's advantages and disadvantages. (The option is the proven method.) Once all the options, along with the advantages and disadvantages, are documented and understood, a formal meeting can be called in which an approval process is conducted among the critical stakeholders. The approval process consists of reviewing each option with the group and explaining their advantages and disadvantages. When more than one option exists, the group should prioritize the options from best to worst. The goal of the step is to achieve group consensus of one or more steps. If group consensus cannot be achieved, then the people performing the research and development options may need to return to the research stages to find more available options. This normally does not need to happen when a good job has been done in the conception, functional mapping, and specification phases. If these early stages are done correctly, then valid options are usually found in the research phase. Fortunately, many companies discontinue the process at this point. Although this may provide an opportunity to cut costs and shorten implementation times, the unpredictability of the outcome can be awkward at times. Many companies simply seem eager to identify that the software has the capability to perform the function. Many companies fail to identify how the function can be used, managed, and implemented. They also fail to determine how reliable the solution might be. The research phase only determines if it is possible.

With positive approval for a specific option, ERP team members and consultants may move forward into the construction stage. This stage will begin preparing the software (and sometimes hardware) for true life cycle testing. The testing step contains the actual prototype business process flow. Specific configuration settings will be adjusted to match the needed configuration.

Ways of looking at the difference between a proof of concept model and prototype are the completeness of the setup and volume of testing. The length of time for the construction phase can vary considerably. Usually the time is very short (less than one day) when using the soft coded capabilities of the software. Additional time must be allowed and software modifications will be made. The length of time to perform necessary software modifications may range from a few minutes to weeks, months, or in rare cases years. Ideally, when all earlier stages of the ERP implementation process have been done well, few situations arise where the construction step requires hard coded software modifications.

Usually the proof of concepts done in earlier steps takes place in some type of alternate environment. The alternate environment is an important part of the construction process. It allows people to segment the construction activities from other important activities going on at the same time during the ERP implementation. The alternate environment can be set up a variety of ways depending upon the technology, ERP software, and operating systems. The number of environments varies from a minimum requirement of one, to as many as 10 or 15. Sometimes an alternate environment is created through libraries, partition of hard disk space, key record identifier within the same database, or additional databases. The concept of using different environments also applies to performing proof of concepts in the research step. Companies that have multiple implementations going on at the same time in different divisions almost always require different alternate environments for testing and prototyping.

The volume of testing involved in the proof of concept model may be no more than one transaction. The prototype should contain the same amount of transactions that would be expected under normal conditions. The configuration settings involved in the proof of concept model should be only enough to prove or disprove valid options. In the testing phase the environment should be set as close to real-life conditions as possible.

The testing process may contain many cycles of testing. ERP team members testing a specific configuration may find that the results were not as expected. They may go back and make further adjustments and test again. This process may repeat itself again and again until the necessary outcome is achieved. Once the process has been thoroughly stabilized and tested, it is ready to receive formal documentation. The formal documentation is then used for the next step, documentation and approval.

In the approval step following the documentation prepared from the testing phase, the critical stakeholders of the ERP team and business process flows will reassemble again to review the results of the test. Many times this is conducted as a demonstration. The documentation created coming out of the testing process is thoroughly reviewed. Discussion takes place between consultants, critical stakeholders, and ERP team members. Should the team decide to reject results of the prototyping and testing process, then it may return to the construction step or even back to the research step. Whether the outcome of the prototyping and testing process is positive or negative, facilitators of the approval meeting should seek to obtain consensus from all members participating in the approval process. It is not necessary to obtain agreement on all issues, but rather all team members in that whatever direction is taken shall support consensus. A healthy analysis will include certain team members that do not agree with the process flow. Be wary of any team that makes a unanimous decision, for group thinking processes may be in place such as those that led to the space shuttle disaster. Should the team decide to accept the outcome of the prototyping and testing process, then the process may move on to the next step: implementation.

During the implementation step the configuration settings developed in the prototyping and testing step are configured for actual conditions as they will be used after the go live date. The configuration settings may be applied immediately after approval or at a future point in time. In some cases, depending on the implementation methodology used, and how the alternate environments are set up, no further adjustments are needed. Some companies choose to accumulate their prototyping and testing configuration settings in their testing environment. When the time comes to go live, using technical functions, the configuration settings are copied over from the prototyping and testing environment into the actual production environment to be used after the go live date. Whatever strategy or situation is used, the configuration settings that have been approved by the team should be documented in a fashion, which will not be disrupted. Many times, in the chaos of the ERP implementation, some team members and consultants can radically rearrange configuration settings, without other ERP team members being aware of the changes. The documentation should be used as an audit trail from which to determine the correct configuration settings of the software just before the go live date.

Questions---

1. What is the purpose of prototyping and testing?
2. When should prototyping and testing take place?
3. How many steps are there to the prototyping and testing process?
4. What does a process flow chart look like for the prototyping and testing process?
5. What does a process flow chart look like for the prototyping and testing process at your company?
6. Who is involved in the conception stage?
7. What is functional mapping? Why is it important?
8. What is the purpose of a proof of concept model?
9. How much testing is enough?
10. What happens in the approval step?
11. Where is testing performed on the new ERP system?
12. What are some advantages of finding more than one way of doing something?

Even when the fire department puts out a fire, you are never better off after the fire than you were before it.

9

Environmental Characteristics

This chapter looks at environmental characteristics from several different perspectives. No matter what type of company, each ERP system tends to develop a certain personality. The particular combination of fundamental concepts such as: ownership, viewpoints, management support, and education contribute to these personalities.

The combination of user ownership and use of an ERP system can quickly bring out the personality of an ERP system. Ownership is the way an ERP user or ERP team member feels about an ERP system. ERP team members with high ownership feel responsible for the performance and quality of the output of an ERP system. ERP team members with low ownership do not feel responsible for the performance or quality of an ERP system. Users with high ownership participate actively in the implementation and day-to-day activities of an ERP system.

The lack of ownership plagues many companies' ERP systems from implementation to end. Consultants often feel frustrated because of the participation of the company's ERP team members. Many factors contribute to the lack of participation, including education, management view of ERP software, management support, technical expertise, training, workloads, culture, vision and missions.

Since an ERP system is highly dependent on people that use it and how they interact with it, high ownership is important for success. A lack of ownership is a warning sign that an ERP system is in trouble. Most companies experience a lack of ownership by the users of the system.

When there is lack of ownership by the users of an ERP system, the IS (Information Systems) function will take over. This produces some interesting characteristics. ERP users will often blame the IS department for problems occurring within the ERP system. The lack of ownership by the users can happen because they are not allowed to take ownership or because they are not capable of ownership functions. In either case adversarial relationships erupt between the users of the ERP system and the members of the IS department.

Figure 9-1 How ERP Is Used

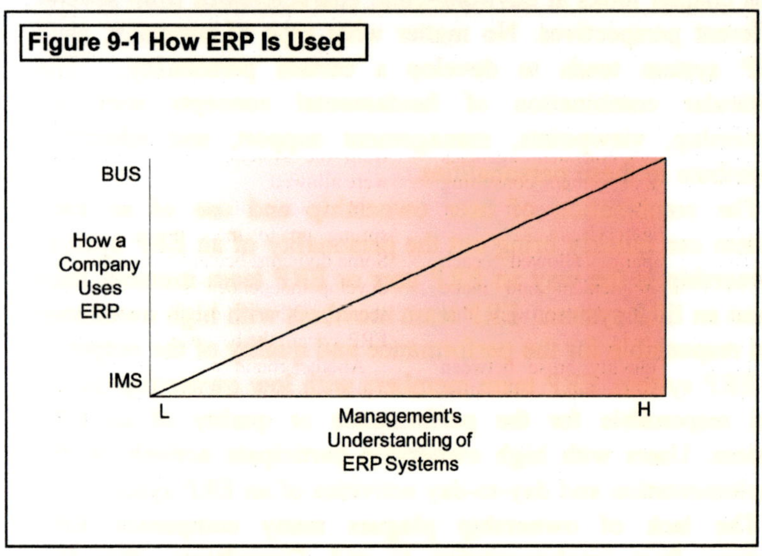

How companies view and use their ERP systems falls between two points as shown in figure 9-1. Some companies view their ERP system as a data collection and storage tool, an information management system (IMS). In environments like this, management has little understanding of what an ERP system is and how it works. In fact, in environments such as this, the term ERP is often missing from the senior management's vocabulary! There is no focus on the quality of input and maintenance of data.

Case Study

Cow Like Environment Wanders Off Course

In 1996, a large American based manufacturer of consumer products decided to go with a tier one ERP vendor to replace their aging home grown legacy system.

They were faced with a complex ERP installation. The company had over 20 manufacturing plants with different management and manufacturing process flows. They had several different manufacturing plants in foreign countries that brought about the need for multi-language and multi-currency.

To aid in the implementation they turned to outside consultant agencies for business management consulting and the ERP vendor for implementation services.

The company allowed each division to implement and make modifications to the software that best fit their needs.

Problems quickly arose between divisions in conflicting functionality. Unable to resolve the issues, the company blamed the ERP vendor for misrepresenting their product. The ERP vendor promptly responded by withdrawing all implementation support services. The implementation effort soon collapsed, leaving deep scars between them.

Beginning in 1997 a second effort was launched using implementation services from the ERP vendor's business partners.

A similar approach was used as the first time, bringing about similar results. Chaos erupted with lack of management support and a host of conflicting issues between different manufacturing divisions.

Faced with other serious market and management problems, the company decided to reorganize the management of the company and dissolve the second implementation effort. A good portion of the management was laid off and a new wave of younger eager managers replaced them.

The new management structure decided to adopt a radically different type of ERP implementation strategy: do-or-die.

A notice was issued to all divisions that they had until December 31st, 1998 to disband their legacy system and move to the new ERP solution. The legacy mainframe system was going to be physically disconnected from the system. No compromises were allowed.

In a wave of panic, new teams sprung up to meet the challenge. Some divisions began to immediately develop independent sub systems in secrecy. Others chose to use the new ERP system the best way they could.

Another round of fresh consultants came in to aid in the implementation effort. Nobody felt that such a radical effort was going to be successful, and it was not.

As of January 1st the legacy system was turned off, leaving the divisions struggling for basic functionality. Operations management and customer service suffered badly, leaving customers questioning the firm's future capability. Unable to enter new customer orders, some divisions started developing paper-based systems.

In order to meet the critical deadline, functionality was simply "programmed" in. Over 1600 programs were modified at the source code level out of the 2100 that came with the system. Some divisions were not even able to perform basic inventory transactions until several months after the go live.

Case Study

Cow Like Environment Wanders Off Course (cont)

Consultants worked with managers over the next year to stabilize the system. A lot of expensive rework was faced by the company in tearing out the independent custom solutions that had been adopted by many of the company's divisions.

Painfully and slowly, progress was made. By the end of 1998, the majority of the divisions were up and running on the new software and most of the company had access to basic functionality such as sales, purchasing, inventory, shop floor control, inventory management, etc.

It looked like they were going to come out of a long deep struggle when, in the first quarter of 1999, the senior management made a startling discovery that made them feel like conductors that just drove their new steam locomotive off a bridge that was half built. They found out that the version of software that they had installed was not supported by the ERP vendor as being year 2000 compliant.

The consultants had warned the company about year 2000 issues but the message never reached key managers that had little participation in the project. Since the ERP vendor was no longer providing support services, no effort was made by them to inform the company.

The senior management quickly learned the graveness of their situation after a meeting with their senior consultants.

Because of the heavy modifications to the system, an upgrade strategy to the ERP vendor's year 2000 compliant software was going to be very difficult.

The most current version was a different system. 1600 new program modifications had to be programmed, tested, and implemented in 10 months. An investigation process was needed to determine which modifications needed to be made and which ones did not. Other program modifications could be eliminated by changing the way some divisions did business or by simple education of the software's capabilities.

Faced with a difficult decision, the senior management decided that only one approach could save them in the amount of time that was available: re-implementation of the software using the year 2000 compliant software without system modifications.

The go ahead was given to issue the ultimatum to the other divisions that they had until December 31st to adopt the latest year 2000 compliant software.

Like the first time, another round of teams and outside consultants sprung up to meet the challenge leaving senior managers wondering if this living hell was ever going to come to an end.

The company struggled financially as the project ate up company profits. In order to stay afloat, the company sold off several divisions and laid off employees to save money.

The after effects were similar to the last implementation effort plagued by extensive rework. By the beginning of year 2000, all remaining divisions were up on the new software but faced serious user morale problems, technical issues, and missing functionality. By the end of 2002 things will probably settle down, making for an expensive overall 7-year implementation effort.

On the other end of the scale management has a thorough understanding of what an ERP system is, how it works, and what to expect from it. Companies and management in this environment view (and use) their ERP system as a strategic and tactical tool for competitive advantage in the marketplace. The ERP system is thoroughly integrated into the functional areas of the enterprise. The ERP system works in harmony with the functional areas of the enterprise as an ERM system.

The combination of user ownership and how a company uses an ERP system tends to produce interesting animal-like characteristics. ERP systems and how companies use them can be classified into one of five different categories: Eagles, Wild Horses, Cows, Monkeys and the Circus.

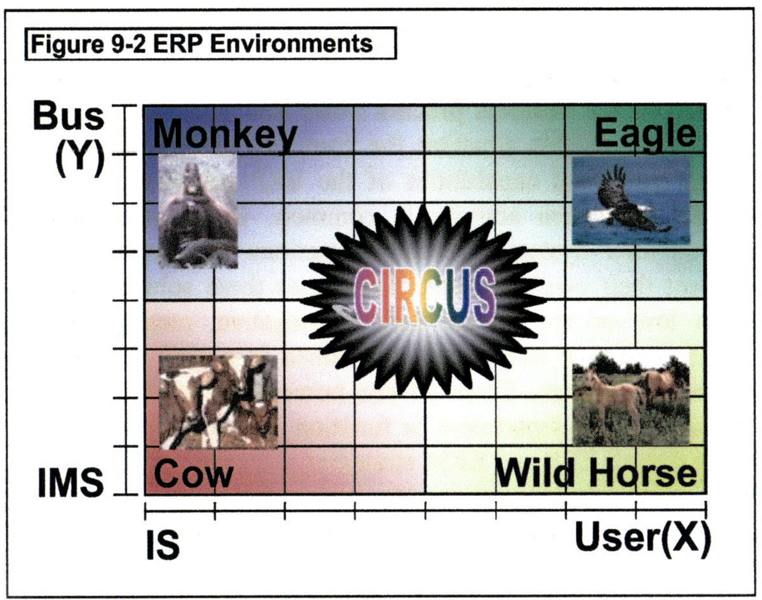

In figure 9-2 the value on the Y-axis determines how the company uses its ERP system. IMS represents information management system. Under this condition the company uses their ERP system simply as the data collection and storage tool. The high side of the Y- axis represents companies that use ERP systems for long-term strategic business management. The X-axis addresses the issue of user ownership. IS represents the lowest value, indicating that the ownership of the ERP system is by the information services function or information technology group. The User, representing the highest value, indicates that the ownership of the ERP system is held by the people and users of the ERP system.

The Eagles represent the rarest group. The users take strong ownership of the system and use it for long-term strategic business management. To put it simply, everything goes well.

The Wild Horses also take strong ownership of the system but use the ERP system as a data collection and storage tool. This particular group is highly resistant to change. This environment fits the classic "people just do not want to change" environment. The people of the organization put more faith in themselves then they do the "system". They take strong ownership of the business process flows and how they should be conducted. In this situation the company cannot reach the designed functional capabilities of the ERP software system. Non-ERP subsystem activity is common. In an attempt to bypass the ERP system, individual functions will develop and implement their own solutions. Sometimes these solutions will drop so low on the Y-axis they go negative, meaning that information is now stored and maintained in a system outside the core ERP system. These ad hoc home made solutions will be specific to the department or function and is not congruent with the overall ERP and ERM strategies.

The Cow group represents the worst-case scenario. Ownership of the system is completely held by the IS function and the ERP system is used as a data collection and storage tool. In this type of environment, the people seem to have trouble learning from their mistakes. The system has little capability to process information and is plagued by data integrity problems. In its place people perform heroic feats of manual data processing in a desperate attempt to keep their business running.

People are pushed right to their theoretical limits and beyond as they approach physiological meltdown.

The Monkey quadrant represents endless red tape and meetings in an attempt to get something done. System ownership belongs to the IS function and they feel that they know how to use the ERP system for long-term strategic business management, even though they don't.

Some companies do not fit the profile of an Eagle, Wild Horse, Cow, or Monkey very well. Their characteristics often contain a little bit of each one. Companies like these fall into the Circus quadrant, which lies in the center. The Circus quadrant is a chaos of mess and turmoil with constantly wandering characteristics.

Figure 9-3 ERP Control

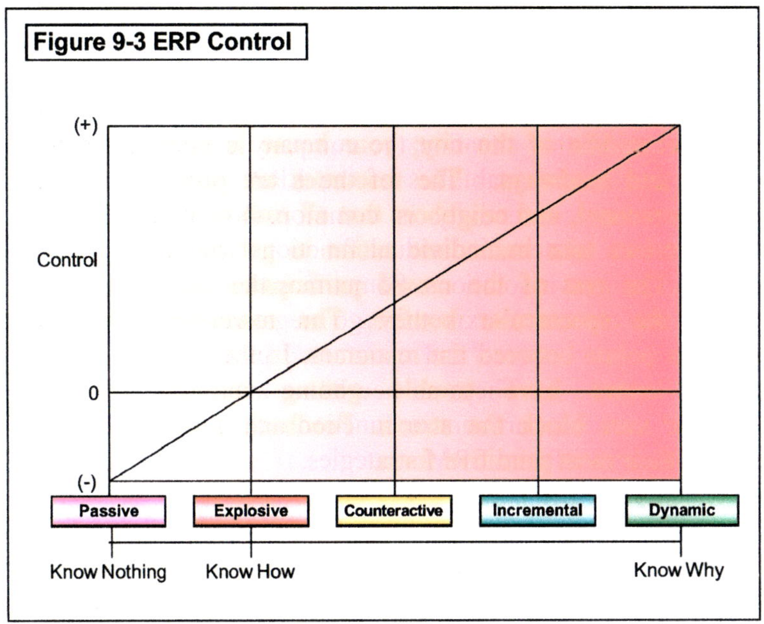

Another way to classify ERP environments is by their controllability. Does the company control the ERP system or does the ERP system control the company? It depends on what type of control technique is in place. There are five basic types of control that apply to ERP systems: passive, explosive, counteractive, incremental, and dynamic. Figure 9-3 shows their relationship to each other. Going from left to right each one represents a higher level of control. Any one particular type of control does not tend to dominate any one company. Companies often tend to exhibit combinations that are next to each other, like passive and explosive, or counteractive and incremental. Companies that control ERP systems can be found on the right hand side. Companies that are controlled by ERP systems can be found on the left hand side.

Passive control is actually not a type of control; it represents the complete lack of control. This is the worst situation for an ERP system to be in. In this type of environment disastrous events happen and management continues on never realizing what is happening. No response is made in situations where they are needed.

Explosive control is something like having your house on fire in the middle of the city; your house is surrounded by resources and roadways. The resources are police, firemen, medical personnel, and neighbors that all rush to your aid. The response crews take immediate action to get the blaze under control. The rest of the crowd participates as bystanders, enjoying the spectacular bonfire. The roadways serve as integration points between the resources. In the chaos of it all, response crews have trouble getting through because bystanders' cars block the streets. Feedback control systems appear in their most primitive form.

Eventually the fire comes under control and is extinguished. The response crews analyze the situation and how they responded in putting out the fire. They take what they learned and incorporate it into further training programs to ensure that their efficiency increases. In time they become quite good at what they do but one fact still remains; they are still fighting fires. Explosive environments are in a constant state of fighting fires. They keep coming, one after another.

Explosive control frequently contains the wrong response. Because of the highly reactive capabilities of the firefighters, unplanned events serve as strong short-term missions, demanding the coordination of resources to extinguish the fire. Like the fire alarm that goes off at the fire stations, it makes little difference whether the event is real or not; the fire fighters are trained to respond aggressively at the sound of that bell.

A demand manager for a chemical company accidentally typed in the telephone number, as the projected demand for a certain customer, into the forecast file. The demand manager left that Friday afternoon completely unaware of the mistake. The weekend material requirements planning was generated and exploded through bills of material to calculate the total raw materials required. When the purchasing function came in Monday morning, they saw the huge requirements for dozens of difficult to obtain chemicals and packaging materials. Without communicating to any other function, they worked furiously to get the material in by the next day by paying high overnight premiums.

Figure 6-4 ERP Control

Control	Event	Action
Passive	Quantity entered in wrong producing abnormal purchasing requirements	No Action
Explosive	ERP system producing gigantic purchasing requirements	Manic rush to order and expedite materials overnight

This is an excellent example of how a company often contains more than one type of control at the same time. Figure 9-4 breaks down the events and relates the appropriate type of control and action. This situation contained passive control because the purchasing department and demand manager never realized that something might be wrong. Despite the abnormality of the situation, people still responded in a fire-fighting mode. It's kind of like firefighters responding to a blaze and trying to put it out when there is none. But in an explosive environment, abnormalities become the norm, making it difficult to tell fact from fiction.

Explosive control is like driving a boat by looking over your shoulder. You can see how fast you are going and if you are going straight or turning a corner but you do not know exactly what is in front of you and when you are going to hit it. These environments do not look forward to see what the problem is and how to avoid it. They make sure the tools are in place to clean up the accident after it happens.

Counteractive control is a significant advancement over explosive control. Counteractive control uses cause and effect relationships. By understanding the cause and effect relationships, the prevention of problems can occur. Total quality management tools first begin to make their appearance. Significant disruption still occurs. Counteractive control can be thought of as launching an investigation after the fire occurred in our example of the house fire. Investigators carefully sift through the ashes to find the remains of a smoke detector. Working with the manufacturer they realize that the smoke detector is made from a type of plastic that warps badly after being heated slightly, causing a complete malfunction of the unit. After learning this, the manufacturer alters the design, allowing the smoke detector to work in extreme heat conditions. Further investigation reveals that the fire started with a space heater that was placed too close to a curtain. In future safety seminars fire officials include their findings.

How would counteractive control take place in our example at the chemical company of the demand manager who typed in the telephone number as the projected demand for the customer? A purchase manager concerned with the abnormal demand begins investigating the ERP system, using a variety of tools, to understand from where all the demand was coming. Eventually he learns that it was coming for a common customer with a very unusual demand. He contacts the demand manager to find out what is going on. The demand manager investigates further and discovers the mistake. They decide to call a planning meeting with the IS department of the company to decide if they can come up with a plan to prevent this from happening in the future. After understanding the problem the IS department develops a simple report that identifies unusual demand (such as a telephone number typed in accidentally) for a customer. The demand manager runs the report after the customer demand has been updated in the forecast file, preventing any more unpleasant surprises for the purchasing department.

Incremental control has all the same characteristics as counteractive plus additional ones. At this stage the characteristics of total quality management are in place. The ERP system has become stabilized but still lacks full control. People clearly understand root causes. Charting key characteristics and documentation are standard. In this type of control one would expect to find:

- Leadership
- Commitment
- Total customer satisfaction
- Continuous improvement
- Total involvement
- Training and education
- Ownership
- Documentation

- Fail proofing success
- Teamwork
- Complex problem solving
- Feedback control systems
- Measurement systems

This situation can be considered "Class A", best of competition or as good as can be achieved. Continuous improvement is good sign that the ERP environment is moving toward incremental control. The users and management of the company "know why" something happens. There is a certain sense of predictability in the system. Good measurement and feedback control systems are in place. The system has good vision and mission statements. People know where they are going, how they are going to get there, and how long it is going to take. Without the basic components of ownership and training in place, incremental control is not practical. Incremental control applies better to a global perspective of an ERP system than it does to a specific module or an event.

One thing that this type of environment does not have is the capability to handle major disruptions to the ERP system such as a corrupted database, change in management, acquisitions or mergers. Companies can lose their sense of direction in an ERP system after years of work in learning how to stabilize and control it. Everything goes smoothly until a rock is tossed into the water. Another type of control is needed to allow things to continue smoothly during disruption.

Dynamic control is the highest level of control and reserved for the very few that become true masters of an ERP system. Users in a dynamic control environment, function more as artisans or scientists than general ERP users. There is a massive drive to understand the "know why" of the system. Cause and effect relationships are clearly understood. This type of control can handle almost any type of disruptive situation. User ownership is very high as are the other characteristics of total quality management (TQM).

Change control management can be found most abundantly here and is sufficient to handle the most extreme change smoothly. There is extensive prototyping and testing process in place. In the other types of control a new ERP process may be introduced after it has been observed to work in a test environment. The dynamic control environment seeks much more that just "proof of concept". Dynamic control will over test ERP process flows to an extreme under all types of conditions. The process flows developed under dynamic control are extremely stable upon implementation, as they are expensive to develop and implement.

Both incremental and dynamic control can be considered as a form of steering. Both types are looking forward for possible signs of danger so the course of the boat can be readjusted to avoid a mishap. The difference between the two is that the level of understanding of what to avoid and when to turn is much better in dynamic control. Using incremental control the driver of the boat changes the course because of an unknown object that lays in its course. Using dynamic control the driver will identify the threat and optimize course corrections that will minimize the delay of the trip, take into account drift of the object due to the current, and movement by the wind.

Because of the tremendous amount of skill required and expense involved, most companies do not seek or cannot achieve dynamic control. Many companies have achieved world-class performance with incremental control, or less, to obtain a competitive advantage in the market place.

Questions--

1. ERP systems are highly dependent upon __________?
2. Management that thoroughly understands ERP will use it for ____________?
3. What is a Monkey? What are some traits?
4. What is an Eagle? What are some traits?
5. What is a Cow? What are some traits?
6. What is a Wild Horse? What are some traits?
7. What is a Circus? What are some traits?
8. What environment most closely matches your company?
9. What is the difference between "know how" and "know why"?
10. What are some traits of a passive environment?
11. What are some traits of a dynamic environment?
12. What are some traits of an incremental environment?
13. What are some traits of an explosive environment?
14. What are some traits of a counteractive environment?
15. What are some traits of a passive environment?
16. What environment most closely matches your company?

Even our future is not what it used to be!
I thought change management was important but that did not mean I wanted to change the way I had always done things!

10

Change Management

Change management is a process of facilitating change within an organization. All organizations that implement ERP must go through some type of change. An ERP system cannot be installed without the capability of an organization to change. This chapter explains basic concepts common to almost all ERP implementations. These concepts include: components of change management, reasons why organizations face change, the types of changes that organizations experience, roles and responsibilities, planning, and execution strategies.

Figure 10-1 Changing Environments

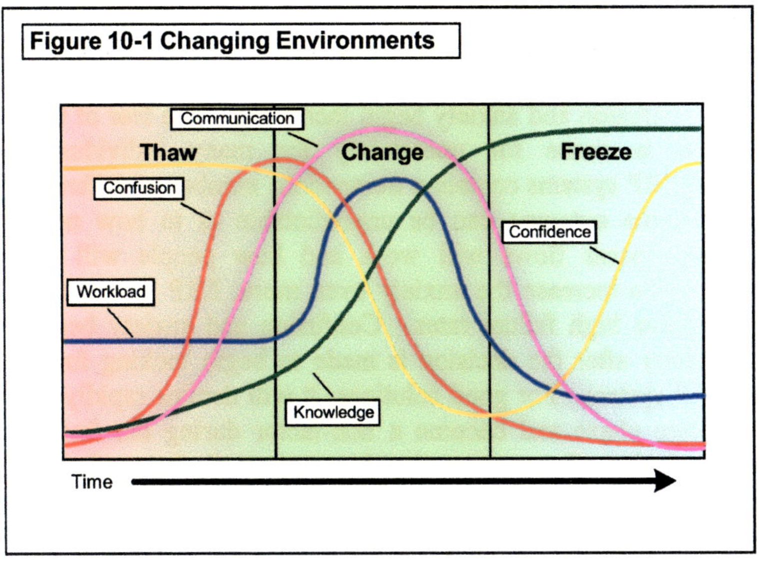

Most companies feel that change management is an important part of an ERP implementation. Ironically, resistance to change from end-users and company employees is a serious problem faced by many ERP implementations. No discussion on ERP implementation change management techniques could be complete without considering how to deal with resistance to change.

The process of change that an organization faces during an ERP implementation can be thought of as a large bell cast out of metal. In its current state its shape is quite inflexible producing a pitch and tone, based upon its physical shape and size. Should an organization need a different bell that produces a slightly different pitch and tone, the situation is not hopeless. Through the coordination of several resources, the organization may remove the bell from the steeple; have it called to a foundry, melted down, re-cast, and re-mounted in the steeple. As with the bell, change in any ERP implementation can be broken down into three phases: thawing of the current activities, changing processes, and freezing to the new characteristic.

The periods of thaw, change, and freeze are ones of great change for any organization. Shortly after the thaw cycle begins, confusion and anxiety begin increasing. The fear of the unknown is cause for uncertainty for many individuals. Because ERP systems contain a tremendous number of different variables, the outcome can be unpredictable as to how new business process flows will work and how people will be affected. To increase the anxiety even more, ERP systems in general have high failure rates. Confusion and anxiety begin immediately after the decision is made to begin looking for a new ERP system. For good solutions, it will decline rapidly in the change phase and become a non-factor during the freeze phase and after. For projects that do not go well, the confusion and anxiety can extend deep into the freeze phase.

The workload that an organization will face during an ERP implementation will be greatest during the change process. Under ideal conditions, the workload will become less in the freeze phase than it was during the thaw phase. However, many companies, reporting from actual conditions, find that their workload in the freeze phase is no better than that during the thaw phase. Careful planning is required to properly manage the substantial increase in workload during the change phase.

Immediately after the announcement of a company to pursue a new ERP system, comes a series of questions. These questions expand the knowledge base of the organization. After the purchase of the software, knowledge increases rapidly during education, training, and implementation of the software. Teachers and consultants, combined with experimentation, provide rapid increases in knowledge acquisition during the change phase. Once process flows have been established, the motivation for knowledge acquisition begins decreasing, which brings an organization into the freeze phase.

An organization's confidence, in regards to a new ERP system, is relatively high during the thaw phase. The high confidence, as further reinforced from software demos and references, begins to deteriorate rapidly in the change phase. The rapid deterioration is usually attributed to unforeseen complex problems with software and hardware systems. Software and hardware problems, combined with other problems, such as lack of ownership and education, can greatly contribute to the deterioration of confidence in the system. Once the system reaches the freeze phase and ERP users realize that the system is going to work and be successful, their confidence begins the process of restoration. Very few ERP projects will have stable confidence from thaw to freeze.

Change in organizations is caused by tension mechanisms that originate from both internal and external factors. Tension mechanisms are anything that creates a motivating drive to go through change when implementing an ERP system. Some external tension mechanisms include:

- Technology factors such as Internet functionality

- Desire to keep up with or stay ahead of the competition
- A mandate to replace a legacy ERP system from a corporate identity
- Customer expectations or requirements
- Completely failed relations with an ERP vendor or service provider
- ERP vendors that went out of business and no longer support

Some internal tension mechanisms include:

- Completely failed relations with an ERP vendor or service provider
- Excessive number of independent software systems faced with integration issues
- Chronic problems with legacy system
- Excessive software modifications to legacy system
- Unsupported legacy system
- Home grown or specially developed systems
- Increase in business growth
- Irresolvable technical issues
- Vision and mission statements
- Corporate culture

Organizations face many different types of changes in the implementation of an ERP system. Organizations will face at least one of the following types of changes:

- Technology changes
- Cultural change - values, views, beliefs
- Change in ownership
- Change in responsibilities
- Business process flow changes

- Change of management
- New visions and mission statements
- Changing of skill sets

Technology provides significant change challenge for many organizations. Technology greatly affects the functionality and capability of ERP systems. New technologies, such as the Internet, and significant improvements in graphical user interface and online data accessibility have created steep learning curves for many organizations. The capability of an organization to absorb such a large amount of knowledge in a short amount of time can provide significant challenges.

The change in corporate culture is often needed to help ensure the success of modern-day ERP systems. In general, ERP systems are greatly misunderstood at all levels of management in an organization. Significant education and training is usually required to manage expectations with functional capabilities and implementation methodologies.

Many organizations face a lack of ownership during an ERP implementation. ERP team members and end users, fearing the unknown, are often slow to embrace new solutions. Through the application of several different management techniques combined with education and training, problems regarding ownership can be greatly reduced or even eliminated.

Changes in responsibilities are bound to occur in ERP implementations because of significant changes to process flows. These changes and responsibilities can create significant disruptions and potential conflict between people and departments. The change in responsibility often lacks clarity, which creates competitive situations. Through proper education, training, and management techniques, disruptions for changes in job responsibilities can be greatly reduced.

Business process flows change for a variety of reasons. One reason is that the software functionality does not match the business process flows. Instead of modifying the software, business process flows are often readjusted. Business process flows are also changed because an ERP implementation provides a great opportunity for process improvements and optimization. A combination of resources from a multiple of sources provides ample opportunity for changes in business process flows.

For the proper implementation of an ERP system the change in management structures are required. Although an ERP system can be installed without any changes to management structures, there are no reported success stories using this strategy. Temporary management structures need to be set up to deal with implementation of the ERP system and adjustment of business process flows. These temporary management structures can be formal or created on the fly in an ad hoc manner. The installation of temporary management structures creates change for company employees. Without careful consideration, conflict can easily erupt between people and departments.

With the coming of the new ERP system comes new vision and mission statements. Some ERP implementations are completely void of mission and vision statements, which can cause ERP team members to wander around as if they were lost in the wilderness without a compass. The creation of vision and mission statements helps bring clarity and direction to the project; however, they can often overlap and create conflict between people and departments. For this reason, vision and mission statements must be carefully formulated to integrate with the overall business strategy, and combined with people that will support them with the proper authority and power.

ERP team members usually must acquire new skill sets before and during the implementation of the software. These skill sets can be classified into technical and application. Application consumes the balk of the change required to develop the proper skill sets. Requiring such a large amount of information in a short amount of time can provide ample opportunities for stress in the need for proper change management. It is important to recognize how fast ERP team members, and organizations, can acquire new knowledge. The rate at which an organization can acquire new knowledge is known as its terminal velocity. Organizations that tried to exceed its terminal velocity bring about frustration and discontent to a project.

Roles and responsibilities

ERP implementations can create an enormous amount of pressure for any organization. This is especially true when the organization has no previous experience with ERP implementations, or worse yet, they have experience with one or more failed ERP implementations. Many companies are struggling to adjust to their new ERP systems in an attempt to keep up with rapidly changing technology. Different levels of management tend to respond differently to change.

The top management of the company in an ERP implementation has a hard time coming to grips with indirect implications of the needed changes. This is why top management support is stressed in so many ERP seminars, books, and articles. They tend to isolate themselves away from the mainstream day-to-day activities of the ERP implementation. They often engage in strategic planning sessions and gather information from their subordinate middle managers. They often expect employees to go along with the necessary changes needed for an ERP implementation. When they find out that end-users reject change management for their new ERP system, they often blame their middle managers. Top management feels betrayed when employees of the company do not respond positively to an ERP implementation.

Middle managers accumulate the pressure for making necessary organizational changes to support an ERP implementation, even though they generally have little idea what is truly required. They are often pulled in several different directions as resource allocation conflicts arise. They are caught in the middle, experiencing mixed feelings because they don't have clear instructions. They receive several different mission statements that conflict with each other. They often have to deal with resistant or withdrawn employees who no longer respond to previous management approaches. Their subordinates often desert them; blame them for the difficulties that they must face.

The employees and ERP team members often feel attacked and betrayed upon the announcement of an ERP implementation. Many respond with resistance, anger, frustration, and confusion. They often become afraid to take risks and experiment for the purpose of learning new things. They experience a loss of traditional relationships and face uncertainty in their future career advancement. To make matters even worse, they now have to become part of the implementation in addition to their normal day-to-day responsibilities.

Guidelines for successful change

ERP implementations are greatly misunderstood. The implementation is slow, expensive, and difficult. There's a tendency to believe that ERP implementations can be quick, painless, and inexpensive. There are several basic guidelines to help facilitate change during an ERP implementation.

- Have good reasons for implementing an ERP system and clearly communicate those reasons to the organization.
- Involve people in the change from the beginning. Employees who are involved a less likely to resist an ERP system. Becoming part of the selection and planning process helps employees to achieve a sense of control.
- Use a well-respected person to facilitate the change. Ideally, this person should have the authority to resolve conflicts in the allocation of resources and

methodologies. This person is usually well respected in the organization and contains a significant amount of knowledge about the business process flows.

- Form ERP teams to help facilitate transition to the new ERP system. These ERP team members should be based upon internal resources of the company.
- Provide education and training on basic concepts of ERP systems for the development of values and behaviors. People need guidance to properly understand the new methodologies that the ERP system will bring. Training brings groups of people together, allowing them to express their concerns and to reinforce newly learned skill sets. Do the same for software functionality.
- Use external consultants to build a critical mass for success. For many companies, there is more power in what an outsider says than from suggestions that come from the people within the company. Outside consultants can cross all political barriers within the company, bringing about the truth. The unbiased success stories that a consultant can bring help to build faith and momentum in the project.
- Clearly communicate the change through the entire organization. Communication of change may come through the development of newsletters, new logos or slogans, and announcements. Recognize and celebrate critical milestones in the ERP implementation.
- Acknowledge and reward people for the struggle and sacrifices that they will have to make during the ERP implementation. Many ERP team members put in numerous hours of overtime dealing with the complex changes that they face.
- Build a critical mass for success by creating small successful projects that lead to bigger and more

complex challenges. By experiencing success in the early phases of the project, an organization will be more open to adopting the changes.

Planning for change

The following activities will help your organization successfully implement complex changes involved with an ERP implementation. The basic steps involve:

- Preparing
- Planning
- Establishing transition structures
- Implementation
- Receiving rewards

Preparing

Prepare employees by communicating the changes that will be upcoming. Establish the correct timing for announcing the changes. Too early can create anxiety and too late can cause ownership issues.

Describe in detail the necessary changes as completely as possible. Identify areas of the business that will be most affected and approach those first.

Conduct research with other companies and study all past ERP implementation attempts within the company. Determine if the company has a positive or negative history in their ability to install ERP systems.

Make readiness assessments of the organizational capability to implement an ERP system. Take a survey to establish the skill sets and readiness of all critical stakeholders and end users. An organization that is not ready for the change can easily fall into denial rather than accept the change.

Don't make unnecessary changes. People need all the stability that they can get during the change. Minimize the amount of changes that the ERP team members may have to face from other areas of the business. Avoid sudden changes in strategy and direction in the early stages. Make sure that other organizational projects will not affect them. Prevent, or reduce, multiple responsibilities from different areas overlapping onto one potential team member.

Planning

Make contingency plans to provide a safety net for the ERP implementation. Most companies spend very little time developing contingency plans. It should be little surprise that company employees feel stressed out when asked to implement an ERP system, with a higher probability of failure, with no contingency plan! That would be like asking your employees to jump out of an airplane without a parachute hoping that they would hit the haystack down below. Contingency plans can greatly reduce the stress for ERP team members, knowing that they will have a safety net to support their fall. Contingency plans allow them to become more daring, forcing them to come out of the resistance stage.

Allow for major impacts of personal performance and employee productivity as ERP team members struggle with high learning curves of new software. Make sure that management expectations are properly aligned with the capabilities of the individuals participating in the project. Placing unreasonable expectations upon ERP team members will only bring about frustration.

Actively encourage employee input through cross-functional communication. Create a plan that will encourage employees to communicate with each other during the ERP implementation. Communication between the ERP team members is most important; however, communication between the ERP team members and the rest of the organization should not be overlooked. Plan a variety of communication opportunities ranging from meetings to email list servers.

Survey the skills and knowledge bases that will be required to implement the ERP system. Provide educational and training programs necessary to build a critical knowledge base.

Establish visions, missions, objectives, and time lines to represent the overall strategy and direction of the implementation.

Establish transition structures

Create an ERP team to help create necessary transitions and to oversee the change. Having a team that can focus on the task of implementing an ERP system helps to bring about progress. The correct structure of the team is important for the success of the project. Teams having members with a high percentage of their time dedicated will outperform teams having members with a low percentage of their time dedicated. In general, small dedicated teams perform better and move faster than large teams with members that dedicate a small portion of their time.

Create and develop temporary policies and procedures for dealing with the change during the ERP implementation. Loosen control and encourage flexibility through the use of experimentation.

Frequently encourage cross communication and obtain feedback. During the active phases of an ERP implementation, daily meetings should take place. For most organizations, implementation of an ERP system is a very different process flow from their normal day-to-day activities. For this reason, organizations should create temporary policies and procedures specifically for dealing with the ERP implementation.

Implementation

Provide the appropriate education and training opportunities for the new skill sets required. The need for education and training extends throughout the implementation from conception to end of life. For many companies, implementation of an ERP system is continuous and ongoing, although it greatly tapers off after the go live date. Educational opportunities can come from a variety of sources including: consultants, formal education classes, experimentation, and research.

Encourage self-management of the ERP team. Although there may be a need for strong centralized leadership in an ERP implementation, because of the complexity, detail task management is often best left to self-management by the ERP team members. Higher levels of management should be reserved for monitoring the project, organizing resources, resolving conflicts, resolving issues, and providing inspirational and motivational support.

Provide ample feedback to establish clarity in the direction the project is moving. Progress of the implementation can be collected from a variety of sources and feedback conducted through a number of different communication channels. Feedback needs to be communicated to ERP team members, consultants and senior management. Regardless of who is receiving the feedback, it should be non-threatening in nature.

Plan for resistance to people who do not want to change. Resistance is common to almost any ERP implementation. Methodologies and techniques should be in place to specifically deal with resistance from ERP team members and company employees. Education on how to deal with resistance is recommended for the senior management through the ERP team members.

Allow ample time for people to examine how they are doing things and methods for change. Most organizations find that the implementation time of an ERP system is much higher than expected. It is relatively rare for a company to complete an implementation on time and on budget. Most companies will exceed their initial estimates, whether they came from internal or external sources such as a consulting agency. Keep in mind that when your company makes the initial work investments in the project planning session, it probably will not be enough.

Actively encourage thought and creativity. Look for ways to promote and implement creativity opportunities for the ERP team members. Use of quality management tools, such as fishbone diagramming, combined with group brainstorming sessions, can provide ample opportunity for the promotion of creativity. The prototyping and testing phase of an ERP implementation also provides great opportunity for additional creativity. The process of creativity is closely connected to change. The process of change is greatly facilitated by a solid foundation of creativity.

If people withdraw from an implementation, be willing to accept their return to the project. Attitudes, values, beliefs all tend to fluctuate during an ERP implementation. Do not expect 100 percent buy in, for this is impossible for some companies. Unless there is a serious problem, most people that withdraw from an ERP implementation will return to it at a later date. Just because team members withdraw does not mean that they are not team players. Withdrawal is a relatively normal occurrence. Their return to the project should be welcomed without criticism.

Encourage collaboration between functional areas to break down barriers between departments. Cross communication can be a valuable tool in understanding business process flows that overlap multiple business silos. An ERP implementation breaks down many of the communication barriers that exist between departments and people. It is a fresh opportunity to begin anew by setting informal rules aside that inhibit communication.

Constantly monitor attitudes and viewpoints the organization to determine how employees are responding to the change. This can be an important activity for measuring the health and well being of the implementation. Negative responses to change should be monitored closely and dealt with by using the appropriate procedures. Be aware of employees or managers eager to build political strongholds of followers for the purpose of undermining the project. Should employees of a company choose to take this approach, especially if there was a good reason, then the ERP implementation probably should have never started. Careful preparation and early phases of the ERP implementation will prevent awkward situations such as this. Prevention is worth a pound of cure, however if it is too late, a pound of cure is worth a ton of rework.

Reward

Create incentives for special efforts. Celebrate critical milestones by creating public displays that acknowledge groups of people who have participated in the project. Reward for ERP team members can be well deserved. Surprisingly, most companies take the time or effort to reward their employees for their extraordinary participation in making an ERP system successful. They should receive some reward above and beyond their normal compensation, because many employees put in more than their fair share of time and effort. Compensation can come in a variety of ways. It is best delivered by understanding the needs of the individuals. Extra compensation should not be so great that it creates jealousy within the rest of the organization.

Dealing with resistance

Resistance from employees comes with almost every ERP implementation. "Why do we have to change?", is a question that has filled top management, project manager, consultants, and ERP team members' ears. We will examine in greater detail stages that employees go through during an ERP implementation and some techniques for dealing with resistance.

Figure 10-2 shows some of the major steps that ERP users go through during an ERP implementation. The first step, denial, occurs after the announcement of the new ERP system. Almost immediately after the announcement, life returns to normal. It is viewed as another passing management fad, nothing that should be taken seriously. For many companies this may be the case, but not for those that wish to be successful in an ERP implementation.

The transition to resistance comes when there is some perceived viewpoint that the new ERP system might actually be implemented. The transition from the denial phase to the resistance phase is actually a good thing, for it shows that employees are responding predictably. Although resistance may not be a good thing it is certainly better than being stuck in the denial stage! The resistance stage is where most companies get hung up. This stage, for many companies, would dominate the entire implementation from conception to end of life. It is a poor way to implement a new ERP system.

Figure 10-2 Stages employees go through

Stage	Activity
Denial	Life as normal
Resistance	Emotions and confusion
Exploration	Creativity, learning, experimentation
Commitment	Planning and execution

During this stage employees are filled with a mixture of emotions and feel confused. Many common types of emotions can be found as well as other characteristics. Some common characteristics that can be found in the resistance stage include:

- Complaints
- Errors
- Anger
- Apathy
- Absence
- Withdrawal
- Anger

- Fear
- Anxiety
- Depression
- Confusion

New ERP implementations attack the way company employees do their jobs. In a blunt way, a new ERP system basically says that employees of the company are not doing a good enough job. Employees who feel threatened can become protective. Just because senior management has more authority and power does not make employees feel any better during an ERP implementation!

Fortunately, there are many good treatment techniques for dealing with resistance, although ironically, few companies choose to use them. This can be attributed primarily to a lack of education and training for leaders of an ERP implementation. Some treatment options include:

- Rituals
- EAP programs
- Accepting overreaction
- Acknowledge loss
- Compensate for losses
- Communicate changes
- Reduce confusion by defining what will end
- Treat the past with respect
- Let people take a piece of the old way with them
- Explain the need for change for the health and well being of the company

Rituals can be used to publicly acknowledge the losses that people are experiencing. During one ERP implementation, a group of ERP team members assembled a time capsule filled with old reports and training manuals from the legacy system and buried it in the cemetery across the road. As they threw dirt on it they told stories about the past. One plant went so far as to assemble its formal documentation from the legacy system to create a bonfire inside the plant. Imagine what a statement that made to the employees of the organization that had experienced great difficulty with their legacy system!

EAP (Employee Assistance Program) is generally a professional counseling service that is conducted through a variety of methods. EAP programs provide employees an opportunity to understand specific stressors leading to dysfunctional behavior. Despite the extreme psychological pressures that ERP team members encounter during an ERP implementation, few companies recognize the need for EAP programs. Employee assistance programs provide necessary counseling during times of stress and change. Many employees tend to hide behind their true feelings or problems.

Employees will often overreact to changes that affect them. When an employee is overreacting, management should perform the function that is required of them, which is listening to the employees. And in many cases there are very good reasons why management should be listening to what employees have to say. Sometimes management will overreact to overreacting employees and attempt a counterattack by labeling them as not being team players. Making such acquisitions against ERP team members is only flirting with disaster in the implementation. Management needs to be accepting of what employees have to say and how it is said. Failure to do so only jeopardizes the project.

Recognizing the losses that employees go through can help bring troublesome employees out of the resistance stage. Recognizing the losses is important because it communicates to the employee that their message has been received. It is a way of acknowledging that communication has taken place. Although the communications may not change the direction of the ERP implementation, it seems that simply because there *was* communication helps to ease people's tension, and that will be affected by the implementation. Recognizing losses becomes a foundation for more progressive communication opportunities.

Recognizing the losses that the employees will face during the implementation brings about opportunities in deciding how to compensate for those losses. This is an adjustment planning process that allows employees to recognize that necessary adjustments will be made that will prevent threatening situations resulting from them being unable to fulfill expected commitments or responsibilities. The issue of time is most common in an ERP implementation. ERP team members wonder how they will have enough time to implement an ERP system in addition to all their other day-to-day responsibilities. Companies can compensate for the loss by allowing employees to use outside clerical assistants or other employees of the company to help them with their day-to-day responsibilities as they focus on the ERP implementation.

Much of the anxiety that employees face is based upon dealing with the unknown. Communicating the nature of the change and how it will take place reduces the unknown factors in the employees' minds. Resistance, in many cases, is simply a sign of a lack of communication.

Defining what will come to an end helps bring clarity to people that will be affected by ERP implementations. Many questions come to mind, that need to be answered, for employees of the company. Questions like: Will business process flows be changing? Will roles and responsibilities be changing? If so, how? Will people be able to continue using the legacy system? What is going to end and how is it going to end is a question that needs to be answered for most of the people that use an ERP system.

The past should always be treated with respect. Although new opportunities may present themselves in the installation of an ERP system; that does not mean the way things were done in the past was wrong or should be attacked, even if they *were* wrong. To attack the way people did things in the past is to attack the people themselves. This will only bring about an adversarial relationship between management and ERP users. Instead management should think of the legacy system as: "the good old days."

Allowing people to take a little piece of the old way with them into the new ERP system is another way to alleviate some of the pain. In most ERP implementations, traditional business process flows are not scrapped. They are usually improved upon. There is a full opportunity to bring old ways into the new ERP system. Many employees do not realize this when faced with the new ERP implementation. Letting people know that they will still be able to perform the same kinds of functions with the new ERP system as with the old helps to bring rest to uneasy minds. This can be done simply through the process of communication. This also recognizes that management is not attacking the way that people did their jobs.

Lastly, it is important that employees understand the reasons for which an organization is implementing a new ERP system. Should there be no good reasons the company can give to employees, then perhaps the company should not be implementing a new system! In all but a few cases it will not be clear to employees why a new ERP system must be implemented. Is it because of technology issues? Or to accommodate future business growth? To increase productivity? All these questions go completely unanswered should the management choose to never speak to their employees.

Planning and execution strategies

The concept of planning is dynamic and varies tremendously from company to company. Each and every ERP project requires a certain degree of planning. The approach of some companies involves way too much planning so that benefits can be realized. The plans consist of so much detail that people spend more time tracking steps than they do performing them!

Other companies have so little planning that they are desperately struggling to understand their next step.

There are three basic types of planning that are used and applied to an ERP system.

- Comprehensive activity sequencing
- Choice objective
- Incremental expansion

ERP projects often begin with comprehensive activity sequencing after the delivery of a new ERP system. The comprehensive activity sequencing begins with a PPS (project planning session) sponsored by the ERP vendor or service provider. It goes by a variety of names, but they are all designed for one purpose: to understand the scope of what needs to be done and the resources it will take to do it. The outcome of the PPS then is forwarded to one or more persons who create a detailed working plan of how to install the software and the resources needed to support it. Sometimes ERP vendors will provide default templates; sometimes those default templates are modified slightly, or completely new plans are created from scratch.

Comprehensive activity sequencing contains a great deal of detailed planning and fits strongly with the project management function. A good example of something that uses comprehensive activity sequencing is the launch, orbiting, and landing of the space shuttle. For example, every activity is carefully planned: when the shuttle will launch, when the astronauts will eat and sleep, what they will do, when they will land, and how their activities will be performed.

Comprehensive activity sequencing consists of one massive objective, usually the go live date of the ERP system, and a series of detailed steps and the subprojects needed to support that objective. Each and every step is carefully planned. This is the implementation plan. The implementation plan consists of:

- Breaking the project into steps
- Assigning sequences
- Assigning tasks
- Calculating resources
- Calculating time
- Assigning dates

Using this strategy, detailed tasks are created and assigned to ERP team members. Each team member is held accountable for his or her task. Each task feeds up to the respective subproject that feeds into the overall objective of the project.

The timing and resources are closely tied together. The option exists to change the timing or alter the resource to achieve a certain schedule. The combination of all this information can produce a PERT (program evaluation and review technique) network. This helps managers to better understand where the critical path exists and how to allocate resources.

Many different types of resources are needed in the implementation of an ERP system. Some of these resource requirements include: hardware, skill sets, facilities, money, and consulting services. Understanding the resources needed is helpful for the functional managers of an organization. Once each type of resource is identified and its amount calculated, a new supply of that resource can be requested from the ERP service provider. Some companies have complete internal capability to implement and maintain an ERP system, while others need continuous assistance from ERP vendors and service providers. Smaller companies tend to need proportionally more help than large corporations with dedicated IS groups.

Companies are usually quite eager to develop a comprehensive activity sequencing strategy, for it helps them to better understand the scope and resources of the project. The process of detailed planning can be a tedious resource consuming process. Unknown variables with technology, services, ERP team participation, and complexities with business process flows can make it almost impossible to create a detailed project plan. Some companies find themselves spending more time planning and documenting what they are going to do than actually doing it! Only people highly skilled in the software, with control of all required resources, strong communication skills, and industry expertise for which the software is being installed, can make this work. For these reasons, most companies do not, or cannot, use comprehensive activity sequencing in their implementation. This is why most companies choose the choice objective or incremental approach.

The choice objective approach takes far less coordination and planning. The choice objective approach can be thought of as a selective objective that may or may not operate independently in supporting higher-level objectives, missions and visions of the company.

Choice objective works based upon the principal of someonc knowing what they want to do and then setting out to do it. The visions and missions are developed for one specific module and do not interface with the overall business strategy. There generally is no preplanning involved and the tasks needed to accomplish the objective are uncovered as people come to them. Communication with other functional areas of the business is limited and occurs only as needed.

Using choice objective, multiple people are often working on different tasks unaware of what other functional areas are doing. The goals are usually small in nature, related to one module. All of these different tasks fall into the category of choice objective because they are not part of an overall strategy as found in the comprehensive activity sequencing.

Incremental expansion contains the most ambiguous objectives. Incremental expansion contains no clear objectives, missions or visions. It can be thought of as something like the Lewis and Clark expedition where their mission was to simply explore the land. How much land was available and where their journey was going to take them was relatively unknown.

Companies using this approach in their ERP systems choose to implement and execute one step at the time before moving on to the next. They live day by day. Planning is conducted by analyzing their past to determine the resources needed to support their future execution strategies. They have no plans for what they are going to do; they simply know that they are going to do something. They are not sure what their next step will be.

Execution is conducted by the events that present themselves. As situations arise and develop, the coordination of resources will focus on those situations. As soon as those situations are resolved, they move on to the next step.

Questions---

1. What is change management?
2. What are three steps to change?
3. Describe the relationship between change and confusion?
4. Describe the relationship between change and workload?
5. Describe the relationship between change and confidence?
6. Describe the relationship between change and knowledge?
7. What is a tension mechanism?
8. What are some tension mechanisms at your company?
9. What is the role of top management in a changing environment?
10. What is relationship between resistance and contingency plans?
11. What is a transition structure?
12. What are 5 things that will help people change?
13. What is the purpose of a ritual? How can it be conducted? Has one been used at your company?
14. What are 5 stages that employees go through during change?
15. What is the worst stage that an employee can be stuck in?
16. What is the best?
17. What are three basic types of planning and execution strategies?

I am so amazed that we paid so much money to get ourselves into so much trouble.

11

Consultants

This chapter defines what a consultant is, how to choose consultants, and how to get the most benefit from them. This chapter will help companies to select better consultants and also help consultants understand their role in an ERP implementation project. The use of consultants in ERP projects, unfortunately, can produce very unpredictable results. Unlike other professions, there are no governmental regulatory agencies for certifying ERP consultants. The lack of standards in the industry can create unpredictable outcomes. The need for ERP consultants is very strong, but because of a company's inability to verify the consultants' capabilities and their high cost, many companies resist the temptation to use them.

Consultants function similar to doctors. They have a responsibility to listen to their clients, diagnose their problems, and recommend a variety of treatments. They work as coaches to bring out the potential in team players and to help them understand the rules of the game. It is a highly specialized game in which sometimes only the consultant knows the rules. The client bears the ultimate responsibility of verifying that the company's problems are within the realm of expertise of that particular consultant or service provider. ERP vendors and service providers also have a responsibility of providing the best possible match between the company's needs and the consultant's capabilities. The company receiving their services should not use the ERP venders and service providers who abuse that privilege. The use of an unqualified consultant in an

ERP project can be most damaging to the implementation, sometimes unrecoverable.

Figure 11-1 Consulting Characteristics

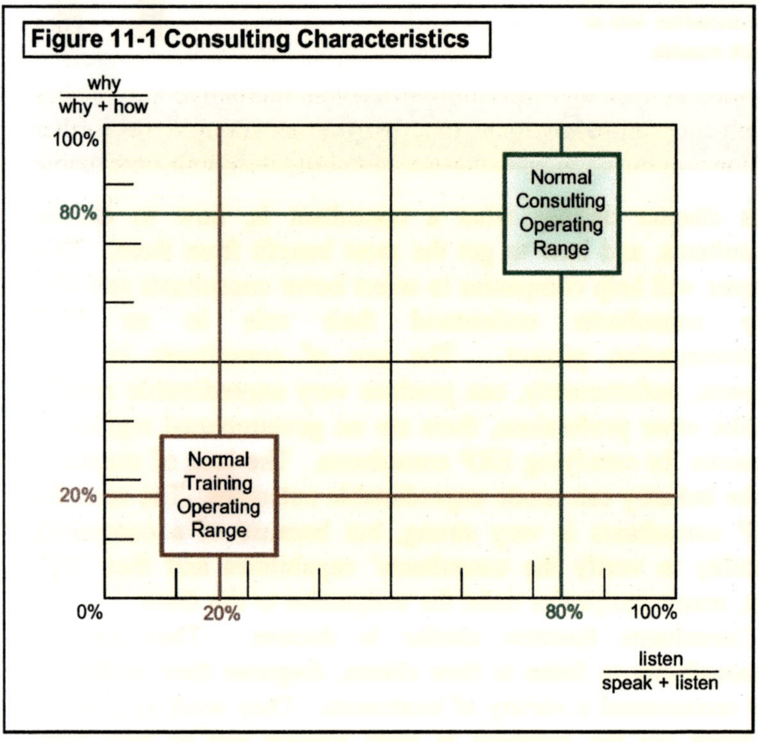

Figure 11-1 illustrates a good operating range for consultants in how they communicate and present knowledge to their clients. Approximately 80 percent of the consultants' time should be spent listening to their clients. In other words, the consultants should not be speaking more than 20 percent of the time. The focus should be on educating the client on the "whys" of the system versus the "hows". Consultants, of course, may be called upon to spend their time speaking and explaining the "hows" of the system. But when consultants go into this mode they become trainers, no longer consultants. A consultant's time is better spent performing education than training. The focus on education helps bring strong conceptual understanding, yielding the full benefits of an ERP system to the ERP core team. The ERP team core members and the functional leaders of the organization should do the training, not the consultants, for good reasons covered later in this chapter.

Good consultants constantly offer you alternative approaches to all the problems that you present to them. In further demonstration of their expertise and skills they will be capable of outlining advantages and disadvantages of each possible alternative. Consultants should provide you with information in a way that allows you to logically choose the method that is best for your company. It is important to keep in mind that *you* are making the decision, not the consultant.

Consultants play useful roles in performing audits. They review your progress and inform you when you are traveling down the wrong track.

Some companies become frustrated when they see consultants spending their time learning about the organization instead of producing the results that they expected. Each consultant needs to spend a certain amount of time with the organization to better understand the organization's needs. Companies restricting the consultant's capability to learn this vital information only jeopardize the consultant's capability to function as a good consultant to the organization.

Good consultants quickly point out potential pitfalls. They may challenge your methodology and your ideas, causing you to think critically. They do this based on their repository of information and experience. They provide you information about other situations, how companies approach them, and the outcome. They will let you know what is abnormal and what is common. Through the use of consultants an organization's members gain the knowledge of that consultant, which can prove invaluable, provided that he or she is a good consultant.

Companies sometimes wonder if the consultant is really performing the function of a consultant. A simple technique to verify if that consultant is providing any kind of useful benefit is to simply keep spending money on the consultant for a long time and see if you are really any better off for it. But even that is not foolproof because a consultant can properly diagnose a problem and recommend an effective treatment without clients taking the responsibility to participate in the treatment for their own benefit. Many consultants struggle with the fact that their clients simply do not want to take the medication that will save them.

Despite an organization's refusal to take their own medication there are still plenty of other strong indicators, especially when combined, that will reveal the consultant as a phony.

Warning signs to watch out for include:

- They create a continuous pattern of work for themselves.
- They receive bonuses on how many billable hours they turn in.
- They complain about how terrible the client is to work for, many times to the client.
- They lie or provide false information.
- They take personal ownership of the project.
- They perform the same function that someone in your company could do.
- They seldom talk to people, spending most of their time working on the computer.
- You have a very uneasy feeling about the decisions that were made for you by the consultant.
- They make personal evaluations on the employees of the company.
- They perform mundane or simplistic tasks such as clerical data entry.

- The company spends a lot of time and money re-implementing software and business process flows.
- They participate in staff disputes completely unrelated to the ERP project.
- They use their certifications or someone else's authority to try to "prove" their point.
- They show signs of psychological disorders.
- Most of the project team and the rest of the organization have a negative attitude towards them.
- They try to implement your cures for you.
- They question your judgment and knowledge frequently in a disrespectful way.

Consultants should not be responsible for making the decisions for you because your company will be living with those decisions long after the consultants have gone on to different projects. Consultants' energies are best suited to the needs for which they were originally required, than for participating in mindless politics and getting involved with disputes between staff functions.

It is better for managers and employees of the companies to train and educate operational level people within their organization. To use the consultant in this function creates a dependency that can destroy the chain of command within an organization. This can become most disruptive when the consultant leaves the organization. It is far better to have the consultant participate at the management level, and have ERP team leaders and functional managers educate and train their own personnel. This forces the supervisory manager of personnel to understand concepts and procedures related to the ERP system and how their people must use it. It also reinforces the chain of command which forces the communication channels to be aligned with their proper sources and destinations.

Consultants should not be used for performing personal evaluations. Consultants, because of their great experience, can compare people to other people that they have worked with at other companies. But these are decisions that the company should make, not the consultant. Company officials are best suited for analyzing all of the different variables in making a good decision regarding a person's capabilities.

The use of consultants to perform direct labor functions can be a costly endeavor. The people of the organization are much better suited to perform the functional activities related to their area. Consultants should be used to help you to define and outline tasks to be performed, not to do them.

It is good to teach the consultant as much about the business as possible. This helps the consultant develop a complete conceptual view of the organization, which is important when dealing with a highly integrated package such as ERP. Each business has its own little quirks and personality. The more the consultants know about the company the better they will be equipped to provide good advice. This, of course, will cost the company money but the benefits in the long run are well worth it.

Education of the consultant should provide information on the functional activities of the business and an understanding of interrelationships between the various functional areas of the business. This helps to reduce fear within the various departments. The more trust that can be built with the consultant, the greater the probability for the success of the project.

Good consultants are excellent troubleshooters and problem solvers. They work together with an ERP team in understanding their problems and helping to solve them. Problem solving sessions begin by properly defining the problem and the related process flows. A good consultant listens to the ERP team members with a concentrated effort. After the consultant has absorbed all of the details from the situation he or she may provide several different solutions.

It is always a good idea to ask your consultant a lot of questions, even after the problem appears to be solved. By asking consultants many questions you encourage their participation, recognize their knowledge, learn more from them, gain concepts from them that can solve problems elsewhere, prevent unnecessary software modifications, and jog their memory to learn even more from them.

Consultants provide three general categories of services: management, application, and technical. The service provider will divide consultants into these three general categories. You can find consultants who can perform two of these functions, however, it is rare to find consultants who can perform all three.

Management consultants focus primarily on the function of management as it relates to the organization of resources and business process flows. Management consultants often participate in project management and will provide high-level direction for the overall successful implementation and use of an ERP system.

Application, or functional, consultants focus on the process of communicating, teaching, demonstrating, and configuring software for the business process flows. A management consultant may consult on how to perform a business process flow where an application consultant would show the company how to perform the business process flow in the new software.

Technical consultants deal with technical issues such as database conversions, source code modifications, communication protocols, operating systems, software installation, hardware systems, and integration programs. Technical consultants work closely with application and management consultants.

Because of the close relationship between the application consultant and a management consultant, application consultants can sometimes end up filling the role of a management consultant and vice versa. It is best to understand the roles of application consultant and the management consultant. Substituting one for the other when they are not qualified can lead to very awkward situations for both the client and the consultant. The same can also be true for application and technical consultants. The company might choose to use a management consultant from an independent source to review the overall implementation on a periodic basis. Application consultants may then come from the ERP vendor or service provider. This combination provides a company with application expertise without placing the application consultants into a situation that may present a conflict of interest for the company.

In choosing the consultant it is a good practice to review several different good candidates for your organization. All too often companies simply accept the first consultant sent by the ERP vendor or service provider, without giving any thought on the long-term repercussions that may occur because of a potential mismatch between the consultant and the organization. ERP team core members and critical stakeholders should be involved in the selection of a good consultant. It is important that the ERP team understand that the consultant will assist them with the project, not do it for them.

Before the process of selecting the consultant the company must have developed a clear definition of what they want to obtain from the consultant. These definitions should have been derived from the early needs analysis and the business integration planning session, which should have occurred in the early stages of an ERP project. It is also helpful to understand any constraints that may keep you from achieving the objectives in the project. Those functional areas with the greatest needs will be the ones that will most likely consume the larger portion of resources from that consultant(s). Estimates of the consultant's time come from the early implementation planning sessions followed by more detailed estimates in the project planning workshop taking place just before the beginning of the implementation.

It is important to create an environment in which the consultant will be successful. All too often companies feel that this is the responsibility of the consultant. Consultants generally have no authority or power over how the work environment is structured. This responsibility must come from the client. The environment includes characteristics such as personalities, personal qualifications, resources, and organizational structure. Consultants should be briefed on the environment that they will be coming into so they will have proper expectations. Some questions that a company can ask to help determine the type of environment for a consultant include:

- Are people of the company relatively open to change? Or are they shocked by it?
- Does top management support the use of sometimes expensive consultants?
- Are the financial resources available to support the long-term use of consultants?
- Is defensiveness exhibited within the ERP team and by management officials?

Consultants can come from a wide variety of sources, sometimes overlooked sources. A list of all possible sources should be considered. Independent references, from other companies, can provide useful insight and quality and service of a particular consultant. The quality of service from one particular consultant company can fluctuate tremendously based upon the individual that performs the services. For this reason it is better to ask for the specific name of the consultant who provided the services. Some sources where consultants can come from include:

- Trade associations
- Professional development societies
- ERP vendors

- Service providers
- System integrators
- Consulting agencies
- Accounting firms
- Educational institutes
- Independent consultants
- Headhunters
- Employment offices
- Other companies
- Newspapers
- Internal company sources
- Past employees
- Retired employees
- New employees
- Websites

After you have compiled a list of consultants, you can narrow them down by many factors. Some important factors to consider or look for include:

- References
- Resumes
- Availability
- Pricing
- Demonstrated competence
- Communication skills

Interviews with consultants can be misleading. A consultant's past history and references can be an indicator (or very misleading) of their capabilities. Sometimes there is just no good way to verify a good consultant without trial and error. The final choice can be most difficult, but it is important not to undervalue the importance of choosing a person that has the right chemistry to help make an organization become successful.

Every company using a consultant seeks to obtain the best benefit from that consultant. Education is an important first step for any consultant coming into an organization. Consultants are like people going to the movie when it is half over. They come in observing the current picture trying to figure out what happened prior to their arrival. The frequency of visits for a consultant may range anywhere from one day per quarter to a full-time commitment. Both the consultants and the client should understand this need.

Each consultant should provide some type of feedback communication through written documentation. The company will need this written documentation to match against the invoices (bills) that are received from the consultant or service provider. The type of memos and status reports needed and how often they are needed should be defined clearly and communicated to the consultant. Too much detail is not always desirable in status reports as it can sometimes cause a consultant to document the project vs. consult for it. A couple of sentences to one paragraph per day should be adequate without over burdening the consultant.

Consultants should be encouraged to be honest and communicate their thoughts and ideas. Consultants with good experience understand that the company will not automatically follow all of his or her recommendations. It is important to build the best relationship possible with the consultant, for your success and theirs depend upon it.

How well an organization benefits from a consultant is dependent upon the consultant and an organization's capability to absorb the consultant's recommendations. Whether a failure to effectively utilize a consultant resides with the organization or the consultant, it does not alter the fact that the company is spending valuable resources without seeing measurable benefits. The company at this point may want to stop using his or her services, or examine how well the company is listening to the advice of the consultant, and find ways to better achieve the objectives of the project.

Questions---

1. List three reasons why consultants are needed in ERP implementations.
2. What is one of the primary responsibilities of a consultant?
3. What is the difference between a trainer and a consultant?
4. Does the consultant make decisions?
5. List five warning signs when searching for consultants.
6. When should consultants engage in employee evaluations?
7. Why is it good to ask your consultant a number of questions?
8. What are the three types of consultants?
9. Where can you find consultants?
10. Why are status reports needed for consultants? How much documentation should be required?
11. How should a consultant be treated?
12. What should you know before hiring a consultant?
13. Who should be involved in the selection of the consultant?

"A project is a problem scheduled for solution" - J.M. Juran
"Plans are worthless, but planning is everything" - President Dwight Eisenhower

12

Project Planning Session

A project planning session is a multifunctional event that serves to recognize the ERP project on a formal basis. One of its primary goals is to develop the project plan. A project is a solution that is scheduled for success. The project planning session is a meeting that usually lasts one or more days and consists of all the critical stakeholders of the ERP system from both internal and external sources. The project planning session will define the main problems with proposed solutions. In the planning session it will be determined what must be done, who will do it, how it will be done, when it will be done, cost of doing it, and the services and materials needed to do it. Output of the project planning session is a formal document, which should be electronic in nature, which will serve as a guide to implement the software and help to build ownership in the system. This chapter addresses all the various events that go into the project planning session and how to perform them.

Companies will attempt to do project planning at all various stages including: before, during, or after the ERP implementation. The ideal time is before the ERP project is started. It is usually performed shortly before or after the software is purchased.

Assemble the Critical Stakeholders

One of the first steps of the project planning session is to assemble the critical stakeholders of the project. The critical stakeholders should include all people who have a direct influence over the project in terms of how the resources should be allocated. It should also include any potential members of the company who may participate, or have an influence on the ERP core team. Notice should be sent out ahead of time through electronic methods informing the necessary people of the company that their participation will be needed in the project planning session. Participation in the project planning session is not an optional exercise. Because of the critical need for strong support in an ERP project, all members having a stake hold in the project need to participate. The full participation of senior management should not be overlooked. All too often it seems that the president of the company, or any other senior manager responsible, expects to stop by to "see how things are going". Any critical stakeholder who refuses participation in the project places the ERP implementation at risk, usually a high-risk. Should refusal to participate result, the necessary actions should be taken to ensure successful participation and to ensure that a conflict of interest does not develop. The project planning session, and the ERP project, simply cannot take place successfully without the participation of the key stakeholders.

Review or Create the Needs Analysis

After the team is assembled a review of the needs analysis should be conducted. Ideally, the needs analysis and output from it should have been performed well before the purchase of the software and the project planning session. If the needs analysis has not been done, then do it now. The needs analysis will essentially be the justification for the project. It will consist of high-level statements as well as specific detail line items related to functional characteristics. The needs analysis should represent all functional areas of the business.

Establish Vision / Mission of the Project

After the team is assembled, determine and document the vision / missions of the project. Ideally, the vision and missions should already be established before the planning session. If they are not, then it should be done now.

The vision should be a global statement that is continuous and ongoing. The mission statements will consist of the major milestones of the project. Mission statements should have specific expiration dates and be measurable in nature so that they do not become vision statements. They can be broken down by functional module. The expected completion date for each module should be documented as expressed by the appropriate critical stakeholders. If the critical stakeholders have not determined a critical completion date, then do the mission statements now and put the date on later. The projected completion date will be calculated in a later step of the project planning session.

Determine Organizational Structure

This section focuses on determining the way that the organization is divided. Some organizations will be clearly separated by geographic facilities. Others may be clearly separated by different business divisions controlled by separate management functions. The purpose of this section is not to create an organizational chart showing a hierarchy of command. It should instead show the major areas of the business that may install the software independently or at different times.

Establish Modules to Be Implemented

Using input from the needs analysis, vision/mission statements, and the organizational structure, the next step is to establish the modules to be implemented. Other independent software packages, that may be interfaced, may also be implemented with the rest of the ERP system. Include all possible sources that will integrate or affect the implementation of the ERP system. The modules of the ERP system may not correlate with the needs of the organization. It may be helpful, or even necessary, to have an ERP system application consultant present to explain what functional need of the organization translates into the appropriate functional module of the ERP software. After the translation has been made, a complete list can be established.

Determine Modular Phasing

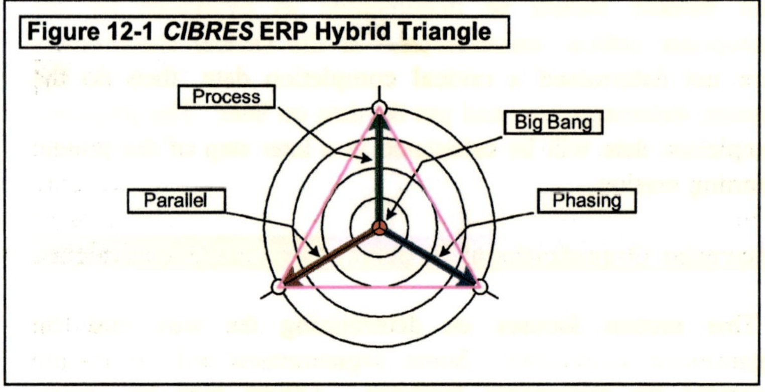

Figure 12-1 *CIBRES* ERP Hybrid Triangle

There are three primary goals for this step. The first goal is to determine the degree of process, phasing, and parallel. Do this by using the CIBRES ERP hybrid triangle as shown in figure 12-1. The second goal is to determine how the functional modules relate to the three fundamental dimensions of the CIBRES ERP hybrid triangle. If there has been a general lack of fundamental ERP education prior to the project planning session, then this will most likely be a lengthy and difficult step. First determine the amount of phasing that will be used. If a form of phasing other than big bang is used, then all of the different phases should be identified as phase one, phase two, phase three, etc. Document functional modules related to each one of the phases. After the amount of phasing is determined, identify the amount of parallel followed by any process (as shown in the CIBRES ERP hybrid triangle) that may be used.

The third goal is to determine the start date of the project. In most cases, if the software has already been purchased, the start date will begin immediately. Input for the start date should come from all critical stakeholders of the system. Consensus should be found among all participants of the project planning session. An estimated completion date may also be documented. If the stakeholders feel uncomfortable about specifying an estimated completion date, it may be postponed. The completion dates will be calculated in later steps.

Establish ERP Core Team

This section has several purposes. They include: determining the structure of the ERP team, assigning ERP corc team members to modules and phases, determining their percentage of participation, adjusting percentage equivalents, and calculating full time equivalents.

First, establish the type of ERP team structure to be used in the implementation. The four classifications of ERP teams are isolated function, lightweight, heavyweight, and the a-team. Each one of these ERP teams can be applied to a number of different implementation methodologies. These four different styles are for the formation of ERP teams, not the way the ERP software is installed. Other positions outside the core ERP team such as: steering committees, management consultant, technical consultant, and application consultant, can be applied and arranged to support any one of these four strategies. Before one is chosen over the other, the advantages and disadvantages should be clearly understood by all critical stakeholders.

After the structure of the team is established, by input from participants of the project planning session, each member must be assigned to a functional area and the percentage of time to be dedicated must be determined. The number of positions and the amount of time that ERP team core members will dedicate can vary considerably from the beginning of the project to the end. This can become quite evident when the project is broken up into phases and one person participates in more than one phase. Different phases may require different participation levels from different people.

Based upon the previously discussed conversion and interface programs, the company may want to dedicate technical resources from within the company. If technical resources are available or are going to be committed from within the company, then those resources should be listed as well.

After the percentage of time is established for each team member, calculate the equivalent percentage. The equivalent percentage recognizes that participation by ERP team members does not have uniform benefits. Individuals with higher participation have more value than individuals with low participation. Using the equivalent percentage allows more realistic values to be established. In some cases low participation can actually be counterproductive because of the high learning curves. At least 50 percent dedication is recommended for an ERP team member. With any amount less than this, a team member may become inactive (meaning participation drops off) and reactive in nature. Figure 12-3 shows the percentage equivalent conversion table for determining the final adjusted percentage of participation.

If the ERP team member participates in more than one area of the ERP project at the same time, then the percentage of time spent in each area should be summed together when determining the adjustment percentage. For example, if John participated in two different areas, 10 percent of his time for each one, his adjusted percentage would be equal to seven percent.

After the percentage equivalents are determined for each team member, the full-time equivalents should then be summed up. The summation will correlate with the number of phases or processes that take place in the ERP implementation. Should the project contain no phasing or process characteristics, then a one-phase summation may be performed.

Figure 12-2 Percentage Equivalents

Estimated Participation %	Adjustment Percentage
0 %	0 %
10 %	0 %
20 %	7 %
30 %	10 %
40 %	20 %
50 %	40 %
60 %	55 %
70 %	70 %
80 %	80 %
85 %	85 %
90 %	90 %
95 %	95 %
100 %	100 %

An example of how this might work could be for the phase one of a financial implementation. Sally plans to dedicate 50 percent of her time, John plans to dedicate 25 percent of his time, and Jennifer plans to dedicate 75 percent of her time. Using the adjusted percentages (figure 12-3) we find that Sally's percentage equivalent is equal to 40 percent, John's percentage equivalent is equal to an estimated 8 percent, and Jennifer's equivalent percentage is equal to an estimated 75 percent. To calculate the full time equivalent, a summation is performed for all the adjusted equivalent percents (.40 + .08 + .75 = 1.23). The total full-time equivalent is then equal to 1.23 people. This is the equivalent of about one person working on the project full time. This calculation should be performed for each phase or process of the project.

Establish Educational / Training Needs

In this step the educational and training needs are established. First determine how much education will be required, the type of education, and the number of participants. Educational classes will generally be predefined standardized training packages. The focus of education should be the critical stakeholders, senior management, and ERP team core members. Some areas to consider for education include:

- Fundamental ERP concepts
- Business management techniques
- ERP functional modules

Make a listing of all the participants who will be attending in each category. ERP educational modules are generally available from ERP vendors and service providers. They are standardized educational programs to help students learn the functionality of the software. Make a complete listing of ERP functional modules with each team member who will be attending. It may be helpful, even necessary, to have an ERP application consultant assist in the assignment of people to ERP functional educational training classes. Education for ERP functional modules should be further broken down by the phase in which the modules will take place.

Figure 12-2 shows a general matrix of how the formulation of educational needs may appear. When determining the total amount of educational needs, the end-users should not be included these figures. Some ERP team members will have the need for both education and training. For ERP team members who will receive both education and training, the educational portion should be included in the educational section and the training portion should be included in the training section.

Figure 12-3 Determining Educational Needs		
Educational Area	Persons	Days
Fundamental ERP Concepts	10	2
Business Management Techniques	7	5
ERP Functional Modules		
Phase 1 - Accounting		
Accounts Payable	5	3
General Ledger	4	3
Accounts Receivable	5	3
Payroll	3	3
Phase 2 - Distribution		
Sales	3	5
Inventory	2	8
Purchasing	3	6
Phase 3 - Manufacturing		
MRP/MPS/DRP	2	5
Forecasting	2	4
Shop Floor Control	3	7
Bills Of Material and Routings	2	9
Engineering Change Orders	2	4
Configuration Management	3	5

After the educational needs are determined, a survey should be taken, using inputs from the critical stakeholders, to determine the total number of people that will need training in each one of the functional modules. The training classes will be specific for the company in that they will teach the users how to use the ERP system specifically for the business. Each training class will be custom developed based on how the software is set up and used. The format for determining training needs for end-users will be similar to the ERP functional modules section found in figure 12-3.

Establish Data Conversion Strategy

The goal in this step is to establish what needs to be converted and how it is going to be done. Almost every functional module will require information from the legacy system. The two primary methods of converting data are manual and electronic. When performing this step it may be helpful to have an entity diagram and file structure specification of the ERP system. Application consultants can provide helpful insight into the critical files that require data for the successful use and implementation of the ERP system. In most cases, either electronic or manual methods may be used. However, before one is chosen over the other, the advantages and disadvantages of each approach should be clearly understood. Some areas to consider for data conversion include:

- Open accounts receivable
- Open accounts payable
- Chart of accounts
- Accounts payable history
- Accounts receivable history
- Open sales orders
- Sales order history
- Open purchase orders
- Purchase order history
- Item master
- Item on hand balance
- Bills of material and routings
- Open engineering change orders
- Engineering change order history
- Open work orders
- Work order history
- Customer master
- Vendor master
- Fixed assets

- General ledger balances
- Employee master files
- Payroll history
- Payroll balances

Many other areas are also available for consideration. It is best to have experienced people from the legacy system working together with application consultants to fully understand the complete need.

Establish Interfaces

The goal of this step is to identify any interfaces that require development. Complementary products, such as a bar coding system, that have pre-established interface programs, should not be included here. This section is for the required interface programs between systems for which none exist. If the ERP implementation strategy contains zero phasing and no process characteristics, it may then require few or no interfaces. Projects that have a high degree of phasing and process characteristics are more likely to contain phasing. Other software packages that need to connect and communicate with the ERP system should be included here. Interface programs can be developed using electronic methods or they can be performed by ERP team members or clerical functions using manual methods. Before one is chosen over the other, the advantages and disadvantages of each approach should be clearly understood. It may be helpful, and in many cases required, to use application consultants or technical consultants to explain critical interface points for the new ERP system. It is best to have company employees with a strong knowledge base of the legacy ERP system working together with knowledgeable ERP application consultants to fully understand the critical interface points.

Perform Work Estimates

This section establishes the work estimates for the ERP project. A wide variety of events are represented that will consume the majority of the resources dedicated to the project. Performing work estimates in ERP systems can be far from an exact science. However, if careful research was done prior to the purchase of the software, general estimates are possible with some degree of accuracy. Communication with outside references can provide estimates of how much work was performed and how long it took. Using these estimates from references combined with experienced honest application and technical consultants, reasonable numbers can be obtained. Estimates should be made for each activity for each phase or process section. Should the project contain no phasing or process characteristics, then only one estimate will be needed for each activity. Some activities, such as installation or war room, may not require estimates for later phases of the project should the project have phasing or process characteristics. The estimates for the work to be performed should be in days. The number of days is not based on how long someone thinks it will take from beginning to end, but rather how long it will take based on a person working full time on that particular event. This is the equivalent of man-hours or in this case, man-days. The following list contains many activities for consideration of work estimates:

- Installation
- Project planning session
- Detailed project plans
- War room
- ERP education
- Answer configuration questions
- Policy formations
- Report equivalents

- Functional mapping
- Testing and prototyping
- Software modifications
- Interfaces
- Database conversion
- Contingency planning
- Documentation
- End-user training
- Audits
- Performance measurements
- Go live
- Post implementation support
- Ongoing education and maintenance

This section will help establish the scope of the project, or how much work needs to be done. With our previous section determining the available amount of resources, we can now move into our next section, which helps us determine the amount of time it will take.

Calculate Consulting Assistance

Most ERP projects benefit from some degree of consultation. This consultation can occur at management, functional, and technical levels. The amount of outside consultation that will be needed is dependent upon many different factors. Some factors that will increase the need for consultants include:

- Large complex installations
- Multilanguage characteristics
- Complex business process flows
- Lack of ownership
- Lack of participation by ERP team members
- Sudden changes in leadership

- Scope creep
- Compressed implementations
- Internal political standoffs
- Technical problems
- Software problems
- Electronic interface programs
- Electronic database conversion programs

The amount of consultation assistance needed for any one ERP project can vary tremendously. When and where a consultant may be needed is very difficult to predict in the early phases of an ERP project. For purposes of increasing ownership and participation, it is better to limit the role of consultants and use them for critical areas. The following guide can be used in selecting the amount of estimated consultation assistance:

- Low - 0% to 16%
- Moderate - 17% to 33%
- High - 34% to 50%
- Turnkey - Over 50%

When consultants perform more than 50 percent of the workload, they begin to stop functioning as consultants and begin functioning more as direct labor for the ERP project. This characteristic can be found in turnkey systems, meaning that the system is implemented through the use of outside resources.

Calculate Project Time

Every ERP project will be affected by three characteristics working together: scope, resources, and time. The scope of the project has already been defined in the previous steps. The available resources have been calculated through percentage equivalents into full-time equivalents. The remaining step is to calculate the completion date. Figure 12-4 shows the relationship between these three important characteristics. Should a company increase its scope of an ERP implementation, then it will need to increase the time or available resources or both. Should a company decrease the available resources used to work on the project, then the scope will need to decrease or the available time will need to increase, or both. By changing any one of the three characteristics, the other two are affected. Since we have calculated the scope and the available resources, we can now determine the implementation time.

Figure 12-4 Relationship Triangle

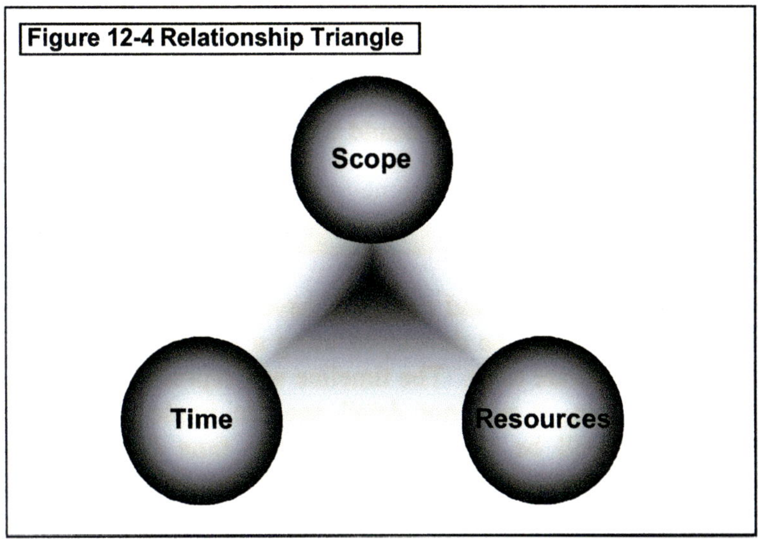

Calculation of the project time is a relatively simple task. The basic formula consists of:

$$\text{Project time} = \frac{\text{Total calculated workdays}}{\text{Total calculated FTEs}}$$

For example, an ERP implementation using a big bang strategy with no process characteristics has a 'total calculated workdays' of 450. The 'total calculated FTEs' have been calculated to be 4.5. The total project time would then be 100 physical days, which, considering weekends, would translate into about twenty weeks based upon a five-day workweek.

This formula should be applied to every phase or process of the project. Presuming that the project times do not overlap, they may all be added together for each phase or process for calculation of the grand total. Should the phases or processes overlap, then the necessary reduction in overall project time should be calculated. Overlapping can take place provided that the different phases or processes of the project cannot compete with each other. For example, say that two phases had a calculated project time of 100 days each with a 50 percent overlap. The total project time would then be 150 days.

Develop Graphical Timeline

Once the scope, time, and resources have been calculated, a graphical timeline may be developed using a variety of project management software tools. The timeline will represent a high-level project plan, it will not detail specific implementation tasks, for this will be developed at a later time during the project. Its purpose is to show major phases or processes, activities, sequence of activities, events that will operate in parallel, start dates, and completion dates.

A graphical timeline is an important part of the project planning session. The graphical representation of the elements of the project helps make it a valuable tool for discussion. In many cases the graphical timeline will be developed outside the project planning session. In some rare cases a highly skilled project planning facilitator will be able to develop the timeline interactively based upon the group discussion.

The timeline should consist of one group of activities for each phase or process of the project. Each group of activities may be sequenced or they may be arranged in parallel. If team members overlap between the different phases, then the groups will need to be held in sequential order. If each phase has dedicated members, then the groups can operate in parallel, shortening the implementation time.

Document All Constraints

In this step all constraints of the project should be documented. A constraint is any business activity or external factor that will inhibit or affect the outcome of the ERP implementation in some negative way. The source of information should come from all the critical stakeholders of the ERP implementation. One of the key factors on which to focus is identifying any activities that will potentially compete for ERP team members' time. Some examples of business activities or problems include:

- Lack of people
- Data integrity problems
- People unwilling to change
- Other implementations
- Change of personnel
- New products or services
- Major capital expansions

- Downsizing
- Corporate buyouts
- Business expansions
- Hardware upgrades
- Change of business process flows

Establish Project Policies

Project policies provide a uniform consistent method for dealing with situations and events that occur in a project. Some areas in which to consider policies include:

- Issue resolution
- Software modification
- Project status meetings
- Weekly communications
- Scheduling consultants
- Documentation

Issue resolution policies have two main categories: internal and external. Internal issue resolution policies deal with all the issues that are within immediate control of the company, and consultants assist in them. They are often related to business process flows requiring management decision. An escalation process allows non-resolvable problems to flow to higher levels of management for decision making.

External issue resolution deals with factors outside the immediate control of the company and consultants. Software functionality problems often fall into this category. An ERP vendor's standard issue resolution policy should be sought and included in the project planning output report.

The software modification policy establishes who has the authority and power to initiate a modification request. An ROI calculation or cost/benefits analysis should be part of the software modification policy. The process of performing cost/benefit analysis discourages any unnecessary software modifications and serves as justification for performing the needed modifications. Also include alternative strategies to performing the software modification. A signature cycle from several key stakeholders should be initiated that will give approval to perform the software modification.

Project status meetings should occur with all critical stakeholders of the project on a weekly basis. Project status meetings serve as a method to review current activities and to discuss issues. During times of high activity, project status meetings may need to occur more frequently. Even after the implementation of the software, many companies still continue to hold meetings to discuss and resolve issues revolving around their ERP system.

Weekly communications should occur, from a centralized source, such as a project manager, in some type of electronic format such as a newsletter. Newsletters allow the organization to follow the progress of the implementation and to help prepare them for what is to come. Several ERP team core members should make contributions to the newsletters in the form of articles. This provides additional insight, for the organization enforces critical thinking and good decision making for the ERP team core members.

Because of the potential high-costs, scheduling consultants should come from an internal source. Sometimes team leaders from different phases or functional modules schedule consultants directly, and in other cases higher level management will do so.

Clearly state a standard policy regarding what should be documented in the project. Key areas to consider for documentation include:

- Issue resolution
- Software modifications
- Configuration settings

- Business process flows
- General communications
- Conversion strategies
- Contingency plans
- Project status meetings
- Training guides
- User guides

Document All Notes and Recommendations

This section serves as a place to document all important notes and recommendations derived in the project planning session. It also serves to accumulate information that does not fit into any other section. It will contain information from ERP team core members, service providers, or the ERP vendor.

The following is an example of how a report from a project planning session may appear.

Gizmo Manufacturing

Project Planning Session

Prepared by John Doe for Gizmo Manufacturing
11-17-2000

Overview and Introduction

On November 10, 2000 Gizmo Manufacturing closed the sales cycle with an ERP service provider with the signing of the contract for the purchase of the KR16 system. On November 17, 2000 Gizmo Manufacturing held a project planning session to identify the goals and objectives and to determine the amount of resources needed for a successful ERP implementation effort.

Critical stakeholders throughout the system have been assembled for the input and creation of the project plan. The output represents the organization's viewpoints and strategies for the KR16 system. The output of this report will require the approval of all critical stakeholders from the different functional areas of Gizmo Manufacturing.

Gizmo Manufacturing manufactures pet accessories and play toys for dogs. In 1994 the company developed a new polymer, for manufacturing in their toys, that was safe and three times more durable than the competition's. The new polymer combined with aggressive marketing has led the company to achieve distribution of their products through most national pet chain stores and smaller private stores.

In 1995 Gizmo Manufacturing purchased Medi-pet, a manufacturer of complex medical support equipment for pet surgeries. Some types of support equipment must be returned for remanufacturing after it has reached its life expectancy. The buyout brought significant challenges as the company attempted to save money by consolidating their ERP systems and IS support staff.

Growth occurred steadily until mid 1998 when the company replaced its centralized year 2000 non-compliant legacy system with a distributed proprietary custom developed solution known as MB5. The MB5 resolved year 2000 issues but brought about a host of serious problems. The MB5 system was faced with chronic data corruption and software support issues. Unable to resolve the issues, Gizmo Manufacturing's customer base started eroding because of poor customer service and production planning capabilities. The irresolvable issues with the MB5 system brought about the strong need for a proven stable commercial ERP system.

Some important details of Gizmo Manufacturing include:

Number of users:	125
Number of plants:	3
Total employees:	650
Environment:	Manufacturing
Sales volume:	$275 million
Current system:	MB5
Current hardware:	LAN

Needs Analysis

Gizmo Manufacturing identified significant justification for the purchase implementation of a new ERP system. Some of the needs identified so far include:

- Stop data corruption
- Consolidate business units onto one system
- Utilize integrated cycle counting programs to improve inventory
- Reduce work effort for month end closing procedures
- Provide better access to data
- Reduce paper output
- Internet access for field service
- Provide stable platform for company growth
- Improve customer service through forecast management
- Utilize vendor supplier analysis tools
- Provide multi-currency function for international markets

- Help manage product change through engineering change order management
- Reduce part shortages through efficient material requirements planning
- Streamline business process flows by using workflow

Vision / Mission of the Project

Vision - to utilize the features and functions of the KR16 system to help develop, establish, and execute the company's long term strategic, tactical, and operational plans for competitive advantage in the market place.

Missions -

- Successfully implement all financial related ERP modules in St. Paul, MN by Oct. 1, 2001.
- Successfully implement all distribution-related functionality such as sales orders, purchase orders, inventory, warehouse management, and basic planning functionality in San Jose, CA by Oct. 1, 2001.
- Successfully implement all manufacturing and distribution related modules in St. Paul, MN by June 1, 2002 over a period of eight months.
- Successfully implement all distribution and manufacturing related modules for Medi-pet in Dallas, TX by June 1, 2002.

Organizational Structure

Gizmo Manufacturing is divided into three primary business units: Medi-pet that resides in Dallas TX, a manufacturing and distribution plant in St. Paul MN, and a distribution plant in San Jose CA. St. Paul MN serves as corporate headquarters providing centralized IS support services, accounting, and payroll functions.

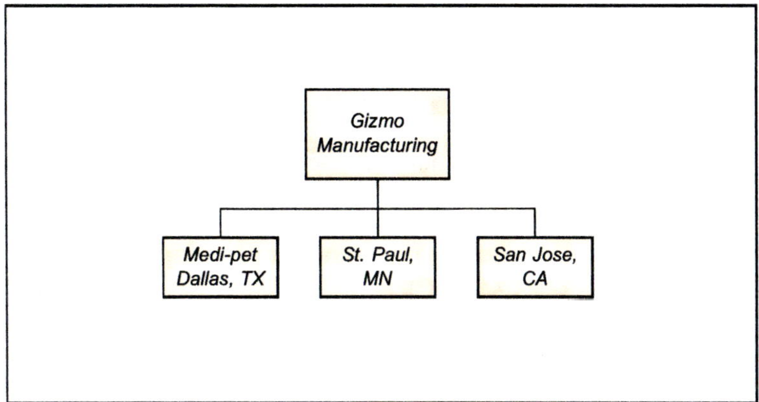

Modules to Be Implemented

Medi-pet Dallas TX –

- Sales order management
- Purchase order management
- Inventory management
- Distribution requirements planning
- MPS/MRP/CRP
- Forecasting
- Field service
- Re-manufacturing

- Engineering change order
- Bills of material and routings
- Configurator
- Shop floor control

Gizmo Manufacturing St. Paul MN –

- General ledger
- Accounts payable
- Accounts receivable
- Payroll
- Fixed assets
- Sales order management
- Purchase order management
- Inventory management
- Distribution requirements planning
- MPS/MRP/CRP
- Forecasting
- Bills of material and routings
- Shop floor control

Gizmo Manufacturing San Jose CA –

- Sales order management
- Purchase order management
- Inventory management
- Distribution requirements planning
- Warehouse management

Modular Phasing

Gizmo Manufacturing will utilize a two-step phased strategy without any process or parallel characteristics. Phase 1 will include accounting functions with operational functions at a different site. Phase two will focus primarily on operational modules at two different sites.

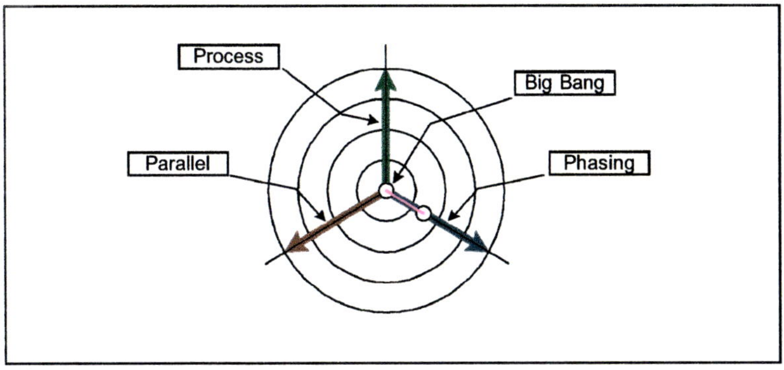

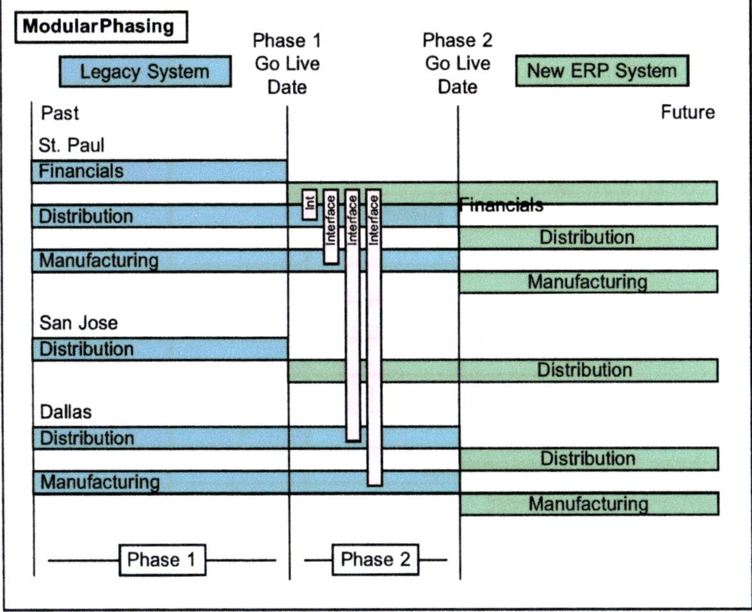

Functional Modules	Phase 1	Phase 2
Medi-pet Dallas TX		
Sales order management		✓
Purchase order management		✓
Inventory management		✓
Distribution requirements planning		✓
MPS/MRP/CRP		✓
Forecasting		✓
Field Service		✓
Remanufacturing		✓
Engineering change order		✓
Bills of material and routings		✓
Configurator		✓
Shop floor control		✓
Gizmo Manufacturing St. Paul MN		
General ledger	✓	
Accounts payable	✓	
Accounts receivable	✓	
Payroll	✓	
Fixed assets	✓	
Sales order management		✓
Purchase order management		✓
Inventory management		✓
Distribution requirements planning		✓
MPS/MRP/CRP		✓
Forecasting		✓
Bills of material and routings		✓
Shop floor control		✓
Gizmo Manufacturing San Jose CA		
Sales order management	✓	
Purchase order management	✓	
Inventory management	✓	
Distribution requirements planning	✓	
Warehouse management	✓	

ERP Team

Gizmo Manufacturing has decided to use a heavyweight strategy for its ERP team. The team will be supported by a steering committee and technical resources. Team members have volunteered or been assigned by the appropriate company official. Their percentage equivalents have been adjusted in the calculation of full-time equivalents. Coverage is provided throughout the duration of the project in both phase 1 and phase 2. The team structure is as follows:

Positions / People	**% Time**	**% Adj**
Steering Committee		
John		
Sue		
Connie		
Executive Sponsor		
Alan		
Project Manager - Phase 1 and 2		**1.00**
Jamie	100 %	100 %
Phase 1 - Total Full Time Equivalents		**3.53**
Gizmo Man St. Paul (Fin.)		**1.78**
Arek	80 %	80 %
Barry	50 %	40 %
Sherry	25 %	8 %
Bill (Technical)	50 %	50 %
Gizmo Man San Jose (Dist.)		**1.75**
Bob	50 %	40 %
Bonnie	40 %	20 %
Kathy	30 %	10 %
Kay	60 %	55 %
Bill (Technical)	50 %	50 %
Phase 2 - Total Full Time Equivalents		**7.00**
Medi-pet Dallas (Man. / Dist.)		**4.30**
Jerry	100 %	100 %
Jim	80 %	80 %
Eric	70 %	70 %
Doug	80 %	80 %
Joanne (Technical)	100 %	100 %
Gizmo Man St. Paul (Man. / Dist.)		**2.70**
Donna	80 %	80 %
Vickie	70 %	70 %
Helena	40 %	20 %
Walter (Technical)	100 %	100 %

Establish Educational / Training Needs

Total educational and training needs have been established. Educational classes will be provided through the ERP vendor and service provider using standardized training classes. The goal of the education classes will be to provide students a conceptual understanding of the features and functions of the software as well as its limitations. Total educational days were calculated from the perspective of resource consumption of the ERP team. Example: if the length of the sales order management class was three days and five people needed to attend it, the total resource consumption from the team would 15 days.

The total training needs in man-days have been calculated also from the ERP team resource consumption perspective. It is the policy of Gizmo Manufacturing and Medi-pet to have all training performed by company employees. Outside consultants will not be used except for assisting in the development and setting up the classes. Since only one instructor will teach the class, the number of days of the class will be equal to the number of days consumed by that team member.

Educational and Training Summary			
	Phase 1	Phase 2	Total
ERP Team educational needs	109	207	316
ERP lead training	18	41	59
Sub total	127	248	375
Total end user training	286	951	1237
Grand Total	413	1199	1612

	Phase 1		Phase 2	
Functional Module Education	People	Days	People	Days
Medi-pet Dallas TX				
Sales order management			5	15
Purchase order management			5	15
Inventory management			5	10
Distribution requirements planning			5	10
MPS/MRP/CRP			5	10
Forecasting			5	10
Field Service			5	10
Remanufacturing			5	15
Engineering change order			5	10
Bills of material and routings			5	5
Configurator			5	10
Shop floor control			5	15
Gizmo Manufacturing St. Paul MN				
General ledger	4	8		
Accounts payable	4	8		
Accounts receivable	4	8		
Payroll	4	12		
Fixed assets	4	8		
Sales order management			4	12
Purchase order management			4	12
Inventory management			4	8
Distribution requirements planning			4	8
MPS/MRP/CRP			4	8
Forecasting			4	8
Bills of material and routings			4	4
Shop floor control			4	12
Gizmo Manufacturing San Jose CA				
Sales order management	5	15		
Purchase order management	5	15		
Inventory management	5	10		
Distribution requirements planning	5	10		
Warehouse Management	5	15		
Total education needs in man days		109		207

	Phase 1		Phase 2	
Functional Module Training	People	Days	People	Days
Medi-pet Dallas TX				
Sales order management			10	2
Purchase order management			10	2
Inventory management			30	1
Distribution requirements planning			10	1
MPS/MRP/CRP			8	1
Forecasting			8	2
Field Service			35	4
Remanufacturing			30	3
Engineering change order			10	2
Bills of material and routings			30	1
Configurator			10	2
Shop floor control			45	5
Gizmo Manufacturing St. Paul MN				
General ledger	8	1		
Accounts payable	8	1		
Accounts receivable	8	1		
Payroll	10	2		
Fixed assets	5	1		
Sales order management			15	2
Purchase order management			10	2
Inventory management			32	1
Distribution requirements planning			5	1
MPS/MRP/CRP			8	1
Forecasting			12	2
Bills of material and routings			28	1
Shop floor control			35	5
Gizmo Manufacturing San Jose CA				
Sales order management	10	4		
Purchase order management	5	2		
Inventory management	15	1		
Distribution requirements planning	8	1		
Warehouse Management	41	4		
Total training needs in man days		18		41

Data Conversion Strategy

Data Conversion Strategy		
From	→	To
Legacy System	Method	New ERP System
Open accounts receivable	Manual	Open accounts receivable
Open accounts payable	Manual	Open accounts payable
Chart of accounts	Manual	Chart of accounts
Accounts payable history	Program	Accounts payable history
Accounts receivable history	Program	Accounts receivable history
Open sales orders	Manual	Open sales orders
Sales order history	Program	Sales order history
Open purchase orders	Manual	Open purchase orders
Purchase order history	Program	Purchase order history
Item master	Manual	Item master
Item on hand balance	Program	Item on hand balance
Bills of material and routings	Manual	Bills of material and routings
Open ECOs	Manual	Open ECOs
ECO history	Program	ECO history
Open work orders	Manual	Open work orders
Work order history	Program	Work order history
Customer master	Manual	Customer master
Vendor master	Manual	Vendor master
Fixed assets	Manual	Fixed assets
General ledger balances	Manual	General ledger balances
Employee master files	Manual	Employee master files
Payroll history	Program	Payroll history
Payroll balances	Manual	Payroll balances

Because of the intensive data corruption problems of the legacy system, manual conversions will be used for all active files. History files, which play an active role and do not require transaction capability, will be converted electronically. The manual conversion strategy will improve the quality of the data, allowing better performance for the new KR19 system. As a secondary side benefit it will provide additional training for the ERP team members. The ERP team members will have primary responsibility for converting the data from the legacy system to the KR19 system. Should time constraints prevail, clerical functions may be used to assist; but those clerical functions must come from within the organization. Outside temporary agencies will not be used.

Data Conversion Strategy Responsibility (Primary)				
		Phase 1	Phase 2	
		SP / SJ	Dallas	St. Paul
Open accounts receivable	Manual	Arek		
Open accounts payable	Manual	Arek		
Chart of accounts	Manual	Arek		
Accounts payable history	Program	Bill		
Accounts receivable history	Program	Bill		
Open sales orders	Manual	Kay	Jerry	Donna
Sales order history	Program	Bill	Joanne	Walter
Open purchase orders	Manual	Bob	Jim	Vickie
Purchase order history	Program	Bill	Joanne	Walter
Item master	Manual	Kay	Jerry	Donna
Item on hand balance	Program	Bill	Joanne	Walter
Bills of material and routings	Manual		Jerry	Donna
Open ECOs	Manual		Jerry	Donna
ECO history	Program		Joanne	Walter
Open work orders	Manual		Eric	Helena
Work order history	Program		Joanne	Walter
Customer master	Manual	Arek		
Vendor master	Manual	Arek		
Fixed assets	Manual	Arek		
General ledger balances	Manual	Arek		
Employee master files	Manual	Arek		
Payroll history	Program	Bill		
Payroll balances	Manual	Arek		

Data conversion for the respective area will be done by the person indicated. The person will work with the other necessary functions to ensure that the data is converted correctly. All converted data, both electronic and manual, will be subjected to testing to ensure integrity and compatibility with the new software.

Interfaces

Because of the high demand for technical resources in developing electronic conversion programs for history needs, the majority of interfaces will be performed manually. Primary responsibility of making sure that interfaces are functioning properly have been assigned and agreed upon by the participants of the project planning session. One interface, from the work order management system to the general ledger in St. Paul, will be conducted electronically because of the massive amount of transactions that take place daily. Should the assigned person not have enough resources to perform the manual interfaces, clerical assistance may be drawn upon from within the company. No external temporary clerical services will be allowed to perform interface functions.

Interface Strategy Responsibility (Primary)						
From					To	
File	Loc	Dir	M/P	Person	Loc	File
Open Sales	SP	➔	Manual	Donna	SP	A/R
Open Sales	DA	➔	Manual	Jerry	SP	A/R
Open Pur	SP	➔	Manual	Donna	SP	A/P
Open Pur	DA	➔	Manual	Jerry	SP	A/P
Inventory	SP	➔	Manual	Vickie	SP	G/L
Inventory	DA	➔	Manual	Jim	SP	G/L
Work Order	SP	➔	Electronic	Walter	SP	G/L
Work Order	DA	➔	Manual	Doug	SP	G/L
Open Purch.	SJ	➔	Manual	Kay	SP	Open Sales

Work Estimates

The work estimates here are based on input from a variety of participants of the project planning session. These estimates were developed from formal documentation that recorded actual implementation effort obtained from a reference, during the sales cycle, by the participants. Although the reference used a slightly different strategy and had different situations, we feel that our adjusted numbers are reasonably accurate.

#	Activity	Phase 1	Phase 2
1	Installation	3	
2	Project planning session	15	15
3	Detail project plans	10	10
4	War Room	4	4
5	ERP education	109	207
6	Answer configuration questions	27	41
7	Policy formations	45	91
8	Report equivalents	21	43
9	Functional mapping	40	68
10	Testing and prototyping	60	140
11	Software modifications	10	22
12	Database conversion	50	120
13	Interfaces	40	86
14	Contingency planning	10	25
15	Documentation	60	120
16	End user training	18	41
17	Audits	20	25
18	Performance measurements	30	37
19	Go live	10	9
20	Post implementation support	40	72
	Total work estimate (man days)	623	1176

The figures represented here are in man-days, not the number of days, it will take to complete that task. Item number 13 - Interfaces - was obtained from the technical programmers who attended the session. Item numbers 16 and 5 came directly from the previous calculations performed in the project planning session. Altogether, Phase 2 appears to be considerably more complex and difficult than Phase 1. This can be expected due to the complex business process flows found at Medi-pet. Their field service and re-manufacturing modules combined with complex engineering change order processes, contributed significantly to the additional workload. Note that these numbers represent a continuous implementation effort. Should the implementation be disrupted or stalled, the workloads would be expected to go up significantly because of the high learning curves.

Consulting Assistance

Gizmo Manufacturing has recognized the important need for ownership and participation in the ERP project. Gizmo Manufacturing also feels that a certain degree of consultation will be beneficial to help ensure knowledge transfer and solve software related problems. Gizmo Manufacturing feels that consultants working as teachers in the early educational classes will be essential in helping the organization understand complete functionality and limitations of the KR19 system. For these reasons Gizmo Manufacturing has decided to use a moderate level of consulting support. Estimates are as follows:

Consulting Support	Phase 1	Phase 2
Total work estimate (man days)	623	1176
Moderate support (20 %)	.20	.20
Total Hours	**125**	**226**

Calculated Project Time

The initial calculations reveal that the scope of the project, the resources allocated, and the available time all appear to be in balance. Output of the calculations is based upon man-days. Given that the number of FTEs remains constant as it was established in this document, the project should be completed by the dates specified in the original mission statements. The calculations also do not include participation of consultants, executive sponsor, steering committee, and the project manager.

$$\text{Project time} = \frac{\text{Total calculated workdays}}{\text{Total calculated FTEs}}$$

Calculated project time	Workdays	FTEs	Project Time
Phase 1	623	3.53	176
Phase 2	1176	7.00	168

These calculations do not include consulting time. Theoretically, implementation time could be lowered by using consultants to perform direct task activities. This, however, will be in direct conflict with Gizmo Manufacturing's ownership policies. The outcome of these calculations has been checked and appears to be relatively consistent with actual figures obtained from references in the sales cycle. We believe them to be accurate to the best of our capability.

Estimated implementation time for Phase 1 has been calculated at 176 days, based upon 3.53 full-time equivalents. This comes out to approximately nine months. Phase 2, despite its much higher workload, came out slightly less at 168 days or about eight and half months. Because of the sequential nature of the phases, total implementation time is expected to be about 1 1/2 years. This includes post implementation support. Actual go live dates should be slightly less.

Estimated starting and go live dates for Phase 1 and Phase 2 have been calculated as follows:

	Start Date	Go Live Date
Phase 1	Jan 1, 2001	Oct 1, 2001
Phase 2	Oct 1, 2001	Jul 1, 2002

Graphical Timeline

ID	Task Name	Duration	Start
1	Gizmo Manufacturing KR19 ERP Implementation	344.2 days	Mon 1/1/01
2	Phase 1 St. Paul Fin - San Jose Dist FTE=3.53	176.2 days	Mon 1/1/01
3	Installation	0.85 days	Mon 1/1/01
4	Project planning session	4.25 days	Mon 1/1/01
5	Detail project plans	2.83 days	Mon 1/8/01
6	War Room	1.13 days	Wed 1/10/01
7	ERP education	30.88 days	Fri 1/12/01
8	Answer configuration questions	7.65 days	Fri 2/23/01
9	Policy formations	12.75 days	Wed 3/7/01
10	Report equivalents	5.95 days	Mon 3/26/01
11	Functional mapping	11.33 days	Tue 4/3/01
12	Testing and prototyping	17 days	Wed 4/18/01
13	Software modifications	2.83 days	Fri 5/11/01
14	Database conversion	14.16 days	Wed 5/16/01
15	Interfaces	11.33 days	Tue 6/5/01
16	Contingency planning	2.83 days	Wed 6/20/01
17	Documentation	17 days	Mon 6/25/01
18	End user training	5.1 days	Wed 7/18/01
19	Audits	5.67 days	Wed 7/25/01
20	Performance measurements	8.5 days	Thu 8/2/01
21	Go live	2.83 days	Wed 8/15/01
22	Post implementation support	11.33 days	Fri 8/17/01
23	Phase 2 Dallas M/D - St. Paul M/D FTE=7.00	168 days	Tue 9/4/01
24	Installation	0 days	Tue 9/4/01
25	Project planning session	2.14 days	Tue 9/4/01
26	Detail project plans	1.43 days	Thu 9/6/01
27	War Room	0.57 days	Fri 9/7/01
28	ERP education	29.57 days	Mon 9/10/01
29	Answer configuration questions	5.86 days	Fri 10/19/01
30	Policy formations	13 days	Mon 10/29/01
31	Report equivalents	6.14 days	Thu 11/15/01
32	Functional mapping	9.71 days	Fri 11/23/01
33	Testing and prototyping	20 days	Fri 12/7/01
34	Software modifications	3.14 days	Fri 1/4/02
35	Database conversion	17.14 days	Wed 1/9/02
36	Interfaces	12.29 days	Fri 2/1/02
37	Contingency planning	3.57 days	Wed 2/20/02
38	Documentation	17.14 days	Mon 2/25/02
39	End user training	5.86 days	Wed 3/20/02
40	Audits	3.57 days	Thu 3/28/02
41	Performance measurements	5.29 days	Wed 4/3/02
42	Go live	1.29 days	Wed 4/10/02
43	Post implementation support	10.29 days	Thu 4/11/02

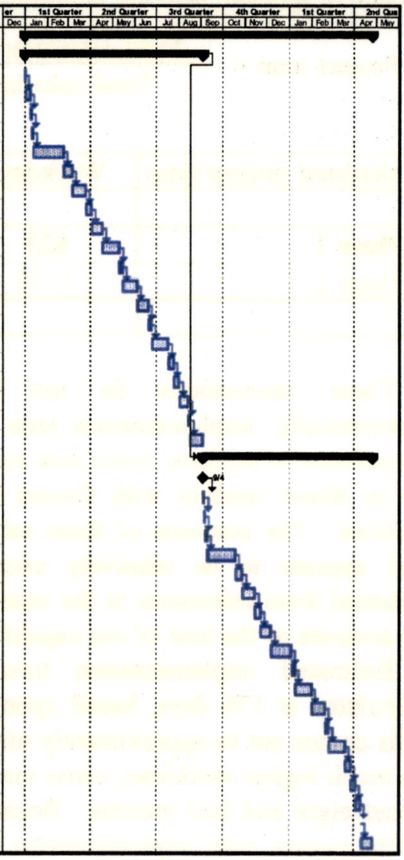

The graphical timeline shown here represents the general sequence of events and phases. It is generated directly from the work estimates and calculations for FTEs. It does not represent a detailed project plan with detailed task activities assigned to ERP team members. Some activities, such as auditing, may be spread out over a further amount of time.

Project Constraints

Several constraining factors have been identified that could affect the successful implementation of the KR19 system. The majority of the participants in the project planning session felt that if the identified factors were monitored and managed carefully they should not affect the success of the KR19 system. Some of factors identified include:

- Massive data integrity problems
- Uncooperative end users
- Lack of organizational buy-in
- Lack of resources
- New capital equipment installations
- Total quality management training
- New product developments
- Increased business growth

Project Policies

Some of the policies have been established for use in the implementation of the KR19 system. The following sections discuss these policies.

Software Modifications -

All software source code modifications will require a cost/benefit analysis before the approval process can start. Upon completion of the cost benefit analysis, signature approvals must be obtained from the project manager, team leader, IS manager, and top senior managers. Documented changes to the source code must be printed out and included with the initial software modifications request form. After the modification has been performed it will be tested for its completeness.

Software modifications that can be performed through standard utilities provided with the ERP system may be done so through the approval of the project manager or team leader. Documentation will be required.

Issue Resolution -

Issue resolution policies will be broken into two main sections: internal and external. All issues that can be resolved internally shall be done so by using the following process:

Team leaders or team members will attempt to resolve issues within their immediate control. Issues outside the immediate control of the team leaders or team members shall be communicated to the project manager using an issue resolution form.

The project manager will review the issue, perform the necessary research, and make the necessary decision. The resolution or decision shall be noted on the issue resolution form and circulated to the ERP team. The project manager will have the full authority and power to resolve issues using his or her discretion.

Issues outside the immediate control of the company, such as software bugs, shall be forwarded to the project manager. The project manager will then initiate a corrective action request from the ERP vendor or service provider. The issue resolution process may be conducted directly by the project manager or delegated at his or her discretion to the appropriate team member. All calls placed with the ERP vendor will be documented in the ERP journal log book, including dates, time, initiator name, vendor contact, call number, and issue.

Documentation -

The following areas will require documentation:

- Consultant activities
- Software modifications
- Weekly ERP team meetings
- Software issues
- Business issucs
- Configuration settings
- Data integrity
- Audit results
- Training manuals
- Changing business process flows
- User guides

Communication -

To ensure effective communication, all ERP team members will be required to attend a weekly ERP team meeting scheduled for Friday of every week. All ERP team members will be required to attend regardless of their participation in the project.

In addition, all ERP team members will be required to write one article per month on the developments in activities occurring within their area of participation.

These articles will then be collected by the project manager for publication in the general newsletter that will be created specifically for the ERP project. This will serve as a monthly update to all interested members of the organization.

Consultants -

All consultants will be required to turn in weekly activity reports. These activity reports will provide daily descriptions of the activities that the consultant performed. Consultants are to turn in their activity summary reports to both a local ERP team member with whom they are working and a project manager. Consultants will be used primarily for education and in the ERP implementation. Their purpose will not be to perform general work activity of the project.

Project Manager -

The project manager has the authority and power to resolve all issues regarding conflicts of resources. In addition, the project manager has the authority and power to allocate additional resources to the project as needed to ensure its success. Should an issue develop between the functional manager and the project manager regarding the allocation of resources for part-time ERP team members, the ruling of the project manager will override that of the functional manager. Should a functional manager wish to appeal the decision, he or she may do so to the executive sponsor and steering committee.

Notes and Recommendations

This document represents the general viewpoints and implementation strategy of Gizmo Manufacturing's KR19 system.

Sudden changes in the leadership of the project, particularly in project management, may have detrimental effects on the outcome of the project.

The resource allocation for phase 1 and phase 2 contains mostly independent resources. At the discretion of the project manager, with the consensus of the executive sponsor and steering committee, Gizmo Manufacturing may elect to begin the phase 2 implementation before the completion of phase 1.

Failure to establish quality data in the new ERP system may have serious detrimental effects on the outcome of the project.

The consultant agency that facilitated the project planning session and prepared this report feels that the work estimates and time lines are conservative figures. The consultant agency feels that the odds of completion ahead of schedule and under budget will be improbable.

Use of Internet technology for selling products over the Internet was originally discussed in the sales cycle that has not been included in the project planning session or part of the implementation strategy. The implementation of Internet sales functions will be considered part of the scope creep and subject to approval before its implementation.

Questions---

1. What are some other names for a PPS?
2. What is one of the primary goals of the PPS?
3. What are some common problems in assembling critical stakeholders?
4. How does determining the organizational structure relate to the PPS?
5. What is the purpose of the percentage equivalents?
6. What are five factors to consider in determining the data conversion strategy?
7. What are five areas to consider for data conversion?
8. What is the purpose of an interface?
9. How is an interface different from a data conversion?
10. How is an interface similar to a data conversion?
11. What are five areas to consider for work estimates?
12. What is an FTE?
13. List six factors that affect the need for consultants?
14. Describe in detail the relationship between time, scope, and resources.
15. What is the formula for calculating project time?
16. Why is planning multi-site ERP implementations more complex than planning single site implementations?

Let's not ask a million questions; instead let's focus on asking the 10 most important ones.

13

Request For Proposal

An RFP (request for proposal) is a questionnaire to an ERP vendor or service provider for an ERP system. Its scope of coverage can have significant variation. In some cases it may be nothing more than a single document with a few high level questions; in these cases it is sometimes called an RFI (request for information). In other cases it has thousands of questions relating to software, hardware, vender, and other characteristics related to the ERP system and supporting products and services. This chapter contains a basic RFP for the reader's review. Although the use of RFPs in ERP implementations can be highly unpredictable, the review of them does serve as a useful tool for learning more about ERP systems and their functionality.

Companies use RFPs to help them better understand the ERP vender and the software and services that they offer. They do this by sending out the same, or very similar, RFP to several different ERP vendors. Upon return, the results will be compiled and compared. By comparing the results, several venders will be disqualified, and the remaining vendors will be subject to further review and analysis.

RFPs are formulated and selected using a variety of techniques, including: internally developed, externally developed, externally purchased boilerplate, and electronic selection techniques. In all cases, except the electronic methods, the RFP will be sent to the ERP vendor or service provider for review. The ERP vendor or service provider will fill out the relevant questions and then return it.

Case Study

ERP Implementation Struggles Despite Good Match

In the fall of 1997 a North Carolina based research and development company decided that it was time to change to a new ERP system.

Several factors were contributing to the need for a new system including an aging legacy system, year 2000 compliance problems, and a growing business.

The company had some unusual business process flows due to its research and development program. It had developed and invented some proprietary machinery, for DNA replication, that received patents. The company designed the equipment with its own in-house CAD department. It then assembled the products based on components sourced from hundreds of different suppliers. The machinery was then *given* away to various customers. Each customer was charged a per cycle rate for the usage of the machine. The company provided free maintenance and service to the machines for their customers.

Because of patent protection, the company was able to quickly grow to three geographical locations and about 200 people and gained control of the world-wide market.

The company was in strong financial position and had top management support for a new ERP system - important elements for a successful ERP implementation. The management of the company considered themselves a "technology company", and understood the importance to keep up with and successfully use technology. The company was well adapted to dealing with extremely complex projects.

Because of their unusual business process flows and the emphasis on doing things "right", they decided to hire an outside consulting firm to help them better understand their options and make an appropriate software selection. They had dealt with the consulting firm for many years and trusted them.

The consulting firm came in and did a complete review of the business and used an electronic selection tool to help find the best match for them. The search was quickly narrowed to just three ERP vendors. Upon further contact and discussion with the ERP vendors, one dropped out, leaving the remaining two.

The electronic selection seemed to show a really good match between both of the ERP vendors. One vendor was a well-known tier two supplier that sold a distributed computing solution that ran on a LAN. The other vendor was a well-known tier one supplier that had a proven centralized computing solution with a new product that just came out that ran on a LAN, providing distributed computing capability.

Both vendors sent pre-sales consultants to answer detailed questions and to perform software demos. The tier two pre-sales consultants struggled in answering basic questions. The tier one pre-sales consultants quickly provided detailed solutions to their questions and wowed them with an impressive demo of their new LAN based product. The choice seemed overwhelmingly clear.

After checking the references provided by the ERP vendor, they discovered a series of highly satisfied customers that implemented the vendor's solutions in less than six months with good results without going over budget.

Case Study

ERP Implementation Struggles Despite Good Match (cont)

The contract with the tier one vendor was signed with a highly experienced local authorized service provider.

Everything looked great. It was a model project. It had a great match in the initial electronic software selection process, top management support, a healthy budget, highly experienced consultants, local service with a proven track record, and great references. It did not look like anything could stop this ERP implementation. But something did.

Shortly after installing the software, they started bumping into technical issues. Programs would not communicate with each other, data would get lost, data would go corrupt, program bugs started appearing, leading to program crashes, security leaks were discovered, and the computer server kept locking up, which brought the entire system down and required a reboot to get started again.

The consultants were very knowledgeable when it came to software functionality related to business process flows but could not provide answers to the host of technical issues that had suddenly appeared. After one and a half years, the management of the company realized that they were faced with a serious problem: two ERP systems that would not work, with the year 2000 quickly approaching. What had gone wrong?

Many things had gone wrong. The outside consulting agency that helped them make the initial software selections with an electronic software selection tool used data that was from the tier one's centralized legacy computing solution. This had been caught by an alert company official but was allowed to pass because both solutions contained "identical functionality" according to the tier one vendor.

All of the references checked had installed the tier one's legacy solution. The vendor only provided controlled phone conferences to verify the quality of its new LAN based product. This was allowed to pass because of the newness of the LAN solution and the high credibility of the ERP vendor. Company officials did not really expect references for the LAN product because of its newness.

All of the experience of the local service provider had been based on the tier one's legacy product. A complete technology review of the LAN based product had been conducted, but no information was available, at the time of purchase, regarding technical problems with the product.

The management accepted the LAN solution more readily than they should have because of their strong drive to be a "technology company". This caused them to overlook many important considerations.

Despite a good match in the initial software selection process and a solid ERP team with top management support, problems plagued the project with no resolution in sight.

The initial software selection process had been primarily functionality based, and based on the wrong product. Important considerations such as track records and reliability of the LAN solution had been overlooked.

The critical mass of the project had been diffused to the dismay of managers who thought that this could never happen to them…

Internally developed RFPs come from the company that will purchase the software. They will examine their existing business process flows, current problems with their ERP system, and long-term strategic business plans. This information will then be compiled and formatted into a single document for the ERP vendor's review. This is sometimes called a company's "wish list".

Internally developed RFPs work well by matching critical business needs with software systems. They can also help to build critical organizational buy in through the input of the different functional areas of the business. They are often shorter than commercial solutions, which further expedites the selection process.

Internally developed RFPs can have disadvantages because they are based on organizational knowledge. Critical changes in technology may be completely overlooked. A company highly focused inward may not think to ask if an ERP vendor has e-commerce support for the sale of their product over the Internet.

To overcome some of these problems, companies turn to externally developed RFPs. Externally developed RFP's generally come from external consulting services. A consultant company will come in and review the company's environment and interview a variety of people within the company. Combining that input with its knowledge base, the consulting company can develop an RFP specifically for the company and send it out to ERP vendors. Externally developed RFPs can, but seldom do, come from other sources such as educational societies and educational institutes.

Externally developed RFPs work well by helping inward focused organizations become less vulnerable to rapidly changing technologies. External consulting resources can provide a fresh unbiased perspective for organizational needs.

Externally developed RFPs can have problems because the quality of service from the outside source can be unpredictable at times. An improper RFP may be created because a consultant company was not keeping up with sudden changes in technology.

The relationships between the ERP vendors and a consultant agency are often unknown to a company seeking these types of services. Some ERP vendors give consultant agencies, or other organizations, a kickback for any new business that they bring them. Because of this, an RFP may be formulated to allow one ERP vendor to score higher than another. The particular ERP vendor with the higher score may or may not be the best choice for that company. The relationships between ERP vendors, service providers, system integrators, and consulting agencies can change rapidly in an unpredictable fashion. A completely independent consultant agency may develop a sudden relationship when the agency learns that a kickback opportunity exists through an ERP vendor.

In other cases the questions in RFPs may be deliberately confusing or vague in nature. In order to "clarify" the questions, the outside consultant agency steps in to cxplain the RFP to the company or the ERP vendor. This allows the consultant agency to rack up additional billable hours against the client that they are serving. Vaguely structured RFPs do little to help companies successfully select ERP software.

An externally purchased boilerplate is an RFP that has been purchased without any, or very little, formulation for a specific company. They usually consist of a significant number of questions and can be obtained from many different sources for relatively low cost. In many cases a company or consultant agency will start with an externally purchased boilerplate and modify it to fit a company's specific needs.

Externally purchased boilerplates have an advantage in that they can be purchased and conveyed to the ERP vendor quickly. The large number of questions that they contain helps to provide insight into the functionality capabilities that one might expect in an ERP system.

Externally purchased boilerplates can be labor intensive for ERP vendors, with all the questions that must be answered.

Because the questions are not targeted specifically for a company, the questions may be somewhat misleading for that company's actual needs. A large number of unnecessary questions can prevent an ERP vendor, service providers, and companies from focusing on the critical issues that will determine the success of an ERP project.

Electronic selection techniques generally do not go by the name of RFPs but are included here because they perform a similar function: to help companies select software. Electronic selection techniques are electronic tools that make recommendations based on a questioning process. The electronic tools may be available through the Internet or through software programs distributed through CD-ROMs or diskettes. Companies providing this type of service range from large consulting agencies to vendors that focus specifically on providing such products. They are generally more expensive than generic boilerplate RFPs.

Electronic selection tools are particularly useful when they contain a large number of ERP vendors and have comparison tools between those vendors. With over 1000 vendors on the market, it would be a time consuming and expensive process to submit RFPs and carry on communications with all of them! Electronic selection tools can narrow a large group of vendors down quickly.

Electronic selection tools have a weakness in that they are usually based on what ERP vendors say their software functionality provides. The same is true for RFPs submitted to ERP vendors. Because of the complexity of ERP systems, there are often many different viewpoints in answering the questions. A particular question might read: "Does the software support ATP capability?" The vendor may answer yes, on the basis that the functionality is supported through a third party provider. A potential customer may interpret "yes" as being built into the base product. With thousands of different viewpoints and questions, misunderstanding is common. Rapidly changing technology and ERP vendor development efforts can make an accurate comparison difficult to almost impossible. Getting the latest up to date information from over 1000 ERP vendors can be a daunting task. Because there are so many different types of functionality in an ERP system, ERP vendors often don't know if their software has a particular functionality!

The structure of a complete RFP can be broken down into several sections: general information and instructions, general system capability, and application specific functionality. All three sections may be combined into one document or they may be delivered to the ERP vendor or service provider as separate documents.

General information and instructions contain information that is non-application and system specific. It has general sections such as: background information, instructions, warranties, guaranties, hardware requirements, installation costs, software pricing, implementation methodologies, training, consulting, references, and vendor profiles.

General system capabilities contain information that applies to or throughout the ERP system. It includes things such as: operating platforms, drill down, data selection, data sequencing, video display formats, report writers, form output, multi-site support, multi-language capability, workflow, database management, etc.

Application specific functionality is where the bulk of most RFPs exist. Anywhere from dozens to thousands of questions may exist. The questions here will cover application specific functionality such as: Are there online inquiries to view transactions posted to the general ledger? Are weekly or smaller buckets available for the display output of an MRP regeneration? Because of the length and the difficulty in answering some application specific questions, it can take some ERP vendors considerable time to complete them.

Answering RFP questions by an ERP vendor can be a frustrating experience, to say the least. Let's consider how an ERP vendor might answer the following question:

Can the system print customs forms for export documentation?

The ERP vendor's software does not contain source code for printing customs forms and the software documentation makes no mention of this capability. The ERP vendor ran into this situation once before with another customer and was able to resolve it by using a shipping acknowledgement report. They set up a user defined table, which appeared on the report as a field, to represent the customs broker, and doing a hard coded change to the print program to say "Custom Form" on the top instead of "Shipping Acknowledgement". The following matrix shows the different options an ERP vendor may have in answering this question.

Solution	"Customs Form"	Customs Broker	Answer
1	Not Required	Not Required	Standard Function
2	Not Required	Required	Partial Function
3	Required	Not Required	Minor Mod
4	Required	Required	Minor Mod

If the "Customs Broker" and "Customs Form" is not required, then they could answer the question as standard functionality. If they are both required, then they should answer the question as a minor modification.

Not knowing what is important to the customer, they could contact them to clarify the question. But often the customer does not know if that is really a problem or not. In no time at all this one question can turn into an all day affair for both the customer and the ERP vendor. With RFPs containing hundreds to thousands of questions, it can become very impractical to try to clarify each and every one of them.

So what happens? If the ERP vendors are actively interested in pursuing the sales cycle, they will tend to answer the question in a way to position them most favorably, in this case, as standard function. Most of the time it is too labor-intensive for companies to verify whether the vendor answered the questions correctly or not according to their own standards. Because of this, most RFPs fade away into history, as the software cycle continues, to never be heard from again. In rare cases, if the software sale is made and the project goes poorly, the customer may come back to the ERP vendor with the RFP saying, "But you misrepresented your software!"

Despite the completeness of many RFPs, they do not seem to ensure the successful use and implementation of an ERP system. They generally tend to focus on the functionality, not how the software is installed, or how to address other critical factors for the successful implementation of an ERP system. Consultants working for ERP vendors and service providers will often shake their heads in dismay as they find themselves sifting through over 100 pages of questionnaires, realizing that despite all their efforts, their ERP project will still most likely bump into serious problems. Companies that verbally express their needs to an ERP vendor can do just as good as companies that used an RFP.

RFPs may not ensure the successful selection implementation of an ERP software system; however they still do have many reasons for use and creation, which include:

- If it is internally developed it can serve to build buy-in and user ownership for key stakeholders.
- By looking at the detail of what a company needs that helps them understand what their needs are for the company overall.
- It can serve as a formal method for documenting the needs of company.
- It can help to establish the overall scope of the ERP project, which is important for calculating the resources and time needed to implement.

- It serves as a historical reference after the ERP implementation to evaluate what they ended up with compared to what they originally requested.
- It can become a useful tool in the development of formal documentation for a company that has none.

The power of the Internet should not be overlooked when requesting RFPs from ERP vendors. As of the time of this publication, the technology had developed to a point where it was just as easy to format RFP questions capable of being displayed through Web browsers over the Internet, as it was to use a word processor. The most significant advantage of using RFPs over the Internet is that all of the results from different ERP vendors can be electronically collected back to one centralized source, allowing the effective comparison of different ERP vendors with the minimal amount of manpower.

The following sample shows how an RFP might appear to an ERP vendor from a potential customer. It includes the three sections discussed here and numerous application specific questions. The sample displayed here is for educational purposes only. It may or may not have application to any particular company engaging in sales activity with an ERP vendor.

Gizmo Manufacturing

Request For Proposal ERP System

Prepared by John Doe for Gizmo Manufacturing
07-28-2000

Table of Contents

Field Service	x
Distribution Requirements Planning	x
Cost Management	x
Payroll	x
Human Resources	x

General Information and Instructions

Introduction

Gizmo Manufacturing has decided to replace its proprietary, in house developed, ERP system with a commercial equivalent or better. The scope of the project includes new software, hardware, and support services to install the software and hardware.

The solution to be provided by the ERP vendor will be a complete ERP solution containing functional modules for all the different areas of Gizmo manufacturing as outlined in this RFP. A fully integrated solution is sought that will allow the company to effectively plan and manage the organization's resources.

Gizmo Manufacturing has decided to adopt a no software modification policy for solution selected. This will require that the software be capable of performing the necessary functions without modification to the source code. The system should be highly flexible with extensive softcoding capability to accommodate the diverse needs of the organization.

The aim of this RFP is to obtain detailed information on software functionality and pricing information for software and some hardware. If the vendor is selected as having a potential solution, they will be invited to participate in a implementation planning session to formulate estimates for consultation assistance based upon the level of help sought and the scope of the implementation project.

Company Details

Gizmo Manufacturing is a manufacturer of pet accessories and play toys for dogs. In 1994 the company developed a new polymer, for manufacturing their toys, that was safe and three times more durable than the competition's. Combined with aggressive marketing, the company has achieved distribution of their products through most national pet chain stores and smaller private ones.

In 1995 Gizmo manufacturing purchased Medi-pet, a manufacturer of complex medical support equipment for pet surgeries. Some types of support equipment must be returned for remanufacturing after it has reached its life expectancy. The buyout brought significant challenges as the companies attempted to save money by consolidating their ERP systems and IS support staff.

Growth occurred steadily until mid 1998 when the company replaced its centralized year 2000 non-compliant legacy system with a distributed proprietary custom developed solution known as MB5. MB5 resolved year 2000 issues but brought about a host of serious problems. The MB5 system was faced with chronic data corruption and software support issues. Unable to resolve the issues, Gizmo Manufacturing's customer base started eroding because of poor customer service and production planning capabilities. The irresolvable issues with the MB5 system brought about the strong need for a proven stable commercial ERP system.

Some important details of Gizmo Manufacturing include:

Number of users:	125
Number of plants:	3
Total employees:	650
Environment:	Manufacturing
Sales volume:	$275 million
Current system:	MB5
Current hardware:	LAN

Instructions

Please reply in a method that is consistent with the content and structure of this RFP. Each section will provide the necessary instructions and questions to complete this RFP. Upon completion of your response, please return to the appropriate contact person at Gizmo Manufacturing.

Vendor Details

Provide the following information as requested:

Contact person ______________________________

Company name ______________________________

Address ______________________________

____

____

____

Phone ______________________________

E-mail ______________________________

Website ______________________________

What is the specific software name(s) and version(s) that will be used to answer this RFP.

What is the current percentage of dollars spent, of sales volume, on research and development?

What was the annual sales volume for the following years?

1995 ______________________________
1996 ______________________________
1997 ______________________________
1998 ______________________________
1999 ______________________________

What is the total number of installs?

What is the total number of service providers or system integrators that provide services working in joint partnership?

How many joint business partnerships exist that support complementary products with integrated solutions?

What is the average customer user acceptance rate? (0 - no acceptance, 10 - full acceptance)

What are average installation times?

Training

Provide the following information as requested:

How many offices conduct training?

Is on site training available?

Are customized training classes available?

Are computerized training and testing that operates on a PC available?

Are computerized training and testing available through the Internet?

Are computerized training and testing available?

Provide any educational course catalog that is available with this RFP that includes dates, times, course descriptions, costs, etc.

Consulting

Provide the following information as requested:

Consultant Type	Typical billing rate
Application	
Technical and Programming	
Project Management	
Temporary Clerical Support	

References

Please provide the contact information for 3 references:

Contact person ____________________
Company name ____________________
Address ____________________
____
____
____
Phone ____________________
E-mail ____________________
Software version ____________________
Platform ____________________
Installation date ____________________

- -

Contact person ____________________
Company name ____________________
Address ____________________
____
____
____
Phone ____________________
E-mail ____________________

Software version ______________________
Platform ______________________
Installation date ______________________

- -

Contact person ______________________
Company name ______________________
Address ______________________
____
____
____
Phone ______________________
E-mail ______________________
Software version ______________________
Platform ______________________
Installation date ______________________

Pricing

Please provide terms and conditions for payment and provide any relevant documentation for standard pricing structures. Note: pricing for implementation consultation services will be considered at a later date should the vender be selected for further consideration.

Cost Type	Amount
Base software product	
Licensing per user	
Maintenance	
Monthly	
Yearly	
Proposed hardware	
Other	
Total	

Warranties and Guarantees

Please include your standard documented warranties and guarantees for your products and services that are offered.

General System Capabilities

This section covers functionality that is non-application specific. When answering the questions please use the following format:

STD - Standard Functionality for the software. This functionality is considered to be part of the normal operating characteristics of the software under the version quoted. STD may be used when changes in softcoding will provide the necessary functionality.

PAR - Partial Functionality for the software. This functionality partially exists and may require minor modification to achieve complete functionality.

MIN - Minor Modification for the software. This functionality does not exist and can be provided through minor modification of the source code. Minor modifications include one-line program changes.

MAJ - Major Modification for the software. This functionality does not exist and can be provided through major modification of the source code. Major modifications require more than one line of code change.

N/A - Not Available for the software. This functionality is not supported or does not exist.

DBS - Database Supports the functionality. Program functionality is not available but the database structure contains the necessary information.

COM - Complementary Product provides the functionality. Functionality is supported through a complementary product, may be through a third party provider, and is integrated requiring no custom programming or specially developed interfaces.

NRE* - *Next Release or future release will provide the functionality.

DIF* - *Different method. Software has the requested functionality but uses a different method for achieving this. Please specify how.

More than one code may be used in answering questions as long as they are not conflicting in nature. Please include any comments or special notes.

Basic Functionality

1. System is fully integrated in all modules. If not, specify which ones.

2. Specify supported operating systems.

3. System and source code is developed using CASE tools.

4. Software code is specifically designed for multi-plant operations without using different environments or duplicating files, allowing each manufacturing division to use the software differently from each other.

5. Barcoding capability for all modules. If not, specify which ones.

6. Ability to handle process flows specific to remanufacturing situations.

7. System logs transaction activity throughout the system for recall and review.

8. Multilanguage. Specify which ones.

9. Multi-currency.

10. Database exporting capabilities using standard formats such as CSV, ASCII. Specify which ones.

11. Database exporting capabilities to popular spreadsheets and word processors. Specify which ones.

12. Can export data directly from videos, and does not require any special programming or scripting, to:

12.1 Common spreadsheets

12.2 Word processors

13. Data dictionary to change data element characteristics such as number of decimals or default values.

14. System uses or has email program that can accept standard email through the Internet.

15. Different configurations of programs can be programmed and saved through the use of soft coding that allows the same program to be run differently.

16. User defined codes that can be attached to records.

17. User defined tables that can be added as a data element to a specific file or table in a database.

18. Simulation capability for financials and supply chain management with out duplicating files.

19. Capability for programs to run as Internet programs through Intranets or the Internet.

20. Sales order entry functions on Internet.

    20.1 Order placement

    20.2 Order lookup and status

    20.3 Quoting

    20.4 Search for inventory items

21. Does sales order entry function on Internet affect licensing costs?

22. Remote dial up.

23. EDI integrated capability.

24. XML capability.

25. Keeps menu history log showing:

    25.1 Menu

    25.2 Program

    25.3 Option

    25.4 User

    25.5 Date

    25.6 Time

    25.7 Terminal

26. System measurement tools for:

    26.1 LAN traffic

    26.2 Menu traveling

    26.3 Total man-hour usage

Database

1. Automatic backup and recovery.
2. Mass database change.
3. Mass database add.
4. Mass database delete.
5. Specify all commercial databases supported.
6. System wide data element name changes.
7. Ability to have more than one environment to support simulation or testing environments.
8. Data logging to see adds, changes, deletes to records.
9. Files or tables contain date stamps in records.
    - 9.1 User ID
    - 9.2 Date
    - 9.3 Time
    - 9.4 Device
    - 9.5 Program

Report Generators

1. Predefined reports included for all functional modules.

2. Modules use the same report generator.

3. Report generator can create ad-hoc reports as needed.

4. Report generator interfaces with data dictionary for consistent field names as found in the ERP system.

5. Can create a standard file such as CSV or ACSII.

6. Can join multiple files or tables together.

7. Has flexible output capability.

    7.1 Add fields

    7.2 Delete fields

    7.3 Calculated fields

    7.4 Move fields

    7.5 Adjust field length

    7.6 User definable headers.

8. Can perform calculations with detail records.

9. Has summary capability.

10. Can generate reports in summary format only without detail.

11. Can perform calculations in summary mode with aggregate records.

12. Multi level data sequencing capability by chosen data element.

13. Data selection using comparison operators integrated with data elements of based on file.

14. Can select unlimited number of specific values.

15. Can specify a range of values.

16. Can perform selections based on wildcards.

17. Can perform page skips based on specific data elements.

18. Uses or has functionality based on SQL.

19. Configuration of custom reports can be saved for reuse.

20. Custom reports can be attached to menu options or icons.

21. Has preview capability to see report output format.

22. Security can control access to files through report writer.

23. Security can control access to fields through report writer.

24. Has capability to update fields in tables or files.

25. Security control for updating fields in tables or files.

26. Integrated function key look up for data fields that can return values to aid data selection.

27. Ability to change fonts.

28. Ability to change font size.

29. Ability to change font color.

30. Can display output in a number of different graphic formats such as bar, pie, chart, etc.

31. Ability to drill down by clicking on a section of a pie or bar chart for more detailed information.

32. Ability to drill down from a summary report to see the detail at the application level.

Security

1. Security control by file or table.
2. Security control by field.
3. Security control by program.
4. Security control by menu.
5. Security control by menu option.
6. Security control by video display or data input panel.
7. Security control by device.
8. Security control by record type based on data field.
9. Signon password.
10. Security hierarchy allowing those with higher security clearance more access.
11. User defined security templates that allow templates to be assigned to a user.

User Interface

1. Suppression of chosen fields that appear on videos.

2. Universal common function keys, such as (F1) revealing a help dialog box.

3. Ability to drill down on data field to find basic field definition information such as:

    3.1 Field name

    3.2 Belong to file

    3.3 Alpha / numeric

    3.4 Character size

    3.5 Valid values

4. Ability to view records in spreadsheet format throughout the system.

    4.1 Font size and color

    4.2 Movable columns

    4.3 Background color

    4.4 User defined templates by video that allow customized views of data

    4.5 Mass updates on videos

    4.6 Mass change on videos

4.7 Mass delete on videos

4.8 Query capability built into the video, supporting basic searches such as =, <>,<,>, etc.

4.9 Specify all of the comparison operators available in the previous question.

4.10 Search windows driven off of data entry fields.

4.11 Records or cells can change color using conditional operators based on data elements.

4.12 Ability to move data entry fields.

5. Ability to change/define tab stops.

6. User definable exit to other programs.

7. Graphical user interface with resizable windows.

8. Mouse support.

9. Field sensitive help.

10. Printing from video.

11. Icon driven.

12. Menu driven.

13. System wide data element name changes for video text.

14. Video specific data element name changes for video text.

15. Ability to attach documents, videos, sounds, text to records.

16. Ability to attach documents, videos, sounds, text to videos.

17. Error checking upon data entry.

18. User defined error checking upon data entry.

19. User defined error messages.

20. Online help with easy recall such as a function key.

21. Online help is user definable.

22. Online help can be attached to icons or menu options.

23. System uses drill down principles throughout the software.

Work Flow

1. Default templates that are application specific available throughout the modules.

2. Sales orders contain standard workflow templates.

3. Purchase orders contain standard workflow templates.

4. Work orders contain standard workflow templates.

5. Accounting contains standard workflow templates.

6. Ability to create and use multiple workflows for documents such as sales, purchasing, work orders, etc.

7. Workflow functionality integrates with email by sending status messages to users.

8. System contains a workflow module for the development of workflows throughout the system.

    8.1 User defined routing capability to specific users.

    8.2 User defined rules allowing decision logic.

    8.3 Logical functions in user defined rules.

    8.4 Sequential process

    8.5 Parallel process

        8.5.1 Split

        8.5.2 Join

8.6 Looping process

8.7 Can pass documents from one user to another.

8.8 Contains hotlinks to programs, menus, videos, etc.

8.9 Action messages sorted by user and department.

8.10 Multiple action code types such as expedite, defer, error, approve, rejected, etc.

8.11 Text based setup.

8.12 Graphical based setup.

8.13 OLE object capability attached to workflow document.

8.14 Workflow can be attached to an event.

8.15 Executions based upon approvals.

8.16 Default message templates.

8.17 Can be assigned to interactive programs.

8.18 Can be assigned to batch programs.

8.19 Multi level approvals.

8.20 Escalation processes.

8.21 Integrated date stamps for steps taken in a workflow pattern.

8.22 Defined workflow patterns based on user selectable objects and activities such as run, queue, message, batch, hold, start, end, logic, functions, etc.

8.23 Workflows exportable to other third party flow charting programs.

8.24 New workflows can be created by copying from one using "same as except" logic.

Application Specific Functionality

General Ledger

1. Ability to drill down to selected detail in the general ledger for a specific account.

2. Balance sheets for every business unit or company.

3. Can review activity from other modules before posting to the general ledger.

4. Can save all monthly transactions electronically for recall and review.

5. Supplementary WIP account ledger by work orders.

6. Has debt equal to credit control at month end.

7. Availability of 13 or more accounting periods.

8. Can store 18 open accounting periods at once.

9. Can open past periods for adjustments.

10. Specify accounting period starting and ending dates.

11. Year-end processing to preliminary clear income accounts.

12. Year-end processing to preliminary clear income accounts for specific business units.

13. Journal entries used to change G/L accounts.

14. Can combine several business units into one income statement showing totals.

15. Flexible report generator used for financial statements allowing changes to output and sequencing.

16. Recurring journal vouchers.

17. Can print and display schedules within the general ledger.

18. Can sort differently for schedules within the general ledger.

19. Can perform data selection for schedules within the general ledger.

20. Logging of all transaction activity with easy recall.

21. Integrates with a variety of inventory management costing techniques such as FIFO, LIFO, average costing, last in, etc. Please specify which ones.

22. Ability to account for several different business units.

23. Allocation of accounts to specific business units.

24. Consolidation of accounts to specific business units.

25. Ability to see income statements by business unit in detail and summary.

26. Can add, delete, change, copy, accounts.

27. Ability to create a hierarchical structure.

28. Ability to compare financial statements electronically at MTD and YTD levels.

29. Has current expense and budgeting data.

30. Has last year's expense and budgeting data.

31. Has next year's budgeting data.

32. Can perform "what if" simulations.

33. Cost analysis showing variance on part numbers for a specific work order.

34. Cost of sales transactions by sales order number and related part numbers.

35. Cost analysis showing actual cost on part numbers for specific work orders or a group of work orders.

Accounts Payable

1. Fully integrated with general ledger.
2. Automated supplier discounting.
3. Check reconciliation.
4. Fully integrated with purchasing.
5. Fully integrated with receiving.
6. Online purchase price variance analysis.
7. 1099 processing for state and federal tax..
8. Void check processing with journal entry updates.
9. Ability to inquire on open invoices a variety of ways.
10. Ability to make partial payments.
11. Payment tracking by due dates.
12. Aging of payables by due date.
13. Automatic payment of recurring payables.
14. Online accounts payable history.
15. User defined coding of invoices.
16. Ability to see all payables by supplier.
17. Integrated multi-currency processing with ability to override.

Accounts Receivable

1. Full integration with sales order management system.
2. Full integration with general ledger.
3. Aging by invoice and due dates.
4. Standard aging report.
5. Standard credit history report.
6. Standard report for past due invoices.
7. Fully integrated with general ledger.
8. Different terms for invoices. Specify.
9. Normal cash posting.
10. Selective cash posting.
11. Ability to see credit balances.
12. Has statement processing.
13. Shows open items by customer.
14. Shows balance forward by customer.
15. Online customer search window by using text.
16. Online customer search window by using customer number.
17. Online customer search window by using phone numbers.

18. Contains several different types of invoicing terms. Specify.

19. Contains due dates and invoice dates.

20. Can specify custom financing.

21. Provides discounts by customers for services and items.

22. Online user defined calculations for discounting.

23. Can see credit history by customers.

24. Ability to make notes by customer in credit management screen.

25. Online aging inquiries by customer.

Payroll

1. Employee master file can perform the following functions:

    1.1 Add

    1.2 Inquire

    1.3 Change

    1.4 Delete

    1.5 Copy using same as except logic

2. Employee contains basic employee information such as:

    2.1 Address

    2.2 Starting date

    2.3 Starting pay

    2.4 Special deductions

    2.5 Social security number

    2.6 Employee ID number

3. Online inquires and reports to see payroll activity by employee by period.

4. Effectivity dates for pay increases or decreases.

5. Can perform payroll processing and check issues in mid-week.

6. Can process and calculate the following deductions:

    6.1 Federal

    6.2 State

    6.3 Local

7. Special logic for processing FICA exemptions.

8. Processing of earned income credits.

9. Both time and attendance reporting integrates with payroll processing.

10. Ability to set up deductions based on:

    10.1 Fixed dollar amount

    10.2 % of gross

    10.3 % of net

    10.4 Special

    10.5 Other user defined

11. End of year or quarter bonus check processing.

12. Online user defined expense reimbursement forms for employees.

13. Employees can fill out expense reimbursement forms online.

14. Ability to integrate online expense reimbursement documents with normal payroll processing.

15. Can track the following hours and print on employee paycheck stub:

    15.1 Holidays

    15.2 Sick days

    15.3 Vacation days

    15.4 Other user defined

16. Can print year to date earnings on paycheck.

17. Can meet EEOC reporting requirements.

18. Can print year to date deductions by type on paycheck.

19. Bonus amounts based on piece rate production.

20. Shop floor control report integrated with payroll for paycheck calculations based on piece rate.

21. Absentee reporting codes include:

    21.1 Maternity

    21.2 Sickness

    21.3 Late

    21.4 Injury

    21.5 Other user defined.

22. Online inquires show total absences by reason code by user defined time period.

23. Absentee reporting system integrated with payroll and makes the necessary payroll deduction based on reason codes for absences.

24. Functionality for union pension accrual schedules.

25. Can issue paychecks manually.

26. Automated methods for handling end of year processing.

27. Can handle government required forms such as:

    27.1 W2

    27.2 941

    27.3 Other

28. Ability to process and make direct deposits.

29. Payment vouchers contain year to date information.

30. W-2 forms can be electronically filed from the software.

31. Ability to handle workmen's compensation claims.

32. Ability to perform payroll processing:

    32.1 Weekly

    32.2 Bi-weekly

32.3 Monthly

32.4 Four week

33. Workmen's compensation claims analysis showing expense by:

    33.1 Employee

    33.2 Manufacturing plant

    33.3 Department

    33.4 Period

34. Ability to do rollover processing for:

    34.1 Vacation

    34.2 Holidays

    34.3 Sick time

35. Ability to cancel checks with reconciliation process.

36. 401K deduction processing.

37. User defined contribution % matching amount.

38. Fully integrated with the general ledger.

39. Payroll transactions are held in suspense for review and approval posting to the general ledger.

Human Resources

1. Online job vacancy management:

    1.1 Initial online request including:

        1.1.1 Job title

        1.1.2 Pay range

        1.1.3 Description

        1.1.4 Request date

        1.1.5 Requirements

        1.1.6 Other user defined

    1.2 Employment application and tracking

    1.3 Job applications can be processed on the Internet

2. Job evaluations.

3. Ability to perform COBRA administration.

4. OHSA health and safety processing.

5. Budgeting tools from employee compensation.

6. New position requisition process is integrated with initial payroll processing for that position.

7. Employee history.

8. Turnover tracking.

Cost Management

1. Ability to perform a cost roll up based on bill of material type such as, manufacturing, prototype, engineering, other.

2. Ability to perform a cost roll up based on routing type such as, manufacturing, prototype, engineering, other.

3. Cost roll ups include special processing logic to accommodate outside vendor processing.

4. Ability to roll up costs with the option to exclude tooling requirements that may be loading in the bills of material or routings.

5. Several different costs based on cost roll ups include:

    5.1 Standard

    5.2 Actual

    5.3 Simulated

6. Variable and fixed overhead are included in cost rollup calculations.

7. Ability to attach additional user defined cost types with costs to part numbers and/or product structures.

8. Ability to perform a net change cost rollup.

9. Ability to perform a gross regeneration cost rollup.

10. A lower level cost change will trigger the recalculation of a higher level cost change.

11. Can perform activity based costing.

12. Selected part number costs can be updated interactively through the use of function keys.

13. Online inquiry can show the cost breakout detail:

    13.1 Material

    13.2 Labor

    13.3 Fixed overhead

    13.4 Variable overhead

    13.5 Machine

    13.6 Outside vendor processing

    13.7 Other user defined

14. Ability to drill down on specific costs to see how they were calculated.

15. Ability to view work order costs by:

    15.1 Material

    15.2 Labor

    15.3 Fixed overhead

    15.4 Variable overhead

    15.5 Other user defined.

16. Ability to update different cost types, for purchased items, such as weighted average, last in, average, etc. based on actual purchase order costs.

17. Ability to update variable or fixed overhead in batch mode by:

    17.1 Labor hours

    17.2 Machine hours

    17.3 Other user defined

18. Ability to assign indirect costs to work centers.

19. Complete selective control, over all transactions, that can be posted to the general ledger.

Fixed Assets

1. Fully integrated with general ledger.
2. Contains several different methods of depreciation. Specify all.
3. Contains automatic end of life processing for assets.
4. Records federal and state depreciation separately.
5. Inquiry capability showing YTD depreciation for one asset.
6. Inquiry capability showing YTD depreciation for a group of assets.
7. User defined coding of assets into groups.
8. Has a fixed asset master.
9. Depreciation can be allocated to business units.
10. Allocations can be done on a percentage basis.
11. Transfer method from one depreciation type to another.
12. Online tax credit analysis.

Sales Management

1. Items and services have user defined classification codes that default in automatically upon sales order entry.

2. Online inquiries that show:

    2.1 Projected sales orders by part number by user defined time period.

    2.2 Projected sales orders by family by user defined time period.

    2.3 Sales orders by part number by user defined time period.

    2.4 Sales orders by family by user defined time period.

    2.5 Shipments by part number by user defined time period.

    2.6 Shipments by family by user defined time period.

    2.7 Planned production by part number by user defined time period.

    2.8 Planned production by family by user defined time period.

    2.9 Actual production by part number by user defined time period.

    2.10 Actual production by family by user defined time period.

2.11 Order shortages by part number by user defined time period.

2.12 Order shortages by family by user defined time period.

2.13 Projected inventory levels by part number by user defined time period.

2.14 Projected inventory levels by user defined time period.

3. Rules driven online backorder release program.

4. Rules driven batch driven backorder release program.

5. Ability to receive customer returns and automatically generate a customer credit or payment.

6. Specific online warranty inquires showing:

   6.1 Open warranties

   6.2 Time remaining

   6.3 Warranties claimed by customer

7. Comparison report between planned sales and actual sales by user-defined period.

8. Can generate mailing lists for customers based on:

   8.1 Part numbers (past sales history)

   8.2 Geographic locations

8.3 Customer families

8.4 Part families

9. Ability to convert primary unit of measure to cost.

10. Ability to convert primary unit of measure to sales dollars.

11. Can drill down and select default contracts to sales orders with the option to override specific areas.

12. Integrated performance measurements for on-time customer shipments.

13. Ability to select a number of different methods or define customer methods for calculating customer on time shipments.

14. Ability to see on time customer shipments by:

    14.1 Customer

    14.2 Part number

    14.3 Family

    14.4 User defined period

    14.5 Other

15. System can automatically generate new quotes based on current contract expirations.

16. Ability to easily renew contracts before, during, or after expiration.

17. System can have many different types of contracts at the same time.

18. Online inquiry show cost, revenue, and profit by:

    18.1 Product families

    18.2 Serial numbers

    18.3 Part numbers

    18.4 Customers

    18.5 Customer families

    18.6 Territories or states

    18.7 Other user defined code

19. Ability to convert primary unit of measure to other units of measures such as pounds, gallons, etc.

20. Ability to convert marketing families into manufacturing families to aid in supply chain management.

21. Ability to define a business plan.

22. Ability to define a sales plan.

23. Can perform ship confirmations that allow inventory to be automatically deducted in real time from stockroom locations.

24. Online inquires show shipped amount and remaining balances against sales orders.

25. Online inquiry to compare sales plan with business plan.

26. Report to compare sales plan with business plan.

27. Ability to specify basic inventory picking strategies such as LIFO, FIFO, largest quantity, least quantity, location order, etc.; specify which ones.

28. Sales order entry programs can perform the following functions at both the header and detail level:

    28.1 Add

    28.2 Inquire

    28.3 Change

    28.4 Delete

    28.5 Copy

    28.6 Copy using same as except logic

29. Online inquiry program allows to see all orders based on:

    29.1 Supplier number

    29.2 Part number

    29.3 Order type

    29.4 Date range

        29.4.1 Order date

        29.4.2 Received date

29.4.3 Expected receive date

29.4.4 Invoice date

29.5 Order number

29.6 User defined codes

29.7 Manufacturing plant

30. Sales order can have multiple detail lines with different:

    30.1 Part numbers

    30.2 Delivery dates

    30.3 Shipping addresses

    30.4 Quantities

31. Sales orders integrate with MRP/DRP/MPS logic for supply chain management.

32. Ability to use cross reference part numbers allowing invoices and shipping papers to print with the customers part number.

33. Ability to drill down directly from a sales order entry screen to see available to promise information for the part in question.

34. Product availability is checked in real time during order entry.

35. Over allocated inventory or no inventory results in a soft error message.

36. Ability to set up rules directing order entry programs to automatically allocate inventory from a different manufacturing plant should the home plant not have enough supply.

37. Ability to manually drill down to other manufacturing locations to check on hand inventory in sales order entry.

38. Special processing logic for dealing with back order releases.

39. Ability to define rules to control the back order release process.

40. Can perform online with option to override

    40.1 Can perform in batch mode

    40.2 Ability to make partial shipments

    40.3 Ability to make only full shipment per line item

    40.4 Ability to make only full shipments per sales order

    40.5 Ability to see all back orders regardless of inventory or manufacturing locations.

41. Rules based error checking in order entry to check for:

    41.1 Defective part numbers

    41.2 Wrong customer number

41.3 Invalid shipping terms

41.4 Invalid pricing information

41.5 Other user defined base on data fields

42. Contains default workflow templates that guide the process through order entry, inventory allocations, ship confirmations, invoices, etc.

43. Sales order header information contains:

43.1 Billing terms

43.2 Carrier

43.3 Sold to

43.4 Ship to

43.5 Bill to

43.6 Special notes

43.7 Credit card numbers

44. Default workflow templates can be adjusted for specific needs.

45. Can perform consolidated pick lists by carrier or customer.

46. Shipping paperwork can provide the following functions:

46.1 Bar coding containing customer part number

46.2 Consolidated bill of ladings

46.3 Billing instructions

46.4 Automatically print special documents like:

46.4.1 Special shipping instructions

46.4.2 HAZMAT safety data sheets

46.4.3 Customer notes

46.5 Customs forms for international shipping

47. Ability to see all sales transaction activity.

48. Ability to define inclusion rules for saving transaction activity.

49. Sales analysis programs can include the entire corporation as well as break out by manufacturing plant.

50. Aggregate sales order activity inquires with drill down capabilities.

51. Ability to issue and process credit memos.

52. Can generate Performa invoices.

53. Through work flow system automatically updates billing system / status after invoice generation.

54. Automated billing based upon user selected billing point identified in sales order processing work flow.

55. Special pricing capabilities:

55.1 By customer

55.2 By product number

55.3 By product characteristics

55.4 By quantity

55.5 By date

55.6 By age

55.7 By other user defined method

56. Commission processing for sale.

57. Notes can be attached to either header or detail.

58. Notes can be drawn from a notes master template with option to override.

59. Ability to create user defined status codes.

60. Sales people have remote dial up or Internet capability to enter sales orders or check sales order status.

61. Blanket order processing for customers.

62. Ability to provide automated substitute item processing during order entry.

63. Ability to code sales orders with user defined codes for future sales history analysis.

64. User defined codes automatically default in from item master for valid part numbers to sales orders.

65. Sales orders have at least five user-defined codes.

66. Sales orders created from sales blanket orders have blanket sales order number in sales order for traceability.

67. Is fully integrated with configuration management.

68. Configuration management processes can take place directly in sales order entry screen.

69. Sales order history can be built that feeds to forecasting module.

70. Ability to withhold certain parts, such as obsolete or prototypes, from normal sales order processing logic.

71. Ability to see total backlog a variety of ways online.

72. Ability to recall serial numbers to determine if products are covered under warranties.

Supplier/Purchasing Management

1. Has the following inspection receiving capabilities:

   1.1 Has receipt inspection capability that allows materials to be received into a routing inspection process before being received into inventory.

   1.2 Inspection process and purchase orders are integrated.

   1.3 Item can be transferred out of receiving / inspection into inventory against a purchase order.

   1.4 Inspection process has user definable inspection steps that allows the routing of parts to inspection / receiving activities.

   1.5 Sampling tables can be attached to parts causing the system to recommend x number of samplings from a lot size of x.

   1.6 Online inquires show the status of parts, quantities, and location in the receipt / inspection process.

   1.7 Inspection / routing process has functionality for the rejection of materials. A return to vendor document is recreated with part numbers, quantities, dates, costs, and reason codes.

2. Vendor scheduling management system can perform the following:

   2.1 Can move MRP recommendation release dates based on predefined rules.

2.2 Different part numbers can be consolidated onto one supplier schedule.

2.3 Ability to define shipping models.

2.4 Can split one item between suppliers based on % rules.

2.5 Automatically generates supplier schedule.

2.6 Supplier schedule is held in suspense for manual overrides and adjustments.

2.7 Ability to set up supplier instructions that are used in the calculation and creation of supplier schedules.

2.8 Supplier analysis tools include:

2.8.1 Online inquires and reports

2.8.2 Shows each vendor's average days late

2.8.3 Shows each vendor's PPV

2.8.4 Shows each vendor's quality

2.8.5 Ability to sort by any of the above

2.8.6 Can perform ABC classification for each of the above with user defined break points.

3. Purchase orders are structured to contain header (information common to all line items) and detail (information specific to line items).

4. Online inquiry programs should show receiving information in aggregate supplier, part number, and manufacturing plant with drill down capability.

5. Purchase order entry programs can perform the following functions at both the header and detail level:

    5.1 Add

    5.2 Inquire

    5.3 Change

    5.4 Delete

    5.5 Copy

    5.6 Copy using same as except logic

6. Online inquiry program allows user to see all orders based on:

    6.1 Supplier number

    6.2 Part number

    6.3 Order type

    6.4 Date range

        6.4.1 Order date

        6.4.2 Received date

        6.4.3 Expected receive date

6.4.4 Invoice date

6.5 Order number

6.6 User defined codes

6.7 Manufacturing plant

7. Receiving program should:

7.1 Integrate directly with receiving inspection processes

7.2 Have PO number

7.3 Item numbers

7.4 Quantities

7.5 Soft error messages for unusual received quantities

7.6 Supplier lot numbers

7.7 Special notes

8. Supplier master to integrate directly with purchase orders and contain the following information:

8.1 Supplier number

8.2 Purchasing terms

8.3 FOB

8.4 Carrier

8.5 Contact name

8.6 Address

8.7 Supplier name

8.8 Supplier telephone number

9. Ability to process and handle non-stock items.

10. Purchase order module and purchase order integrates direction with MRP and DRP planning logic.

11. Ability to handle consignment inventory by issuing a payable upon usage of material.

12. Requisitions use the following features:

    12.1 Ability to place requisitions online

    12.2 Integrated approval processing

    12.3 Generation of PO from requisitions

13. Has blanket order processing logic:

    13.1 MRP release can be performed against open blankets

    13.2 Purchasing users can perform PO releases against open blankets

14. Price break logic capability for supplier / part / quantity combinations.

15. Ability to have several different ship-to's for the same purchase orders.

16. Option to print different ship-to locations on the PO.

17. Ability to perform drop shipments.

18. Automation for handling purchase order changes.

    18.1 Automatic revision number change for detail line

    18.2 Option to automatically reprint or resend PO

19. Purchase order management integrates with outside special vendor processing.

20. Ability to automatically include special packaging or processing instructions for the supplier on or with the PO.

21. Ability to enter quotes.

22. Ability to transform quotes into PO with a few keystrokes.

Maintenance Management

1. Integrates with capacity and material planning systems allowing them to plan accordingly for planned or unplanned machine downtime.

2. Integrates with inventory and accounting.

3. Integrated with fixed assets.

4. Machines are defined and set up in the fixed asset master.

5. Can automatically generate preventive maintenance work orders based upon:

    5.1 MRP output

    5.2 Capacity output

    5.3 Reported machine cycles

    5.4 Time intervals

6. Auto generation of maintenance schedules based upon predefined rules.

7. Maintenance work orders can be generated in batch mode based on scheduled output.

8. Maintenance work orders can be generated online interactively based upon scheduled output.

9. Maintenance kits can contain:

    9.1 Materials

9.2 Labor

9.3 Tooling

9.4 Special work instructions

10. Maintenance kits can be assigned to equipment.

11. Maintenance kits attach automatically to maintenance work orders for specific machines.

12. Ability to automatically substitute pre-approved parts in work order generation for parts that are out of stock.

13. Supplier lot numbers can be attached to machine serial numbers.

14. Ability to trace from machine serial number to supplier lot numbers or vise versa.

15. Parts carried on the system as part numbers can be consumed through normal reporting and inventory transactions.

16. System automatically consolidates total purchasing requirements after preventive maintenance schedule is generated.

17. MRP purchasing requirements and maintenance requirements can be seen on a single screen for purchase order execution for purchasing agents.

18. Complete maintenance history can be online for analysis and review.

Capacity and Resource Planning

1. Capacity planning can provide:

    1.1 Routings integrated with the master production schedule to calculate load.

    1.2 Spare parts demands (that consume capacity) are included in capacity calculations.

    1.3 Ability to use different units of measure other than time based such as hours, minutes, days, etc.

    1.4 Online inquires show both summary and detail of capacity loads by toggle or drill down capability.

    1.5 Recognizes routings that are going through ECO.

    1.6 Planning buckets for online inquires and reports can be defined as:

        1.6.1 Days

        1.6.2 Weeks

        1.6.3 Months

    1.7 Online inquires contain the following information:

        1.7.1 Total capacity consumed

        1.7.2 Capacity consumed by planned orders

        1.7.3 Capacity consumed by released orders

        1.7.4 Total capacity available

1.7.5 Work center

1.7.6 Work center description

1.8 Ability to see information in summary and to drill down to see detail (pegging).

1.9 Ability to see work center loads using graphics.

1.10 Ability to automatically create capacity availability by day based on work center capacity and number of hours per day or shift.

1.11 Ability to manually create or override capacity availability by day.

1.12 Ability to classify work centers based on importance.

1.13 Capacity consumption that considers utilization and efficiency in its calculations.

1.14 Capacity planning based on shop calendar that distinguishes between working and non working days.

2. Resource planning can provide:

2.1 Online inquiry for showing resource load and resource availability.

2.2 Ability to drill back from resource loads to the driving demand.

2.3 Resource profiles can be created manually.

2.4 Resource profiles can be automatically created based on routings.

2.5 Ability to use different units of measure for the same part or family

2.6 Online inquires show both summary and detail of resource loads by toggle or drill down capability.

2.7 Planning buckets for online inquires and reports can be defined as:

   2.7.1 Days

   2.7.2 Weeks

   2.7.3 Months

2.8 On-line inquires contain the following information:

   2.8.1 Total resource consumed

   2.8.2 Resource consumed by planned orders

   2.8.3 Resource consumed by released orders

   2.8.4 Total resources available

   2.8.5 Work center

   2.8.6 Work center description

2.9 Ability to see information in summary and to drill down to see detail (pegging).

2.10 Ability to see resource loads using graphics.

2.11 Ability to automatically create resource availability by day based on work center capacity and number of hours per day or shift.

2.12 Ability to manually create or override resource availability by day.

2.13 Resource planning is based on a shop calendar that distinguishes between working and non working days.

2.14 Ability to use forecasting as input in calculating resource loads.

2.15 Option to include or exclude on hand inventory in resource requirement calculations.

Forecasting

1. Online inquires to review output of forecast generation for manual, review, modification, or deletion.

2. Online inquiry showing variance between actual sales orders and forecast by user defined time horizon.

3. Online inquiry showing variance between actual sales orders and forecast by user defined time bucket.

4. Different forecasting techniques such as weighted average, exponential smoothing, etc. Specify which ones.

5. Forecasting technique based on seasonality.

6. Ability to manually override the forecast.

7. Forecasting pyramids that allow the viewing of aggregate data with the ability to drill down to detail by:

    7.1 Families

    7.2 Locations

    7.3 Sales dollars

    7.4 User defined.

8. Ability to mark key areas of the forecast with graphics or text messages.

9. Uses forecast consumption logic.

10. Has a special processing technique to handle past due sales orders when using forecast consumption logic.

11. Forecast can be based on total demand from sources including:

    11.1 Sales orders

    11.2 Interplant demand

    11.3 Service orders

    11.4 Spare part usage

12. Forecasts for component parts can be included as a source of demand in MRP calculations.

13. Simulation capability

14. User defined forecast types.

Master Production Schedule

1. Firm planned order logic that the system does not change.

2. Has selection logic that allows the inclusion or exclusion of any part.

3. Ability to integrate remanufacturing work orders into daily MPS.

4. Has selection logic that allows the inclusion or exclusion of any family.

5. MPS schedule accuracy measurement system. Can be measured as: number of orders completed on time on quantity per period / total number of order due per same period.

6. System recognized differences between supply and demand and provides the following action messages through online inquires:

    6.1 Order

    6.2 Expedite

    6.3 Defer

    6.4 Past Due

    6.5 Cancel

    6.6 Increase

    6.7 Decrease

7. User definable planning horizon.

8. Are there any limitations on how long the planning horizon can be?

9. User definable planning buckets that can use any combination of :

   9.1 Days

   9.2 Weeks

   9.3 Months

10. Capability of recognizing and processing the following types of demand:

    10.1 Dependent

    10.2 Sales orders

    10.3 Forecast

    10.4 Interplant

11. Has online inquires that show quantities and dates of:

    11.1 Master scheduled work order receipts

    11.2 Sales orders

    11.3 Forecasts

    11.4 Dependent demand

    11.5 Other master scheduled items

11.6 Interplant

11.7 Firm planned orders

12. Ability to drill from a planning screen to demand sources such as:

    12.1 Forecast

    12.2 Sales order

    12.3 Work orders

    12.4 Interplant

    12.5 Dependent demand

13. Displays in spreadsheet format for the following:

    13.1 Future available balance

    13.2 Available to promise

    13.3 Accumulated available to promise

    13.4 Forecast

    13.5 Sales orders

    13.6 Interplant

    13.7 Future work order receipts

    13.8 Beginning balance

13.9 Firm work orders

13.10 Dependent demand

13.11 Purchase orders

14. Displays in spreadsheet format both the results of following system recommendations and the results of not following them.

15. Has special logic to support a multi-level master schedule including final assembly schedule.

16. System makes recommendations, based on a working calendar, that distinguish between working and non working days.

17. Online inquires to see aggregates of the master production schedule by families for:

    17.1 Sales

    17.2 Interplant

    17.3 Work Orders

    17.4 Forecasts

    17.5 Dependent demand

18. Ability for one master scheduled item to belong to more than one family.

19. Online inquiry for family and its subfamily at the same time.

20. Has planning bill logic.

21. Planning bills contain effectivity dates for parents.

22. Planning bills contain effectivity dates for components.

23. Master planning logic can display and process decimal quantities.

24. Option to round or not to round to the nearest quantity when processing decimals.

25. Planning horizons can be adjusted to be longer than the longest cumulative lead time of the product.

26. Online inquires or batch programs can calculated the longest cumulative lead-time for an MPS item base on bill of materials and lead times for lower level components.

27. Online inquiry with drill down shows MPS orders by different dates such as:

    27.1 Start date

    27.2 Finish date

    27.3 Order date

28. Basic order quantity modification logic:

    28.1 Min

    28.2 Max

    28.3 Multiple

28.4 Lot for Lot

28.5 Periods of supply

28.6 Fixed order quantity

28.7 User defined

Material Requirements Planning

1. Pegging capability that allows the drilling to higher level demands.

2. Can recognize and incorporate phantom logic into MRP calculations.

3. Phantom logic can be turned on or off in MRP regeneration.

4. Hold codes, that cause MRP to ignore on hand inventory, that can be assigned to:

    4.1 Part numbers

    4.2 Lots

    4.3 Locations

5. Ability to factor in yield into MRP calculations.

6. Ability to factor projected scrap into MRP calculations.

7. Can plan for tooling requirements like a normal inventory item.

8. System recognizes differences between supply and demand and provides the following actions messages through online inquires:

    8.1 Order

    8.2 Expedite

    8.3 Defer

8.4 Past Due

8.5 Cancel

8.6 Increase

8.7 Decrease

9. MRP processing logic utilizes low level code logic.

10. MRP integrates with effectivity dates found in the bill of materials.

11. Basic order quantity modification logic:

    11.1 Min

    11.2 Max

    11.3 Multiple

    11.4 Lot for Lot

    11.5 Periods of supply

    11.6 Fixed order quantity

    11.7 User defined

12. Can use firm/planned order logic.

13. Displays in spreadsheet format for the following:

    13.1 Future available balance

    13.2 Available to promise

13.3 Accumulated available to promise

13.4 Forecast

13.5 Sales orders

13.6 Interplant

13.7 Future work order receipts

13.8 Beginning balance

13.9 Firm work orders

13.10 Dependent demand

13.11 Purchase orders

14. Can show through videos and reports, total future and current purchase order quantities by family and part number.

15. Can show through videos and reports, total future and current purchase order dollars by family and part number.

16. Ability to drill down from aggregate exception message video to detail message video.

17. MRP planning and execution videos have access to the following information on screen or through function keys:

    17.1 Part number

    17.2 Description

    17.3 Unit of measure

17.4 Make or buy code

17.5 Planner or buyer code

17.6 Order policy

17.7 Reorder point

17.8 Lead time

17.9 Current balance (real time)

18. Time phased planning screens can show material sitting in inspection waiting to be received into the system.

19. Ability to drill down through planning screens to see purchase order details.

20. Has both net change and regenerative capabilities.

21. Ability to do selective net change or regenerative by part number and family.

22. System has online inquires showing both bucketed and non-bucketed formats.

23. System has reports showing both bucketed and non-bucketed formats.

24. System makes recommendations based on a working calendar that distinguishes between working and non working days.

25. User defined planning horizon that is incorporated into net change and regenerative MRP runs.

26. User defined planning buckets allow the selective combination of days, weeks, and months.

27. MRP logic considers effectivity dates in bills of material.

28. Ability to do data selection for specific bill types in MRP regeneration or net change.

29. MRP logic recognizes remanufacturing work orders and can add several different parts back to inventory based on one work order.

30. Are there any limitations on how long the planning horizon may be?

31. User definable planning buckets that can use any combination of:

    31.1 Days

    31.2 Weeks

    31.3 Months

Distribution Requirements Planning

1. Distribution planning logic works similar to a single level MPS and shares same source code and programs.

2. Basic order quantity modification logic:

    2.1 Min

    2.2 Max

    2.3 Multiple

    2.4 Lot for Lot

    2.5 Periods of supply

    2.6 Fixed order quantity

    2.7 User defined

3. MRP planning and execution videos have access to the following information on screen or through function keys:

    3.1 Part number

    3.2 Description

    3.3 Unit of measure

    3.4 Make or buy code

    3.5 Planner or buyer code

    3.6 Order policy

3.7 Reorder point

3.8 Lead time

4. Displays in spreadsheet format for the following:

    4.1 Future available balance

    4.2 Available to promise

    4.3 Accumulated available to promise

    4.4 Forecast

    4.5 Sales orders

    4.6 Interplant

    4.7 Future work order receipts

    4.8 Beginning balance

    4.9 Firm work orders

    4.10 Dependent demand

    4.11 Purchase orders

5. Each item number can be planned differently.

6. Each manufacturing plant can use different planning parameters, such as order quantity size.

7. DRP system seamlessly integrates with the MPS.

8. Ability to define supply / demand sources.

9. DRP planning generations can be performed by net change.

10. DRP planning generations can be performed by gross regeneration.

11. System has ability to use sales orders and purchasing orders to ship and receive distribution products between branches.

12. Distribution sales orders and purchase orders are joined together by a common reference number.

13. Ability to see total shipping unit of measure, through reports or on-line, between plants by:

    13.1 Volume

    13.2 Dollars

    13.3 Weight

    13.4 Pallets

    13.5 Cases

    13.6 Other user defined

14. Are there any limitations on how long the planning horizon can be?

15. User definable planning buckets that can use any combination of:

    15.1 Days

    15.2 Weeks

15.3 Months

16. Has ability to manage transportation capacity in graphical format.

17. Ability to drill down from a summary transportation screen to a detail screen showing:

    17.1 Part number

    17.2 Dates

    17.3 Quantities

    17.4 Demand plant

18. Ability to setup "rate schedules" allowing the continuous shipment of product between branches.

Product Data Structures

Bills of material------------------------------

1. Has parent / child relationships up to 12 layers deep. If less than 12, specify.

2. Bill of material editing programs that allow:

    2.1 Addition

    2.2 Deletion

    2.3 Change

    2.4 Copy

    2.5 Same as/except logic

3. Bill of material editing programs allow drill down capability to lower or higher levels.

4. Logging history for bill of material changes that allow online lookup by users.

5. Multi level where used inquiry.

6. Multilevel where used report.

7. Single level where used inquiry.

8. Single level where used report.

9. Ability to define a part as a bulk item bypassing inventory transactions.

10. Dynamic updating of low level codes during BOM changes allowing proper calculation of MRP logic.

11. Can assign default consumption inventory location by part number.

12. Supports phantom logic.

13. Phantom levels are highlighted or identified on bill of material inquiry screens.

14. Bills of material integrated with shop floor control.

15. Bills of material integrated with work orders.

16. Bills of material integrated with engineering change order management.

17. Online inquiry screen allows users to type in a parent quantity and see the usage throughout a multilevel bill and show current on hand quantities with calculated shortages.

18. Ability to identify material substitutes that allows work orders to automatically use different substitute parts when shortages occur.

19. Ability to store the following information at the component level in the BOM:

    19.1 Bubble number

    19.2 Special notes

    19.3 Assembly sequence number

    19.4 Pick sequence number

19.5 Drawing numbers

19.6 Setup Instructions

19.7 Revision numbers

20. Unit of measure ability at parent level.
21. Unit of measure ability at component level.
22. Effectivity dates at the parent level.
23. Effectivity dates at the component level.
24. Supports modularization of bills of material.
25. Bills of material can be set up that reflect the production of several parts from one parent item.
26. Ability to have multiple bill types such as:

26.1 Engineering

26.2 Manufacturing

26.3 Remanufacturing

26.4 Prototype

26.5 Other user defined

27. Ability to drill back to the item master through the BOM inquiry and maintenance screens.

28. Ability to do a part number search and pull back part numbers to the bill of material maintenance screens.

29. User defined decimal capability up to 6 places through the use of a data dictionary.

30. Bill of material has a batch size field that allows different bills for different size batches.

Routings--------------------------------------

31. Detail routings inquiry / maintenance screens contain the following fields:

    31.1 Machine hours

    31.2 Man hours

    31.3 Work center

    31.4 Routing type

    31.5 Sequence numbers

    31.6 Tooling

    31.7 Part number

    31.8 Number of machines

    31.9 Number of operators

32. Resource profiles can contain user defined units of measure such as pounds, gallons, square feet, etc.

33. Yield factors can be assigned to routing steps.

34. Can have several different routing types for the same part such as:

    34.1 Manufacturing

    34.2 Alternate

    34.3 Engineering

    34.4 Master

    34.5 Other user defined

35. Ability to use one routing as a "master" for a family of parts.

36. Ability to "connect" component parts in the BOM to specific routing steps in the routing.

37. Work centers are part of the routings steps.

38. Work centers have a work center master where basic work center maintenance is performed.

39. Work centers are considered a business unit and must be defined in the business' unit master.

40. Routings for phantoms are allowed.

41. Multiple alternate routings are allowed.

42. User defined decimal capability to the routings up to 4 places through the use of a data dictionary.

43. Ability to define overlapping routing steps.

44. Ability to define splits in routing processes.

45. Routings have a batch size field that allows different routings for different size batches.

46. Revision level field is part of the header information in routing inquiry and maintenance screens.

47. Functionality to accommodate outside subcontracting.

48. Routing detail integrates with a default note master. User has the ability to drill down and pull in default text master templates.

49. Text master templates can be overridden by user for specific operation routing steps.

50. Number of operators per routing step can be entered, and fully supported, as a decimal quantity.

51. Number of machines and routing step can be entered and fully supported, as a decimal quantity.

52. Routing editing programs that allow:

    52.1 Addition

    52.2 Deletion

    52.3 Change

    52.4 Copy

    52.5 Same as except logic

53. Logging history, for routing changes, that allows online lookup by users.

54. Routings have sub sequence number that allows multiple operation steps to take place within one work center.

55. Routings are integrated with engineering change order management.

56. Tooling requirements can be loaded by operation.

57. Effectivity starting and ending dates for individual routing steps.

58. Effectivity starting and ending dates for the entire routing connected to the parent part number.

59. Specific routing steps can be flagged to trigger outside special vendor processing. Integrates with purchase order management.

Inventory Management

1. Unlimited unit of measure conversion capability by part number.

2. Ability to specify units of measure for each functional module such as sales, inventory, purchasing, shop floor control, MRP. Specify which ones.

3. Contains default workflow templates that allow a new part to flow from one department to another, allowing the correct information to be added. Workflow template is integrated with e-mail functionality.

4. Material can be scrapped, with integrated reason codes.

5. Online history shows transaction details such as when, by whom, part number, quantities, etc. for ALL transactions to inventory items.

6. Fully supports cycle counting:

    6.1 ABC analysis with automatic frequency counting code assigned to part numbers.

    6.2 Automatic adjustments can be made in batch mode for a large number of parts.

    6.3 Counted quantities can be held in suspense for review and can be released for automatic inventory adjustments.

    6.4 Cycle counting sheets are created showing part numbers, locations, and on hand quantities.

6.5 Cycle counting process contains workflow that has individual steps from cycle count generation to completion.

6.6 Online inquires provide filter capability to show the cycle counts at different steps.

6.7 Online inquires provide filter capability to show the part numbers at different cycle counting steps.

7. Inventory accuracy can be calculated as: inventory accuracy = number of locations out of tolerance / number of locations.

8. Tolerance is user definable.

9. Ability to measure inventory accuracy by:

    9.1 Part number

    9.2 Inventory location

    9.3 Manufacturing plant

    9.4 Entire company

    9.5 Responsible manufacturing or inventory manager

    9.6 Families

10. Location master allows transactions to only valid inventory locations.

11. System has basic inventory transaction capabilities:

    11.1 Issue

11.2 Adjustments

11.3 Transfers between manufacturing plants.

11.4 Transfers between inventory locations.

11.5 Ability to reclassify inventory from one part number to another.

11.6 Ability to adjust cost up or down for part or lot.

12. Contains several different costing methods such as:

12.1 LIFO

12.2 FIFO

12.3 Weighted Average

12.4 Last In

12.5 User defined

13. Ability to turn on or off location master.

14. Annual physical inventory process.

14.1 Prints tags with part numbers, quantities, and locations.

14.2 Has suspense file that allows the review and approval before inventory adjustments are posted.

14.3 Built in adjustable work flow in defining steps and process flow.

14.4 Ability to issue tags out and receive them back in.

14.5 Online inquires have filters that show part numbers counted, locations and tags.

14.6 Final inventory adjustments can all be performed at once in batch mode.

15. System has user defined hold codes that can be applied to:

15.1 Parts

15.2 Locations

15.3 Lots

16. Basic inventory inquiry screens show real time demand or supply from the following sources:

16.1 Sales orders

16.2 Purchase orders

16.3 Work orders (both supply and demand)

17. System provides for lot control and traceability.

17.1 Certain parts can be designated as lot control items and cause lot transactions to occur in any module that has inventory transactions.

17.2 Lot expiration dates.

17.3 Default expiration time periods that default from the part number to the lots upon lot creation.

17.4 Individual lots for one part number can be put on hold while other lots are allowed transactions.

17.5 Online inquires that allow users to trace from the parent lot numbers all the way to supplier lot numbers.

17.6 Where used inquiry shows all the places where a lot has been used.

17.7 System forces the use of lot numbers if lot control is turned on for a part number.

17.8 Inventory allocation methods for sales and shop floor control can be done by:

17.8.1 Lot number

17.8.2 FIFO

17.8.3 LIFO

17.8.4 Other user defined

17.9 Different types of lot numbers can be set by part such as:

17.9.1 Year-month-day format / sub ID

17.9.2 Next number

17.9.3 Other user defined

17.10 Lot control functionality can also be used for serial number control.

Field Service

1. Field service module is a fully integrated non-third party provider.

2. Uses the system's standard inventory master.

3. Integrated with sales order management.

4. Can classify parts as

    4.1 New

    4.2 Used

    4.3 Refurbished

    4.4 Other user defined

5. Automated dial up support systems such as fax on demand or helpful information.

6. Ability to set up trucks as a separate business unit with their own inventory locations, costs, part numbers, etc.

7. Can attach the following activity to machine serial numbers:

    7.1 Call history

    7.2 Machine configuration

    7.3 Replacement parts

    7.4 Serviced by technician

    7.5 Service order history

8. Ability to look up warranty information as text or scanned documents from OEM suppliers.

9. Field service personnel has full access to the system via dial up networking or through Internet.

10. Online inquires have filters that support inquires by:

    10.1 Customer

    10.2 Machine numbers

    10.3 Serial numbers

    10.4 Special coding

    10.5 Call number

    10.6 Service numbers

    10.7 Incident type

    10.8 Other user defined code

11. Scheduling tools can schedule field technicians.

12. Scheduling tools use 7 x 24 format videos.

13. Both days and hours can be blocked out (such as holidays).

14. Technicians can be scheduled for specific locations.

15. Tools for providing rapid online real time estimations for repairs for waiting phone customers.

16. Ability to connect common problems and resolutions to customer profiles.

17. Phone support users can drill down through customer profiles to read detail problem resolution text messages.

18. Ability to see online and through reports costs by

    18.1 Customer

    18.2 Jobs

    18.3 Machines.

19. Triggers for call service management people to call customer for preventative maintenance.

20. System can automatically generate preventive maintenance schedule based on predefined rules.

21. Calls can be:

    21.1 Opened like a job

    21.2 Modified to include parts, labor, instructions

    21.3 Closed out

22. Call orders use default work flow templates that can be modified.

23. Ability to identify orders as rush, ship overnight.

24. Caller ID that brings up default customer profile with drill down capability for:

24.1 Contact information

24.2 Last customer orders

25. Can record meter readings.

26. Meter readings integrate with preventive maintenance schedule.

27. Can calculate the following failure statistics by part number:

27.1 MTBF

27.2 MTFF

27.3 MTBI

27.4 MTTR

28. Can calculate the following failure statistics by serial number:

28.1 MTBF

28.2 MTFF

28.3 MTBI

28.4 MTTR

29. Performance measurement reports showing:

29.1 Number of failures by month

29.2 Average field response time

29.3 Average call response time

29.4 Average open order time

29.5 Total orders processed per month

30. Automated escalation processes.

31. Ability to classify machines as active or inactive for field service planning.

Shop Floor Control

1. Ability to transact a work order pick list from pull locations to WIP locations in a single keystroke by the user.

2. Ability to override part numbers and quantities on a work order pick list from pull locations to WIP locations.

3. Phantom logic is used in the creation of parts lists.

4. Special tooling requirements print out on the shop floor work order and show in online inquires.

5. Online inquires and reports to show shortage by planner.

6. Online tools to check for shortages before work orders are released.

7. Tooling consumed based amounts specified in routings.

8. All cost related activity can be transacted to the general ledger though integration.

9. Ability to see all work order related transactions from history.

10. Bubble numbers show in online inquires for work order parts lists.

11. Ability to process remanufacturing products:

    11.1 Work order can produce multiple recoverable parents.

    11.2 Remanufacturing activity does not conflict with accounting activities.

11.3 Ability to classify recoverable parts for future statistical analysis.

11.4 Item returned for remanufacturing can be marked as belonging to a customer.

11.5 Remanufacturing items can be tracked by new serial number that traces to original serial number.

12. Bubble numbers show in work order printouts.

13. Assembly sequence number shows on work order inquiry screens.

14. Assembly sequence number shows on work order printouts.

15. Ability to retain an unlimited amount of work order history.

16. All phantom items that contain routings are merged into the parent item during routing creation for a work order.

17. Parts list can be different from a BOM by performing manual changes.

18. Routings on work orders can be different from the routing master by performing manual changes.

19. Phantom logic is supported in routing processing for work orders up to 12 layers deep.

20. Routing editing programs that allow:

    20.1 Addition

    20.2 Deletion

20.3 Change

20.4 Copy one work order

20.5 Copy a range of work orders

20.6 Same as/except logic

21. Materials can be issued out of inventory or WIP locations showing by a work order.

22. Online inquires show issued amounts and remaining balances to work orders.

23. Production reporting capability showing an item as completed to a stockroom or inventory location.

24. Ability to do production reporting by operation step.

25. Online inquires can show production quantities completed at operation steps and remaining balances.

26. Materials can be issued against a work order as scrap.

27. Scrap transactions can be performed against work orders with reason codes.

28. Online inquires show total scrap and yield per work order.

29. Online history show when scrap transaction were performed and by whom, with reason codes.

30. Parent completions, component issues, and material scrap can all per performed as actual regardless of the planned quantity.

31. Basic soft error edit checking logic occurs for unusual transaction quantities.

32. Ability to use specific basic inventory picking strategies such as LIFO, FIFO, largest quantity, least quantity, location order, etc. Specify which ones.

33. System has the ability to use pre-flush for work order component parts.

34. System has the ability to use backflush for work order component parts.

35. Ability to define simple rules for the automatic sequencing of shop orders for group technology or reduce setups.

36. Online inquires have filters to locate work orders by:

    36.1 Order number

    36.2 Planner number

    36.3 Parent part number

    36.4 Component part number

    36.5 Several different user defined codes

    36.6 Starting date range

    36.7 Completion date range

    36.8 Work centers

    36.9 Status (release through completion)

37. Ability to sequence work orders on reports and videos in the order that they should be executed.

38. Work order generation copies over bills of material and routings with all related information such as notes.

39. Both bills of material and routings can be modified at the work order level.

40. Default work flow templates that can be modified through softcoding for normal work order process flow.

41. Online inquires show the quantity completed of parent item with remaining balances.

42. Online inquires show the quantity issued of component item with remaining balances.

43. Summarized pick list can be issued for a range of work orders.

44. Summarized pick list is held in a suspense file that allows the user to recall the pick list by pick list number and issue or move all the materials to a WIP location with only a few keystrokes.

45. Simplistic production reporting tools capable of backflushing through the bill of material. No work order creation is necessary.

46. Open shop orders under an ECO change can be highlighted or identified through integration of the ECO module.

47. Work order start and finish dates can be manually changed.

48. Online reporting of labor and machine hours.

49. Dispatching lists by work center can be sorted by start and due dates.

50. Summary reports show all open work orders with a variety of sorting techniques.

51. Variety of work order variance analysis tools:

    51.1 Parent item

        51.1.1 Original work order vs. actual

    51.2 Component parts

        51.2.1 Original work order vs. actual

        51.2.2 Bill of material vs. actual

    51.3 Labor hours

        51.3.1 Original work order vs. actual

        51.3.2 Bill of material vs. actual

    51.4 Machine hours

        51.4.1 Original work order vs. actual

        51.4.2 Bill of material vs. actual

52. Variance dollars can be transacted to the general ledger and accumulated by account number.

Configuration Management

1. Ability to integrate directly with sales order management providing configuration management capability direction within a sales order.

2. Ability to configure products with an almost infinite number of configuration techniques.

3. Ability to automatically calculate cost of the product based on the configuration of the product.

4. Ability to automatically calculate price of the product based on the configuration of the product.

5. Ability to quickly recall historic configuration based on past sales order history by customer.

6. Configuration management logic works for quotes and estimations.

7. Configuration management will automatically create lower level demand work orders.

8. All work orders created from configuration management are cross-referenced through the "master" work order and/or sales order.

9. Ability to set up "characteristics" or segments such as length, color, size, etc.

10. Ability to use if then logic to associate "characteristics" with manufacturing part numbers and assemblies.

11. Ability to generate soft errors based on incompatible combinations.

12. Can create new item numbers and add them to the item master automatically from the configuration management module.

13. Can create new bills of material and add them to the bill of material master automatically from the configuration management module.

14. Can create new routings and add them to the routing master automatically from the configuration management module.

15. Ability to update feature percents in planning bills of material based on usage.

16. Ability to define new items or calculate quantities based on user defined mathematical calculations. Example: length x width x height = volume.

Engineering Change Order Management

1. Different types of implementation strategies such as:

    1.1 Inventory use up

    1.2 Implementation based on specified date

2. Online inquiry tool allows the selection of ECO by:

    2.1 Past history

    2.2 Open ECOs

    2.3 Transition coordinator

    2.4 Reason codes

    2.5 Other user defined classification codes

    2.6 ECO number(s)

    2.7 Originator

3. Ability to drill into prototype bill of material.

4. Uses the same bill of material file as MRP.

5. Ability to drill into prototype routing.

6. Is integrated with:

    6.1 Shop floor control

    6.2 Material requirements planning

6.3 Master production scheduling

6.4 Bills of material

6.5 Routings

6.6 Capacity and resource requirements planning

7. Ability to archive inactive bills of material.

8. Global search and replace capability for component part numbers.

9. Global search and replace capability for parent part numbers for bills of material.

10. Global search and replace capability for parent part numbers for routings of material.

11. Global search and replace capability for routing steps in routings.

12. Has user definable approval routing process.

13. Approval routing is integrated with e-mail.

14. Batch global search and replace update can be performed automatically upon last approval from approval routing.

15. Global search and replace can update more than parents, components, and routings steps. Specify which fields.

16. Analysis tools to classify and summarize reason codes for ECO changes.

17. Can enter requests for ECOs online.

18. Requests can be converted to live ECOs by interactive user approval.

19. Requests can be converted to live ECOs by batch job.

Questions---

1. What does RFP stand for?
2. What does RFI stand for?
3. What is the difference between an RFP and an RFI?
4. What are some problems with RFPs?
5. What are some advantages of using RFPs?
6. Where do RFPs come from?
7. What is the primary type of questions asked by an RFP?
8. Why does an RFP not ensure success?
9. What is a boilerplate? What are some advantages and disadvantages of using them?
10. What are the different types of RFPs?
11. What is the structure of an RFP?
12. Why do some ERP venders and service providers dislike answering RFPs?

We considered and used quality programs in the past, but we never really thought of using quality for principles in our ERP system...

14

Total Quality Management

Total Quality Management (TQM) is a technique for enhancing customer satisfaction and continuous improvement within a company. The concept of TQM applies widely to many different needs within a company, including ERP systems. Historically speaking, TQM principles have been applied to ERP systems very poorly by both ERP vendors and the companies that adopt ERP systems. The TQM philosophy differs from traditional management philosophies as it involves everyone's participation. It creates a win-win environment for all the participants of the team, providing overall value to the system.

It has structured techniques and processes that satisfy the needs of internal customers and leads to the satisfaction of external customers. Participants must be committed to its use and focused on the successful implementation of an ERP system. The effective use of TQM provides a much higher quality ERP implementation that functions properly upon first use, on time, with less cost, and more overall value. More importantly, TQM ensures satisfaction of all participants, including ERP vendors, service providers, systems integrators, team members who implement the software, and the company that purchased the software.

Characteristics of TQM are fundamentally common to all different types of business process flows and ERP functional modules. TQM applies to much more than just a discrete product or characteristic; it's for the overall system.

Figure 14-1

Deming's 14 Points For Management	Juran's 10 Steps For Quality Improvement	Crosby's 14 Steps to Quality Improvement
1. Create consistency of purpose for improvement of product and service.	1. Build awareness of the need an opportunity for improvement.	1. Make it clear that management is committed to quality.
2. Adopt the new philosophy.	2. Set goals for improvement.	2. Form quality improvement teams with representatives from each department.
3. Cease dependence on inspection to achieve quality.	3. Organize to reach the goals (establish a quality council, identify problems, appoint teams, designate facilitators).	3. Determine where current and potential quality problems lie.
4. End the practice of awarding business on the basis of price tag alone. Instead, minimize total cost by working with a single supplier.	4. Provide training.	4. Evaluate the cost of quality and explain its use as a management tool.
5. Improve constantly and forever every process for planning, production, and service.	5. Carry out projects to solve problems.	5. Raise the quality awareness and personal concern to all employees.
6. Institute training on the job.	6. Report progress.	6. Take actions to correct problems identified through previous steps.
7. Adopt and institute leadership.	7. Give recognition.	7. Establish a committee for the zero defects program.
8. Drive out fear.	8. Communicate results.	8. Train supervisors to actively carry out their part of the quality improvement program.
9. Breakdown barriers between staff areas.	9. Keep score.	9. Hold a "zero-defects day" to let all employees realize that there has been a change.
10. Eliminate slogans, exhortations, and targets for the workforce.	10. Maintain momentum by making annual improvement part of the regular systems and processes of the company.	10. Encourage individuals to establish improvement goals for themselves and their groups.
11. Eliminate numerical quotas for the workforce and numerical goals for management.		11. Encourage employees to communicate the management obstacles they face in attaining their improvement goals.
12. Remove barriers that rob people of workmanship. Eliminate the annual rating or merit system.		12. Recognize and appreciate those who participate.
13. Institute a vigorous program of education and self improvement for everyone.		13. Establish quality councils to communicate on a regular basis.
14. Put everybody in the company to work to accomplish the transformation.		14. Do it all over again to emphasize that the quality improvement program never ends.

The origins of modern day Total Quality Management can be attributed to three men: Deming, Juran, and Crosby. Their work in the United States and Japan has affected almost every area of modern day business management. Although the complete scope of their work is subject for many textbooks and is not included here, the chart shown in figure 14-1 summarizes the main points of each pioneer.

Some of the concepts related to TQM that are covered in this chapter, have received extensive attention in other chapters of this book. Those sections will be covered only briefly while other sections receive more detail.

It seems incredible that the same companies that develop and manufacture products with quality defect rates in the parts per million cannot install and maintain a computer system that will be valuable in the overall health and growth of their company. There is a high correlation between ERP failure and non-use of TQM principles in ERP system design and development. To be successful with an ERP system companies need to learn and understand the concepts of Total Quality Management and how to apply them to ERP systems.

TQM principles are the main factors that greatly increase the probability of a successful ERP system. Generally speaking, they can be grouped into these major classifications:

- Leadership
- Commitment
- Total customer satisfaction
- Continuous improvement
- Total involvement
- Training and education
- Ownership
- Fail proofing
- Teamwork
- Visual quality tools
- Quality function deployment

Leadership

Having strong leadership is critical for the overall success of an ERP system. The leadership role senior management plays for an ERP system is often greatly misunderstood. Successful ERP implementations will have one or more senior managers closely involved in the installation and maintenance of ERP system. The senior manager has the authority and power to resolve conflicting needs in the allocation of resources for the ERP system, and does so as needed. Too often senior management takes the role of only providing motivational support for those involved in the implementation of an ERP system. This is not enough. ERP implementations that go poorly always do so in the absence of good management.

Commitment

To be successful with an ERP system, commitment must come from team members, management, financial resources, ERP service providers, and computer resources.

Lack of commitment of ERP team members is noticeable in most ERP implementations. To ensure rapid and smooth implementation, team members must be capable of dedicating 60 to 100 percent of their time to the ERP project. Lower committed times of 20 to 30 percent, or less, do not work well because of the high learning curves required for ERP implementations. Figure 14-2 shows the relationship between the success of a project and the amount of time that team members dedicate to it.

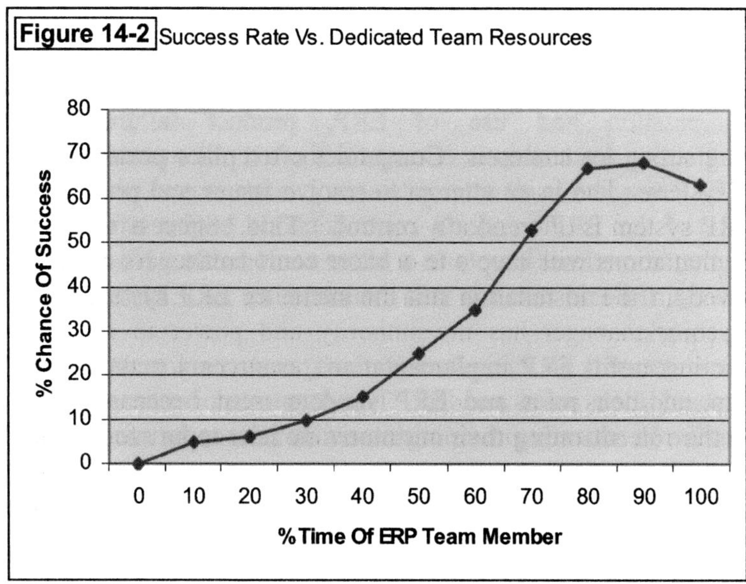

Figure 14-2 Success Rate Vs. Dedicated Team Resources

Total customer satisfaction

The most important concept of total customer satisfaction is understanding who the customer is and what the customer's role is. The customer of an ERP system is the company who has purchased it and intends to use it for their business. ERP systems are complex in nature and are not well supported by traditional customer service techniques.

As common consumers of the market, when we purchase products we generally expect the company that we purchase the product from to provide services and directions in making that product successful for its intended use. ERP systems are not that simple. The success of an ERP system is highly dependent upon the leadership, commitment, and implementation technique by the company that purchased it. Generally, ERP vendors do not have the authority or power to tell their customers how they may or may not use or install an ERP system.

Because many companies do not understand their role in the implementation and use of ERP, product failure and dissatisfaction are common. Companies often place pressure on their ERP vendors in an attempt to resolve issues and problems outside of the ERP vendor's control. This begins a vicious cycle that sometimes erupts to a bitter court battle. No matter who wins, the end result is still the same: an ERP system that doesn't work.

For successful ERP implementations, customers must better understand their roles and ERP vendors must become more aggressive in educating their customers on how to be successful with an ERP system.

Continuous improvement

The concept of continuous improvement is understood well by world-class companies but rarely applied effectively to ERP systems. There is a strong effort by companies to fix ERP systems, which often leads to layers and layers of complex software modifications. Eventually the complexity becomes so great that companies are forced to abandon the ERP system and implement a new one. This is not continuous improvement.

Continuous improvement in an ERP system is the process of better learning how to use the ERP system for long-term competitive advantage in the marketplace without making unnecessary software modifications. Success is rarely invented or obtained overnight. Small simple installations can show large scale improvement in a period of three to six months, while larger complex installations may take five or ten years. No matter what the size of an organization or its complexity, when it comes to ERP systems, continuous improvement is shown in small incremental steps.

Total involvement

The process of total involvement is well suited for ERP systems. The installation of an ERP system can be thought of as being similar to designing a complex product for your customer. An ERP system may be sold as a standard package; but the way that it will be installed and how it will be used requires significant design work. The overall quality of the installation will be greatly improved by the involvement of all affected parties. Companies that attempt to install ERP systems while keeping end-users in the dark during the design process, have notably higher failure rates. The process of communicating how an ERP system will affect people, and the changes required, gives concerned parties an opportunity to recognize mistakes and avoid costly decisions.

Total involvement has many important benefits in the early design phases including: less rework, higher user acceptance, less training, faster implementation times, higher success rates, better performance, and less post implementation support.

Training and education

ERP system training can be thought of as what button to push and when it should be pushed. Education can be thought of as the reason for pushing that button and how it relates to the overall system. Companies will all too often attempt to use training as a substitute for education or vice versa. The results are usually dismal. ERP systems need both.

ERP systems should begin with education for the team core members. It is important to understand the overall design and functional capabilities of a new ERP system. Once those functional capabilities are clearly understood, the core team members will be in a better position to implement the ERP system and develop training programs.

ERP training programs are the classes designed specifically for the company using the ERP system. These classes will show in detail how to use the software for specific business process flows. These ERP training programs cannot use standard ERP vendor supplied training programs, for those are oriented towards education, not training. ERP training programs must be custom developed for almost every situation. Educational training classes provided by ERP venders are focused on the functionality of the system and how it works in a general sense, not specific for a company.

Ownership

Overall company satisfaction in an ERP system correlates strongly with end-user ownership. Companies where the ownership has shifted from the end-users of the system to the Information Systems (IS) function, suffer from a barrage of mistakes and rework. These types of environments have trouble learning from their mistakes and often occupy their time in endless political meetings and red tape.

Companies with high end-user ownership will use their ERP system for long-term strategic business management. These types of companies are rare, making it difficult to learn from another's success.

A complete lack of ownership will lead to catastrophic results. When the ERP system is no longer supported by the end-users, management, and the ERP vendor, death is almost certain to occur.

Fail proofing

Fail proofing in ERP systems is a process of taking small incremental steps, ensuring that they will be successful, leading up to bigger and more costly steps. Because of the complexity of an ERP system and the amount of organizational change required, these systems can not be instantly turned on. Installing ERP systems works something like a train; it takes time to build up momentum or to slow down.

Building momentum in an ERP project is much easier if there is something to cheer about. With careful planning each and every step is ensured success in the implementation phase. As organizational members see these incremental steps taking place successfully, it becomes much easier for them to place their trust in the ERP project.

One of the primary reasons that companies bypass fail proofing the process is the belief that ERP systems can be installed quickly and cheaply. One dollar of prevention spent on fail proofing strategies can be worth several thousand dollars of expensive fixes and rehabilitation.

Through the flexibility of modern day ERP systems, numerous opportunities are available for the fail proofing of business process flows. Hard coded software, workflow, validation tools, error codes, and user defined error messages can all greatly reduce the errors that occur in an ERP system. Most often this is not enough to preserve the quality and integrity of an ERP database. Aggressive training for accurate transactions is still important so long as humans are involved in creating transactions in an ERP system.

Teamwork

ERP vendors, consultants, management and ERP team members must all work together for successful ERP implementation. Successful communication is required for this to happen. How to arrange the ERP team is generally given little thought in an ERP implementation. Quite interestingly, traditional TQM concepts of teamwork where team members are allowed to communicate and make decisions outside of the direct line of management supervision has not worked well for ERP implementations.

Because of the complexity of ERP systems, they require a massive amount of coordination and synchronization of organizational resources. These organizational resources are often badly stressed between finding time to implement the ERP system and keeping the business running.

These conflicting needs require the decision making capability of the management responsible for the overall organization and implementation of the ERP system. Successful ERP implementations will usually have a strong senior manager of the company coordinating and synchronizing activities with the power and authority to resolve conflicting needs of personnel resources. Without the strong centralized resource guiding the ERP team, individual functions and team members tend to become lost in the chaos. Teamwork is most important, but works best when clear direction is present.

Visual quality tools

Visual quality tools help us to solve problems and to find cause and effect relationships that we typically would not see or understand without the use of these tools. Some common TQM tools include:

- Fishbone (cause and effect) diagram
- Pareto charts
- Statistical process control

Cause and effect diagrams offer an approach to problem solving that helps to give us structure and identify root causes. Cause and effect diagrams are also known as fishbone diagrams because of their shape. Fishbone diagrams help us to solve problems by providing us an examination method based on several different categories that are created during the creation of the fishbone diagram.

Cause and effect diagrams are most helpful in brainstorming sessions with lots of different people. The tool provides a method of recording different people's ideas in graphical format.

The basic design of the cause and effect diagram is shown in figure 14-3. On the left-hand side we have the effect, which is the problem that we are trying to find causes for. At the edges of the skeleton, along the top and bottom, are the major categories of causes. As we work our way towards the center we find causes of the causes, or root causes.

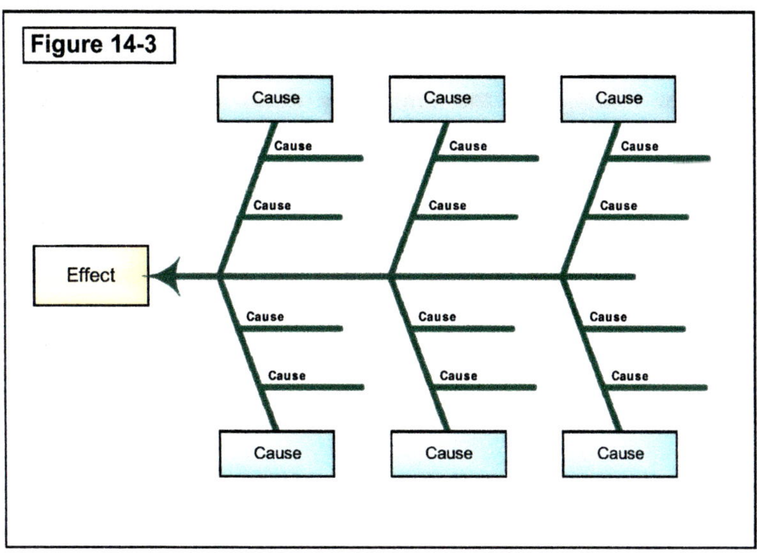

Figure 14-3

As a facilitator, working with a group during the brainstorming session, it is important to ask the five whys. The five whys is a process of asking why something is five times to reveal the root cause. Exposing the root cause is one of the primary goals of using a fishbone diagram. By identifying the root cause we can often correct or fix the problem more easily. Companies that do not spend enough time identifying root causes may unnecessarily spend their time and money treating symptoms of ERP problems rather than the root causes. A company's effort should be directed at correcting the root problems rather than the treatment of symptoms.

The following example illustrates the process of asking the five whys to resolve a problem in an ERP system for a sales order entry program.

Effect: Pricing does not work properly in sales orders.

Question 1: Why does pricing not work properly?
Cause: Some customers receive the wrong price.

Question 2: Why do some customers receive the wrong price?
Cause: Pricing for the effectivity dates is not managed properly.

Question 3: Why are effectivity dates not managed properly?
Cause: Because nobody updated the setup tables when John went on vacation.

Question 4: Why did no one set up the tables?
Cause: Because there is no teamwork.

Question 5: Why is there no teamwork?
Cause: Because top management does not support education for teamwork in this company.

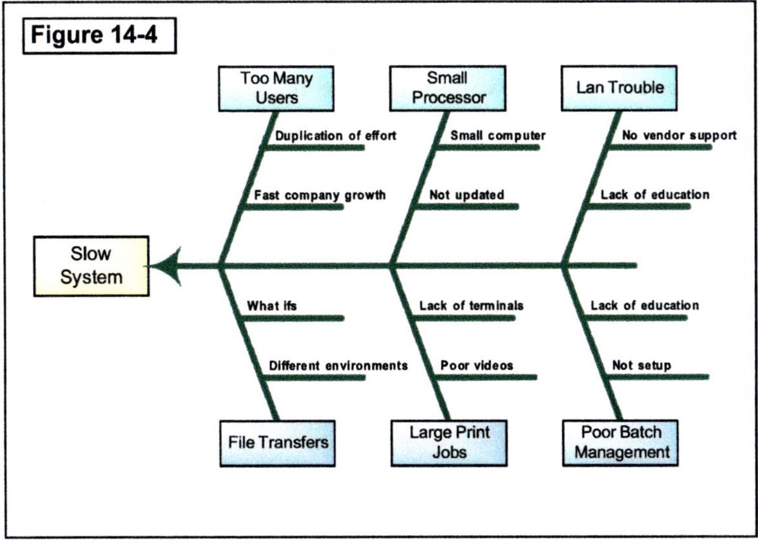

Figure 14-4 shows a completed fishbone diagram for an ERP system that was faced with performance problems because of long processing times. The system was too slow for the company for a variety of reasons. The main causes can be found on the outside edges of the fishbone diagram in the squares. Additional causes, for the main cause, can be found on the inside of the fishbone diagram.

Pareto analysis the process for identifying the most important problem areas. It is based on the principle that a relatively few factors will account for a large percentage of the total problems with. The idea is to focus an organization's efforts on resolving the most important ones. The Pareto analysis is often referred to as the 80-20 rule. It is based on the fact that 80 percent of the problems come from 20 percent of the items. For example, 80 percent of dissatisfied ERP users can be traced to the 20 percent that cause the problems.

In ERP systems it is useful to prepare a chart that shows the number of occurrences by category, arranged in the order of frequency. Figure 14-5 shows how a Pareto chart can be constructed based on complaints of ERP systems. With the data collected we see that management is viewed as a significant source of problems in the successful use and implementation of an ERP system. Efforts would focus on the management of the company. This might be done through the use of education. After resolving the issues found in management we would then move on to the next major category. Companies that take the time to construct Pareto charts usually find them quite interesting and revealing.

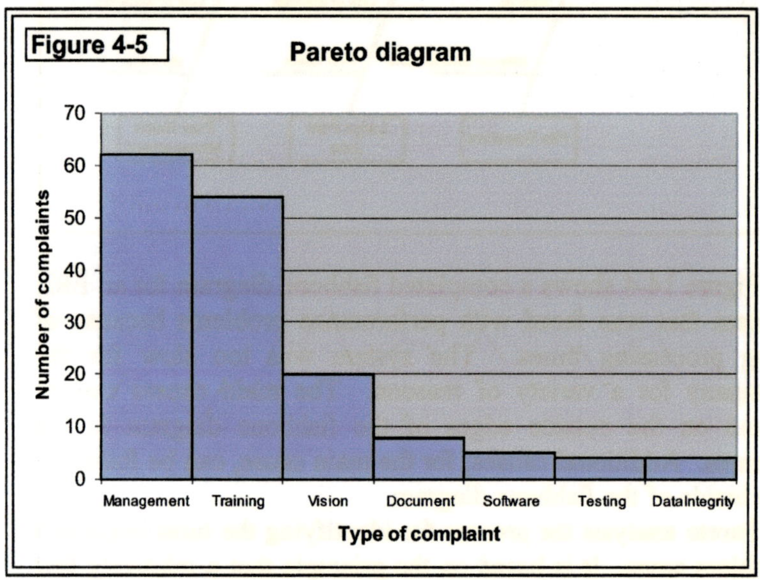

Statistical process control charts, or SPC charts, are graphical tools used to identify abnormal variables that occurred in the system. SPC charts are a considerably more advanced system of measurement than Pareto charts. SPC charts can be used to monitor the number of defective invoices posted to the general ledger, percentage of sales orders shipped on time, schedule accuracy, action messages in MRP and MPS, and much more.

The concept of SPC charts applies strongly to many different functional areas of an ERP system but historically has never been used. The concept of SPC applies strongly to ERP systems for two reasons. The first reason is that there are a large number of different areas in an ERP system that work well for SPC measurement systems. The second reason is that a computer program can access and calculate the data with little effort from the user. Companies are generally more concerned with applying SPC concepts to the product that they make or services they provide than for their ERP system. Figure 14-6 shows an example of a SPC chart as it applies to measuring percentage of sales orders shipped late.

Figure 14-6 SPC Chart

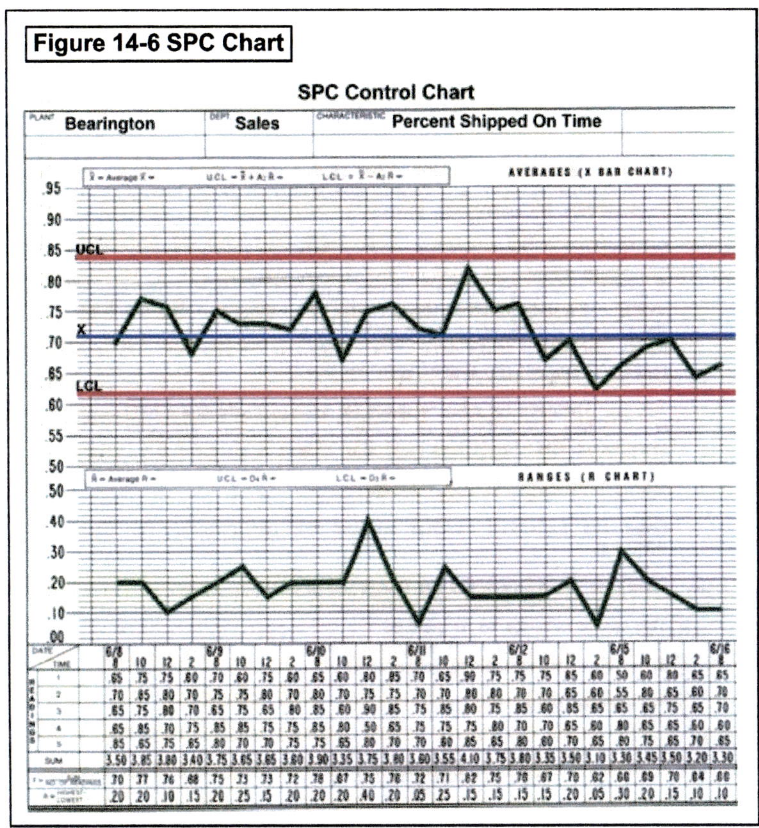

SPC charts can take many different forms. However, on the surface they are quite similar. Each chart has an average line, which represents the process average, and upper and lower control lines. The lower control line is called the lower control limits or LCL for short. The upper control line is called the upper control limits or UCL for short. The use of these charts involves taking periodic samples and calculating appropriate sample statistics to be plotted on the chart. When sample statistics fall between the UCL and the LCL, the process is said to be in control. Many types of processes will not have a LCL, for the lowest possible value will always be desirable, such as the percentage of sales orders shipped late. Mathematical calculations exist for calculating the LCL and the UCL based upon sampling data or capability studies. The LCL or UCL may also be set manually as deemed appropriate by the management of the company.

When values exceed either the LCL or the UCL it is appropriate action to begin an investigation to locate and understand the probable cause. Through the use of statistics a plotted value that exceeds either the LCL or the UCL indicates that abnormal fluctuation has taken place that has a corresponding cause. Anything falling between the LCL and the UCL can be considered normal fluctuation. If the LCL and UCL have been set manually, through a management directive, then the abnormal fluctuations outside the UCL or LCL may or may not have a corresponding cause.

Quality function deployment

Quality function deployment (QFD) is an excellent tool for solving problems, making decisions, and planning for ERP systems. QFD goes by many other names including: voice of customer, house of quality, customer driven engineering, matrix product planning, and decision matrix. Quality function deployment is a technique for identifying customers' (internal and external) needs and using a system to determine how to best to fulfill those needs with available resources. It gives everyone in an organization a road map showing how each step from design through delivery interacts with the objectives of the ERP system.

Quality function deployment takes a look at a series of problems and uses matrices to break them into specific action assignments. These assignments create the minimum level of effort for satisfying the customer. QFD translates qualitative organizational requirements into appropriate technical requirements. Through the use of QFD, shorter implementation cycles, lower costs, and higher productivity can be achieved.

Figure 14-7 The QFD Matrix

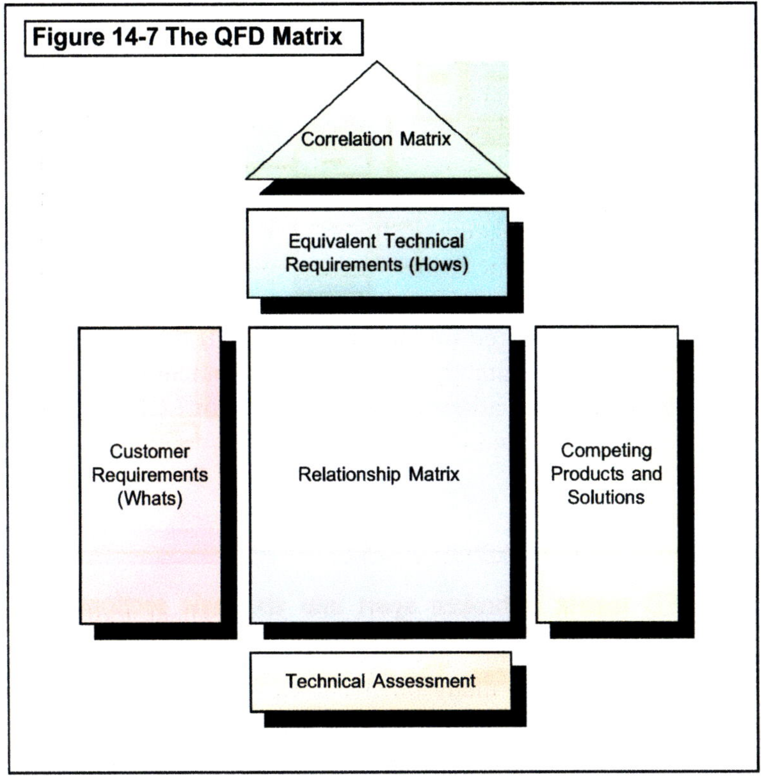

Matrices may be added or subtracted depending upon the needs of the organization. The use of QFD can be thought provoking but is seldom used in the selection and implementation of ERP systems.

Figure 14-8 Hows and Whats

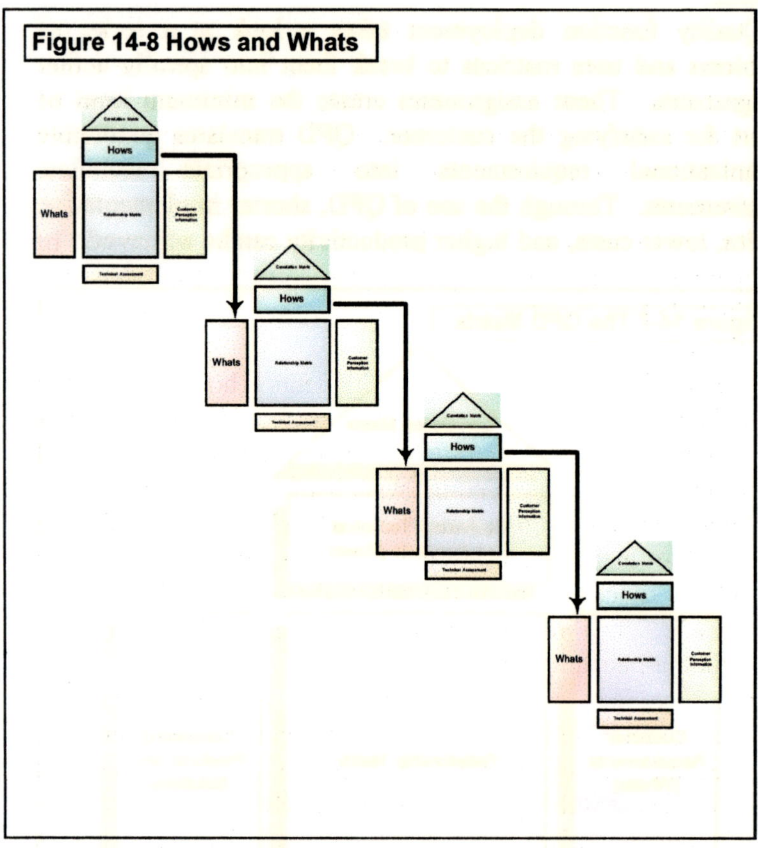

The QFD matrix is broken apart into six basic sections as shown in figure 14-7. They create the foundation building blocks for the QFD process. The six components are:

- Customer requirements (whats)
- Equivalent technical requirements (hows)
- Relationship matrix
- Correlation matrix

- Technical assessment
- Competing products and solutions

The process begins with the most important part, the customer requirements (whats). The customers may be either internal or external to an organization. Requirements can be thought of as a wish list. This section is usually already completed when an organization begins its search for a new ERP system.

For each one of the wish list items an analysis is made of competing products and solutions. The results of that analysis are included to the far right in the competing products and solutions box.

The equivalent technical requirements (hows) are then plotted across the top into the equivalent technical requirements box. Each one of the equivalent technical requirements will correspond with one item on the wish list found to the left.

After the completion of the 'whats' and 'hows', the relationship matrix can be created. Every combination is considered for each item on the 'what' list with each item on the 'how' list. The results are one of three options for each combination: negative, neutral, or positive.

The technical assessment box at the bottom reveals the specific target value of the equivalent technical requirements. The technical assessment box can reveal characteristics that may or may not be possible with today's technology. The correlation matrix at the top, existing as a triangle, examines relationships between each one of the technical requirements. As with the relationship matrix, one of three options will exist for each combination: negative, neutral, or positive.

From a learning perspective, QFD is usually broken into four matrices. They are called design, details, process, and production. Each cycle consists of the same matrix. Two important parts of the matrix are the 'hows' and the 'whats'. 'Whats' are the organizational requirements and the 'hows' are ways of achieving them. Each part of the QFD cycle uses the same basic matrix arrangement. As the transition is made from one cycle to another, the 'hows' are transferred to the 'whats' section of the next matrix. Figure 14-8 shows this process of transferring the hows of one matrix to the whats of the next matrix.

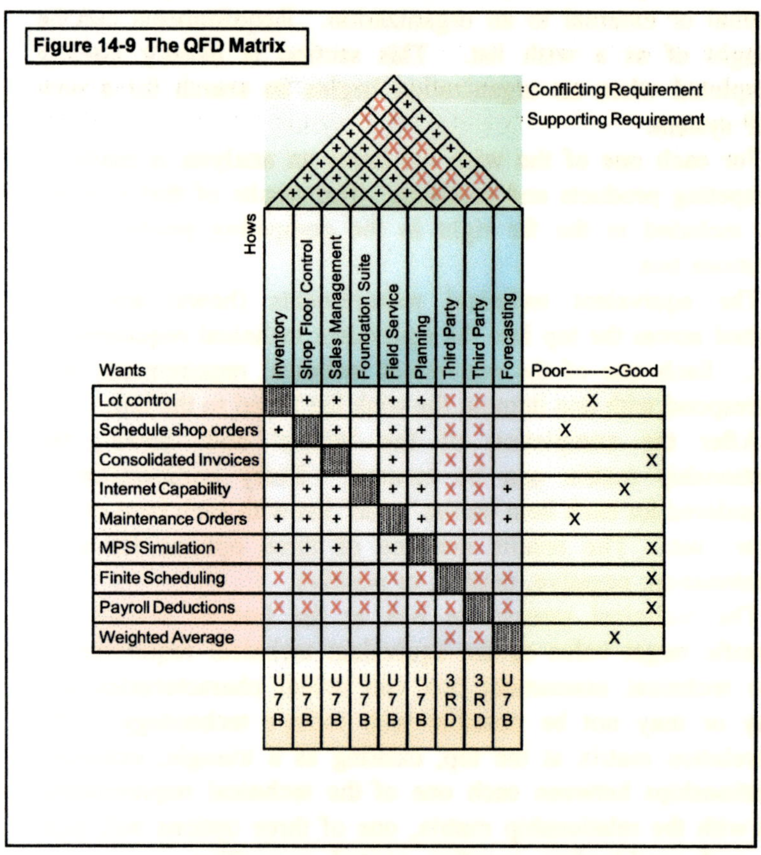

Figure 14-9 The QFD Matrix

An important concept is that the customers' needs and wants are connected together through the entire process of designing and implementing an ERP system. Figure 14-9 demonstrates how the QFD matrix could be used in the evaluation of an RFP returned by an ERP vendor. On the left-hand side, the company has listed some of the most important characteristics that they desire in a new ERP system. Solutions are shown across the top. The ERP vendor was unable to meet the basic needs of the customer: payroll deductions and finite scheduling. These two solutions were presented as a third party provider. One of the primary drivers in selecting a new ERP system for this particular company was the high need for integration. As a result, a variety of conflicting requirements show up as red X's revealing that integrated solutions were not available between the third party providers and the rest of the functional modules of the ERP system.

Questions---

1. What is TQM?
2. What does RFI stand for?
3. What are some of the major principles of TQM?
4. Why would TQM not be applied to many ERP system implementations?
5. Who were the three pioneers in the field of quality?
6. How is a customer defined in an ERP implementation?
7. What is the concept of fail proofing success?
8. What is a fishbone diagram?
9. What are the two main parts of a fishbone diagram?
10. What is a Pareto chart?
11. What is statistical process control?
12. What is quality function deployment?
13. How do the 'hows' and 'whats' fit into quality function deployment?
14. What is the most mathematically complex quality visual tool?

Where we think we may be tomorrow may not be what we think today because today was not what we thought...

15

ROI Techniques

Return on investment (ROI) is a mathematical technique for determining the suitability of making an investment. It is an estimate of the financial benefit of money spent on a particular proposed project. Generally, an ERP system's ROI calculations come into play during the software selection and justification process. Because of the enormous expense of purchasing and implementing an ERP system, a company's senior management may turn to some quantitative rationale for making such a significant investment.

There is considerable debate about the suitability of using ROI for the justification of ERP systems. Somewhat surprisingly, given the enormous amount of time and money needed to implement an ERP system, many companies purchase and implement them without making any ROI calculations. This was especially true prior to the year 2000 when companies were racing to implement new ERP systems that could handle year 2000 calculations. Sudden changes in technology, scope of project, change in business, and other factors can quickly invalidate any previous ROI calculations. Because of the extreme variation, the number of variables, and the qualitative characteristics of the variables, coming up with accurate and stable ROI calculations can be difficult to impossible.

Implementing an ERP system purely for the purpose of return on investment of the ERP system can seldom show a positive return on investment. For example, a company may choose to purchase, implement, and maintain an ERP system over a five-year period for a total of $6.2 million investment.

The new ERP system, because of better integration and streamlined technology, will enable a company to save 5.5 full-time positions for a period of 3.5 years. Each position costs the company $42,000 per year in employee benefits. The total savings is equal to $808,500. Clearly, the total costs incurred in the project did not pay for the savings that the system incurred. This is typical of most ERP implementations. In fact, many ROI calculations that are based purely on the ERP systems, go negative.

So, if ERP systems cannot pay for themselves, why do companies purchase and install them at all? One of the most important reasons is the potential for increased customer and operational efficiency. For example, let's say a company carries $54 million worth of inventory to supply their customers and manufacturing plants. Through the effective implementation of an ERP system, combined with effective operations management, they may be able to take the $54 million worth of inventory and reduce inventory to $23 million while providing the same level of customer service. Through the reduction of inventory, the company was able to gain $31 million for its $6.2 million investment in an ERP system. The total realized gain was $24.8 million.

How much an ERP system will benefit an organization's operational efficiency can be subject to much debate. The success of using an ERP system to increase operational efficiency is highly dependent upon the people systems that support the ERP system, because an ERP system can be thought of as a people system. The capability to successfully benefit from an ERP system is not necessarily dependent upon a new ERP system. For this reason companies can potentially realize the same great gains that they have with their current ERP system without making any investment in a new ERP system!

Most organizations find a decline in productivity after the immediate implementation of an ERP system. This is because the new ERP systems are usually more complex and difficult to master than the legacy systems to which people are accustomed.

The steep learning curves usually result in errors and delays. Organizations can struggle badly for the first three to 12 months after going live as ERP users struggle to learn the software. Customer orders may be entered wrong or delayed, inventory levels may go up, and operational efficiency may decrease. ROI calculations that companies perform to justify ERP systems rarely consider the decrease in operational efficiency after the go live of an ERP system.

Few companies will ever see a quick payback of the ERP system. Many companies realize that ERP specific application functionality such as customer service management, inventory management, manufacturing, and supplier management provides the greatest opportunities for return on investment.

Despite the unreliability of ROI calculations, ROI can still play an important role in building a critical mass of support from some of the most critical stakeholders: senior management. Senior management often looks for something more solid than someone's vague opinion that it is time for a new ERP system. ROI calculations fit that need well. ROI calculations give senior management a quantitative basis for justifying such an expensive investment. With senior management's buy-in and support, the overall probability of a successful implementation and use of an ERP system increases substantially.

There are two fundamental considerations to keep in mind when performing ROI calculations. The first is that ROI analysis, no matter how expensive, complex, or thorough, is no better than the basic assumptions used in determining the amount of the investment and the anticipated increased earnings or cost reductions. The second is that any accurate ROI calculations should only include those costs that are truly relevant to the investment decision being evaluated.

Although ROI calculations may not accurately represent the purchase and implementation of an entire ERP system, they do tend to work well for making small component decisions, such as a software modification. The process of using ROI calculations can provide considerable insight and justification for otherwise unnecessary investments of activity time and money.

Companies often make unnecessary software modifications. This is because the mindset of many companies is such that they think of ERP systems as highly automated streamlined systems that should reduce or eliminate human interaction or support. When companies find that the ERP system does require human intervention, they often attempt to program out the person needed to achieve that functionality. It is not uncommon for a $20,000 dollar modification to be performed, with no payback over the life of the modification, to be initiated with nothing more than single breath or a sticky post note memo from a functional manager, IS manager, or project manager. Performing ROI calculations helps to slow the pace so that the organization can consider the full impact of making such changes.

Although there are many good reasons for the elimination of efficient manual systems, it is not always justifiable to do so. The process of using people to perform redundant tasks, in many cases, can be more cost-effective than seeking technical customized program solutions.

Figure 15-1 shows a cost benefits analysis for making a software modification to replace the clerical function in sales order management. First, all the various costs of creating a custom program solution are identified. These costs include costs from internal and external sources such as: technical programming, testing, documentation, and training. After the initial setup costs are calculated, the annual maintenance costs must also be considered. The annual maintenance costs can be calculated as 20 percent of the initial setup cost times five years or the life expectancy of the software modification. In figure 15-1 the total accumulated costs over a five-year period are $27,820. Upon completion of the total accumulated costs, the estimated savings regain must then be considered. These are the benefits. The primary benefits from labor savings will extend over a five-year period. The total calculated savings comes to $11,700. The total realized savings or gain comes to a negative $16,120. Because total realized gain is a negative amount, this indicates that making this software modification would be undesirable from a cost perspective.

Figure 15-1 Cost / Benefits Analysis			
Software Modification	Hours	Cost/Hr	Extend
Cost of making modification			
External Technical Programming	40	$185	$7,400
External Technical Testing	20	$185	$3,700
External Technical Documentation	10	$185	$1,850
Internal Training	16	$40	$640
Internal Documentation	8	$40	$320
Total			$13,910
Annual Maintenance Cost For 5 Years			
= (20% of setup cost) x (5 years)			$13,910
Total Cost For 5 Years			**$27,820**
Estimated Savings or Gain			
Labor Savings For 5 Years	780	15	**$11,700**
Total Realized Savings or Gain			**-$16,120**

Some of the advantages and disadvantages of the cost / benefit analysis method can be stated as following:

Advantages

- Easy to calculate and understand.
- Good rough indicator for preliminary investment screening.
- Measures cash recoverability.

Disadvantages

- Does not properly recognize the time value of money.

- Limited capability to compare and rank.
- Does not consider variation in future gains.

Another technique, called the payback method, calculates the time it will take for a new investment to pay for itself. The formula for calculating it is relatively simple and straightforward:

$$\text{Payback period} = \frac{\text{Original net investment}}{\text{Annual earnings after tax} + \text{depreciation}}$$

The three parts of the equation needed to calculate the payback period is the original net investment, annual earnings after tax, and the depreciation.

Figure 15-2 shows the basic spreadsheet needed to determine the input for the payback period. The gross investment is the complete sum of all anticipated costs. It includes the cost of the software, related hardware, consulting and training services, licensing fees, and other costs.

The net investment simply considers any deduction that must be made for salvageable hardware or materials.

The determination of annual depreciation costs takes the net investment to be depreciated divided by the life expectancy of the system. ERP life expectancies can range from three to 15 years, with an average between five and seven years.

The savings and benefits of a new ERP system are all the labor dollars saved and increased gains in computer and operational efficiency.

The gross cash savings less cash tax expenses considers the deductions for the tax expenses for the labor savings.

Figure 15-2 Payback Method	
Gross Investment	
Cost of ERP software	$1,350,000
Cost of new computer hardware	$50,000
Cost of consulting and training services	$1,555,000
Total gross investment	**$2,955,000**
Net Investment	
Gross investment	$2,955,000
Salvage value of old systems	$10,000
Total net income	**$2,945,000**
Determination of Annual Depreciation Costs	
Gross investment	$2,955,000
Less salvage value	$10,000
Net investment to be depreciated	$2,945,000
Expected life of system	5 years
Annual depreciation = ($2,955,000 / 5)	**$589,000**
Savings and benefits of new ERP system (annual)	
Elimination of four full time positions	$160,000
Elimination of three temp clerical positions	$60,000
Increased operational efficiency	$120,000
Total savings and benefits	**$340,000**
Gross cash savings less cash tax expense (cash flow)	
Gross cash labor savings	$340,000
Less cash tax expense	$112,000
Annual earning after tax	**$228,000**

Going back to our original payback period formula in transferring the appropriate numbers from our spreadsheet from figure 15-2, we are able to calculate the payback period.

$$\text{Payback period} = \frac{\text{Original net investment}}{\text{Annual earnings after tax + depreciation}}$$

$$\text{Payback period} = \frac{\$2{,}945{,}000}{\$228{,}000 + \$589{,}000}$$

$$\text{Payback period} = 3.6 \text{ Years}$$

The final figure comes out to a relatively attractive (for ERP systems) 3.6 years. Using simple spreadsheets, investment decision-makers can perform a variety of 'what if' situations that can affect the outcome. For example: what would the payback period be if only two full-time jobs were eliminated and an additional $325,000 had to be paid for software licensing fees?

Some of the advantages and disadvantages of the payback method can be stated as follows:

Advantages

- Easy to calculate and understand.
- Good rough indicator for preliminary investment screening.
- Measures cash recoverability.
- The use of time series can help evaluate investment for risk.
- Places emphasis on earlier cash flows.

Disadvantages

- Does not properly recognize the time value of money.
- No recognition of benefits of earnings after investment has been repaid.
- Limited capability to compare and rank alternative investments.

The return on investment ratio method is another simple way for ERP investment decision-makers to measure a return on investment. The formula is based on net savings or earnings after depreciation and tax costs divided by the total net investment as shown in the following equation:

$$\text{ROI} = \frac{\text{Net savings after depreciation and tax}}{\text{Net Investment}}$$

By returning to figure 15-2 we can obtain the necessary information to complete the formula:

$$\text{ROI} = \frac{\$228{,}000}{\$2{,}945{,}000}$$

$$\text{ROI} = 7.7\%$$

Some of the advantages and disadvantages of the ROI ratio can be stated as follows:

Advantages

- Recognizes accounting profit and loss effect of investment.

- It is consistent and relates well to accounting data.
- Easy to calculate.

Disadvantages

- No capability to recognize the time value of money.
- Assumes the benefits of the investment last for the depreciable life of the asset.
- Does not weigh the amounts or timing of cash flows.

The present value technique considers the present and future value of money. The difference between the present value methods and accounting and payback methods is that the present value technique takes into account the time value of money. Because the present value method takes into account the value of money in relation to time, the expenses and benefits must be identified by time.

Some of the advantages and disadvantages of the present value method can be stated as follows:

Advantages

- Properly recognizes the time value of money.
- It gives weight to both timing and amounts of cash flows.
- Handles ranking and comparison of investment projects.

Disadvantages

- More difficult to calculate and learn.

- Does not merge well with accounting principles regarding profit and loss effects.
- Assumes money can be reinvested at the same rate of return to discount the project.

Questions--

1. What does ROI stand for?
2. What is ROI used for?
3. What are some factors that make ROI unreliable?
4. What is a cost / benefit analysis?
5. What are some advantages of the cost / benefit analysis?
6. What are two fundamental considerations to consider during ROI calculations?
7. What are some advantages to the payback period method?
8. What is the formula for the payback period?
9. What is the accounting method?
10. What are some disadvantages of the accounting method?
11. What is the difference between the present value method and others?
12. What are some disadvantages of using the present value method?

ERP: like a vast network of plumbing. Integration is the pipeline and information is the fluid. Forever flowing in many directions...

16

Integration and Relationships

Integration is essential to an ERP system to achieve the functionality for which it was designed. The amount of integration in an ERP system can be somewhat staggering for newcomers and seasoned practitioners as well. This chapter examines the relationships between various functional modules that make up an ERP system.

Figure 16-1 ERP Concept Triangle

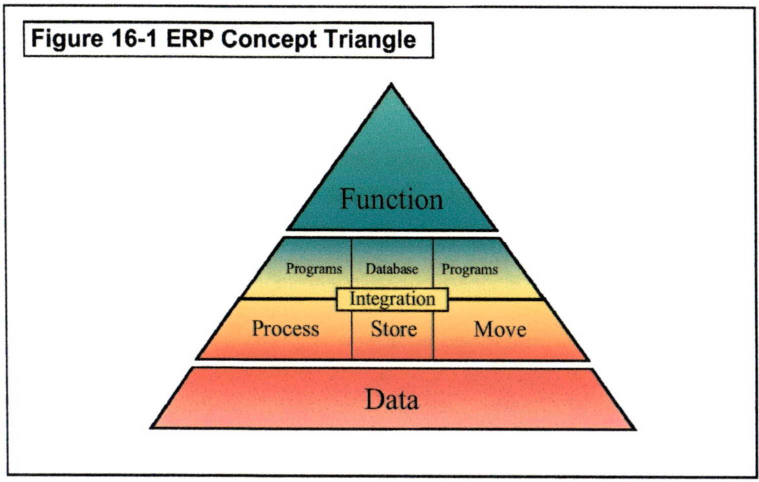

The amount of integration that exists between two different functional modules in an ERP system varies considerably from module to module. Some modules have extremely strong integration between them, while others have no integration between them. The integration between programs and the database provides functionality in an ERP system as shown in figure 16-1.

Integration is achieved through interfaces in an ERP system. Integration is an important foundation characteristic of an ERP system. Through the use of integration, ERP systems achieve communication, therefore bringing functionality to an ERP system. Integration is achieved through a variety of interfacing techniques including, communication protocols, software, Internet, workflows, etc. Integration can be thought of as bringing together two different systems (or modules) so that they act as one.

Interface is the communication process between two different points. Interfaces exist at multiple levels, between functional modules of an ERP system, computer platforms, and different software packages. Interfaces use a variety of communication technologies to exchange information between two points. Interfaces directly support integration of an ERP system. An interface can be thought of as two devices with a connector between them.

It can be very difficult to make hard coded software changes on highly integrated systems. Because of the deep integration, one little change can create an entire chain reaction of unforeseen side effects that are sometimes not all detected until years afterwards. The effect can be something like dropping a ping-pong ball into a room full of mousetraps. This is one reason why some ERP vendors are very slow to change functionality in their core software and why software modifications are not recommended except when necessary.

Integration exists on several different levels. The type of integration will be based upon the desired functionality of the modules. Some different types of integration include:

- Primary
- Workflow
- Independent functional
- Complementary

Primary integration is the integration that is provided directly by the ERP vendor between two functional modules. It is hard coded and built directly into the software. An example of primary integration may include a sales order entry screen where an ERP user presses on a function key on top of a part number field to drill down into a search window that allows the selection of the correct part number. The search window integrates with the inventory item master. By selecting one part number the ERP user can pull it back directly into the sales order. Generally speaking, because it is hard coded, there is usually limited flexibility in changing primary integration. Usually, ERP users will simply choose to use it or not.

Figure 16-2 Workflow Integration

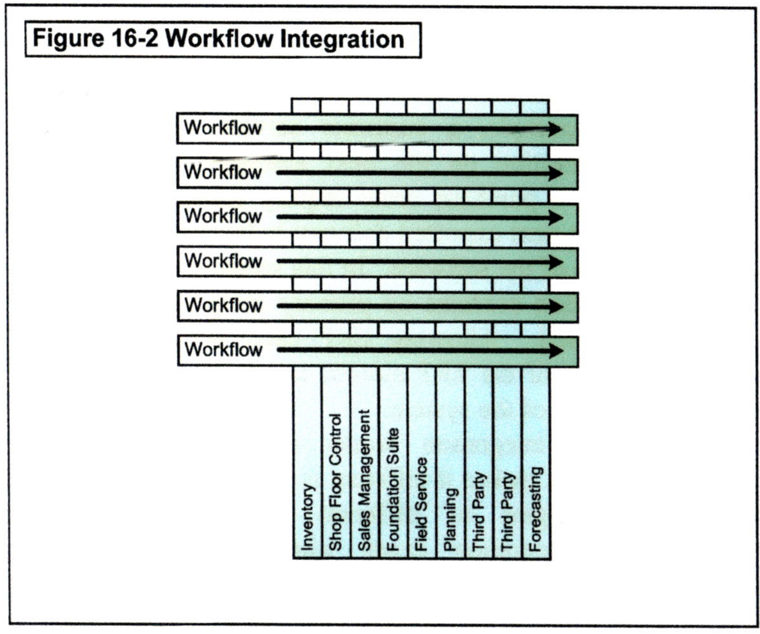

A trait of primary integration is that both the sending and receiving programs are developed using the same consistent patterns and standards, such as using a case tool. Integration is not always between two different programs, in many cases it will live between programs and the database.

Workflow integration can cross several functional modules to combine functional activities into one process flow. It is used to combine a variety of activities, features, and functions into a certain sequence providing function in itself. Some types of workflow use primary integration to lock business process flows into an unchangeable pattern. Many other types of workflow are highly flexible in nature and can be programmed using conditional operators. Workflow may also be specific to a module or specific documents. Different types of documents that often contain workflow include: sales orders, purchase orders, work orders, etc. Figure 16-2 shows how the process of workflow can cross many different functional modules.

Independent functional integration is based upon the principal of ERP users belonging to a functional area of the business using functional software from a different area of the business. For example, a customer service representative looking for information on the next available shipment of material may use a purchase order inquiry screen to get the latest details of the next expected delivery independently of any integrated features of the software. In this scenario independent functional integration contains no primary integration; or if it does, it is not used. Allowing ERP users access to other functional modules of the ERP system can greatly expand the overall functionality of the system.

Complementary integration works similarly to primary integration; but what makes it different is how the integration is established in origins of different functional modules. Complementary integration exists when a pre-established communication channel conducts information or data from one functional module to another module that is of a different origin by design. For example, a company may want to expand its overall ERP system functionality by the addition of a bar coding system. The bar coding system is not part of the original ERP system. The bar coding system is provided by a third party provider. The development methods used for the bar coding system were much different than those used for the ERP system. Simply by looking at the source code of the ERP system and the bar coding system, one could see that they were developed using different methodologies even if they used the same programming language. In complementary integration, interfaces are pre-established, meaning that they require no further development by the company that purchases them. The software is installed and with a few adjustments communication can begin between the third party system in the ERP system.

Figure 16-3 Integration

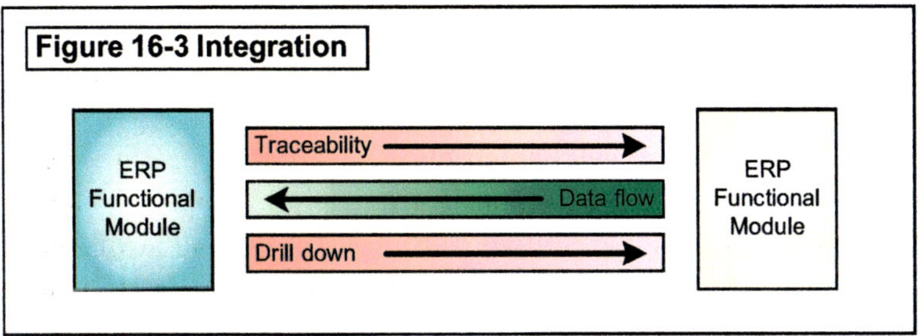

An integration relationship matrix is shown in figure 16-4. It shows the level of integration and relationship structure between different functional modules of an ERP system. It represents many of the more popular ERP functional modules. The matrix is not totally complete in nature, for some ERP systems have more than 75 functional modules. It is representative of the need for integration between modules. Some ERP systems, which are lacking integration, would not achieve the same scores as found in figure 16-4. The integrating relationships shown are largely based upon primary integration. Modules that are highly integrated with each other receive higher scores than those with a small or weak level of integration. Data flow between integrated modules in an ERP system tends to be in more than one direction.

Figure 16-4 Integration Relationship Matrix

0-3: Little to no integration **4-6**: Drill down, auxiliary relationship **7-9**: Drill down, data is transferred, primary relationship	Address Book	Accounts Payable	Accounts Receivable	General Ledger	Payroll	Human Resources	Fixed Assets	Forecasting	MPS	Finite Scheduling	MRP	DRP	CRP	Bills of Materials	Product Routings	Project Management	Inventory Management	Barcoding	Warehouse Man.	Customer Ser. Man.	Configuration Man.	Supplier Management	Work Order Man	ECO	Preventative Manten.	Transportation Man	Field Service	Report Writer
Address Book		9	9	7	9	9	2	9	0	3	0	5	0	0	0	6	5	4	5	8	0	8	8	7	3	8	8	9
Accounts Payable			5	9	0	1	1	0	0	0	0	1	0	0	0	3	0	0	2	2	0	9	5	0	5	6	2	9
Accounts Receivable				9	2	0	0	0	0	0	0	1	0	0	0	3	0	0	2	9	0	2	1	0	0	2	5	9
General Ledger					9	1	9	0	0	0	0	1	0	0	0	0	9	3	2	3	0	3	9	0	2	2	5	9
Payroll						9	0	0	0	0	0	0	0	0	0	0	0	2	0	0	0	0	9	0	0	0	0	9
Human Resources							0	0	0	0	0	0	0	0	0	0	0	0	0	0	0	0	3	0	0	0	0	9
Fixed Assets								0	0	0	0	0	0	0	0	1	5	0	0	5	0	0	0	0	8	0	5	9
Forecasting									9	5	7	9	3	9	0	0	9	0	0	9	0	5	2	0	0	2	7	9
MPS										9	9	9	8	7	2	2	9	0	2	9	4	4	9	9	0	4	2	9
Finite Scheduling											9	7	9	9	9	0	9	0	1	9	0	2	9	9	0	4	2	9
MRP												9	9	9	0	1	9	0	0	9	2	9	9	9	1	4	1	9
DRP													2	9	0	0	9	0	2	9	0	9	2	9	2	6	9	9
CRP														0	9	2	0	0	0	2	3	7	9	9	7	0	9	9
Bills of Materials															9	0	9	0	2	7	2	7	9	9	3	0	9	9
Product Routings																1	9	2	0	0	2	6	9	9	2	0	1	9
Project Management																	2	0	0	2	0	2	5	0	0	0	3	9
Inventory Man.																		9	9	9	9	9	9	9	9	7	9	9
Barcoding																			7	6	0	6	6	2	5	5	5	9
Warehouse Man.																				9	0	9	9	2	3	6	1	9
Customer Ser. Man.																					9	9	9	5	2	9	9	9
Configuration Man.																						0	9	8	1	0	6	9
Supplier Management																							9	5	3	4	3	9
Work Order Man																								9	7	5	9	9
ECO																									0	2	7	9
Preventative Mainten.																										0	7	9
Transportation Man																											2	9
Field Service																												9
Report Writer																												

In well-integrated systems, traceability and drill down functions allow ERP users to drill back to the source of data. Two ERP modules that are integrated, supported by an interface that communicates in both directions, is known as a bi-directional interface, or bi-directional integration. Bi-directional integration is common between many ERP modules. However, the majority of the data flow generally tends to be from one module to another.

The following paragraphs examine the strong relationships between ERP modules that have received scores of seven or higher in figure 16-4.

ERP Module	Data Flow	ERP Module
All ERP Modules	→ Drill Down ←	Report Writer

Report writers, sometimes called report generators, can interface with almost all ERP modules. General report writers allow ERP users to specify specific files that are associated with a particular ERP module. The capability to specify any file gives great flexibility in determining the output of a report. Other report writers are hard coded to operate only one or several specified files. Hard coded report writers contain less flexibility. Some report writers have the capability to drill down back to the source data. This can be particularly helpful when the ERP user not only wants to view the total records, but also the detail behind those total records. This of course, is done on screen, working as a print preview, before the report is actually printed out.

ERP Module	Data Flow	ERP Module
	→	
Address Book	Drill Down	Accounts Payable
	←	

Data flows from the address book to various accounts payable functions. Sometimes the address book is separated into what is called the supplier master. The supplier master contains key information on how payment should be processed for that particular vendor. Vouchers can be entered in accounts payable pulling default information directly from the address book or supplier master. Some of the default information includes customer number, payment terms, pay to addresses, and more. Drill down capability allows ERP users to drill down into the address book, giving them the capability to select vendors and new default information.

ERP Module	Data Flow	ERP Module
	→	
Address Book	Drill Down	Accounts Receivable
	←	

Accounts receivable receives information from the address book somewhat similarly to accounts payable except that the difference is based upon customers instead of suppliers. Just as with accounts payable, a certain section of the address book may be partitioned and called the customer master. The customer master will contain default information about the customer and how to process invoices for payment to the company. Default information will include bill to information, payment terms, customer number, and more. Drill down capability allows ERP users to drill down into the address book, allowing them to select customers when trading invoices.

Sometimes a system will do this automatically from the sales order module.

ERP Module	Data Flow	ERP Module
Address Book	→	Payroll
	Drill Down	
	←	

Payroll receives information from the address book for employee information. Information that will travel from the address book to payroll includes employee name, employee number, employee address, employee phone number, etc. Additional information may be buried in the address book in the area known as the employee master. Some systems place this in the address book and other systems will create a separate file. Employee master information can be built by directly drilling down into the address book going back to the employee ID and relevant information. Employee master information may include Social Security number, tax area, marital status, salary, etc.

ERP Module	Data Flow	ERP Module
Address Book	→	Human Resources
	Drill Down	
	←	

Just as with payroll, human resources uses the address book to pull in default information. Human resources may also interact strongly with the employee master file just as it did with payroll. A wide variety of functions can interact with the address book. Almost any function that needs to use an employee ID number can interact with the address book or employee master. Some common functions in human resource management that use drill down capability into the address book include benefits, employee history, wage administration, health and safety data, employee turnover, job specifications, etc.

ERP Module	Data Flow	ERP Module
Address Book	→	Forecasting
	Drill Down	
	←	

Address book information flows to the forecasting files through a variety of techniques. A key piece of information is customer ID number. Forecasts that contain the customer ID numbers allow ERP users to do forecasting by customers. Information may be drawn from the address book and directly through sales order management. Some forecasting systems will examine the sales order history and generate forecasting, including customer ID number, into the forecast file. The ID number obtained in the sales order history files comes directly from the address book. Some forecasting systems will allow ERP users to load forecast manually by customer ID number using drill down capability.

ERP Module	Data Flow	ERP Module
Address Book	→	Customer Service Management
	Drill Down	
	←	

Address book information is used in a wide variety of ways in customer service management. The primary flow of information is from the address book to customer service functions. Of key importance is the customer ID number. This is used on a variety of inquiry screens as well as for placing customer orders. Upon placing the customer order, drill down capability allows ERP users to select the correct customer ID. Basic information that is transferred from the address book to the sales order includes customer ID, name, address, classification codes, billing instructions, special notes, etc.

ERP Module	Data Flow	ERP Module
Address Book	→ Drill Down ←	Supplier Management

Address book information is used in a wide variety of ways in supplier management. The primary flow of information is from the address book to supplier management functions. Of key importance is the supplier ID number. This is used on a variety of inquiry screens as well as for placing purchase orders. Upon placing the purchase order, drill down capability allows ERP users to select the correct supplier ID. Basic information that is transferred from the address book to the purchase order includes supplier ID, name, address, classification codes, payment instructions, special notes, etc.

ERP Module	Data Flow	ERP Module
Address Book	→ Drill Down ←	Work Order Management

Work order management draws data from the address book for a variety of purposes. In some systems, work orders are directly connected to sales orders. The connection between sales orders and work orders provides the needed information on whom the work order is for. This is done by pulling in the customer ID number that comes into the sales order, which in turn got it from the address book. Work orders also use the address book for employee ID numbers. Some companies choose to organize their work orders by planner or supervisor numbers, which are the same thing as employee ID numbers. Production reporting for work orders also uses address book information. Some companies report production by employee number. Using error-checking logic, the system checks the address book to determine if the employee ID number is a valid number. Address book numbers come in automatically to work orders, with drill down capabilities, or manually.

ERP Module	Data Flow	ERP Module
Address Book	→	ECO
	Drill Down	
	←	

Engineering change orders (ECOs) function similarly to work orders. Some companies choose to organize engineering change orders by people responsible for managing them or by their originators. This information is usually specified manually through drill down capability into the address book. Employee ID numbers are further used in approval processing. Approval processing takes the ECO and routes it to several employees seeking their approval. Upon approval the ECO is implemented causing updates to develop materials and routings. Approval processing templates are usually set up ahead of time and attached to the ECO as they are requested. The majority of address book information comes in through drill down capability.

ERP Module	Data Flow	ERP Module
Address Book	→	Transportation Management
	Drill Down	
	←	

Transportation management may obtain address book information for carriers. Carrier ID numbers may be pulled directly into transportation management documents that specify transportation carriers. Information may also be obtained manually through drill down capability.

ERP Module	Data Flow	ERP Module
Address Book	→	Field Service
	Drill Down	
	←	

Field service uses the address book through a variety of ways using several different modules. Field service makes active use of work orders, call service management, customer sales orders, and maintenance management. Some functionality, such as scheduling of technicians in the field, may use the address book directly.

ERP Module	Data Flow	ERP Module
Accounts Payable	→	General Ledger
	Drill Down	
	←	

A variety of information flows from the accounts payable module to the general ledger. Some kinds of information include: account ID, document numbers, division ID's, transaction dates, amounts, and sometimes address numbers. Good integration brings drill down capability from the general ledger back to accounts payable. Navigating into one account, ERP users should have the capability to drill down back into accounts payable detail to learn more about the on hand balances and how they have evolved.

ERP Module	Data Flow	ERP Module
Accounts Payable	←	Supplier Management
	Drill Down	
	→	

The relationship between accounts payable and supplier management is very strong. The primary flow of information is from purchase orders to the accounts payable module. A variety of information flows from supplier management including: document numbers, addresses, supplier IDs, dates, and dollar amounts. Drill down capability exists from the accounts payable ledger back to purchase order details. This allows ERP users to understand from where specific payment commitments are coming. The integration between accounts payable and purchasing is important to any ERP system in companies that purchase any type of material or service.

ERP Module	Data Flow	ERP Module
Accounts Receivable	→	General Ledger
	Drill Down	
	←	

Accounts receivable passes many different types of information to the general ledger. Some key pieces of information that are typical include: account ID's, document numbers, division numbers, transaction dates, and dollars. Drill down capability from the general ledger allows ERP users to drill back into the accounts receivable module to identify from where dollars and transactions have come in creating the totals found in the general ledger.

ERP Module	Data Flow	ERP Module
Accounts Receivable	→	Customer Service Management
	Drill Down	
	←	

A strong relationship exists between the accounts receivable module and the customer service management module. The key relationship comes with the sales orders that are entered in the system. As sales orders are entered into the system, the accounts receivable module receives many different types of information from the sales order, including: document, address number, invoice dates, transaction dates, and dollar amounts. Drill down capability allows ERP users to drill back into the sales order itself to understand from where dollars and balances found in accounts receivable are coming.

ERP Module	Data Flow	ERP Module
General Ledger	←	Payroll
	Drill Down	
	→	

The payroll module sends data to the general ledger. A variety of information is generated during payroll processing to be sent to the general ledger. Some of this information includes account numbers, dates, dollars, and more. Good integration will have drill down capability from the general ledger back to payroll processing so that ERP users can understand from where the balances were generated.

ERP Module	Data Flow	ERP Module
General Ledger	← Drill Down →	Fixed Assets

Fixed assets passes depreciation amounts to the general ledger. Fixed assets are depreciated over time using predefined rules. Every year assets will depreciate a certain degree allowing the value of that asset to be reduced by the amount of its depreciation. Some ERP software systems will automatically generate the depreciation amount based upon the depreciation rules and the type of assets. Once the depreciation amount is known, then journal entries can be made and passed to the general ledger for update in the balances. Drill down capability should exist with good integration, allowing ERP users to understand where the on hand balances in the general ledger came from as it relates to the fixed assets.

ERP Module	Data Flow	ERP Module
General Ledger	← Drill Down →	Inventory Management

The general ledger receives inventory transaction information translated into financial dollars through journal entries. The information flows from the inventory management module to the general ledger. What creates the initial data flow are inventory transactions. Inventory transactions are based upon several different inventory management transaction techniques including: issues, transfers, cost adjustments, and reclassifications. All of this activity translates into financial activity. This activity is captured through journal entries and then eventually sent to the general ledger. Good integration allows ERP users in the general ledger to drill back down through journal entries into the inventory management module, allowing them to see the transactions that took place contributing to the balances found in the general ledger. Information that is sent to the general ledger from the inventory management module includes dollars, dates, and document numbers.

ERP Module	Data Flow	ERP Module
Payroll	↔	Human Resources
	Drill Down	
	↔	

Payroll and human resources have tight integration in that data flow and drill down capabilities are bi-directional, meaning that a large bulk of the information flows both ways. In some ERP systems, the payroll system and the human resource management function are so tightly integrated that they exist as one module. In other systems they contain tight integration that is still technically classified as separate modules that use integration to communicate with each other. An example of how human resource management sends data to the payroll system is for new job openings. New job openings often contain information regarding the wage rates, hours, and other compensation. This information will exist as a document in the human resource management module until the person is hired, at which time information will then be transferred to the payroll module, along with the employee ID and relevant information to begin the payroll cycle. An example of how information is transferred from the payroll module to the human resource management module is for attendance and time keeping. The payroll module must track specific hours in days that people work so those payroll amounts can be calculated with proper deductions. When time cards show that a person is sick or absent, that information is accumulated in the payroll module and sent to the human resource management module for further evaluation and monitoring. Drill down capability exists from both modules.

<table>
<tr><th>ERP Module</th><th>Data Flow</th><th>ERP Module</th></tr>
<tr><td rowspan="3">Work Order Management</td><td>→</td><td rowspan="3">Payroll</td></tr>
<tr><td>Drill Down</td></tr>
<tr><td>←</td></tr>
</table>

The work order management module sends information to the payroll module. Some companies use their work order management module to track time and attendance for their employees. By doing this they can also track the amount of time that employees spend working on certain jobs for the company. Another reason for using the work order management module is for piece rate bonuses. Piece rate bonuses are productivity incentives for workforces for meeting productivity goals. Based upon predefined rules, workers may receive bonuses for meeting productivity targets plus additional bonuses, sometimes, for work done above and beyond the productivity goals. Good integration will allow ERP users in the payroll module to drill back down into the work order management module to locate specific time and attendance entries for specific work orders. The work orders will be linked through journal entries to the payroll module. Some productivity bonuses are based on pieces instead of hours worked. When based on pieces, the concept of bonuses still remains the same.

ERP Module	Data Flow	ERP Module
Fixed Assets	→ Drill Down ←	Preventive Maintenance

Preventive maintenance receives information from the fixed assets master for determining what types of equipment need maintenance and schedules. The fixed assets master serves as a listing of all capital assets that a company owns. They are usually expensive in nature and require some type of attention. Drill down capability should exist in the preventive maintenance module that allows ERP users to drill back down into the fixed assets master to review specific details about the fixed assets and any specific notes.

ERP Module	Data Flow	ERP Module
Forecasting	→ Drill Down ←	MPS

Forecasting can provide large amounts of data for the MPS module. Forecasting data, containing part numbers, dates, and quantity flow directly to the MPS for further processing. The MPS will examine the total demand found in the forecast file and perform calculations based upon planning parameters and on hand inventory. Good integration will have drill down capability from the MPS to the forecasting file. In situations where finite scheduling is performing as the master production schedule, it will play a similar role, taking the place of MPS.

ERP Module	Data Flow	ERP Module
Forecasting	→	MRP
	Drill Down	
	←	

Conceptually speaking, integration between forecasting and MRP is similar as between forecasting and MPS. In many cases, the same source code is used to perform the integration. The difference comes in what level of the product structure, as defined by the bills of material the demand enters in to. Forecasting at the MRP level usually includes service and spare part components or independent demand. Data flow is from the forecasting file to MRP with drill down capability running from MRP to forecasting. For most companies the relationship between forecasting in MRP is much weaker than forecasting and MPS.

ERP Module	Data Flow	ERP Module
Forecasting	→	DRP
	Drill Down	
	←	

Forecasting can provide large amounts of data for the distribution requirements planning (DRP) module. Forecasting data, containing part numbers, dates, and quantity, flow directly to DRP for further processing. DRP will examine the total demand found in the forecast file and perform calculations based upon planning parameters and on hand inventory. The DRP module can connect many different geographical locations for management of the supply chain. The information that flows from forecasting into DRP helps provide higher levels of customer service for anticipated demand of inventory items. Good integration will have drill down capability from the DRP to the forecasting file.

ERP Module	Data Flow	ERP Module
Forecasting	←	Bills of Material
	Drill Down	
	→	

Bills of material (or planning bills) are used in forecasting for the management of families and groups of inventory items. Planning bills of material are set up with a parent item and several children. Each of the children contains a certain planning percentage. The planning percentages for all children will add up to 100 percent. When the forecast is created, programs examine the forecast demand and explode through the planning bill of material. This will give the forecast for all of the children of that family or parent item. The data flow is from the planning bill of material to the forecast generation program. The forecast generation program uses the planning bill primarily as a parameter input for calculating the total forecast demand for the children. Good integration will have drill down capability from the forecasting file back into the planning bills of material so that ERP users will be able to understand how forecasting quantities were calculated.

ERP Module	Data Flow	ERP Module
Forecasting	←	Inventory Management
	Drill Down	
	→	

Forecasting integrates with the item master found in the inventory management module. Data is transferred from inventory management to forecasting files in the form of part numbers and descriptions. Validation processes may take place inside forecasting to insure that part numbers are correct when people enter them manually. In addition, some systems use the item master to code and classify the parts into groups and families. Some forecasting systems will take these codes and classifications to create families that contain aggregate forecast of all the parts that make up that code or classification. Drill down capability usually exists in the form of search windows that allow ERP users to search for part numbers based upon text description or classification codes.

ERP Module	Data Flow	ERP Module
Forecasting	←	Customer Service Management
	Drill Down	
	→	

Forecasting plays a strong role in the integration of customer service management. Large amounts of data flow from customer service management into the forecasting file through forecasting generation procedures. Forecast modules examine the past historical demand of inventory items and customers and based upon that demand, generate a forecast using one of several different forecasting techniques. These forecasts then help to plan future customer demand, providing higher levels of customer service. Information also flows from forecasting to customer service management on an inquiry basis. Certain customer service representatives may inquire on the forecast to help provide information on future product availability. Good integration will allow automated methods of the transfer of historical demand into the forecasting file using one of several different forecasting generation techniques. Customer service representatives also have capability to drill down into the forecasting file to see further details.

ERP Module	Data Flow	ERP Module
Forecasting	← Drill Down →	Field Service

The integration between forecasting and field service is similar to that found between forecasting and customer service management. Field service often uses inventory items that come from all different levels of the bill of material. The nature of demand created by field service is independent. For this reason forecasting systems need to be aware of this additional demand in order to generate a complete forecast. Field service often uses sales orders, found in customer service management, to provide the sales to customers. The sales orders will then feed back into the forecasting process as historical demand. The integration through sales orders to the forecasting file provides an indirect method of integration that avoids the duplication of additional source code development for the ERP vendors. Good integration will have drill down capability from the forecasting file back to field service sales orders that show original demand.

ERP Module	Data Flow	ERP Module
MPS	→ Drill Down ←	Finite Scheduling

Integration between the MPS (master production schedule) and finite scheduling varies from situation to situation. In some ERP systems the MPS module and finite scheduling will be merged into one. In other ERP systems MPS and finite scheduling will remain distinctly separate modules. In these cases the primary information flow tends to be from the MPS to the finite scheduler. The finite scheduler will read the MPS and apply various rules to reschedule work orders. This is a common strategy used in complementary finite scheduling programs that serves to expand the functionality of core ERP functions. When existing as separate modules the data will flow from the MPS to the finite scheduling module. Good integration will allow drill down capability back to the MPS for traceability of activity occurring in the MPS.

<table>
<tr><th>ERP Module</th><th>Data Flow</th><th>ERP Module</th></tr>
<tr><td rowspan="3">MPS</td><td>→</td><td rowspan="3">MRP</td></tr>
<tr><td>Drill Down</td></tr>
<tr><td>←</td></tr>
</table>

MPS and MRP (material requirements planning) are strongly integrated with each other. Some ERP vendors, because of the strong integration needs, will develop MPS and MRP into a single module or program. Data flows from the MPS to the MRP module in the form of part numbers, dates, and quantities. MRP will then take this demand and explode it through the bill material, creating lower level demand for purchasing and other work orders. A formal industry recognized standard for drill down capability in MRP is known as pegging. Pegging provides ERP users the capability to drill down through MRP back to higher levels of demand found in the MPS. Using pegging, ERP users gain better understanding of how calculations were performed in MRP and the nature of the demand found in the MPS.

ERP Module	Data Flow	ERP Module
MPS	←→	DRP
	Drill Down	
	←→	

Integration between MPS and DRP (distribution requirements planning) accommodates highly intensive bi-directional data flows. DRP uses the MPS to identify sources of demand in distribution and manufacturing plants. DRP will take this demand and apply it to distribution rules that specify where to obtain product and in what quantities. MPS will use the DRP output in calculation of total requirements for inventory items in the MPS. DRP may be combined with sales orders, forecasting, and work orders to create the total demand found in the MPS. Drill down capability should exist in both directions to allow ERP users to understand the nature of demand, which is creating the output in MPS or DRP. The functionality of DRP and MPS is similar and many ERP vendors will use a single program to provide both DRP and MPS functionality.

ERP Module	Data Flow	ERP Module
MPS	→	CRP
	Drill Down	
	←→	

Integration between MPS and CRP (capacity requirements planning) provides key capacity planning capability for organizations. The CRP module obtains part numbers, dates, and quantities in the MPS. The information is then applied to product routings, which contain work centers and capacity consumption figures, for the total calculation of capacity consumption by time period. Information primarily flows from the MPS to CRP. Drill down capability is needed in both directions. In the CRP module, ERP users need to drill down back to the MPS to obtain further details on specific part numbers, dates, quantities, etc. In the MPS module, ERP users need to drill down into CRP to see capacity loads by work center to understand how certain part numbers may be affected by capacity constraints.

ERP Module	Data Flow	ERP Module
MPS	← Drill Down →	Bills of material

Bills of material play a needed role when companies operate their MPS by what is known as a multilevel MPS. A multilevel MPS has several master scheduled items existing at different levels in the bill of material. MPS obtains information from the bill of material to understand the structure and quantity per relationship of the children. By using this information MPS can calculate the correct requirements for lower level MPS items. Good integration will allow ERP users in the MPS module to drill back down to the bill of material for multilevel MPS items.

ERP Module	Data Flow	ERP Module
MPS	← Drill Down →	Inventory Management

Enhanced functionality is gained in MPS through integration of inventory management. MPS interfaces with inventory management in several different ways. One method is for obtaining on hand inventory for proper calculations and MPS. Another way is through integration to the item master. Some companies organize their MPS items into families or categories that allow ERP systems to generate a specific MPS for a product family. Specific planning parameters, such as order size, are usually stored in the inventory master. On hand inventory is usually displayed directly in the MPS module. However, because the MPS is usually static, drill down capability is needed into the inventory management module to find the current on hand quantities.

ERP Module	Data Flow	ERP Module
MPS	←→	Customer Service Management
	Drill Down	
	←→	

Integration between the MPS and customer service management is important for achieving good customer service for any manufacturing organization. The level of integration is thoroughly intensive because of the bi-directional data flow and bi-directional drill down needs. The MPS obtains specific demand oriented information; such as part numbers, dates, and quantities; for calculations and recommendations for appropriate production. Once the calculations are complete in MPS, information then flows back to customer service management for order fulfillment and promise deliveries. Generally speaking, data flow from the MPS back up to customer service management is a manual process facilitated by drill down capabilities. Of most interest to customer service representatives are specific quantities and dates of availability for part numbers. Good integration will allow an ERP user in the MPS module to drill back down to customer service management to locate specific sales orders, creating the demand in the MPS module.

ERP Module	Data Flow	ERP Module
MPS	←→ Drill Down ←→	Work Order Management

Communication and integration between MPS and work order management can be intensive in the need for bi-directional data flow and drill down capabilities. Data flows from the MPS into work order management for the creation of work orders based upon MPS output. Key pieces of information that work order management uses from the MPS for creating work orders are part number, dates, and quantities. Work orders are created for the purpose of fulfilling demand generated by the MPS. MPS obtains information from work orders for monitoring remaining balances and checking for out of balance situations in the supply chain. If a work order is not completed as expected, MPS may make a series of recommendations such as: expedite, increase quantity, defer, etc. ERP users operating in the MPS module need drill down capability for obtaining details on supply and work orders or work orders with problems. ERP users operating in the work order management module need drill down capability into the MPS to completely understand the source of demand, its dates, and quantities.

ERP Module	Data Flow	ERP Module
MPS	← Drill Down ←→	ECO

Integration between MPS (master production schedule) and ECO (engineering change order) is usually achieved through one or more modules that reside between the ECO module and the MPS module. The two modules that may help to bridge the integrating gap include work order management and bills of material. Depending upon the ERP system and the way that an organization uses it, information may flow from the ECO module to the bills of material and then to work order management, which then provides the information to the MPS. In other situations, the ECO will provide the information directly to work orders and bills of material at the same time. Both will then pass the information to MPS. Drill down capability provides ECO users information on anticipated production of items that may be affected by the ECO. Drill down capability from the MPS into the ECO provides MPS users with knowledge of open and future ECOs that may affect the MPS.

ERP Module	Data Flow	ERP Module
Finite Scheduling	← Drill Down →	Product Routings

Finite scheduling faces most of the same critical integration points as MPS with one important difference: product routings. Because of the nature of finite scheduling, which allows it to dynamically reschedule the MPS based on predefined rules and capacity limitations, it requires access to the routings, which provide work center and capacity consumption data. Using the information obtained from the product routings, finite scheduling may dynamically reschedule workloads based upon available capacity and capacity consumption rates established in the product routings. Drill down capability allows ERP users to obtain routing specific information from the finite scheduling module.

ERP Module	Data Flow	ERP Module
MRP	←	DRP
	Drill Down	
	↔	

MRP (material requirements planning) examines the output from DRP (distribution requirements planning) for calculation of total planned work orders and purchase orders. The calculations performed by MRP based upon the input from DRP will allow MRP to correctly calculate fulfillment requirements for regional distribution and manufacturing centers. Drill down capability allows ERP users in the MRP module to identify sources of demand that are arriving through DRP. ERP users working in the DRP module need capability to drill down into MRP to obtain supply information for their respective regional distribution or manufacturing center.

ERP Module	Data Flow	ERP Module
MRP	→	CRP
	Drill Down	
	↔	

Integration between MRP and CRP (capacity requirements planning) provides key capacity planning capability for organizations. The CRP module obtains part numbers, dates, and quantities from MRP. Information is then applied to product routings, which contain work centers and capacity consumption figures for the total calculation of capacity consumption by time period. Information primarily flows from MRP to CRP. Drill down capability is needed in both directions. In the CRP module, ERP users need to drill down back to the MRP to obtain further details on specific part numbers, dates, quantities etc. In the MRP module, ERP users need to drill down into CRP to see capacity loads by work center to understand how certain part numbers may be affected by capacity constraints.

ERP Module	Data Flow	ERP Module
MRP	← Drill Down →	Bills of material

The functionality of MRP is highly dependent upon bills of material. Without the integration between the two, MRP could not exist. MRP uses the bill material in an explosion process to determine the correct quantities and dates needed to support higher-level demand. It will make recommendations for work orders and purchase orders depending upon various planning parameters and the bill of material structure. Good integration will allow ERP users to drill down into the bill of material from MRP planning and execution screens. This allows MRP users to obtain product-structuring information that allows them to better understand output found in the MRP module.

ERP Module	Data Flow	ERP Module
MRP	← Drill Down →	Inventory Management

Enhanced functionality is gained in MRP through the integration of inventory management. MRP interfaces with inventory management in several different ways. One method is for obtaining on hand inventory for proper calculations in MRP. Another way is through integration to the item master. Some companies organize their MRP items into families or categories that allow ERP systems to generate a specific MRP for a product family. Specific planning parameters, such as order size, are usually stored in the inventory master. On hand inventory is usually displayed directly in the MRP module. But because the MRP is usually static, drill down capability is needed into the inventory management module to find the current on hand quantities.

ERP Module	Data Flow	ERP Module
MRP	↔ Drill Down ↔	Customer Service Management

Integration between MRP and customer service management is important for achieving good customer service for any manufacturing organization that sells lower level components for replacement or service. The level of integration is thoroughly intensive because of the bi-directional data flow and bi-directional drill down needs. The MRP obtains specific demand oriented information; such as part numbers, dates, and quantities; for calculations and recommendations for appropriate production or purchase. Once the calculations are complete in MRP, the information then flows back to customer service management for order fulfillment and promise deliveries. Generally speaking, data flow from MRP back up to customer service management is a manual process facilitated by drill down capabilities. Of most interest to customer service representatives are specific quantities and dates of availability for part numbers. Good integration will allow an ERP user in the MRP module to drill back down to customer service management to locate specific sales orders, creating the demand in the MRP module.

ERP Module	Data Flow	ERP Module
	←→	
MRP	Drill Down	Supplier Management
	←→	

The integration between MRP and supplier management provides enhanced functionality in supplier management functions, particularly for determining the amount of demand for calculation of purchase order quantities. Purchase orders may be generated directly from recommendations created by MRP. MRP passes critical information such as: quantity, part numbers, and dates. Using this information, purchase order documents are created and then released to various suppliers for fulfillment. Data flows from purchase orders back to MRP during MRP regeneration. Should the date or quantity of a purchase order be out of balance in the supply chain, MRP might recommend the necessary adjustments. MRP users need drill down capability to see sources of supply and supplier management. ERP users working in the supplier management module need drill down capability into MRP to understand sources of demand. As previously discussed, the drill down capability from supplier management into MRP is often referred to as pegging.

ERP Module	Data Flow	ERP Module
	←	
DRP	Drill Down	Bills of Material
	→	

Some ERP systems use bills of material as a relationship structure between various supply and demand plants. Other ERP systems use a similar approach, except they use a separate file and call it a bill of distribution. Whatever approach the ERP vendor uses, data will flow from the bills into the DRP module. This will happen during DRP generations. ERP systems first look for demand and then establish the supplier plants based upon the bill of material or bill of distribution. Thorough integration will allow ERP users to drill back into the bills so that relationships can be established, reviewed, or adjusted between supply and demand plants.

ERP Module	Data Flow	ERP Module
DRP	←	Inventory Management
	Drill Down	
	→	

Enhanced functionality is gained in DRP through integration of inventory management. DRP interfaces with inventory management in several different ways. One method is for obtaining on hand inventory for proper calculations in DRP. Another way is through integration to the item master. Some companies organize their DRP items into families or categories that allow ERP systems to generate a specific DRP for a product family. Specific planning parameters, such as order size, are usually stored in the inventory master. On hand inventory is usually displayed directly in the DRP module, or modules that interface with DRP. However, because the DRP is usually static, drill down capability is needed into the inventory management module to find the current on hand quantities.

ERP Module	Data Flow	ERP Module
DRP	←→	Customer Service Management
	Drill Down	
	←→	

Integration between the DRP and customer service management is important for achieving good customer service for any organization involved in the distribution of its products. The level of integration is thoroughly intensive because of the bi-directional data flow and drill down needs. The DRP obtains specific demand oriented information; such as part numbers, dates, and quantities; from sales orders for calculations and recommendations for appropriate requisition. Once the calculations are complete, DRP information then flows back to customer service management for order fulfillment and promise deliveries. Generally speaking, data flow from DRP back up to customer service management is a manual process facilitated by drill down capabilities. Of most interest to customer service representatives are specific quantities and dates of availability for part numbers. Good integration will allow an ERP user in the DRP module to drill back down to customer service management to locate specific sales orders creating the demand in the DRP module.

ERP Module	Data Flow	ERP Module
DRP	↔	Supplier Management
	Drill Down	
	↔	

The integration between DRP and supplier management provides enhanced functionality in supplier management functions, particularly for determining the amount of demand for calculation of purchase order quantities. Purchase orders may be generated directly from recommendations created by DRP. DRP passes critical information such as: quantity, part numbers, and dates. Using this information, purchase order documents are created and then released to various suppliers for fulfillment. Data flows from purchase orders back to DRP during DRP regeneration. Should the date or quantity of a purchase order be out of balance in the supply chain, DRP might recommend the necessary adjustments. DRP users need drill down capability to see sources of supply in the supplier management module. ERP users working in the supplier management module need drill down capability into DRP to understand sources of demand.

ERP Module	Data Flow	ERP Module
DRP	←	ECO
	Drill Down	
	↔	

Integration between DRP and ECO (engineering change order) is usually achieved through one or more modules that reside between the ECO module and the DRP module. The two modules that may help to provide the integrating gap are work order management and bills of material. Depending upon the ERP system and the way that an organization uses it, information may flow from the ECO module to the bills of material and then to work order management, which then provides the information to the DRP. In other situations the ECO will provide the information directly to work orders and bills of material at the same time which both will then pass the information to DRP. Drill down capability provides ECO users information on anticipated production of items that may be affected by the ECO. Drill down capability from the DRP into the ECO provides DRP users knowledge of open and future ECOs that may affect the DRP.

ERP Module	Data Flow	ERP Module
DRP	←	Field Service
	Drill Down	
	↔	

Field service integrates through the customer service management module into the DRP module. Customer service management is used for the tracking of shipments of field replacement parts. The customer service management module may also be used to receive returned components back into the system for repair or credit. DRP will recognize this return and add it to the future projected on hand inventory. Field service technicians need drill down capability into DRP to obtain availability information for service and replacement parts. ERP users working in DRP need drill down capability into field service to identify sources of demand.

ERP Module	Data Flow	ERP Module
	←	
CRP	Drill Down	Product Routings
	→	

CRP (capacity requirements planning) integrates tightly with product routings by obtaining part numbers, work centers, and capacity consumption rates for the calculation of total capacity used based on input from the product routings and MPS. Information flows from product routings to CRP for capacity calculations. ERP users working in the CRP module need drill down capability to understand product routing structures and how they affect CRP calculations.

ERP Module	Data Flow	ERP Module
	←	
CRP	Drill Down	Supplier Management
	→	

CRP is used in supplier management occasionally in a variety of ways. Some companies create product routings for purchase materials that instruct people on how to route received materials through the receiving area. The steps may include such events as packaging, inspection, and staging for put away. Creating product routings for receiving allows companies to plan capacity for critical areas such as expensive inspection equipment. Another way that companies use CRP and supplier management is to monitor their suppliers' capacity. Based upon the number of purchase orders and the type of products that the company is purchasing, companies can get a capacity load for their suppliers. People working in the CRP module need drill down capability into the supplier management module to identify upcoming purchase orders that will be received into the system or to help manage outside suppliers.

ERP Module	Data Flow	ERP Module
CRP	↔ Drill Down ↔	Work Order Management

CRP integrates tightly with work order management in its need to satisfy bi-directional data flow and drill down capabilities. During CRP generations the CRP module reads work orders with their corresponding attached product routings. These product routings on the work order serve as tracked import in calculating the total capacity needs of a work center. Data flows back up to the work order management module manually through the review of capacity loads in CRP. ERP users working in CRP may choose to reschedule work orders to a different time period with greater capacity availability. Users working with work order management need drill down capability into CRP for identifying workloads as they relate to particular work orders. Although there seems to be a significant need for effective capacity management, few companies use capacity requirements planning to manage their work orders.

<table>
<tr><th>ERP Module</th><th>Data Flow</th><th>ERP Module</th></tr>
<tr><td rowspan="3">CRP</td><td>←</td><td rowspan="3">ECO</td></tr>
<tr><td>Drill Down</td></tr>
<tr><td>↔</td></tr>
</table>

Capacity requirements planning interfaces with ECO indirectly through product routings. Engineering change orders that modify product routings can affect capacity requirements planning. The new configuration of the product routings is established in the engineering change order. Upon approval, the production routing is modified, having a direct impact on capacity requirements planning. Changes in product routings through engineering change orders can have a significant impact on the capacity requirements planning module. People managing engineering change orders need drill down capability into capacity requirements planning to see what work centers may be affected. People working in capacity requirements planning need drill down capability to identify which engineering change orders may be affecting the capacity in the future.

<table>
<tr><th>ERP Module</th><th>Data Flow</th><th>ERP Module</th></tr>
<tr><td rowspan="3">CRP</td><td>←</td><td rowspan="3">Preventative Maintenance</td></tr>
<tr><td>Drill Down</td></tr>
<tr><td>→</td></tr>
</table>

Capacity requirements planning needs information from preventive maintenance schedules in order to calculate realistic load conditions. Production equipment generally must stop production for routine maintenance. Preventive maintenance procedures can consume production at capacity. The use of integration capacity requirements planning can receive the schedules to adjust capacity consumption accordingly. ERP users working with capacity requirements planning need drill down capability to detect the portion of capacity that is consumed by preventive maintenance activities. Generally speaking, few companies have need, or use, this level of integration. Therefore many ERP vendors do not provide this integration.

ERP Module	Data Flow	ERP Module
CRP	← Drill Down →	Field Service

Integration between the CRP and field service can work similar to that of CRP and work order management. In fact, field service modules often use work order management tools for planning and execution of field service activities. The field service module may use capacity requirements planning for scheduling technicians that work in the field. By applying standards to routine maintenance jobs, capacity loads for technicians can be determined. The primary flow of data is from field service, often through work orders, to capacity requirements planning. Drill down capability allows CRP users to identify all the jobs and related details by technician.

ERP Module	Data Flow	ERP Module
Bills of Material	→ Drill Down ←	Product Routings

Some companies have the need to attach part numbers directly to routing operation steps found in the product routings. Through the use of integration, ERP users can drill down into the bill of material for the parent item specified in the product routings and select component parts on that bill of material.

This functionality is particularly helpful for facilitating work order reporting in manufacturing facilities that have large complex assemblies, such as automobiles, with long production lines.

ERP Module	Data Flow	ERP Module
Bills of Material	← Drill Down →	Inventory Management

Bills of material integrates with inventory management for two primary reasons: development speed and quality. Bills of material can be developed faster by using search and drill down techniques into inventory management. Quality is improved by the process of using validation against the item master for part numbers that are entered into a bill of material. Validation processes make sure that each and every part is a valid part number. Various fields from the item master may also default into the bill of material detail line.

ERP Module	Data Flow	ERP Module
Bills of Material	→ Drill Down ←	Customer Service Management

Customer service management sometimes takes advantage of integration with the bills of material for creating kits. Kits are standard packages of items that customers purchase. By using bills of material, parent child relationships can be established. This allows sales order entry personnel to enter in one parent item, which will then be used to retrieve the children from the kit bill of material. Drill down capability is needed from customer service management so customer service representatives can identify kit bill of material structures. In some systems, this can be done automatically upon entering the parent item for a kit bill of material.

ERP Module	Data Flow	ERP Module
Bills of Material	→	Supplier Management
	Drill Down	
	←	

Supplier management sometimes takes advantage of integration with the bills of material for creating kits. Kits are standard packages of items that are purchased from suppliers. By using bills of material, parent child relationships can be established. This allows purchase order entry personnel to enter in one parent item, which will then be used to retrieve the children from the kit bill of material. Drill down capability is needed from the supplier management module so purchasing agents can identify kit bill of material structures. In some systems, this can be done automatically upon entering the parent item for a kit bill of material.

ERP Module	Data Flow	ERP Module
Bills of Material	→	Work Order Management
	Drill Down	
	←	

Bills of material can be used extensively in work order management. Bills of material flow to work orders for the creation of parts lists. ERP users managing work orders may then choose to override certain part numbers on the parts lists to reflect current materials that will be used for the work order. Drill down from the work order management module into the bills of material can be helpful for ERP users to determine the standard configuration in which something is put together or manufactured. A variety of information is transferred from the bill of material to a work order. Some of this information includes parent part number, component part numbers, quantities, and issue codes.

ERP Module	Data Flow	ERP Module
Bills of Material	←	ECO
	Drill Down	
	←→	

ECO (engineering change order) integrates with bills of material by providing integrated change management updates to the bills of material. Engineering change orders are entered into the system with instructions regarding what bills of material need to be changed and how those changes should be performed. After the ECO has been approved, utility programs can then perform mass updates to the bill of material file. Drill down capability is needed from the ECO to determine the current configuration of the bill of material and drill down capabilities are needed from the bills of material into the ECOs so ERP users can find detailed information regarding changes that were made to the bill of material.

ERP Module	Data Flow	ERP Module
Bills of Material	→	Field Service
	Drill Down	
	←	

The field service module uses bills of material very similarly to the way that work order management uses bills of material. Field service functions often use standard work order systems of an ERP system. Field service technicians often have the need to look up bills of material to identify how specific machines or products are assembled.

ERP Module	Data Flow	ERP Module
Product Routings	← Drill Down →	Inventory Management

Product routings use integration to obtain part numbers from item masters in inventory management to validate good part numbers. Information flows from inventory management to product routings by ERP users using search windows and drill down techniques to pull back valid part numbers into the routing. Program logic, operating in the background, may validate part numbers against the item master to insure that they are valid.

ERP Module	Data Flow	ERP Module
Product Routings	→ Drill Down ←	Work Order Management

Product routings interface with work order management by transferring product routings directly to work orders through the use of integration. ERP users may then modify those product routings that have been attached to work orders to reflect changes. Specific types of information that are transferred from the product routings include: part numbers, work centers, machine times, man-hours, and sequence numbers. ERP users working with work order management need to have drill down capability to manually attach product routings to work orders. A variety of inquiry screens are also usually needed.

ERP Module	Data Flow	ERP Module
Product Routings	←	ECO
	Drill Down	
	↔	

Product routings have a direct interface with engineering change order management. Engineering change orders are entered into the system as documents. ERP users attach product routings to the engineering change order and specify the necessary changes to be conducted. After the engineering change order has been approved, mass updates can be performed throughout the system to update all product routings specified in the engineering change order. Good integration allows ERP users to inquire on product routings within the engineering change order module itself. ERP users also need drill down capability from product routings into ECOs to learn more about changes that have been performed to product routings. The primary data flow is from ECO to product routings; however, some systems may have data flow from product routings into the ECO, depending upon how product routings are adjusted or set up in an ECO.

ERP Module	Data Flow	ERP Module
Inventory Management	←	Barcoding
	Drill Down	
	←	

Barcoding systems have the need for strong integration with inventory management. Depending upon the technology used, barcoding systems can integrate with an ERP system much differently than the other functional modules of the ERP system. The majority of data flow between barcoding and inventory management consists of inventory transactions. These transactions contain basic information such as part numbers, quantities, locations, and costs. Sometimes this information is transferred immediately to the inventory management module. In other cases, where barcode scanners operate as stand alone units, the information is uploaded at a later period. Barcoding systems need drill down capability into inventory management for part number validation. Quite often the validation process takes place in batch mode after the uplink is performed. Only more sophisticated barcode systems with online inquiries can provide real-time validation processes.

<table>
<tr><th>ERP Module</th><th>Data Flow</th><th>ERP Module</th></tr>
<tr><td rowspan="3">Inventory Management</td><td>➔</td><td rowspan="3">Warehouse Management</td></tr>
<tr><td>Drill Down</td></tr>
<tr><td>🡐</td></tr>
</table>

Warehouse management uses inventory management for purposes of setup and validation. The primary need is for validation of part numbers and inventory locations. Program logic working in the background validates part numbers and locations. Should an error occur, the system might alert the user through a hard coded or soft coded error message. Classification codes may be used from the item master to organize warehouse items into logical groupings. Warehouse management personnel need drill down capability and search windows to help locate valid part numbers.

ERP Module	Data Flow	ERP Module
Inventory Management	→ Drill Down ←	Customer Service Management

Customer service management interfaces with inventory management primarily for saleable inventory items for sales orders. Inventory management may transfer a variety of information to sales orders, including: price, costs, part number, description, inventory location, and category codes. Customer service representatives need drill down capability and searchable windows for locating inventory items to place on sales order detail lines. Background program logic can provide the integrity checking of part numbers against the item master. This ensures that only valid part numbers are entered into sales orders.

ERP Module	Data Flow	ERP Module
Inventory Management	→ Drill Down ←	Configuration Management

Integration between inventory management and configuration management is primarily used for validation of part numbers and configuration management. Other information, related to the part number from the item master, may also be transferred, such as the part number description. Drill down capability with searchable windows is most helpful when specifying specific parts to use in configuration management.

ERP Module	Data Flow	ERP Module
Inventory Management	➔ Drill Down ←	Supplier Management

Inventory management provides several key pieces of information for use in supplier management for inventory items. Through integration, information may be transferred from the item master to purchase orders. Some of the information transferred may include part number, description, costs, primary supplier, and category codes. ERP users working in supplier management need drill down capability and search windows to locate inventory parts and pull them back into the purchase order.

ERP Module	Data Flow	ERP Module
Inventory Management	➔ Drill Down ←	Work Order Management

Integration between inventory management and work order management is provided through the transfer of information related to inventory items. Once work orders are entered into the system, for inventory items, several pieces of information may be transferred from the inventory master. These pieces of information include part number, description, address book numbers for supervisors and planners, and category codes. ERP users working within work order management need drill down capability into inventory management to select part numbers for work orders. Work orders also interface indirectly with inventory management through bills of material and product routings. Work order entry programs may also use validation processes for new part numbers that are entered into work orders. The work order program will validate the part number entered against the item master to ensure it is a good part number.

ERP Module	Data Flow	ERP Module
Inventory Management	↔ Drill Down ↔	ECO

The need for integration between inventory management and ECOs is strong because of its bi-directional data flow and drill down needs. People performing engineering change orders need drill down capability into inventory management in the form of searchable windows to allow the proper selection of inventory part numbers needed for change. By selecting one of the parts shown in the searchable windows, they can easily be returned to the engineering change order. After the engineering change order is approved, it may automatically perform updates to the item master. Some of these updates may include revision numbers, part number changes, text description changes, and category code changes. ERP users operating in inventory management need drill down capability to drill down into the ECO to find out additional details of why and how specific part numbers were changed.

ERP Module	Data Flow	ERP Module
Inventory Management	→ Drill Down ←	Preventative Maintenance

Preventive maintenance processes integrate with inventory management for inventory items that are carried in stock and identified in the item master. Preventive maintenance packages, or kits, may contain a series of parts and materials needed for maintenance of equipment. These kits may be created manually by using drill down capabilities into inventory management, selecting one part at a time, or the integration may exist indirectly by using a predefined kit similar to a bill of material.

ERP Module	Data Flow	ERP Module
Inventory Management	→ Drill Down ←	Transportation Management

The transportation management module has the need to integrate with the inventory management module to obtain transportation management related information. Some types of information that may be stored in the item masters or auxiliary files include palette configuration, weights, volumes, and default carriers. By examining documents from other areas of the system and obtaining information from the inventory management module, total weight in volume requirements can be obtained as well as potential carriers. The transportation management module needs drill down capability into inventory management to obtain transfer kit related information. The data primarily flows from inventory management to the transportation management module.

ERP Module	Data Flow	ERP Module
Inventory Management	→ Drill Down ←	Field Service

The need of field service to integrate with the inventory management module is similar to many other modules that integrate with inventory management; however, the technique may be different. Because field service people often work in the field far away from distribution and manufacturing centers, the need for Internet connectivity is higher for them than ERP users working in other modules. Field service technicians need drill down capability into inventory management modules to review characteristic information and notes related to field service. Field service technicians may place orders for parts and supplies through other modules. The primary flow of data is from inventory management to field service. This flow of data may go through other modules before arriving at the field service module. Field service often uses other modules for its needs. Some of these modules include preventive maintenance and sales orders.

<table>
<tr><th>ERP Module</th><th>Data Flow</th><th>ERP Module</th></tr>
<tr><td rowspan="3">Barcoding</td><td>→</td><td rowspan="3">Warehouse Management</td></tr>
<tr><td>Drill Down</td></tr>
<tr><td>←</td></tr>
</table>

Barcoding systems may interface with warehouse management for the purposes of transacting pull and put away requests. Through advanced functionality of warehouse management, material put away and pull lists can be optimized for the most efficient use of manpower. The completion of these pull and put away requests may be done through using barcoding systems. Within the warehouse management module, drill down capability is helpful for viewing barcoding transactions. Primary flow of data is from barcoding into warehouse management. Key pieces of information may include pick list number, date, time, user ID, and completed quantities. Many types of warehouse management functions are provided directly by inventory management techniques found in the inventory management module.

ERP Module	Data Flow	ERP Module
Warehouse Management	← Drill Down →	Customer Service Management

Warehouse management has a strong interface with customer service management because it provides a significant amount of information for warehouse management. Many times, ERP users working in warehouse management will generate a pick list based upon carriers. Sales orders found in customer service management provide part numbers, quantities, and carrier numbers. Drill down capability allows warehouse management personnel to obtain specific details for part numbers on sales orders. These specific details may include special shipping information, safety data sheets, or other special packaging instructions.

ERP Module	Data Flow	ERP Module
Warehouse Management	← Drill Down →	Supplier Management

Warehouse management interfaces with the supplier management module through purchase order receipts. Purchase order receipts generate the signal to produce a warehouse put up request. By consolidating all of the purchase order receipts, efficient put away techniques may be performed by warehouse personnel using generated outputs from the warehouse management system. Key pieces of information that are transferred from the PO receipt file to the warehouse management system include part numbers, quantities, PO numbers, and locations. Good integration allows drill down capability from warehouse management systems into supplier management programs such as inspection routing status and receipts status file.

ERP Module	Data Flow	ERP Module
Warehouse Management	←→ Drill Down ←→	Work Order Management

The integration between warehouse management and work order management can be a communication intensive process for some companies having large warehouses and manufacturing operations because of the need for bi-directional data flow and drill down capabilities. Manufacturing work orders that are ready to be released generate pick list requests, which are sent to the warehouse and consolidated with other pick lists to help increase efficiency and reduce overhead. Some key pieces of information that are transferred include part numbers, order number, quantities, and descriptions. After the order is picked, all of the materials (sometimes called a kit) are then transferred to a manufacturing location using inventory transfer programs driven by the original work order number. After the materials have been consumed in the manufacturing process, parent items, and sometimes subassemblies, are then recognized as completed on the work order, which generates a put away request for warehouse management. Warehouse management will recognize this put away request and consolidate it with other put away requests. Drill down capability is needed from work order management to identify the status of pick requests and fulfillment statuses. The warehouse management personnel need drill down capability to obtain more detailed information on work orders which are driving put away and pick requests.

ERP Module	Data Flow	ERP Module
Customer Service Management	← Drill Down →	Configuration Management

Customer service management has a strong integration with configuration management because configuration management helps configure sales orders, which are used in customer service management. Configuration management is the process of configuring customer sales orders based upon predefined rules, usually using inventory part numbers. Using a series of 'if then' conditional statements and boolean logic, rules are created which drive the configuration process. Configuration management is often used in the sale of complex capital equipment. A customer service representative may enter a sales order for a piece of equipment that requires configuration. Based upon predefined rules established in configuration management, the sales order will ask a series of questions which, when answered provide a configured sales order for the customer. The primary data flow is from configuration management to the sales orders. Key pieces of information transferred include part numbers, quantities, and prices. Drill down capability is usually provided automatically by the configuration process. Additional drill down capability that allows ERP users to drill down directly into the rules matrix established in configuration management allows for the quick dynamic configuration of rules that drive the configuration process.

ERP Module	Data Flow	ERP Module
Customer Service Management	↔	Supplier Management
	Drill Down	
	↔	

Customer service management and supplier management need strong integration with each other because of bi-directional data flow and drill down requirements. Strong integration between these two modules is needed more so for distribution types of environments. Customer service management, in some ERP systems, may dynamically generate a sales order based upon a purchase order from a demand plant that exists within the company. Customer service agents often need drill down capability into supplier management to identify future purchase orders that will deliver needed materials for customers. Large data flows occur between customer service management going to supplier management. ERP systems can automatically generate recommendations to purchase materials should on hand inventory not be enough to supply customer demand. Purchasing agents need drill down capability from supplier management into customer service management to see what customer orders are outstanding. Some ERP systems will automatically notify customer service representatives or warehouse personnel when the purchase order has been received to fulfill a customer order.

ERP Module	Data Flow	ERP Module
Customer Service Management	→	Work Order Management
	Drill Down	
	↔	

Enhanced customer service management can be achieved through the integration of work orders for manufacturing types of environments. ERP systems can generate work orders for sales orders either directly, or through another module such as MPS, based upon sales order detail lines. The connection of work orders to customer sales orders can provide traceability useful for ERP users working in either customer service management or work order management. Drill down capability into work order management is useful for customer service representatives. This gives them additional details on the work order, providing higher levels of customer service. Drill down capability into customer service management from work orders allows manufacturing personnel to gain more complete understanding of customer requirements.

ERP Module	Data Flow	ERP Module
Customer Service Management	→ Drill Down ↔	Transportation Management

Transportation management has a strong relationship with customer service management. Data flows from customer service management carrying information from sales orders as input to the transportation management module. Using this input the transportation management module can organize sales orders by carrier numbers and routes, providing opportunities for better customer service and reduced transportation costs. ERP users working in transportation management need drill down capability to see specific details regarding customer sales orders. ERP users working in customer service need drill down capability into transportation management to see the latest details on shipping schedules. The primary flow of data is from customer service management to transportation management.

ERP Module	Data Flow	ERP Module
Customer Service Management	←	Field Service
	Drill Down	
	←	

The integrating relationship between customer service management and field service tends to be different from integrated modules of an ERP system. Integration is not provided through software, but more through human intervention and ERP users. This is because customer service management can work as a sub component of field service. The capability to function as a sub component allows customer service management and field service to exist almost as a single module. The primary flow of data is from field service to customer service management. Information that may flow from field service includes customer IDs, part numbers, dates, quantities, and service charges. Drill down capability is needed by field service personnel to identify open sales orders and provide basic customer service functions.

ERP Module	Data Flow	ERP Module
Configuration Management	→	Work Order Management
	Drill Down	
	↔	

Configuration management integrates with work order management by specifying certain combinations of work orders to support customer sales orders. Based upon the configuration of a sales order, configuration management will use its rules to determine what combination of work orders is needed to support sales orders. Good integration will connect all lower level work orders with the parent work order that connects with a sales order. Information that is passed from configuration management to work order management includes work order header information, bills of material, and routings. Drill down capability from configuration management into work order management is needed to help ERP users working in configuration management to identify open work orders that may be affected by changes in base rules set up in configuration management. Drill down capability from work orders into configuration management is not as critical but is useful to help understand how work orders are generated based upon the rules specified in configuration management. The primary flow of data is from configuration management to work order management.

<table>
<tr><th>ERP Module</th><th>Data Flow</th><th>ERP Module</th></tr>
<tr><td rowspan="3">Configuration Management</td><td>←</td><td rowspan="3">ECO</td></tr>
<tr><td>Drill Down</td></tr>
<tr><td>↔</td></tr>
</table>

The integrating relationship between configuration management and ECO is most similar to the integrating relationship between bills of material and ECO. Just as formal change management is provided in bills of material by ECO, so is configuration management change by ECO. The primary flow of information is from the ECO module to configuration management. An ERP user enters an engineering change order into the system and specifies the necessary changes and reasons for the changes. Upon receiving approval, the engineering change order automatically reconfigures rules found in configuration management. Drill down capability is needed in the ECO module to identify rules that may change in configuration management. Drill down capability is needed in configuration management to identify any rules that may be changing, or have changed because of ECO activity. Although the need for formal change management in configuration management through ECO is just as great as it is for bills of materials and product routings, few ERP systems, if any, provide this important integration link. One reason why ERP vendors do not provide this link is that the configuration management process tends to be highly unstable beyond the capabilities of control ability of the ECO module. There is also a general lack of awareness in the industry for this type of integration.

ERP Module	Data Flow	ERP Module
Supplier Management	↔	Work Order Management
	Drill Down	
	↔	

Supplier management can have a significant level of integration with work order management because of its need for bi-directional data flow and drill down capabilities. A process known as outside vendor processing places strong demand for integration between these two modules. In outside vendor processing, work orders are generated that require some type of outside operation, such as painting or machining. Upon generation of the work order, information will flow from the work order management module to the supplier management module, which will then create an open purchase order for the materials that leave the plant to have outside operations performed on them by a supplier. The part is delivered to the supplier. The supplier will perform the necessary operations, and then the parts will be returned to the company to be received on the purchase order, which will then send information back to the work order updating it showing that the outside operation has been completed. Drill down capability is needed from the work order management module into the supplier management module to identify all purchase orders that support work orders. Drill down capability is needed from the supplier management module into the work order management module to help coordinators and purchasing agents understand specific details regarding open purchase orders with their suppliers.

ERP Module	Data Flow	ERP Module
Work Order Management	←	ECO
	Drill Down	
	←→	

Integration between work order management and ECO provides enhanced functionality for the ECO module. Future and open work orders are subject to product and routing restructuring changes based upon engineering change orders. Because of the dynamic nature of the work order management module, integration with the ECO module can be extremely complex in the programming needed to support the integration. For this reason, many ERP vendors do not include this integration with their ERP product. Upon entry in an ECO document and receiving approval to perform the changes, then the ECO module will pass the changes to specific work orders that are affected in the work order management module. Information that may be passed includes part numbers, quantities, work centers, operation hours, and sequence numbers.

Good integration will allow ERP users in the ECO module to drill down into the work order management module to identify work orders that may be affected by the ECO change. ERP users working in the work order management module may benefit from drill down capability to obtain more detailed information on work orders that were restructured to the ECO module.

ERP Module	Data Flow	ERP Module
Work Order Management	←	Preventative Maintenance
	Drill Down	
	←→	

Work order management interfaces with preventive maintenance by supporting and executing preventive maintenance schedules. Preventive maintenance schedules are automatically generated based upon maintenance needs of equipment. Work orders, which record material consumption and labor hours applied, are used to record activity applied to one or more machines. The primary data flow is from the preventive maintenance module to the work order management module. Key pieces of information transferred include: equipment IDs, part numbers, work instructions, and dates. Good integration will allow ERP users in the preventive maintenance module to drill down into the work order management module to find all supporting work orders. ERP users in the work order management module need drill down capability to identify how certain work orders fit into the overall preventive maintenance schedule.

ERP Module	Data Flow	ERP Module
Work Order Management	←	Field Service
	Drill Down	
	←	

The work order management module provides enhanced functionality by integrating with field service. Work orders serve to record activity performed out in the field by service technicians. Field service technicians may access work orders directly through the Internet to report activities against work orders and to complete them. ERP users working in field service need drill down capability into the work order management module to obtain more specific details on the jobs that need to be performed. The primary data flow is from field service to the work order management module. The relationship of field service to the work order management module is similar to that found between preventive maintenance and work order management.

ERP Module	Data Flow	ERP Module
ECO	➔ Drill Down 🡐	Field Service

For some types of companies, especially those that manufacture and service large complex assemblies, the ECO and the field service modules need strong integration. Engineering change orders that are entered into the system to alter the design of a product can have a significant impact on products that are already operating in the field. A good example of where ECO can be used for field service is for a manufacturing recall. The engineering change order will specify the reason for modification of the product and how to do it. It may require new work orders or the reactivation of closed work orders. The primary flow of data is from the ECO module to field service. Field service has a strong need for integration that will allow them to drill back down into ECO to obtain additional details.

<table>
<tr><th>ERP Module</th><th>Data Flow</th><th>ERP Module</th></tr>
<tr><td rowspan="3">Preventative Maintenance</td><td>➔</td><td rowspan="3">Field Service</td></tr>
<tr><td>Drill Down</td></tr>
<tr><td>🡐</td></tr>
</table>

The preventive maintenance module can greatly enhance the functionality of field service through good integration. Preventive maintenance is an essential part of many field service programs. The preventive maintenance schedule will alert field service personnel of the appropriate time to perform preventive maintenance on equipment out in the field. The preventive maintenance module may then interface with work the order management module for execution. The field service function needs drill down capability into the preventive maintenance module to obtain scheduling information for field service technicians. The primary data flow is from the preventive maintenance module into the field service module. In many cases, this may be done simply through drill down capabilities from field service to the preventive maintenance module. The types of information it will pass back to the field service module include equipment ID, dates, special notes, locations, and kit information.

Questions--

1. What is integration?
2. What is an interface?
3. How is an interface and integration different?
4. How is an interface and integration the same?
5. What are four examples of an interface?
6. What is an example of primary integration?
7. What is an example of workflow integration?
8. What is an example of independent functional integration?
9. What is an example of complementary integration?
10. What are the relationships between traceability, data flow, and drill down?
11. What is drill down?
12. What is traceability?
13. How many relationships exist with an integration level of 7 or higher?
14. What is the most integrated module of an ERP system?
15. What is the least integrated module of an ERP system?

ERP… its not just a job, it's an adventure of a lifetime…

17

Internet

The introduction of the Internet for ERP systems and businesses is revolutionizing the way that many companies do business and how they use their ERP systems. The technology of the Internet has evolved rapidly, providing many features and functions that ERP systems were missing. The merging of Internet and ERP technologies has become a rapid movement that has allowed some ERP vendors to present a single integrated product that contains an ERP system with seamless integrated Internet functionality. This chapter reviews some history of the Internet and examines how the two started merging to provide enhanced business functionality.

The original Internet (ARPANET) was conceived in the late 1960s and faced a long gestation period to finally be birthed into mainstream use in the early 1990s. In the early 1980s educational institutions started using NSFNET (National Science Foundation Network). Growth exploded at this stage but still remained relatively unknown to the rest of us. In 1990 hypertext came to age and by 1992 the Internet Society was chartered and the World Wide Web created. The long awaited child finally arrived in 1993 through the use of directory and database services, registration services, and graphical user interface called "Mosaic for X". By the year 2000 Internet had matured to a young adult, captivating the attention of millions of users worldwide. When we look at other types of communication technology such as television, radio, newspaper, etc., nothing has come close to the explosive growth of the

Internet. Internet technology is the most adopted communication technology in the history of mankind.

In 1995, ERP was nothing more than a casual acquaintance of the Internet. In 1996 and 1997, customers began asking ERP vendors for Internet capability. ERP vendors responded by adding Internet functionality to their software in 1998 and 1999. By the year 2000 the relationship between ERP and Internet was well developed, as Internet functionality became mainstreamed in ERP sales.

But what kind of relationship is it? Have ERP vendors completely fallen in love with the Internet? And how do ERP customers feel about the relationship?

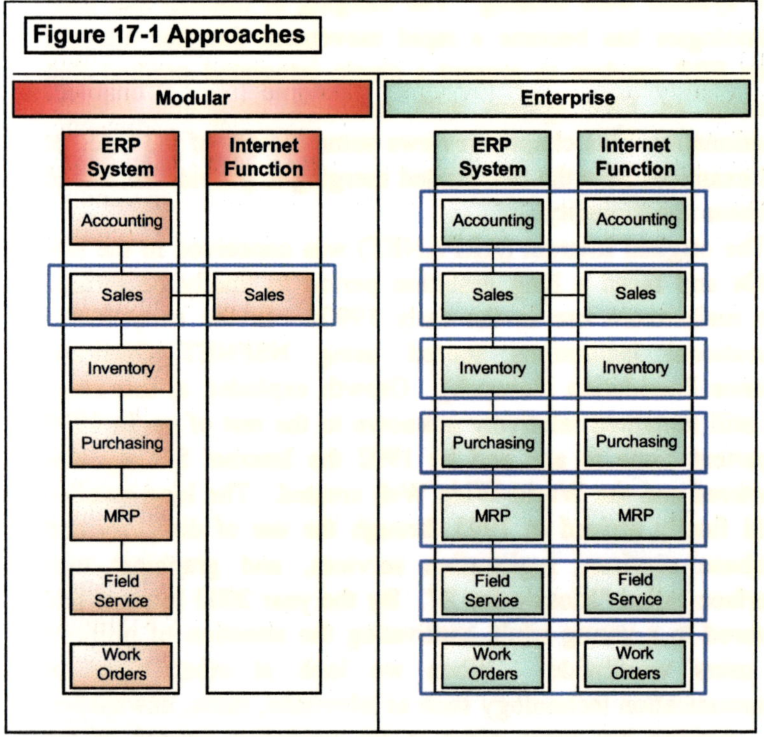

Practically every single ERP vendor with more than one percent market share has adopted some type of Internet strategy. ERP vendors have taken two approaches in developing a relationship with the Internet: modular and enterprise.

With the modular approach, as shown in figure 17-1, ERP venders have developed Internet solutions for key strategic areas such as customer service management with order entry. These solutions are generally developed independent of the software system sold by the ERP vendor. They may be developed in-house through the ERP vendor or they may be purchased from a third party supplier. Both solutions bring benefits by providing additional functionality. The disadvantage is the solutions bring additional complexity and integration issues.

The enterprise solution seeks to duplicate the entire functionality of the ERP system to become Internet enabled. All functions are provided for, such as sales, purchasing, forecasting, financials, manufacturing, etc. These systems may be considered 100 percent Internet enabled. Some ERP vendors have focused all their resources solely on creating Internet solutions, while others have chosen to expand their product offerings by adding Internet functionality. The vendors that have added Internet functionality usually retain their traditional software systems.

As of the beginning of year 2000, few companies had chosen to trust their prized ERP systems completely to the uncharted territory of the Internet. The process of developing complete ERP Internet functionality while simultaneously maintaining their traditional ERP systems has been staggering for ERP vendors. The complexity of ERP systems has tripled for some ERP vendors because they have chosen to provide complete ERP Internet functionality and traditional ERP functionality with both running on different operating systems.

Having the capability to operate on different computer operating systems while still being able to cross communicate synchronizing files between the two, does greatly increase the overall functionality of an ERP system. But increased functionality does not mean increased quality. The development of functionality that has no benefit is a waste. As of the beginning of year 2000 no customers of ERP systems were claiming that they saw an increase of the overall quality with such a strategy.

This situation can be considered a love triangle. The ERP venders have been married to their traditional systems for years as the Internet has quickly caught ERP vendors' attention. With the ERP vendors' resources being stretched thin, the quality of the relationships have become strained as the quality of ERP products struggle.

The subject of e-commerce is often confused with e-business. The definition of each varies depending on the source. It is the responsibility of the customer to properly understand how e-commerce or e-business is marketed and defined from a vendor's perspective.

E-business can be defined as the complete process of marketing and promoting your company's product or service through the use of the Internet and websites. It includes on-line catalogs, product reviews, product information, performance characteristics, etc.

E-commerce is the process of doing commercial transactions through the use of Internet and websites. Internet commercial transactions include such things as quantities, credit card numbers, dates, part numbers, etc. E-commerce is a function of e-business.

The use of the Internet can have many potential advantages for ERP systems, including:

- Reduced maintenance
- World wide access
- Less hardware dependencies
- Customer service management
- Supplier management

Use of Internet technology can dramatically impact the way that ERP systems are installed and maintained. Traditional ERP systems require clients (computers or dumb terminals which receive information) to have special software or hardware to interpret the data stream from the servers. Using Internet technology, virtually all of the software maintenance on the client computers has disappeared. Now, any computer with a web browser can access the ERP system and perform the necessary functions. This can be a tremendous timesaving for IS departments, reducing the overall cost of ownership in an ERP system. As an additional bonus, the ERP system can now operate off of any computer system that is capable of using a web browser. Some companies may choose to achieve this effect using an intranet while others choose to hook their ERP systems up to Internet connections to allow ERP users to access their ERP systems from any place in the world. Having direct access to an ERP system through the Internet can raise many security concerns.

Customer service management can use Internet technology in a number of different ways to help promote a companies' e-business and e-commerce strategies. Some ways that companies are using Internet technology to promote their products or services include:

- Product information
- Online sales
- Customer support
- Configuration management

Online transaction capability to sell products can greatly reduce the ordering cost. Lower ordering cost allows companies to set lower minimum order quantities, which allows them to expand their market shares to reach more customers.

A variety of customer service support techniques can be integrated with Internet functionality. Some companies may choose to publish articles or maintenance updates about their products or services for users to access worldwide. Some companies will provide a "knowledge garden". A knowledge garden is a specific area set up on a website that contains a large collection of supporting product information available for general customer use.

Many computer companies have chosen to perform the function of configuration management online. This allows consumers to configure their computers specifically to their needs with the ability to receive the price of their configuration online. Operating from predefined rules, online configuration management allows consumers to only choose compatible configurations that a company can sell.

The ability to take companies' product catalogs and publish them for general availability to the Internet greatly reduces direct mailing costs and allows much faster updates. Simple search techniques can also greatly speed location of specific products or services in large catalogs. This continuously becomes more and more practical as Internet connections increase in speed.

Supplier management can benefit greatly from the use of Internet. The RFP chapter in this book gives an example of how a company can use Internet technology to collect information from a variety of vendors for the purpose of deciding which vendor products will best fulfill their needs. Some companies have been able to decrease sourcing time by several months by giving their vendors access to their ERP systems through the Internet.

The use of Internet technology can affect the functionality in ERP systems in the following areas:

- Multi-language
- Multi-currency
- Hardware
- Workflow

Because the Internet can give customers and suppliers access to your ERP system worldwide, multi-language and multi-currency problems can quickly arise as companies from international markets start using your ERP system online. Business process flows can also change significantly as companies find new ways of doing business with suppliers and customers over the Internet. A good example is when companies send confirmation notices by email for the products that have been shipped. Flexible workflows are needed in ERP systems for companies making transitions to Internet based business strategies.

Questions--

1. What is ARPANET?
2. When did Internet technology come to ERP systems?
3. What are two different approaches in how Internet technology is used in ERP systems?
4. What is a client?
5. What is a server?
6. What is the relationship of a client to a server?
7. What are some reasons for so many ERP venders adopting Internet functionality in their products?
8. What are some functional areas of an ERP system that can greatly benefit from the use of Internet technology?
9. How can email be used with functional modules of an ERP system?
10. What is e-commerce?
11. What is e-business?
12. What are three advantages of the Internet in ERP systems?
13. What are four special considerations when deciding to use an ERP system on the Internet?

Things tend to get better when companies find ways to measure the characteristics they want to improve...

18

Diagnostic and Measurement Systems

This chapter covers the different options that practitioners have available to them for troubleshooting and measuring characteristics of ERP systems. As an increased number of companies learn more about their ERP problems, they tend to become more demanding in measuring the progress that they make. Measurement systems for ERP systems measure ERP specific and operational characteristics of a company. How well a company uses an ERP system will directly contribute to the success of a company's ERM system as described in *Chapter 1: Introduction to Enterprise Resource Planning.* How well a company can control its ERP / ERM system will directly contribute to the type of environment the company achieves. Refer to *Chapter 9: Environmental Characteristics* for more information on the different perspectives of environmental characteristics.

Companies become interested in diagnostic and measurement systems for three general categories of reasons:

- Events
- Improvements
- Comparisons

Events are situations that happen within an ERP system that creates disruption to the normal business process flows. An example may be a customer who was charged the wrong price for a product after an unauthorized ERP user decided to change the pricing for that customer. Some helpful tools include:

- Tracing
- Tracking
- Date stamps
- History logging
- Menu logging

Several different tools exist within ERP systems to help companies understand how disruptive events occur, allowing them to identify the root cause of the problem.

Tracing is a methodology for connecting two records that have something in common. Manufacturing processes that use lot control functionality usually have tracing capabilities. Drill down capability may be used to facilitate tracing functionality. Tracing works based upon the principle of newest to oldest record.

Tracking is similar to tracing and the two are often confused with each other. Tracking is also a methodology of connecting two records that have something in common. Drill down capability may be used to facilitate tracking functionality. Tracking works based upon the principle of oldest to newest. Tracking can be thought of as a hunter tracking wild game in the wilderness. The hunter first identifies the oldest footsteps and then continuously "tracks" to newer footsteps until the hunter finds the prey.

Date stamps contain basic information such as, date, time, terminal, program, user, etc. The information is usually attached to the corresponding record in a file or table. Date stamps by themselves have no history tracking / tracing capability. Date stamps only show the last identity to change or update a record in a database. Each time that record is changed or updated, the history is lost and replaced with the most current information. Date stamps work well when records experience little change, and detection of a problem occurs quickly. Date stamps in highly changing environments can quickly become an ineffective method for diagnosing something that went wrong.

History logging, also known as journal, is a methodology that records all additions, deletions, and changes to the records in a file or database. History logging can be particularly more useful than date stamps because it gives a complete history of all the activity that has been happening to a particular record in a table or file. Some systems allow every single field in the record to be duplicated, allowing ERP users the capability to see the exact changes occurring within the record over its entire life history. While history logging can be very effective as a diagnostic tool, most companies find the storage capabilities of modern day computers to be inadequate, or too expensive, to store all of the history for any length of time. Larger corporations may have over one million computer transactions taking place every day. In such environments usually only article files will have the history logging functionality turned on. Most ERP systems use history logging for tracking activity performed on inventory items.

Menu logging works similarly to history logging except it is based upon the activity of a user who is traveling from one menu to another instead of logging the changes performed to records in files or tables. Menu history information accumulates, showing all menus and options that an ERP user selected. The user ID, date, time, menu option, and program ID are usually recorded. The number of data elements is often smaller than the amount collected in history logging from other files. However, despite the smaller amount, menu history files can soon become overwhelming because of the large number of users traveling over many different menus. Menu logging does not inform investigators what records were changed and by whom they were changed.

Improvements and comparison information requires higher-level diagnostic and troubleshooting tools than required for eventful situations. For many companies, improvement activities in ERP systems consist of making hundreds of micro-improvements specific to a business process flow or functional area of a business. For many companies, all of these micro-improvements do not sum up to an overall improvement for the company, as many of the individual micro-improvements will conflict with each other. Measuring the overall progress of a company and how well it uses its ERP system requires companies to measure the overall system rather than specific targeted areas. Measurements and drive for improvements, of course, may still be performed at the micro-level; however, they should not be done without understanding how those micro-improvements are contributing to the big picture: a successful ERM system.

A variety of sources exist for companies to obtain high-level comparison information for their ERP/ERM systems. Some of these options include:

- Consulting agencies
- Educational institutes and societies
- Electronic diagnostic tools

Consultant agencies have historically been heavily used to help troubleshoot ERP/ERM systems at a high level. Consultants and consultant agencies can work well for receiving independent unbiased information on how well a company's ERP/ERM system is working when a trusting relationship exists between the consultant agency and the company. Consultants will document the situation and recommend areas for improvement, working from experience or sometimes from predefined checklists.

Educational institutes and professional societies can provide opportunities for networking and benchmarking. Some educational institutes can perform very similar functions as the consulting agencies. Professional societies can provide numerous contacts, which can allow companies to visit other companies to determine benchmarking opportunities for their ERP/ERM systems.

Electronic diagnostic tools measure a variety of characteristics found within an ERP/ERM system. Some electronic tools are very rudimentary and do little more than plot values on graphs, based upon how ERP users answered questions. Other electronic diagnostic tools are much more sophisticated, allowing ERP users to obtain detail diagnostic information for targeted areas with multiple levels of comparison information in areas such as software and industry standards. Price ranges for such tools can fluctuate significantly, ranging from free to several thousand dollars. The quality of electronic diagnostic tools can also fluctuate significantly.

Sections 18.1 – 18.16 discusses the CIBRES scorecard tool in detail. The CIBRES scorecard tool is an advanced diagnostic tool that allows companies to effectively obtain diagnostic information on their ERP systems.

Questions---

1. What are three general categories of reasons for diagnostics and measurements in ERP systems?
2. What are some tools for use with events?
3. What is the difference between tracing and tracking?
4. What is an example of tracing?
5. What is an example of tracking?
6. What is the difference between history logging and menu logging?
7. How are history logging and menu logging similar?
8. What is a date stamp?
9. Which method is best suited for networking when obtaining high-level diagnostic information?

18.1

Introduction and Instructions for Use

Overview

How are we doing? Compared to what? That's a very good question. Seeking these answers brings opportunities for

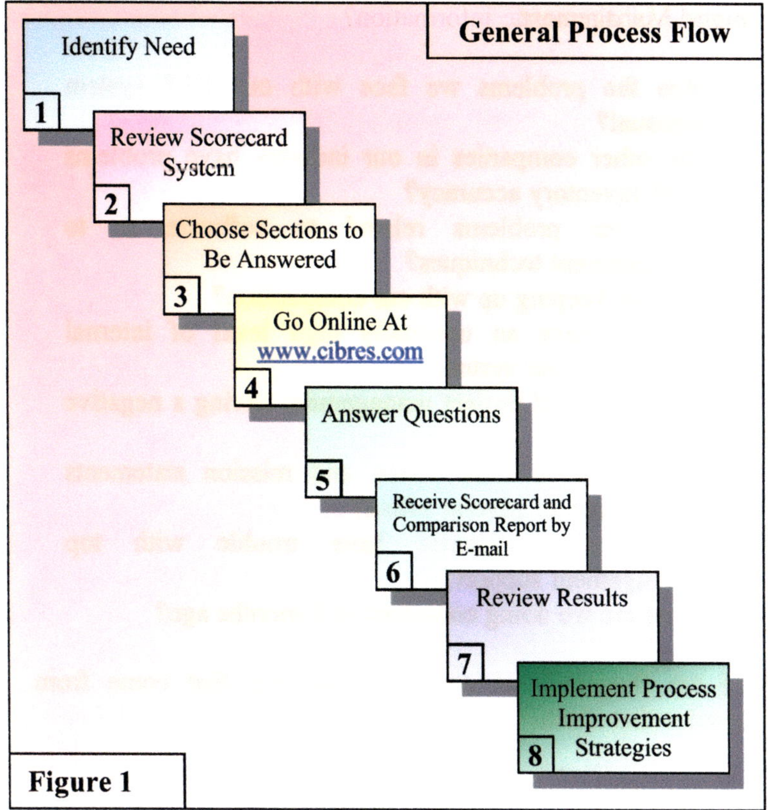

Figure 1

process improvements and competitive advantage in the marketplace. Figure 1 gives a general process flow of how the Scorecard System For World Class Enterprise Resource Management works.

Identify Need

Most companies and practitioners that purchase this book will already have identified a need at least in a general sense. Review of the material presented in this book and the results through the scorecard and comparison report can further refine that need. The following are examples of questions that identify the need for the Scorecard System For World Class Enterprise Resource Management.

1. Are the problems we face with our ERP system unusual?
2. Do other companies in our industry have problems with inventory accuracy?
3. Are our problems related to software or to management techniques?
4. Are we keeping up with our competition?
5. Do we have an unusually high level of internal support for our system?
6. Is our style of project management having a negative impact?
7. Does lack of clear vision and mission statements really have an adverse effect?
8. Do other companies have trouble with top management support?
9. How are we doing compared to 6 months ago?

There are thousands of questions like this that come from companies that identify the need.

Review Scorecard System

Under this step the participant reviews the overall process and different areas to participate in. This is a process of browsing through the sections and becoming familiar with the different chapters and learning how the scorecard system works using internet technology.

Choose Sections to Be Answered

Your needs will determine what sections should be answered. All sections should be answered for companies and practitioners seeking overall global perspectives of their ERP systems and how they interact with the functional activities of the business. Participants that have identified a need in specific areas may participate in those particular sections.

Go Online At www.cibres.com

This is one of the most beneficial features of this publication, the ability to enter your answers electronically and receive results back by e-mail. There is no charge for going online or receiving the standard scorecard and comparison reports by e-mail. It is recommended that you review the latest updated instructions online. The website performs best using Internet Explorer 4.0 or later. First goto http://www.cibres.com

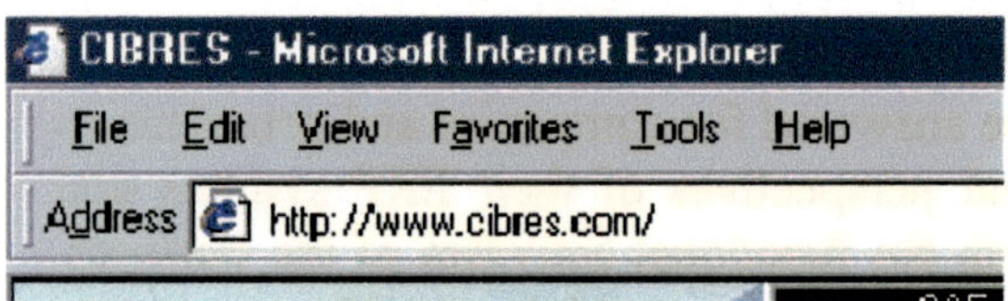

Then look for the ERP Scorecard button and click it.

After that you will come to a page where you will receive the latest updates and instructions.

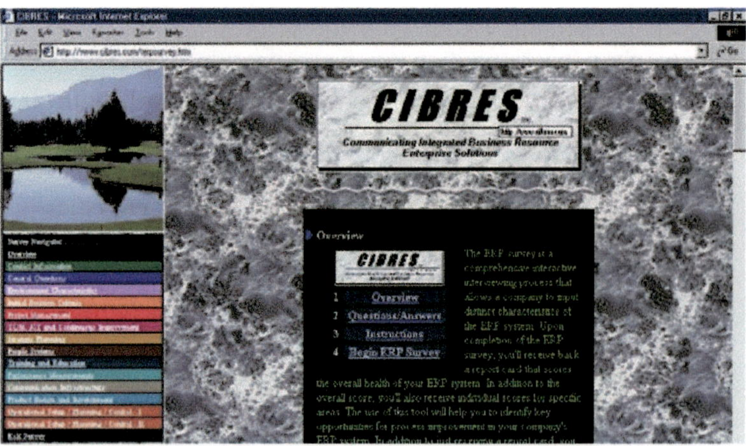

Answer Questions

There are 3 basic ways of answering questions:

1. Fill in the blank, usually free form text. This is used for answers where selections do not work well such as the Contact Information section.
2. Select from a list of options. This is used for situations that cannot be represented well using a scale score system for characteristics such as operating system used or type of software.
3. Select from the 0 to 10 scale. This is the most common type of selection process used. In this publication it appears using the following format:

0	1	2	3	4	5	6	7	8	9	10

The following can be used as a general guide in choosing a value in the 0 to 10 scale:

0-2 Does not exist - Characteristic could produce beneficial results but is not used.
3-4 Faulty - Characteristic functions very poorly producing inadequate results.
5-6 Passable - Characteristic is in place but does not produce expected results.
7-8 Worthy - Characteristic performing well with occasional problems.
9-10 Superb - Characteristic has achieved the highest results obtainable. Characteristic cannot be improved further.

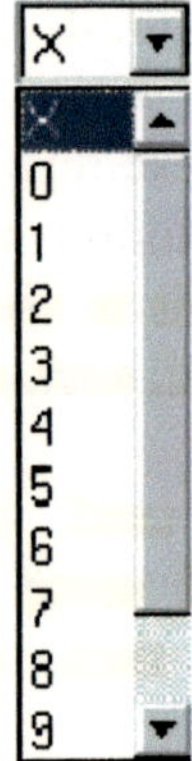

Online, the 0 to 10 scale will be represented by a drop down selection box. Almost all questions using the 0 to 10 scale score contain qualifiers or indicators of a particular response. This is to ensure more stable answers and comparisons. In some rare cases the 0 to 10 scaled score is presented in reverse order, 10 being the lowest and 0 the highest. The letter X indicates the question has not been answered.

Please note that the Contact Information section must be answered to obtain results. Without completion of this section the answers to a particular section cannot be associated with the proper company / person / e-mail address.

Some questions are repeated. They may be worded differently or similarly within the same section or different sections.

Receive Scorecard and Comparison Report by E-mail

Once the questions have been answered comes the exciting part, receiving your results! Some of the major features of the Scorecard and Comparison Report include:

1. Detail line item results
2. Sectional scores
3. Averages of all participants
4. Averages for industry
5. Averages for software
6. Recommendations and notes

Sample Report

CIBRES Inc.
http://www.cibres.com
Communicating Integrated Business Resource Enterprise Solutions

P.O. Box 493
Eau Claire, WI 54702

www.cibres.com
service@cibres.com

ERP Survey ---- Scorecard and Comparison Report

Question	Your Score → Result	Survey Ave → Study Ave	Your Score Compared To Survey Average → Study Dif	Score For Your Specific Industry Based On ERP Survey Average → Ind. Ave	Your Score Compared To Industry Average → Ind. Dif	Score For Your Specific Software Based On ERP Survey Average → Soft Ave	Your Score Compared To Software Average → Soft Dif
F1	Other ---> Specify						
F1S1	Impact Encore						
F2	3.2						
F3	60	12.6	47.4	31.5	28.5	31.5	28.5
F4	0	0	0	2.5	-2.5	2.5	-2.5
F5	Operations						
F5S1	(Other)						
F6	6	6	0	6.5	-0.5	6.5	-0.5
F7	X						
F8	X						
F9	3	4.5	-1.5	4.5	-1.5	4.5	-1.5
Sec Score (%)	38	41	-3	42	-3	42	-3
Recommendations	Procedure - hold cross functional meetings to understand ERP problems. Procedure - use change control control management system for program modifications Training - hold an ERP basics class for senior management.						

Reviewing Results

In reviewing your results you should look for weak areas, how you compare to the study average, industry average, and software average. Sectional scores are based on percentage of 100. 100 being the highest achievable score for any section. Some answers that cannot be included in calculations (such as software type) are left blank. How you answer the questions determines what recommendations show up. Some questions will not generate recommendations while others generate recommendations based on predefined parameters built into the scorecard and comparison system.

Implement Process Improvement Strategies

After receiving your results you should decide on how to implement your process improvement plan should you need one. Some basic steps that can be considered in your process improvement plan include:

1. Form goals and objectives using information from the scorecard and comparison report while being consistent with your company's overall business strategy
2. Create a corrective action process that will bring about change using techniques such as education, training, documentation, project management, software setup, etc…
3. Use an assessment system to review forward motion. Many options are available from participating in the Scorecard System For World Class Enterprise Resource Management again to developing specific measurement systems for the characteristic that is being measured. In other cases measurement systems will already be in place open for inspection at your company.
4. Establish a periodic review process (such as monthly) to review the progress made. Such review sessions should include the participation of the Senior Management of the company with the authority and power to resolve conflicts in allocation of resources.

18.2

Questions and Answers

How long does it take to get the results back?

It depends on how the questions are answered. The results can take anywhere from several hours to several weeks.

Will my company's results remain confidential?

Absolutely, the results of your company's output will remain strictly confidential.

I am concerned about the security of receiving my results by e-mail. Do I have other options?

Yes, a number of different options exist from electronic encryption to certified mail.

How long will it take to complete?

It largely depends on the quality of the desired output and the availability of the information. Some companies choose to hold cross functional meetings to obtain the most accurate results possible while others chose to elect a single individual to decide the answers. Companies taking the most care in answering the questions obtain the highest quality results. The actual inputting of the answers generally takes a couple of hours or less.

How much will this cost?

The cost is free. This includes the report card / comparison report.

Does my company really need this?

Most likely yes. On average, about 75% of all companies' ERP systems will not succeed or fail to meet expectations. Some companies will never realize why!

How much detail is available on the comparison report?

It depends on the nature of the ERP software. You are much more likely to obtain comparison information on major ERP vendors vs. very small or obsolete systems. Comparison information will still always be available comparing your results to industry average.

Can I complete part of it on-line and then come back at a later time to fill out the rest?

We recommend that all of the information be collected ahead of time so the answers can be completed in one session.

Can I perform this process again in 6 months to see the improvement in my ERP system?

Yes. A self to self comparison report is available upon special request.

Will this tell me the performance of my ERP software?

Although the Scorecard system contains many questions related to ERP software, the goal is to measure the *ERP system* that includes people and processes. The management of the resources determines the overall performance of the ERM (Enterprise Resource Management) system.

Do I get a better score if I use all "10's" for my answers?

No. In fact, this will only lower your score. 10 does not necessarily mean a higher score. In some cases 10 represents the lowest outcome and 0 represents the highest. In other cases the response only indicates a correlation to one preexisting condition or another.

I looked at all the questions; it seems kind of large; can I take just the part that my company is interested in?

Yes. Because the Scorecard system is modular in design it gives the capability to be taken in parts. The initial contact page must always be filled out first before the following modules are completed. The internet computer servers need this information to connect the data to the organization participating in the Scorecard system.

ERP, It's not just a job, it's an adventure of a lifetime.

18.3

Contact Information

This section is used to identify the participant's information and to bind the results together from the entire process. Without this basic information the results cannot be obtained.

First Name: ______________________________________

Last Name: ______________________________________

Title: ______________________________________

Company: ______________________________________

Address: ______________________________________

City/State/Zip: ______________________________________

Phone: ______________________________________

Fax: ______________________________________

E-mail: ______________________________________

Web Address: ______________________________________

Notes: ______________________________________

____

ERP is like farming, hard work, patience and good weather make for a bountiful harvest.

18.4

General Questions

A-1 How did you find out about this ERP Scorecard system?

____

A-2 What method of notification is desired? (Note: Charges apply to anything other than E-Mail notification.)

____E-Mail with attached Excel document
____E-Mail Encryption (Excel)
____E-Mail TXT
____Overnight Fedex Printed
____Overnight Fedex Electronic TXT
____Overnight Fedex Electronic (Excel)
____Overnight Fedex Electronic Encryption
____US Mail Printed
____US Mail Electronic TXT
____US Mail Electronic (Excel)
____US Mail Electronic Encryption (Excel)
____Other ---> Specify

____

It's not what we know that hurts; it's what we know that just ain't so.
-Kin Hubbard

18.5

Environment Characteristics

F-1 What ERP software do you use? (SAP, BAAN, JBA) If your system has been developed in house then specify:

____

F-2 What version is used? (A7.3.1, 2.43,)

____

F-3 What is the current status of your ERP system. (Note: the questions answered here should be consistent with this answer. 0 - under implementation, 3 - 3 months after implementation, 12 - months after implementation, etc..)

____

F-4 How many program modifications have been performed?

____

F-5 What function or position does the IS department report to? (Quality, Operation, CFO)

____

F-6 In a general sense, how is the ERP system viewed. (0 - not accepted at all, 10 - fully embraced by all users of the system.)

0	1	2	3	4	5	6	7	8	9	10

F-7 What was the level of consultation availability before the go live of the ERP system? (0 - none at all, 10 - unlimited access.)

0	1	2	3	4	5	6	7	8	9	10

F-8 What was the level of consultation availability after the go live of the ERP system? (0 - none at all, 10 - unlimited access.)

0	1	2	3	4	5	6	7	8	9	10

F-9 What was the level of training given to the implementation team members before the go live of the ERP system? (0 - none at all, 10 - unlimited access.)

0	1	2	3	4	5	6	7	8	9	10

F-10 What was the level of training given to the implementation team members after the go live of the ERP system? (0 - none at all, 10 - unlimited access.)

0	1	2	3	4	5	6	7	8	9	10

F-11 What was the level of training given to the end users before the go live of the ERP system? (0 - none at all, 10 - unlimited access.)

0	1	2	3	4	5	6	7	8	9	10

F-12 What was the level of training given to the end users after the go live of the ERP system? (0 - none at all, 10 - unlimited access.)

0	1	2	3	4	5	6	7	8	9	10

F-13 What is the total number people that use the system?

____

F-14 What is the quality of the relationship between your company and the ERP software vendor or vendors? (0 - non working relationship, 10 - cooperative joint strategic planning.)

0	1	2	3	4	5	6	7	8	9	10

F-15 How many geographical locations will be represented? (Number of different manufacturing plants, or distribution facilities, or other)

____

F-16 How many program modifications have been made to the software system? (0 - no program modifications, 10 - system has been heavily modified, if system has been developed in house then use 10)

0	1	2	3	4	5	6	7	8	9	10

F-17 Has an ERP training class been given for the senior management of the company? (0 - no training class offered, 10 - training class give by a professional resource)

0	1	2	3	4	5	6	7	8	9	10

F-18 Are lengthy communication delays, based on need, often experienced because of computer hardware? (0 - critical information routinely delayed, 10 - no delays in interactive or batch processes)

0	1	2	3	4	5	6	7	8	9	10

F-19 Does the ERP system process information interactively or by using batch processes? (0 - highly interactive, 5 - 1/2 of each, 10 - highly batch)

0	1	2	3	4	5	6	7	8	9	10

F-20 Do people / teams / departments act in a fashion that is best for the company vs. what is best for the individual, team, or department? (0 - people / teams / departments act in a fashion that is best for the company, 10 - people / teams / departments act in a fashion that is best for the person / team / department)

0	1	2	3	4	5	6	7	8	9	10

F-21 Does the company actively use principles of integrated supply chain management? (0 - no integrated supply chain management, 10 - integrated supply chain management used extensively)

0	1	2	3	4	5	6	7	8	9	10

F-22 Are the information networks and communication systems reliable? (0 - extremely unreliable, 10 - communication and/or information network has never experienced a communication disruption)

0	1	2	3	4	5	6	7	8	9	10

F-23 Is the organization primary focused on the customer? (0 - people seldom worry about the customer, 10 - the customer is an obsession by everyone in the company)

0	1	2	3	4	5	6	7	8	9	10

F-24 Has information been standardized to ensure consistency? (0 - inconsistencies are found constantly, 10 - all databases and information systems have been standardized)

0	1	2	3	4	5	6	7	8	9	10

F-25 Is data integrity of the databases of importance? (0 - poor data integrity is often found, 10 - documentation, procedures, audits are performed that keep the database in peak condition)

0	1	2	3	4	5	6	7	8	9	10

F-26 Does the company engage in international sales or service and international sourcing? (0 - company is completely domestic, 10 - company actively communicates and engages in activity with foreign customers and suppliers)

0	1	2	3	4	5	6	7	8	9	10

F-27 Does the entire organization share a common vision and mission statements? (0 - visions and missions are not shared or they do not exist at all, 10 - universal understanding of the organization's visions and mission by all functional areas)

0	1	2	3	4	5	6	7	8	9	10

F-28 Which selection best matches your industry? (See Appendix A for your specific 2 digit SIC industry code)

____

____Other ---> Specify

____

F-29 What is the annual sales amount for your company? (Round to nearest amount. Answer represents millions of dollars per year.)

____

F-30 Who had the most influence in deciding what software package to purchase?
____Senior Management
____IT or IS Department
____General Users
____Consulting Agency
____Middle Management
____Other ---> Specify

____

F-31 From whom was the software purchased?
____Software company direct
____Value added reseller
____Other ---> Specify

____

F-32 What is the operating system for your ERP software system?
____DIGITAL/VMS
____HP MPE
____HP UX
____IBM AIX
____IBM OS/400
____MVS
____NOVELL/Netware
____OS/2
____SUN
____OS/Solaris
____UNIX
____VM
____VSE

____Windows NT
____Other ---> Specify

____

F-33 What is the primary hardware platform for your ERP software system?
____AMD
____Amdahi
____Compaq
____Data General
____Dell
____Hewlett-Packard
____Hitachi Data Systems
____IBM AS/400 IBM
____RS/6000, SP2
____IBM mainframe
____Intel
____NCR
____Sequent
____Siemens Pyramid
____Sillicon Graphics
____Sun Unisys
____Other ---> Specify

____

F-34 What is the primary database for your ERP software system?
____Oracle
____Infomix
____Sybase
____IBM DB2 Family
____MS SQL Server
____MS Access
____Other ---> Specify

____

F-35 Who is the primary supplier of professional consultation services?
____Software company direct
____Value added reseller
____Other ---> Specify
____

F-36 How would you rate the vendor reputation based on actual experience? (0 - so poor its unratable, 10 - the best that could possibly be achieved)

0	1	2	3	4	5	6	7	8	9	10

F-37 How would you rate the vendor vertical industry expertise based on actual experience? (0 - so poor its unratable, 10 - the best that could possibly be achieved)

0	1	2	3	4	5	6	7	8	9	10

F-38 How would you rate the vendor stability based on actual experience? (0 - so poor its unratable, 10 - the best that could possibly be achieved)

0	1	2	3	4	5	6	7	8	9	10

F-39 How would you rate the vendor service quality based on actual experience? (0 - so poor its unratable, 10 - the best that could possibly be achieved)

0	1	2	3	4	5	6	7	8	9	10

F-40 How would you rate product reputation based on actual experience? (0 - so poor its unratable, 10 - the best that could possibly be achieved)

0	1	2	3	4	5	6	7	8	9	10

F-41 How would you rate product performance based on actual experience? (0 - so poor its unratable, 10 - the best that could possibly be achieved)

0	1	2	3	4	5	6	7	8	9	10

F-42 How would you rate the time to implement based on actual experience? (0 - so poor its unratable, 10 - the best that could possibly be achieved)

0	1	2	3	4	5	6	7	8	9	10

F-43 How would you rate the post implementation cost based on actual experience? (0 - so poor its unratable, 10 - the best that could possibly be achieved)

0	1	2	3	4	5	6	7	8	9	10

F-44 How would you rate the product flexibility based on actual experience? (0 - so poor its unratable, 10 - the best that could possibly be achieved)

0	1	2	3	4	5	6	7	8	9	10

F-45 How would you rate the product training requirements based on actual experience? (0 - so poor its unratable, 10 - the best that could possibly be achieved)

0	1	2	3	4	5	6	7	8	9	10

F-46 How would you rate the critical capabilities and functions based on actual experience? (0 - so poor its unratable, 10 - the best that could possibly be achieved)

0	1	2	3	4	5	6	7	8	9	10

F-47 How would you rate total cost of ownership based on actual experience? (0 - so poor its unratable, 10 - the best that could possibly be achieved)

0	1	2	3	4	5	6	7	8	9	10

F-48 How would you rate 3rd party support based on actual experience? (0 - so poor its unratable, 10 - the best that could possibly be achieved)

0	1	2	3	4	5	6	7	8	9	10

F-49 How would you rate ease of integration with other products based on actual experience? (0 - so poor its unratable, 10 - the best that could possibly be achieved)

0	1	2	3	4	5	6	7	8	9	10

F-50 How many networking personnel (People that manage communication networking devices between computers.) are dedicated to the system? (If two people are dedicated 50% then answer as 1 etc..., 1 - 1, 10 - 10, 100 - 100)

____

F-51 How many people are dedicated as a help desk function? (If two people are dedicated 50% then answer as 1 etc..., 1 - 1, 10 - 10, 100 - 100)

____

F-52 How many people are dedicated as technical function (These people develop applications, write code, perform database conversions, etc..)? (If two people are dedicated 50% then answer as 1 etc..., 1 - 1, 10 - 10, 100 - 100)

___

F-53 How many people are dedicated to the function of security, setting up new users, restriction access, etc..? (This includes hardware and software security.) (If two people are dedicated 50% then answer as 1 etc..., 1 - 1, 10 - 10, 100 - 100)

___

F-54 How many people does the company employ? (1 - 1, 10 - 10, 100 - 100)

___

When we decided to purchase, we never thought we would still be trying to figure how to use it 5 years later.

18.6

Initial Decision Criteria

K-1 What role did the vendor reputation play in the decision to purchase the ERP software? (0 - was not a factor and was not considered, 10 - critical to the final decision)

0	1	2	3	4	5	6	7	8	9	10

K-2 What role did the vendor experience in your industry play in the decision to purchase the ERP software? (0 - was not a factor and was not considered, 10 - critical to the final decision)

0	1	2	3	4	5	6	7	8	9	10

K-3 What role did the stability of the vendor play in the decision to purchase the ERP software? (0 - was not a factor and was not considered, 10 - critical to the final decision)

0	1	2	3	4	5	6	7	8	9	10

K-4 What role did vendor service quality play in the decision to purchase the ERP software? (0 - was not a factor and was not considered, 10 - critical to the final decision)

0	1	2	3	4	5	6	7	8	9	10

K-5 What role did product reputation play in the decision to purchase the ERP software? (0 - was not a factor and was not considered, 10 - critical to the final decision)

0	1	2	3	4	5	6	7	8	9	10

K-6 What role did product performance play in the decision to purchase the ERP software? (0 - was not a factor and was not considered, 10 - critical to the final decision)

0	1	2	3	4	5	6	7	8	9	10

K-7 What role did implementation time play in the decision to purchase the ERP software? (0 - was not a factor and was not considered, 10 - critical to the final decision)

0	1	2	3	4	5	6	7	8	9	10

K-8 What role did post implementation cost play in the decision to purchase the ERP software? (0 - was not a factor and was not considered, 10 - critical to the final decision)

0	1	2	3	4	5	6	7	8	9	10

K-9 What role did product flexibility play in the decision to purchase the ERP software? (0 - was not a factor and was not considered, 10 - critical to the final decision)

0	1	2	3	4	5	6	7	8	9	10

K-10 What role did product training requirements play in the decision to purchase the ERP software? (0 - was not a factor and was not considered, 10 - critical to the final decision)

0	1	2	3	4	5	6	7	8	9	10

K-11 What role did critical capabilities or special functions play in the decision to purchase the ERP software? (0 - was not a factor and was not considered, 10 - critical to the final decision)

0	1	2	3	4	5	6	7	8	9	10

K-12 What role did total cost of ownership play in the decision to purchase the ERP software? (0 - was not a factor and was not considered, 10 - critical to the final decision)

0	1	2	3	4	5	6	7	8	9	10

K-13 What role did 3rd party support play in the decision to purchase the ERP software? (0 - was not a factor and was not considered, 10 - critical to the final decision)

0	1	2	3	4	5	6	7	8	9	10

K-14 What role did ease of integration with other products play in the decision to purchase the ERP software? (0 - was not a factor and was not considered, 10 - critical to the final decision)

0	1	2	3	4	5	6	7	8	9	10

K-15 What role did software demonstrations play in the decision to purchase the ERP software? (0 - was not a factor and was not considered or was not performed, 10 - critical to the final decision)

0	1	2	3	4	5	6	7	8	9	10

K-16 What role did independent references play in the decision to purchase the ERP software? (0 - was not a factor and was not considered or was not performed, 10 - critical to the final decision)

0	1	2	3	4	5	6	7	8	9	10

K-17 How many vendors made the short list for consideration for purchase? (0 - 0, 1 - 1, 2 - 2, 3 - 3, 10 - 10)

0	1	2	3	4	5	6	7	8	9	10

K-18 What were some of the most significant factors for choosing the final ERP software over others?

____

I seem to have been only like a boy, playing on the seashore and diverting myself in now and then finding a smoother pebble or a prettier shell, whilst the great ocean of truth lay all undiscovered before me.

-Isaac Newton

18.7

Project Management

B-1 How clear is the vision statement for the ERP system. (0 - none at all, 10 - clearly understood by everybody.)

0	1	2	3	4	5	6	7	8	9	10

B-2 How clear is the mission statement for the ERP system. (0 - none at all, 10 - clearly understood by everybody.)

0	1	2	3	4	5	6	7	8	9	10

B-3 Were clear milestones established through the original implementation process. (0 - none at all, 10 - clearly understood by everybody.)

0	1	2	3	4	5	6	7	8	9	10

B-4 How many different people were responsible for project management?

____

B-5 Was project management provided by an internal or external resource?

____Internal

____External

____Both

B-6 How many times did a change in project management take place from one person to another?

____

B-7 Did the person or people responsible for project management receive some type of training for project management in ERP systems? (0 - no training at all, 10 - extensive training)

0	1	2	3	4	5	6	7	8	9	10

B-8 Did the person or people responsible for project management have organizational knowledge about the company and products? (0 - no knowledge at all, 10 - very extensive knowledge)

0	1	2	3	4	5	6	7	8	9	10

B-9 Did the person or people responsible for project management have authority and power to directly control conflicting needs of implementation team members? (0 - no authority at all, 10 - complete authority and power)

0	1	2	3	4	5	6	7	8	9	10

B-10 Did team building activities take place during or before the implementation process? (0 - no team building, 10 - extensive team building and training)

0	1	2	3	4	5	6	7	8	9	10

B-11 Did formal weekly team meetings take place during the implementation process? (0 - no team meetings, 10 - meetings held weekly without failure)

0	1	2	3	4	5	6	7	8	9	10

B-12 Were internally developed checklists developed during or before the implementation process to audit missing functionality of the software? (0 - no checklist developed, 10 - formal checklist developed)

0	1	2	3	4	5	6	7	8	9	10

B-13 Did an external consultant agency provide checklists during or before the implementation process to audit missing functionality. (0 - no checklist provided, 10 - formal checklist provided covering all needs)

0	1	2	3	4	5	6	7	8	9	10

B-14 Was a separate computer room set up for training and testing? (0 - no computer room setup, 10 - computer room setup)

0	1	2	3	4	5	6	7	8	9	10

B-15 Was a timeline highlighting critical milestones developed and communicated? (0 - no timeline was developed, 5 - timeline developed but not communicated, 10 - timeline developed and communicated)

0	1	2	3	4	5	6	7	8	9	10

B-16 Was a newsletter used to communicate project news? (0 - no newsletter used, 5 - sporadic appearances, 10 - regular publication and distribution without failure)

0	1	2	3	4	5	6	7	8	9	10

B-17 Did the people responsible for doing the work, participate in the planning? (0 - no, 10 - extensive involvement in the planning)

0	1	2	3	4	5	6	7	8	9	10

B-18 Was the entire team allowed to help develop the vision and mission statements for the project? (0 - no involvement, 10 - extensive involvement)

0	1	2	3	4	5	6	7	8	9	10

B-19 Have clear project objectives been developed and communicated? (0 - no development, 10 - developed and communicated)

0	1	2	3	4	5	6	7	8	9	10

B-20 Has a detailed task list been developed that supports the project objectives? (0 - no development, 10 - developed and communicated)

0	1	2	3	4	5	6	7	8	9	10

B-21 Have all the required resources to support the project objective been identified, documented, and communicated? (0 - no development, 10 - developed, documented, and communicated)

0	1	2	3	4	5	6	7	8	9	10

B-22 Have risk areas been identified with contingency plans documented? (0 - no identification, 10 - identified, documented, and communicated)

0	1	2	3	4	5	6	7	8	9	10

B-23 Did signoff of the project plan occur for all critical stakeholders? (0 - no signoffs performed, 10 - signoffs performed)

0	1	2	3	4	5	6	7	8	9	10

B-24 Is some process of change control management in place to communicate and adjust the project plan? (0 - no change control management in place, 10 - change control in place, changes documented and communicated)

0	1	2	3	4	5	6	7	8	9	10

B-25 Are subprojects carefully selected in the early stages of the project that have a high probability of success? (0 - subprojects are not scheduled based on the probability of success, 10 - scheduling successful subprojects in the early stages of the project are considered critical for success of the overall project)

0	1	2	3	4	5	6	7	8	9	10

B-26 Does an open issue log exist that is easily accessible to all members of the project team? (0 - no issue log exists, 10 - issue log exists and is open to all project members for inspection)

0	1	2	3	4	5	6	7	8	9	10

B-27 Is focus to remain on time and on budget or to meet the needs of the company? (0 - on time and on budget, 5 - somewhere in between, 10 - meet the needs of the company)

0	1	2	3	4	5	6	7	8	9	10

B-28 Is an issue resolution process used? (0 - we have no clear issue resolution process, 10 - our issue resolution policy is documented and followed closely)

0	1	2	3	4	5	6	7	8	9	10

B-29 Did an overall planning workshop take place so the company could understand the complete magnitude of the project before the project started? (0 - no planning workshop performed, 10 - planning workshop took place with documented output)

0	1	2	3	4	5	6	7	8	9	10

B-30 Is it clearly understood who is responsible for specific project tasks? (0 - no understanding, 10 - very clear understand by all team members)

0	1	2	3	4	5	6	7	8	9	10

B-31 Have target dates slipped or been met on time? (0 - target dates have never been met, 10 - a target date has never been missed)

0	1	2	3	4	5	6	7	8	9	10

B-32 Have periodic audits been performed before and after the go live date of the ERP system? (0 - an audit has never been performed, 10 - comprehensive audits are regularly scheduled and performed without fail)

0	1	2	3	4	5	6	7	8	9	10

B-33 Do other business functions and projects often interfere with the implementation and maintenance of the ERP system? (0 - other projects are constantly interfering, 10 - other projects and business functions never interfere)

0	1	2	3	4	5	6	7	8	9	10

B-34 What level of control exists within the project? (0 - highly reactive fire fighting, 10 - dynamic integrated change control management with no surprises)

0	1	2	3	4	5	6	7	8	9	10

B-35 Do project team members perform the tasks from their own work stations or from a designated project working area? (0 - own work stations, 10 - designated project working areas)

0	1	2	3	4	5	6	7	8	9	10

B-36 Are major milestones celebrated? (0 - milestones not recognized or communicated, 10 - team celebrates well together with each milestone achieved)

0	1	2	3	4	5	6	7	8	9	10

B-37 What is the general conversion strategy from the legacy system to the new ERP system? (multiple choice)
____Parallel Process
____Cut Over

B-38 Have conference room pilots been used to completely test the software? (0 - we do not do this, 5 - partially, 10 - complete integrated enterprise testing)

0	1	2	3	4	5	6	7	8	9	10

B-39 Is there a documented cost justification strategy in place for program modifications? (0 - no, 10 - we have a documented cost justification strategy that must be followed before modification can be made. Signature cycle approval process must be followed)

0	1	2	3	4	5	6	7	8	9	10

B-40 Are project team members for the ERP implementation process, before the go live, considered dedicated resources? (0 - team members dedicated 0% time, 10 - our team members dedicate 100% of their time)

0	1	2	3	4	5	6	7	8	9	10

B-41 Was there a pre ERP class/seminar for senior management? (0 - no, 10 - yes)

0	1	2	3	4	5	6	7	8	9	10

B-42 How much training was provided to the team members in understanding the software applications? (0 - not enough, 10 - enough to completely satisfy the team members)

0	1	2	3	4	5	6	7	8	9	10

B-43 For team members that were fully dedicated to the project, was some type of job security process communicated to the dedicated members? (n/a - we had no fully dedicated members, 0 - no, 10 - yes)

0	1	2	3	4	5	6	7	8	9	10

B-44 What type of project management strategy best matches your implementation and future process improvements? (1 - Functional Organization, 2 - Lightweight Project Manager, 3 - Heavyweight Project Manager, 4 - Tiger Team) See diagrams on the web.

____ 1 Functional Organization
____ 2 Lightweight Project Manager
____ 3 Heavyweight Project Manager
____ 4 Tiger Team

8-42 How much training was provided to the team members in understanding the software applications? (0 - not enough, 10 - enough to completely satisfy the team members)

___ 1 Functional Organization
___ 2 Lightweight Project Manager
___ 3 Heavyweight Project Manager
___ 4 Tiger Team

Hockey is an exciting sport, and its style is exciting. But it is not a good management style - Philip Crosby

18.8

TQM, JIT and Continuous Improvement

C-1 Is the process of operations management using computer information systems considered to be a key component for developing a competitive advantage in the market place? (0 - not considered to be important, 10 - believed to be critical to the success of the company)

0	1	2	3	4	5	6	7	8	9	10

C-2 Are managers and users constantly looking for ways to improve operational effectiveness through the use of computer resource management? (0 - never looking, 10 - always looking)

0	1	2	3	4	5	6	7	8	9	10

C-3 Are consistent stable messages received from top management providing clear direction? (0 - no messages or mixed messages, 10 - long term consistent message)

0	1	2	3	4	5	6	7	8	9	10

C-4 Do people accept responsibility to take corrective action for problems that will adversely affect the company without prompting from the management? (0 - no sense of responsibility, 10 - responsibility is accepted without prompting)

0	1	2	3	4	5	6	7	8	9	10

C-5 Are managers and users looking to sources outside the company establishing realistic benchmarks? (0 - no search performed, 10 - continuous process to establish new benchmarks)

0	1	2	3	4	5	6	7	8	9	10

C-6 Are benchmarks understood by all stakeholders of the organization? (0 - no communication in place, 10 - clearly understood)

0	1	2	3	4	5	6	7	8	9	10

C-7 How often do benchmarks get changed? (0 - do not exist or are never changed, 10 - dynamically change as conditions change)

0	1	2	3	4	5	6	7	8	9	10

C-8 Are people at all levels of the organization inspired to reveal areas of improvement? (0 - people are not inspired, 10 - people are inspired and communicate areas for improvement)

0	1	2	3	4	5	6	7	8	9	10

C-9 Is process improvement initiated and driven by factors other than financial reasons? (0 - driven purely by financial reasons, 10 - driven by factors other than financial reasons)

0	1	2	3	4	5	6	7	8	9	10

C-10 Is there a process of eliminating non-value added activities? (0 - no attempt to eliminate non-value added activities, 10 - relentless effort to eliminate non-value added activities)

0	1	2	3	4	5	6	7	8	9	10

C-11 Do annual plans include the dedication of a portion of resources for the purpose of continuous improvement? (0 - no dedication, 10 - portion of resource are dedicated for every planning period)

0	1	2	3	4	5	6	7	8	9	10

C-12 Does sharing between departments of resources, occur without the direction of upper or mid management? (0 - no resource sharing, 10 - top or middle management must get involved for resource sharing to occur)

0	1	2	3	4	5	6	7	8	9	10

C-13 Do employees take direct action to make improvements within their immediate work area? (0 - no direct action is taken, 10 - direct action is taken without constraint)

0	1	2	3	4	5	6	7	8	9	10

C-14 Is management constantly looking for ways to tear down barriers for process improvement? (0 - management is not looking, 10 - management is constantly looking)

0	1	2	3	4	5	6	7	8	9	10

C-15 What percentage of the new process improvement ideas, that are implemented, remain in effect for 6 months or greater? (0 - 0%, 1 - 10%, 2 - 20%, 3 - 30%, 10 - 100%)

0	1	2	3	4	5	6	7	8	9	10

C-16 Is customer feedback openly encouraged and infrastructure in place to support corrective actions? (0 - customer feedback is not accepted or welcomed, 10 - customer feedback is received and corrective action is taken)

0	1	2	3	4	5	6	7	8	9	10

C-17 Are formal tools in place to educate employees on customer needs and expectations? (0 - employees are not educated for customer needs and expectations, 10 - a formal documented process is in place to educate employees on customer needs and expectations)

0	1	2	3	4	5	6	7	8	9	10

C-18 Are journal logs kept by customer, which record all complaints and how the problem was resolved? (0 - no logs are kept, 10 - logs maintained containing both complaints and resolutions)

0	1	2	3	4	5	6	7	8	9	10

C-19 Is the search for new innovative methods of customer feedback always present? (0 - new methods for customer feedback are never considered, 10 - new methods of customer feedback come up on a regular basis)

0	1	2	3	4	5	6	7	8	9	10

C-20 Does the primary customer contact representative have the authority to initiate a corrective action request? (0 - customer contact representative has no authority to initiate a corrective action, 10 - customer contact representative has complete authority)

0	1	2	3	4	5	6	7	8	9	10

C-21 Does the marketing function consider JIT, TQM, and ERP to be important as a competitive advantage against competitors? (0 -the marketing function does not understand JIT, TQM, and ERP, 10 - marketing has clear understanding of JIT, TQM, and ERP and aggressively promotes these techniques)

0	1	2	3	4	5	6	7	8	9	10

C-22 Are long term relationships being sought with vendors for the purposes of improving quality and lowering costs? (0 - there is no commitment to developing long term relationships, 10 - strong relationships continuously sought and currently exist)

0	1	2	3	4	5	6	7	8	9	10

C-23 Is the average lead time for all products continuously reduced? (0 - lead times are growing worse on average, 5 - lead times have stayed about the same 10 - lead times have continuously dropped.)

0	1	2	3	4	5	6	7	8	9	10

C-24 Are shipping costs to the customer decreasing? (0 - shipping costs are growing worse on average, 5 - shipping costs have stayed about the same, 10 - shipping costs have continuously dropped.)

0	1	2	3	4	5	6	7	8	9	10

C-25 Since five years ago or the start of the company, have inventory turns increased? (0 - inventory turns are growing worse on average, 5 - inventory turns have stayed about the same, 10 - inventory turns have continuously dropped.)

0	1	2	3	4	5	6	7	8	9	10

C-26 Are kanbans used? (0 - kanbans apply to this environment but are not used, 10 - kanbans apply to this environment and are used, n/a - kanbans do not apply to this environment)

0	1	2	3	4	5	6	7	8	9	10

C-27 Are lot sizes continuously decreasing in size? (0 - on average they are growing in size, 5 - on average they are staying about the same, 10 - on average they are decreasing in size)

0	1	2	3	4	5	6	7	8	9	10

C-28 Are lead times continuously decreasing? (0 - on average they are growing in length, 5 - on average they are staying about the same, 10 - on average they are decreasing in length)

0	1	2	3	4	5	6	7	8	9	10

C-29 Is standardization of parts used? (0 - there never has been any effort to standardize parts, 5 - effort has been made in the past and benefits still exist today, 10 - standardization of parts is a continuous process)

0	1	2	3	4	5	6	7	8	9	10

C-30 Is a program in place to increase the stability of the manufacturing process to obtain more reliable completion dates? (0 - no program in place, 10 - program is in place and good progress has been made in increasing process stability)

0	1	2	3	4	5	6	7	8	9	10

C-31 Are engineering change orders examined to identify trends and patterns for the purpose of cutting their numbers? (0 - engineering change orders are not examined for trends or patterns, 10 - engineering change orders are monitored consistently by the use of graphs and charts that are open to the public)

0	1	2	3	4	5	6	7	8	9	10

C-32 Are inspection activities being reduced, or at a bare minimum, because the quality of the product can be trusted? (0 - there is no trust in the product, 10 - no inspections are performed because of outstanding quality)

0	1	2	3	4	5	6	7	8	9	10

C-33 Is there a formal program in place to eliminate scrap and rework while increasing yields? (0 - no effort is being made to reduce scrap, 10 - people at all levels of the organization are looking for ways to increase operational efficiency through the reduction of waste)

0	1	2	3	4	5	6	7	8	9	10

C-34 Does each functional area of the company perform root cause analysis to understand the cause of problems? (0 - no functional areas of the business perform root cause analysis, 10 - all functional areas perform root cause analysis)

0	1	2	3	4	5	6	7	8	9	10

C-35 Does data collected in tracking measurements or process control charts serve as focal points in discussions for process improvement? (0 - tracking measurements or process control charts are never subject of discussion, 10 - tracking measurements or process control charts are considered critical in meetings to discuss process improvement)

0	1	2	3	4	5	6	7	8	9	10

C-36 Are cause and effect diagrams used? (0 - have never been used and people have no understanding of cause and effect diagrams, 10 - cause and effect diagram are scattered through the company publicly posted)

0	1	2	3	4	5	6	7	8	9	10

C-37 Are the most significant problems of each department posted in plain sight with supporting TQM data tracking the situation with potential solutions or improvement opportunities? (0 - departments have never considered themselves to have problems, 10 - all functional areas post problems with supporting TQM data)

0	1	2	3	4	5	6	7	8	9	10

C-38 Are a variety of TQC tools used? (0 - no TQC tools are used, 10 - a wide variety of TQC tools are used and matched for the job)

0	1	2	3	4	5	6	7	8	9	10

C-39 Are flow charts used to document processes and bring better understanding? (0 - flow charts have never been used, 10 - flow charts are used extensively)

0	1	2	3	4	5	6	7	8	9	10

C-40 For accident prone processes, is there an effort to "mistake proof" the process? (0 - mistake proofing is not performed, 10 - mistake proofing is a company wide campaign reaching into all functional areas of the business)

0	1	2	3	4	5	6	7	8	9	10

C-41 Are facilities and manufacturing processes continuously improved to reduce handling and transfer of materials? (0 - no efforts have ever been made to improve material handling, 10 - material handling and transfer has been reduced to almost nothing)

0	1	2	3	4	5	6	7	8	9	10

C-42 What is the general organizational level of the warehouse and/or staging areas? (0 - disastrous chaotic mess, 10 - clean, neat, organized allowing the expeditious location and transfer of materials)

0	1	2	3	4	5	6	7	8	9	10

C-43 Are low setup time, high quality, and flexibility important considerations for production equipment when performing ROI analysis? (0 - these factors not considered to be important, 10 - as part of company policy, these factors must be considered before an expenditure can be approved)

0	1	2	3	4	5	6	7	8	9	10

C-44 Have production lines been set up so that simple visual tools are in place to expedite the process of troubleshooting? (0 - there is extensive need, but nothing has been done, 10 - numerous visual tools exist for the process of troubleshooting)

0	1	2	3	4	5	6	7	8	9	10

C-45 Are jigs, tools, and fixtures stored at the point of use? (0 - these are often some distance away and often difficult to locate, 10 - stored at the point of use)

0	1	2	3	4	5	6	7	8	9	10

C-46 Is there a program in place to continuously search for ways to reduce setup and changeover times? (0 - no effort is made to reduce setup and changeover times, 10 - the search for ways to reduce setup and changeover times is an ongoing process)

0	1	2	3	4	5	6	7	8	9	10

C-47 Is there a preventive maintenance program for plant and equipment? (0 - preventative maintenance is not performed, 10 - well planned and executed preventative maintenance programs exist)

0	1	2	3	4	5	6	7	8	9	10

C-48 Are machine breakdowns carefully analyzed for cause so future breakdowns will be prevented through the use of preventive maintenance? (0 - machine break downs are not analyzed for cause, 10 - breakdowns are analyzed, understood, documented, and incorporated into preventive maintenance programs)

0	1	2	3	4	5	6	7	8	9	10

C-49 Are materials for manufacturing processes stored at the point of use? (0 - materials must be transferred from some warehouse, 10 - almost all materials can be found within the immediate area of use)

0	1	2	3	4	5	6	7	8	9	10

C-50 Is cleanliness of facility an important task? (0 - cleaning is ad hoc and performed when people get around to doing it, 10 - cleaning is performed on a regular schedule without fail backed up by clear documentation)

0	1	2	3	4	5	6	7	8	9	10

C-51 Is mix modeling production and scheduling used to better meet customer demands? (0 - the concept of mix modeling production is not known in this company, 10 - mix modeling production is used wherever possible)

0	1	2	3	4	5	6	7	8	9	10

C-52 Does operations management wait for key pieces of information before decisions can be made? (0 - production lines often stand still while waiting for information, 10 - downtime never occurs because of a lack of critical information)

0	1	2	3	4	5	6	7	8	9	10

C-53 Is there a systematic effort to reduce the overall number of suppliers? (0 - number of suppliers is increasing or staying the same, 10 - an aggressive program is in place and significant reductions have been made in the number of suppliers)

0	1	2	3	4	5	6	7	8	9	10

C-54 Is there a communication program in place to promote JIT and TQM with suppliers? (0 - suppliers are not encouraged to participate in JIT or TQM, 10 - a program is in place and a significant number of suppliers has adopted JIT and TQM)

0	1	2	3	4	5	6	7	8	9	10

C-55 Is quality placed before price when negotiations take place with suppliers? (0 - price dominates with little discussion regarding quality, 10 - quality tends to dominate discussions with price being only a secondary consideration)

0	1	2	3	4	5	6	7	8	9	10

C-56 Do long term contracts with suppliers reside over short term contracts? (0 - contracts are only for short term immediate need, 10 - contracts are for long term including life of product, multi-month, and multi-year)

0	1	2	3	4	5	6	7	8	9	10

C-57 Is there any kanban activity with suppliers? (0 - kanban is not used for suppliers, 10 - kanban is used whenever possible and includes electronic kanban capability)

0	1	2	3	4	5	6	7	8	9	10

C-58 Are suppliers allowed to participate in the design of new products? (0 - suppliers are not considered in the design of new products, 10 -suppliers participate and provide most useful insight in the design of new products)

0	1	2	3	4	5	6	7	8	9	10

C-59 Are long term future projections shared with suppliers? (0 - suppliers are not allowed to have this type of information, 10 - future projections are shared with suppliers to reduce shortages, improve quality, and reduce cost)

0	1	2	3	4	5	6	7	8	9	10

C-60 Do suppliers receive release schedules from planning systems? (0 - no release schedules are used, 10 - release schedules are actively used)

0	1	2	3	4	5	6	7	8	9	10

C-61 Are there any certification programs in place for suppliers? (0 - no certification programs are in place, 10 - every supplier must go through a certification process)

0	1	2	3	4	5	6	7	8	9	10

C-62 Are delivery quantities being reduced from suppliers resulting in more frequent deliveries? (0 - no effort is being made to reduce delivery size, 10 - delivery size has decreased substantially and is expected to expand to other vendors)

0	1	2	3	4	5	6	7	8	9	10

C-63 Are the overall supplier shipping costs decreasing over time? (0 - shipping costs are very unpredictable often containing emergency or overnight surcharges, 10 - shipping costs conform closely to expectations showing a general decreasing trend)

0	1	2	3	4	5	6	7	8	9	10

C-64 Is there a supplier report card program in place? (0 - supplier report card is not in use, 10 - supplier report cards are used aggressively often resulting in improved performance)

0	1	2	3	4	5	6	7	8	9	10

C-65 Do suppliers often analyze the company's product to lower cost, make improvements or lower response time? (0 - suppliers have never seen our product, 10 - suppliers make recommendations to our product on a regular basis)

0	1	2	3	4	5	6	7	8	9	10

C-66 Does communication flow freely between the company and the supplier? (0 - communication must often flow between several different layers of management on both sides before reaching the right person, 10 - there are direct lines of communication in place bypassing layers of management)

0	1	2	3	4	5	6	7	8	9	10

C-67 Is work often performed at a work station without some type of authorization? (0 - work stations are often operated with out authorization and in conflict with the company's needs, 10 - no work is ever performed without a prior authorization)

0	1	2	3	4	5	6	7	8	9	10

C-68 Is every effort made to resolve quality problems from where they originate or are they passed on for someone else to fix? (0 - quality problems are passed on to someone else for fixing, 10 - intense effort is made to not pass on defective parts and to fix the quality problems from where they originate)

0	1	2	3	4	5	6	7	8	9	10

C-69 Are production quantities for kanbans and work orders followed? (0 - overproduction is a constant problem, 10 - production always follows amounts found on kanban cards and work orders consistent with company needs)

0	1	2	3	4	5	6	7	8	9	10

C-70 Are common functional work centers being broken up into manufacturing cells where needed? (0 - similar functional work centers are always grouped together, 10 - ways of combining different functional work centers into manufacturing cells are constantly sought)

0	1	2	3	4	5	6	7	8	9	10

C-71 Is mix modeling production a strong consideration in the design of manufacturing processes and production equipment selection? (0 - mix modeling production is never considered, 10 - mix modeling production is always kept in mind)

0	1	2	3	4	5	6	7	8	9	10

C-72 Have routings for both materials and information flow become more complex? (0 - material and information flows are complex and no improvements have been made, 10 - material and information flows are continuously simplified)

0	1	2	3	4	5	6	7	8	9	10

C-73 Is there a tendency to keep bills of materials flat or to use phantoms to achieve a similar effect? (0 - bills of materials are complex and do not use phantoms, 10 - bills of materials are flat and use phantoms wherever needed)

0	1	2	3	4	5	6	7	8	9	10

C-74 Are needless work orders eliminated? (0 - no reduction of work orders has occurred because of process simplification, 10 - several work orders have been combined into one after manufacturing processes have been simplified or combined)

0	1	2	3	4	5	6	7	8	9	10

C-75 Does top management encourage the use of activity based costing? (0 - top management does not encourage activity based costing, 10 - top management actively promotes the use of activity based costing)

0	1	2	3	4	5	6	7	8	9	10

C-76 Are quality problems and process improvement activities performed by the appropriate teams? (0 - often assigned or performed by wrong team, 10 - organizational agreement exists on what teams should examine quality problems and improvement activities)

0	1	2	3	4	5	6	7	8	9	10

C-77 Do benchmarks exist throughout the company? (0 - no benchmarks exist, 10 - benchmarks are found in all functional areas of the business)

0	1	2	3	4	5	6	7	8	9	10

C-78 Is a calibration program in place to ensure that accurate data is obtained? (0 - no calibration programs or processes exist, 10 - calibration processes can be found wherever calibration principles can be applied)

0	1	2	3	4	5	6	7	8	9	10

C-79 Are there any programs to automate data collection tasks? (0 - no effort has been made, 10 - numerous automated data collection projects have been implemented with the search always continuing)

0	1	2	3	4	5	6	7	8	9	10

C-80 Have all main business processes been streamlined to eliminate all waste? (0 - no effort has been made to eliminate waste, 10 - numerous automated data collection projects have been implemented with the search always continuing)

0	1	2	3	4	5	6	7	8	9	10

C-81 Do all processes in the company perform at or above 6 sigma? (0 - below six sigma, 10 - at or above six sigma)

0	1	2	3	4	5	6	7	8	9	10

C-82 Has fear been completely driven out of the organization? (0 - fear is common, 10 - fear is seldom found)

0	1	2	3	4	5	6	7	8	9	10

C-83 Is there a formal procedure for eliminating process constraints? (0 - no process, 10 - procedure exists and is applied)

0	1	2	3	4	5	6	7	8	9	10

C-84 Is the concept of continuous improvement applied to operations management? (0 - continuous improvement is not used for operations management, 10 - continuous improvement is used extensively in operations management)

0	1	2	3	4	5	6	7	8	9	10

C-85 Are quantitative measurement systems used widely to identify problems AND to show that the corrective action produced expected results? (0 - quantitative measurements systems are not used with corrective action techniques, 10 - the two are considered to be an intricate bond and actively practiced)

0	1	2	3	4	5	6	7	8	9	10

C-86 Are current technologies for data collection and data process being used, where applicable, to identify improvement areas? (0 - new technologies are not considered or applied, 10 - company is constantly on the lookout for new technologies to aid in process improvement to be applied where needed)

0	1	2	3	4	5	6	7	8	9	10

C-87 Is the number of acceptable production defects known and is that goal met? (0 - nobody knows what is an acceptable amount of production defects, 10 - the number of production defects is always less than the acceptable amount)

0	1	2	3	4	5	6	7	8	9	10

C-88 Do quality measurements include parts per million (PPM) reporting? (0 - nobody here has ever heard of PPM and it is not used, 10 - PPM is common and is applied where appropriate)

0	1	2	3	4	5	6	7	8	9	10

C-89 Are the number of acceptable supplier defects clearly understood by the supplier and is the goal achieved? (0 - we just deal with defects as we come across them, 10 - supplier goals are clearly understood and achieved)

0	1	2	3	4	5	6	7	8	9	10

C-90 Is the cost of quality measured throughout the entire company? (0 - cost of quality is not measured, 10 - cost of quality is measured and goals achieved)

0	1	2	3	4	5	6	7	8	9	10

C-91 Are on-time deliveries measured and tracked? (0 - our company does not have or use these measurements, 10 - on time deliveries are carefully measured and tracked without fail)

0	1	2	3	4	5	6	7	8	9	10

C-92 How much emphasis is placed on the measurement of labor efficiency or labor deviations? (0 - our company does not have or use these measurements, 10 - labor efficiency and/or deviations are carefully measured and tracked without fail)

0	1	2	3	4	5	6	7	8	9	10

C-93 How much emphasis is placed on the measurement of machine efficiency or machine deviations? (0 - our company does not have or use these measurements, 10 - machine efficiency and/or deviations are carefully measured and tracked without fail)

0	1	2	3	4	5	6	7	8	9	10

C-94 How much emphasis is placed on the measurement of defects per person? (0 - our company does not have or use this measurement, 10 - defects per person are carefully measured and tracked without fail)

0	1	2	3	4	5	6	7	8	9	10

C-95 How much emphasis is placed on the measurement of purchased price variance? (0 - our company does not have or use this measurement, 10 - purchase price variance is carefully measured and tracked without fail)

0	1	2	3	4	5	6	7	8	9	10

C-96 How much emphasis is placed on the measurement of manufacturing overhead rate? (0 - our company does not have or use this measurement, 10 - manufacturing overhcad rate is carefully measured and tracked without fail)

0	1	2	3	4	5	6	7	8	9	10

C-97 Are production outputs, including quality and quantity, posted for public viewing? (0 - production quality and quantity are kept secret, 10 - always posted with out fail for public inspection)

0	1	2	3	4	5	6	7	8	9	10

C-98 Is days on hand inventory measured? (0 - this is not measured, 10 - measured on a regular basis without fail)

0	1	2	3	4	5	6	7	8	9	10

C-99 Is total asset turnover measured? (0 - this is not measured, 10 - measured on a regular basis without fail)

0	1	2	3	4	5	6	7	8	9	10

C-100 Are plans in place with clear priorities for attaining operational excellence to improve quality, lower response time, and lower total cost? (0 - no plans and no priorities exist, 10 - clear plans and priorities are understood by all critical stakeholders)

0	1	2	3	4	5	6	7	8	9	10

C-101 Is there a procedure in place to establish new goals for operational or organizational excellence? (0 - no procedure in place, 10 - procedure in place and clearly followed)

0	1	2	3	4	5	6	7	8	9	10

C-102 Are many different areas such as benchmarking, customer requirements, process capability, and supplier requirements considered for process improvement? (0 - many different areas are not considered, 10 - numerous areas are always considered for process improvement)

0	1	2	3	4	5	6	7	8	9	10

C-103 Do customer expectations and needs blend smoothly with the planning process? (0 - no, 10 - planning process blends smoothly and remains consistent with customer needs)

0	1	2	3	4	5	6	7	8	9	10

C-104 Is benchmark data used to help establish target areas for process and quality improvements? (0 - no, 10 - benchmark data is a key to help determine process and quality improvements)

0	1	2	3	4	5	6	7	8	9	10

C-105 Do people from all different parts and levels participate in process improvement activities? (0 - we do not have process improvement activities, 10 - people from all levels and parts participate)

0	1	2	3	4	5	6	7	8	9	10

C-106 In order to meet future process improvement targets, are the kind and amount of technology, training, and education understood so targets goals can prioritized? (0 - we are not sure where we are or where we are going with technology, training, and education, 10 - we have clear understanding where we are, where we are going, and when we are going to get there)

0	1	2	3	4	5	6	7	8	9	10

C-107 Is planning for improvements also considered a process that can be improved upon? (0 - no, 10 - yes, and is documented and understood by all critical stakeholders)

0	1	2	3	4	5	6	7	8	9	10

C-108 Are the number of acceptable supplier defects clearly understood by the company and is the goal achieved? (0 - we just deal with defects as we come across them, 10 - supplier goals are clearly understood by the company and achieved)

0	1	2	3	4	5	6	7	8	9	10

It is better to be frightened now then killed hereafter.
-Winston Churchill

18.9

Strategic Planning

D-1 Do all key people, representing all functional areas of the business, participate in the development of the business strategy? (0 - no people or only one person is responsible, 10 - all functions working together as a team)

0	1	2	3	4	5	6	7	8	9	10

D-2 Is the business strategy clear enough so that it is not subject to confusion or interpretation? (0 - very unclear, 10 - clearly understood)

0	1	2	3	4	5	6	7	8	9	10

D-3 Does communication take place to inform all critical stakeholders of the business strategy? (0 - no communication, 10 - extensive communication with follow ups)

0	1	2	3	4	5	6	7	8	9	10

D-4 Does the strategic business plan adjust for situations and events that will affect the business? (0 - no adjustments, 10 - dynamic change synchronization consistent with situations and events)

0	1	2	3	4	5	6	7	8	9	10

D-5 Are strategic business plans developed directly under the company's control or delegated to an outside source? (0 - delegated to an outside source, 10 - managed directly by the company)

0	1	2	3	4	5	6	7	8	9	10

D-6 Are large capital investment projects driven by the thought of developing a longterm competitive advantage in the marketplace? (0 - driven by other factors, 10 - driven by long term competitive advantage)

0	1	2	3	4	5	6	7	8	9	10

D-7 Are core business strategies reexamined on a regular basis? (0 - business strategies not considered, 10 - reexamined on a regular basis or as conditions dictate)

0	1	2	3	4	5	6	7	8	9	10

D-8 Is cross edit checking performed between the different business strategies to check for compatibility? (0 - no cross edit checking, 10 - extensive cross edit checking)

0	1	2	3	4	5	6	7	8	9	10

D-9 Are business strategies reviewed by senior management as a team? (0 - never reviewed, 10 - reviewed 8 or more times per year)

0	1	2	3	4	5	6	7	8	9	10

D-10 What level of integration exists between the business strategy as it relates to the functional areas of the business? (0 - dysfunctional and opposing, 10 - synchronized integration)

0	1	2	3	4	5	6	7	8	9	10

D-11 Are internally developed budgets consistent with business plans? (0 - dysfunctional and opposing, 10 - synchronized integration)

0	1	2	3	4	5	6	7	8	9	10

D-12 Does the business plan act as a compass to provide a sense of direction and final destination? (0 - business plan does not exist and/or has no sense of direction, 10 - clear direction with destinations understood)

0	1	2	3	4	5	6	7	8	9	10

D-13 Does the longest cumulative lead time for operations planning exceed that found in the business plan? Note: the longest cumulative leadtime should consider factors other than products/services such as facility expansion. (0 - leadtime is much longer than the business plan, 5 - about the same, 10 - leadtime is much shorter than the business plan)

0	1	2	3	4	5	6	7	8	9	10

D-14 Are business plans created based on supporting concerns that have been internally documented? (0 - no documentation, 10 - concerns clearly documented)

0	1	2	3	4	5	6	7	8	9	10

D-15 Are budgets developed by department? (0 - budgets do not exist or are not broken down by department, 10 - budgets are broken down by department)

0	1	2	3	4	5	6	7	8	9	10

D-16 How often are budgets checked for proper tracking? (0 - budgets do no exist or are not tracked, 10 - budgets are tracked monthly or more frequently)

0	1	2	3	4	5	6	7	8	9	10

D-17 Do sales projections flow up to the overall financial projections for the company? (0 - sales projections are not considered, 10 - sales projections have direct impact on financial projections)

0	1	2	3	4	5	6	7	8	9	10

D-18 Do compensation plans tie in with strategic business plans or do they act independently? (0 - tie in with strategic business plans, 10 - act independently)

0	1	2	3	4	5	6	7	8	9	10

The reason that talk is so cheap is because supply greatly exceeds demand.

18.10

People Systems

G-1 How well developed are the political and social structures that make distinctions between working classes AND inhibit the process of communication? (0 - highly developed structures that prevent cross functional communication, 10 - open and unrestricted communication patterns)

0	1	2	3	4	5	6	7	8	9	10

G-2 Are team meetings held on a regular basis for purposes of information exchange? (0 - no team meetings, 10 - meetings are held on a regular basis)

0	1	2	3	4	5	6	7	8	9	10

G-3 Is training provided on an annual basis to educate people, at all levels of the organization, on how to participate in teams? (0 - no team training, 5 - team training took place but no future plans to repeat the training, 10 - team training has been performed every year for the last 3 years and planned for the next 4 years)

0	1	2	3	4	5	6	7	8	9	10

G-4 Did the process of team training remain consistent or did the content and structure change as the organization gained a better understanding of team processes? (0 - no team training, 10 - repeated team training has taken place with adaptation taking place each time)

0	1	2	3	4	5	6	7	8	9	10

G-5 Is maintaining or developing strong channels of communication an important company objective understood and practiced by the company? (0 - never stated as an objective or practiced, 10 - clearly understood and practiced)

0	1	2	3	4	5	6	7	8	9	10

G-6 Are lengthy communication delays, based on need, often experienced? (0 - critical information routinely delayed, 10 - no delays in communication)

0	1	2	3	4	5	6	7	8	9	10

G-7 Does communication take place between team members and suppliers of the company? (0 - no communications, 10 - communications occur continuously without restrictions)

0	1	2	3	4	5	6	7	8	9	10

G-8 Does active bi-directional communication take place between managers and peers? (0 - no communication, 10 - active bi-directional communication)

0	1	2	3	4	5	6	7	8	9	10

G-9 Are reward systems in place to encourage communication? (0 - no reward system, 10 - reward system in place and understood by all people)

0	1	2	3	4	5	6	7	8	9	10

G-10 Are job titles and roles supportive of a teamwork environment? (0 - highly conflicting with a team environment, 10 - job titles and roles directly support team environments)

0	1	2	3	4	5	6	7	8	9	10

G-11 Does each work team have clear objectives or missions? (0 - no missions or objectives, 10 - all teams have objectives or missions)

0	1	2	3	4	5	6	7	8	9	10

G-12 Do teams meet for the purposes of problem solving related to the objectives or missions of the team? (0 - never meet, 10 - meet to solve problems with regular frequency)

0	1	2	3	4	5	6	7	8	9	10

G-13 Are teams capable of self direction? (0 - require extensive management direction and support, 10 - completely self directed)

0	1	2	3	4	5	6	7	8	9	10

G-14 Do teams look inward to their own performance for purposes of process improvement? (0 - require extensive management direction and support, 10 - completely self directed)

0	1	2	3	4	5	6	7	8	9	10

G-15 Do teams have a documented procedure in obtaining feedback from both internal and external suppliers and customers? (0 - no process or documentation in place, 10 - process and documentation in place and commonly used)

0	1	2	3	4	5	6	7	8	9	10

G-16 Are the requirements for suppliers and customers, both internal and external, commonly understood by the teams? (0 - teams have no understanding, 10 - team has exceptionally good understanding)

0	1	2	3	4	5	6	7	8	9	10

G-17 Do the teams have internally developed performance measurements to monitor their own performance? (0 - no performance measurements exist, 10 - team has performance measurements in place and posted for public viewing)

0	1	2	3	4	5	6	7	8	9	10

G-18 Do company and employees work together and understand the importance of building long term employee/company relationships? (0 - employees and company often conflict, 10 - employees and company work together for mutual benefit without conflict)

0	1	2	3	4	5	6	7	8	9	10

G-19 Do teams have the capability to respond quickly in reorganizing their resources for sudden changes in supply or demand? (0 - no capability to respond, 10 - can respond quickly)

0	1	2	3	4	5	6	7	8	9	10

G-20 Do all people in the company understand who the important customers are and what makes the company's products distinct from the competitors? (0 - less than 5% of the people understand, 10 - 100% of people understand who the key customers are and what makes the products distinct)

0	1	2	3	4	5	6	7	8	9	10

G-21 Are basic employee activities such as resignations, sickness, lateness, absenteeism, and employee moral measured on a regular basis? Are those measured results then compared with previous measurements? (0 - no measurements performed, 10 - measurements performed on a regular basis, comparisons and understanding occurs)

0	1	2	3	4	5	6	7	8	9	10

G-22 Have all the people of the company from all levels of management received training on the concept of work teams? (0 - no training has been performed, 10 - all people from all functional areas of the business have received training and understand the concept of work teams)

0	1	2	3	4	5	6	7	8	9	10

G-23 Did a confidentiality agreement have to be signed in order to receive consultation services from the software vendor? (0 - no confidentiality agreement had to be signed, 10 - confidentiality agreement had to be signed)

0	1	2	3	4	5	6	7	8	9	10

G-24 Did a contract services agreement have to be signed limiting where your company can seek services or who provides those software services or consultation? Note: sometimes this is included in the initial software sales contract. (0 - no contract services agreement had to be signed, 10 - contract services agreement had to be signed)

0	1	2	3	4	5	6	7	8	9	10

G-25 Do the layers of management tend to be flat or multilevel? (0 - very flat , 10 -multi layer management having 4 or more layers)

0	1	2	3	4	5	6	7	8	9	10

G-26 Do reward systems recognize both team and individual performance combined? (0 - recognizes one or the other or none, 10 - both are recognized)

0	1	2	3	4	5	6	7	8	9	10

G-27 Does the company have teams that are used throughout the organization? (0 - no, 10 - teams are used throughout the organization)

0	1	2	3	4	5	6	7	8	9	10

G-28 Do people tend to be organized into organizational silos or process teams? (0 - people are organized into silos, 10 - people are organized into process teams)

0	1	2	3	4	5	6	7	8	9	10

G-29 Does the company use a single compensation program? (0 - company has lots of compensation programs, 10 - only one compensation program is used)

0	1	2	3	4	5	6	7	8	9	10

G-30 Are people trained and understand how to work in a paperless environment? (0 - no training or understanding, 10 - people have been trained, understand thoroughly, and execute actions in a paperless environment)

0	1	2	3	4	5	6	7	8	9	10

If you think education is expensive, try ignorance.
-Derek Bok

18.11

Training and Education

H-1 Does management aggressively support education for new techniques and technologies? (0 - no top management sponsorship, 10 - top management sponsorship is very evident)

0	1	2	3	4	5	6	7	8	9	10

H-2 Does the process of internal education work in a bi-directional fashion between layers of management? (0 - no education or education in only one direction, 10 - training classes are held from both a top town and a bottom up perspective)

0	1	2	3	4	5	6	7	8	9	10

H-3 Are educational classes adjusted for the level of knowledge contained by the team members? (0 - no adjustments are made, 10 - surveys are conducted before class so the classes can be calibrated precisely)

0	1	2	3	4	5	6	7	8	9	10

H-4 Are the training classes held for the sole purpose of education or do they integrate tightly with strategic business plans causing changes in behavior? (0 - held for the purpose of education, 10 - held for the purpose of strategic business plans)

0	1	2	3	4	5	6	7	8	9	10

H-5 Are adequate financial resources available to support educational ventures? (0 - education is unsupported by financial resources, 10 - education is never limited because of limited financial resources)

0	1	2	3	4	5	6	7	8	9	10

H-6 Are the results of either internally or externally conducted audits taken into consideration in the determination of educational training needs? (0 - audits are not considered at all, 10 - audit results are considered and examined to help determine educational needs)

0	1	2	3	4	5	6	7	8	9	10

H-7 Are training and education organized to promote cross training within departments? (0 - cross training is not performed, 10 - cross training is encouraged and conducted)

0	1	2	3	4	5	6	7	8	9	10

H-8 Do educational classes promote the thinking in what is best for the company vs. what is best for the individual, team, or department? (0 - people / teams / departments are trained to think in what is best for the company, 10 - people / teams / departments are trained to think in what is best for the person / team / department)

0	1	2	3	4	5	6	7	8	9	10

H-9 Is top management committed to establishing lifelong learning for people and teams? (0 - life long learning is not considered, 10 - lifelong learning is considered critical and reflected in multiyear budgets)

0	1	2	3	4	5	6	7	8	9	10

H-10 Has all senior management been trained in integrated resource management? (0 - no training performed, 10 - complete training with clear understanding and application of principles of integrated resource management)

0	1	2	3	4	5	6	7	8	9	10

We used our measurement systems like a drunk uses a streetlight - for support, not illumination.

18.12

Performance Measurements

I-1 Do the results of the performance measurements feed back to the teams and people that are responsible? (0 - measurements are not used or feedback does not take place, 10 - measurements are used and feedback occurs with each measurement)

0	1	2	3	4	5	6	7	8	9	10

I-2 Are external customer service goals measured and used to identify process improvement opportunities? (0 - measurements are not used, 10 - measurements are used and always considered in process improvement opportunities)

0	1	2	3	4	5	6	7	8	9	10

I-3 Do performance measurements tend to be focused on internal processes and operation vs. outside customer based measurements? (0 - focused on internal processes, 10 - focused on outside customer based measurements)

0	1	2	3	4	5	6	7	8	9	10

I-4 What % of the sales orders are shipped complete? (0 - 0%, 10 - 10%, 100 - 100%)

____

I-5 What % of orders are shipped on time? (0 - 0%, 10 - 10%, 100 - 100%)

____

I-6 Do measurements, objectives, and accountability all exist for the sales plan? (0 - none of this exists, 5 - partial, 10 - all of this exists)

0	1	2	3	4	5	6	7	8	9	10

I-7 Do measurements, objectives, and accountability all exist for the production plan? (0 - none of this exists, 5 - partial, 10 - all of this exists)

0	1	2	3	4	5	6	7	8	9	10

I-8 Do measurements, objectives, and accountability all exist for the master production schedule? (0 - none of this exists, 5 - partial, 10 - all of this exists)

0	1	2	3	4	5	6	7	8	9	10

I-9 What is the accuracy of the master production schedule? (0 - 0%, 10 - 10%, 100 - 100%)

____

I-10 What is the accuracy of the overall supplier deliveries? (0 - 0%, 10 - 10%, 100 - 100%)

____

I-11 Do measurements, objectives, and accountability all exist for supplier delivery performance? (0 - none of this exists, 5 - partial, 10 - all of this exists)

0	1	2	3	4	5	6	7	8	9	10

I-12 What is the accuracy of the bills of material? (0 - 0%, 10 - 10%, 100 - 100%)

I-13 Do measurements, objectives, and accountability all exist for bills of materials? (0 - none of this exists, 5 - partial, 10 - all of this exists)

0	1	2	3	4	5	6	7	8	9	10

I-14 Do measurements, objectives, and accountability all exist for inventory accuracy? (0 - none of this exists, 5 - partial, 10 - all of this exists)

0	1	2	3	4	5	6	7	8	9	10

I-15 What is the accuracy of the inventory? (0 - 0%, 10 - 10%, 100 - 100%)

I-16 Do measurements, objectives, and accountability all exist for routing accuracy? (0 - none of this exists, 5 - partial, 10 - all of this exists)

0	1	2	3	4	5	6	7	8	9	10

I-17 What is the accuracy of the routings? (0 - 0%, 10 - 10%, 100 - 100%)

When one door closes another door opens; but we so often look so long and so regretfully upon the closed door, that we do not see the ones which open for us. - Alexander Graham Bell

18.13

Communication Infrastructure

J-1 Is there a communication channel in place between customers and employees, and employees and suppliers? (0 - no communication structure in place, 10 - communication structure in place and actively used by employees)

0	1	2	3	4	5	6	7	8	9	10

J-2 Are two way radio communications systems used to coordinated resources between various functions such as manufacturing and material support or quality and receiving? (0 - we do not have radio communications, 10 - radio communications are used to coordinate resources wherever possible, short simple communication standards have been developed to represent various situations)

0	1	2	3	4	5	6	7	8	9	10

J-3 Do voice mail systems exist so that people may leave and receive messages? (0 - we have phones but no voice mail systems, 10 - we have voice mail systems providing basic phone mail support such as offsite voice retrieval)

0	1	2	3	4	5	6	7	8	9	10

J-4 Does the company have basic email functions available to ALL people of the company? (0 - only some people have email, 10 - all people receive and have access to email during or shortly after their new employee orientation)

0	1	2	3	4	5	6	7	8	9	10

J-5 Is the email system capable of basic intermediate functions such as broadcast groups and file attachments? (0 - we do not have email or our system does not have these capabilities, 10 - our email system contains these capabilities)

0	1	2	3	4	5	6	7	8	9	10

J-6 Is the email system linked to the outside world allowing communication with suppliers, vendors, friends, and family? (0 - our email only works internally or we do not have an email system, 10 - with our email system we can communicate freely with the outside world)

0	1	2	3	4	5	6	7	8	9	10

We could hardly wait to get up in the morning. - Wilbur Wright

18.14

Product Design and Development

L-1 Are phase in and phase out techniques used in conjunction with engineering change order management? (0 - phase in and phase out is not used, 10 - phase in and phase out is used extensively with engineering change orders)

0	1	2	3	4	5	6	7	8	9	10

L-2 Is the quantity of engineering change orders used to monitor the quality of the initial product development process? (0 - no, 10 - yes and our company lowered the number of ECOs over historical levels because of improvements made in the initial design phase)

0	1	2	3	4	5	6	7	8	9	10

L-3 Are TQM techniques applied to engineering change orders? (0 - no, 10 - yes, whenever possible across all product lines)

0	1	2	3	4	5	6	7	8	9	10

L-4 Is engineering change order management considered seriously and reflected by the manager to whom the people responsible for engineering change coordination report? (0 - engineering change order management is not considered to be important, 10 - yes, engineering change order management is considered seriously and the people responsible report to managers or functions that have an intense interest)

0	1	2	3	4	5	6	7	8	9	10

L-5 Is there a documented process flow for engineering change order management? (0 - no, 10 - clear documented policy exists and it is followed closely)

0	1	2	3	4	5	6	7	8	9	10

L-6 Are causes for delays in product development schedules monitored and tracked so that aftermath can be projected and planned for? (0 - our company does not worry about what can happen from delays in product development, 10 - delays are monitored carefully so that disruptions and adjustments can be planned for and communicated)

0	1	2	3	4	5	6	7	8	9	10

L-7 Does the product engineering function circulate information on how new designs will effect manufacturing process capability and capacities with planning and scheduling functions? (0 - this information is not shared, 10 - this information is circulated and shared resulting in few unplanned surprises)

0	1	2	3	4	5	6	7	8	9	10

L-8 Is product engineering design capacities considered for the development of the sales and operation plan? (0 - this information is not shared, 10 - this information is circulated and shared resulting in few unplanned surprises)

0	1	2	3	4	5	6	7	8	9	10

L-9 Are the planning and scheduling systems important functions and completely understood from the viewpoint of engineering managers? (0 - engineering managers have limited understanding of these functions and have received no training, 10 - very complete understanding of planning and scheduling systems)

0	1	2	3	4	5	6	7	8	9	10

L-10 Does product engineering and planning systems share common databases such as part numbers and bills of materials so the changes made by engineering are immediately reflected in the planning and scheduling systems? (0 - engineering uses a separate system, 10 - integrated changed management promoted by common databases resulting in synchronized planning and scheduling systems)

0	1	2	3	4	5	6	7	8	9	10

L-11 As soon as a new product is approved to begin the design process, are the known or stable parts of the design allowed to flow through the planning and scheduling system? (0 - nothing is allowed to flow to the planning and scheduling systems until the design is complete, 10 - stable portions of the design are allowed to flow into the planning and scheduling systems before all the design work is done)

0	1	2	3	4	5	6	7	8	9	10

L-12 Are different bills of materials used to specify requirements for prototypes, manufacturing, field service, etc...? (0 - we only use one bill even though we need different bills for different functions, 10 - different bills are used for different functions wherever needed)

0	1	2	3	4	5	6	7	8	9	10

L-13 Are the quality and reliability of the product verified before the product is released for manufacturing and shipment? (0 - we only worry about quality and reliability of the product if something happens after it has been released, 10 - quality and reliability of the product is completely demonstrated through statistical methods)

0	1	2	3	4	5	6	7	8	9	10

L-14 Are the first manufacturing runs carefully watched and monitored to obtain yields, quality, setup problems, production rates, etc... information for improvement opportunities? (0 - we treat first manufacturing runs of new products just like any other, 10 - new manufacturing runs are subject of interest for everybody in the plant for analyzing improvement opportunities)

0	1	2	3	4	5	6	7	8	9	10

L-15 Do new products receive adequate funding to bring the project to completion? (0 - new product projects are very sporadic and start and stop often depending on the funding, 10 - new product projects are properly funded resulting in stable schedules)

0	1	2	3	4	5	6	7	8	9	10

L-16 Are initial product development schedules developed based on input from all the different functions that will be affected? (0 - we just develop the schedules and worry about who will be affected later on, 10 - all new product development schedules are carefully reviewed so that input can be obtained by any function that will be affected by the schedule)

0	1	2	3	4	5	6	7	8	9	10

L-17 Are competitors' products carefully analyzed to obtain benchmarking data? (0 - we never look to see what our competitors' products can do, 10 - we are constantly monitoring our competitors' products and watching for new benchmarking data OR we have no competitors)

0	1	2	3	4	5	6	7	8	9	10

L-18 Is quality function deployment used to examine customer and product requirements? (0 - we are not sure what this is and have not received training, 10 - we use quality function deployment wherever the opportunity presents itself)

0	1	2	3	4	5	6	7	8	9	10

L-19 Are marketing and design engineering people aware of what the customer would like to have and what the customer must have? (0 - the customer has differences between what they would like to have and what they must have but we are not sure what that is, 10 - we have a clear understanding of what the customer would like to have and what the customer must have)

0	1	2	3	4	5	6	7	8	9	10

L-20 Do marketing and design engineering people understand what new features and functions of the product that will excite the customer? (0 - we are not sure what excites the customer, 10 - we have a clear understanding of what excites the customer)

0	1	2	3	4	5	6	7	8	9	10

L-21 Do product development teams consist of a variety of functions so that a broad set of requirements can be developed for the new product? (0 - we do not use product development teams, 10 - all functions that will be affected by new products can be found on the product development team so complete requirements can be obtained)

0	1	2	3	4	5	6	7	8	9	10

L-22 Is the concept of concurrent engineering used wherever practical? (0 - we are not sure what concurrent engineering is and have not received training on this, 10 - we understand this concept and use it wherever practical)

0	1	2	3	4	5	6	7	8	9	10

L-23 Are the best suppliers known and are those suppliers brought into the design process? (0 - we just pull in any supplier that we think might work, 10 - we have detailed supplier lists compiled through years of experience that we use to determine the best suppliers to bring into the design process)

0	1	2	3	4	5	6	7	8	9	10

L-24 Are measurement systems in place to track the new product development process? (0 - we have no measurement systems, 10 - we have a number of measurement systems that we actively use such as time to market, design stages, total designs, etc...)

0	1	2	3	4	5	6	7	8	9	10

L-25 Do product development teams have access to costing information that includes both real costs and simulated costs from proposed design changes/new products? (0 - our product design team does not have access to this information, 10 - our product design team has access to this information and uses it readily)

0	1	2	3	4	5	6	7	8	9	10

L-26 Do product development teams meet on a regular basis to get updates, solve problems, communicate, etc..? (0 - we meet sporadically in an unpredictable fashion, 10 - our product development team always meets on a regular basis and will meet more frequently if the need calls for it)

0	1	2	3	4	5	6	7	8	9	10

The whole is often greater than the sum of the parts. That seems to be our case, since we have yet to find our parts!

18.15

Operational Setup / Planning / Control

M-1 Do planning systems work off of shared databases that all functions can use to help meet customer demands? (0 - not all functions have access to view our planning systems, 10 - all functions have access to view our planning systems)

0	1	2	3	4	5	6	7	8	9	10

M-2 Is there a documented sales and operations plan that explains the reason for the plan, how it happens, and who does it? (0 - we do not have sales and operations plan, 10 - we have a clear documented plan and it is understood by all stakeholders)

0	1	2	3	4	5	6	7	8	9	10

M-3 Do the sales and operation meetings occur in a systematic fashion? (0 - we don't do this or we try a new process almost every time, 10 - we have a well defined pattern of events that is repeated in almost every meeting)

0	1	2	3	4	5	6	7	8	9	10

M-4 Are the sales and operation meetings preplanned to avoid scheduling conflicts? (0 - we don't do this or people are always missing from the meeting, 10 - people seldom miss a meeting, if they do there is a backup to take their place)

0	1	2	3	4	5	6	7	8	9	10

M-5 Is the agenda distributed before the sales and operation meeting takes place? (0 - we don't do this, 10 - agendas are distributed without fail)

0	1	2	3	4	5	6	7	8	9	10

M-6 Do the discussions of the sales and operation meetings rotate around commonly understood units of measure? (0 - we often are confused because of different units of measure, 10 - units of measure are never a problem)

0	1	2	3	4	5	6	7	8	9	10

M-7 Do people review the progress of new designs at the sales and operations meeting? (0 - we do not worry about new designs at the meeting, 10 - new product designs often come up for discussion)

0	1	2	3	4	5	6	7	8	9	10

M-8 Are the discussions at the sales and operations meeting a consolidation of other meetings for the functions participating? (0 - no preparation or communication takes place before the meeting, 10 - for each function represented adequate preparation has taken place within that function)

0	1	2	3	4	5	6	7	8	9	10

M-9 Like any other process, is the sales and operation planning subject to investigation for process improvement opportunities? (0 - we have never considered process improvement for our sales and operations planning process, 10 - we often find new ways to improve the process and we document those ways)

0	1	2	3	4	5	6	7	8	9	10

M-10 Does abnormal fluctuations take place for each of the functions thfat are part of the sales and operation planning? (0 - any particular function can be unpredictable as to what is going to happen, 10 - each function has clear accountability and usually acts/performs in a predictable fashion)

0	1	2	3	4	5	6	7	8	9	10

M-11 Are different what if scenarios regarding the marketplace considered for the creation of future projections in sales and operations planning? (0 - we do not worry about what is going to happen in the marketplace, 10 -we are always prepared for the changes in the marketplace and are prepared for each possible outcome)

0	1	2	3	4	5	6	7	8	9	10

M-12 Are major disruptions usually known before the sales and operations meeting takes place? (0 - it seems like we always find out about major disruptions in the meeting, 10 - we always receive notice of major disruptions before the meeting takes place)

0	1	2	3	4	5	6	7	8	9	10

M-13 Does the master production schedule work in synchronization with the production plan? (0 -these two act completely independent of each other, 10 - the master production schedule functions in a way that is consistent with the production plan)

0	1	2	3	4	5	6	7	8	9	10

M-14 Is the concept of time fences used that restrict changes in near term and allow more flexibility long term? (0 - we do what every the customer wants no matter what the impact, 10 - the concept of time fences are well understood, documented, and followed)

0	1	2	3	4	5	6	7	8	9	10

M-15 Do the battles and struggles found in the sales and operation meetings come to some resolution? (0 - deadlocks are often experienced upon the closing of the meeting, 10 - resolution and consensus is always reached before the meetings come to a close)

0	1	2	3	4	5	6	7	8	9	10

M-16 Are the results of the sales and operations meetings posted or distributed to all critical stakeholders? (0 - the only people that know about the meeting are the people that attend, 10 - notes of the meeting are communicated to all concerning parties)

0	1	2	3	4	5	6	7	8	9	10

M-17 Do the different levels (aggregate vs detailed) within the sales and operations plan measure up in total? (0 - it seems like there is always a mismatch between the different levels, 10 - different levels are always in synchronization with each other)

0	1	2	3	4	5	6	7	8	9	10

M-18 Are inventory and backlogs both considered in the sales and operations planning meetings? (0 - these are not considered, 10 - these are always part of our overall plan)

0	1	2	3	4	5	6	7	8	9	10

M-19 Are past fulfilments, current activity, and future projections all considered in sales and operations planning? (0 - these are not considered, 10 - these are always part of our overall plan)

0	1	2	3	4	5	6	7	8	9	10

M-20 What is the level of integration between the projections found in the sales and operations plan and the financial plans? (0 - completely nonintegrated, act independently, 10 - completely integrated, one cannot change without the other changing)

0	1	2	3	4	5	6	7	8	9	10

M-21 Does the financial function share the same database/databases that other functions do such as sales, purchasing, inventory, etc...so information is not duplicated? (0 - data is often duplicated between the financial function and other areas of the business, 10 - the same database is used avoiding duplication of information)

0	1	2	3	4	5	6	7	8	9	10

M-22 Are traditional financial measurements no longer playing a significant role in determining the health of the business? (0 - traditional measurements such as those relating to scales of economy dictate business decisions, 10 - financial measurements are now used that are consistent with JIT/TQM processes)

0	1	2	3	4	5	6	7	8	9	10

M-23 Do all transactions that affect financials flow directly into the financial software module? (0 - our system does not have this capability, 10 - our financial modules can collect almost all transaction activity through the use of integration)

0	1	2	3	4	5	6	7	8	9	10

M-24 Do material receiving transactions integrate back through receiving, purchasing, and accounts payable? (0 - this process is not integrated, 10 - this process flow is all integrated)

0	1	2	3	4	5	6	7	8	9	10

M-25 Is the final cost of the product calculated by considering the cost of labor for the product? (0 - this process is not integrated, 10 - this process flow is all integrated)

0	1	2	3	4	5	6	7	8	9	10

M-26 Do work order completions serve as a trigger to move inventory from a wip account to a finished goods account in the general ledger? (0 - this process is not integrated, 10 - this process flow is all integrated)

0	1	2	3	4	5	6	7	8	9	10

M-27 Do customer shipment transactions update on hand inventory as well as initiate the customer billing processes through accounts receivable? (0 - this process is not integrated, 10 - this process flow is all integrated)

0	1	2	3	4	5	6	7	8	9	10

M-28 Are cash flow plans based on the sales and operations plan and updated at least monthly? (0 - our cash flow plans are not based on the sales and operations plan, 10 - our cash flow plans integrate tightly with the sales and operations plan)

0	1	2	3	4	5	6	7	8	9	10

M-29 Are any simulation tools used to obtain financial information based on planning and operations data? (0 - we do not have this capability, 10 - we use simulation tools extensively to obtain financial information that we use in key strategic business decisions)

0	1	2	3	4	5	6	7	8	9	10

M-30 Is there a general effort to eliminate nonvalue added activities and to promote continuous process improvement for the financial processes? (0 - there is no general process to improve financials, 10 - there are continuous efforts to eliminate nonvalue added activities and process improvement activities)

0	1	2	3	4	5	6	7	8	9	10

M-31 Is simulation capability applied to sales and operations planning allowing the review of several different strategies so the impact on the supply chain can be evaluated? (0 - we do not have this capability, 10 - we have this capability and we use it)

0	1	2	3	4	5	6	7	8	9	10

M-32 Is available to promise information used to review the impacts of accepting new unplanned customers orders? (0 - we do not have this capability, 10 - we have this capability and we use it extensively)

0	1	2	3	4	5	6	7	8	9	10

M-33 Is rough cut capacity used to validate changes in the MPS before MRP is run? (0 - we do not have this capability, 10 - we have this capability and we use it)

0	1	2	3	4	5	6	7	8	9	10

M-34 Is capacity requirements planning (CRP) used as a tool when reviewing the need for new capital production equipment and/or for hiring production labor? (0 - we do not have this capability, 10 - we have this capability and we use it)

0	1	2	3	4	5	6	7	8	9	10

M-35 Is the changing of various planning factors, such as lot size or safety stock, tested and simulated to review impact on the supply chain? (0 - we do not have this capability, 10 - we have this capability and we use it)

0	1	2	3	4	5	6	7	8	9	10

M-36 Do one or several people have clear responsibility for the forecast? (0 - no one is really responsible for the forecast, 10 - it is very clear to all critical stakeholders who is responsible for the forecast)

0	1	2	3	4	5	6	7	8	9	10

M-37 Do the people responsible for the forecast have a clear understanding of the product, customers, market, and manufacturing processes? (0 no one is really responsible for the forecast, 10 - have clear understanding of all those areas listed)

0	1	2	3	4	5	6	7	8	9	10

M-38 Is the demand represented by the forecast complete in nature? (0 - our forecast only considers customer demand, 10 - our forecast includes other demands such as spare parts, field service, warranties, etc....)

0	1	2	3	4	5	6	7	8	9	10

M-39 Is there a variety of statistical forecasting methods available for use such as weighted average, exponential smoothing, etc....? (0 - we do not have different methods available, 10 - we have several different methods available and we chose the best one for the item)

0	1	2	3	4	5	6	7	8	9	10

M-40 Is the right part number used for lower level demands such as field service in forecasting and order entry? (0 - we never seem to have the right part number, 10 - the right part number is always used in forecasting and order entry for lower level items)

0	1	2	3	4	5	6	7	8	9	10

M-41 Are any unusual characteristics of forecast quantities or part numbers documented? (0 - these are not documented, 10 - these are documented and easily accessible by other functional areas)

0	1	2	3	4	5	6	7	8	9	10

M-42 Do the person/persons responsible for the forecast also participate in product development and management meetings? (0 - never participate, 5 - occasionally, 10 - always without fail)

0	1	2	3	4	5	6	7	8	9	10

M-43 Is forecast accuracy measured at both the aggregate and detail levels? (0 - we do not measure forecast accuracy at all, 5 - we measure one but not the other, 10 - both are measured and tracked carefully)

0	1	2	3	4	5	6	7	8	9	10

M-44 Do marketing and sales work hard to help establish good solid sales plans? (0 - marketing and sales do not have a sales plan, 10 - we have great sales plans that always keeps our customers satisfied)

0	1	2	3	4	5	6	7	8	9	10

M-45 Are sales plans compared to actual sales? (0 - no, 10 - sales plans are compared to actual sales with differences noted and communicated)

0	1	2	3	4	5	6	7	8	9	10

M-46 Is the sales planning process efficient in keeping clerical and bureaucratic activities to a minimum within the sales force? (0 - we have lots of bureaucracy and clerical overhead, 10 - our sales planning process runs smoothly)

0	1	2	3	4	5	6	7	8	9	10

M-47 Do sales compensation programs influence the sales plan in a negative way? (0 - our compensation programs often get us into trouble as a company, 10 - sales compensation programs do not affect the sales plan in a negative way and do not conflict with the strategic business plans)

0	1	2	3	4	5	6	7	8	9	10

M-48 Does the sales force actively promote connections of customer demand systems with our supply system through the used of EDI, internet, or other wherever possible? (0 - we do not promote any type of linking, 10 - good progress has been made in this area with demonstrated benefits)

0	1	2	3	4	5	6	7	8	9	10

M-49 Do the totals of sales plans agree with the totals of forecasts? (0 - these are mismatched, 10 - these are always in synchronization)

0	1	2	3	4	5	6	7	8	9	10

M-50 Does the sales function work tightly with forecasting, manufacturing, and marketing to communicate customer information to establish sound sales and operations planning? (0 - this is not done, 10 - these functions work together tightly to establish sound sales and operations planning)

0	1	2	3	4	5	6	7	8	9	10

M-51 Does the sales function review their performance to plan monthly or more frequently? (0 - this is not done, 10 - this is done without fail)

0	1	2	3	4	5	6	7	8	9	10

M-52 Are any unusual characteristics of the sales plan documented so that they can be examined and changed as needed? (0 - this is not done, 10 - this is done without fail)

0	1	2	3	4	5	6	7	8	9	10

M-53 Do sales and marketing participate in establishing time fences? (0 - no, 10 - on a regular basis without fail)

0	1	2	3	4	5	6	7	8	9	10

M-54 Is there a standard operating procedure for dealing with unusual spikes or slumps in demand? (0 - no, 10 - well documented and communicated)

0	1	2	3	4	5	6	7	8	9	10

M-55 Are customer orders processed quickly relative to what the customer expects? (0 - no, 10 - yes, without fail)

0	1	2	3	4	5	6	7	8	9	10

M-56 Are customer orders carefully monitored for quality of correctness? (0 - our orders have many mistakes, 10 - yes, and those results are posted for public inspection to further eliminate mistakes)

0	1	2	3	4	5	6	7	8	9	10

M-57 Is characteristic information related to sales change orders measured and organized into meaningful data? (0 - we do not measure this, 10 - yes, we can see the kind of changes, whether those changes came from internal or external sources, and how many changes)

0	1	2	3	4	5	6	7	8	9	10

M-58 Is it clear who is responsible for the master production schedule? (0 - no, 10 - well documented and understood by all critical stakeholders)

0	1	2	3	4	5	6	7	8	9	10

M-59 Does the master scheduler have a good background and training with the products, manufacturing processes, planning systems, and the customers? (0 - no, 10 - the person/persons responsible for this have complete knowledge in all of these areas)

0	1	2	3	4	5	6	7	8	9	10

M-60 Does the master scheduler work closely to assist the sales and operation planning process? (0 - no, 10 - yes, and responds as needed for important input)

0	1	2	3	4	5	6	7	8	9	10

M-61 Does the master scheduler carefully watch for feedback to detect material or capacity problems? (0 - no, 10 - yes, communicates these situations as needed to the appropriate functional areas)

0	1	2	3	4	5	6	7	8	9	10

M-62 Does the master scheduler work with sales and marketing in developing planning bills? (0 - no, 5 - sometimes, 10 - whenever possible)

0	1	2	3	4	5	6	7	8	9	10

M-63 Are abnormal fluctuations monitored, tracked, and posted through the use of TQM tools for the MPS? (0 - no, 10 - always without fail)

0	1	2	3	4	5	6	7	8	9	10

M-64 Does the master scheduling have a certain firming period starting at the present and flowing out to some period in the future? (0 - we do what ever the customer wants regardless of impact, 10 - we monitor the firming period carefully and hesitate in making changes)

0	1	2	3	4	5	6	7	8	9	10

M-65 Is there an approval routing process for changes in the firm period of the MPS? (0 - who ever needs a change in the MPS can just make the change, 10 - changes to the MPS inside the firm period must be intensively communicated and approved by all critical stakeholders)

0	1	2	3	4	5	6	7	8	9	10

M-66 Are buffers such as safety stock, safety lead time or over planning used to manage variations in supply/demand chain? (0 - we are constantly running out of commonly used or ordered items, 10 - we know where our variations occur and use the best policy to manage these variations)

0	1	2	3	4	5	6	7	8	9	10

M-67 Are all levels of the master schedule planned for in the MPS? (0 - as far as we know they are, 10 - we know that they are because we took actions after having researched this concern and documented our findings)

0	1	2	3	4	5	6	7	8	9	10

M-68 Does the production plan synchronize with the MPS? (0 - these two act independently of each other, 10 - these two work together tightly following standard production planning rules)

0	1	2	3	4	5	6	7	8	9	10

M-69 Does the master schedule generated at least weekly using weekly buckets or smaller? (0 - no, 10 - we generate using weekly buckets or smaller for our immediate horizon)

0	1	2	3	4	5	6	7	8	9	10

M-70 Do the bill of materials cause any problems in master scheduling or forecasting? (0 - we are constantly bumping into bill of material problems that disrupt our MPS and forecasting, 10 - we have tight control over the bill and seldom have problems)

0	1	2	3	4	5	6	7	8	9	10

M-71 Is forecast consumption logic applied? (0 - we have never used or considered this, 10 - we use forecast consumption logic wherever applicable)

0	1	2	3	4	5	6	7	8	9	10

M-72 Are planning bills of materials used? (0 - we never have used or considered this, 10 - we use planning bills wherever applicable)

0	1	2	3	4	5	6	7	8	9	10

M-73 Is the final assembly coordinated with the master schedule? (0 - no or we are not sure, 10 - these two act in a coordinated fashion)

0	1	2	3	4	5	6	7	8	9	10

M-74 Is mix model production used where needed? (0 - we have never considered this or it is not used, 10 -we use this technique wherever it applies)

0	1	2	3	4	5	6	7	8	9	10

M-75 Is a master production schedule meeting held at least weekly and attended by all critical stakeholders? (0 - we do not hold MPS meetings, 5 - we hold meetings and people are often missing, 10 - our meetings are held without fail and attended by all stakeholders)

0	1	2	3	4	5	6	7	8	9	10

M-76 Do material planners have good understanding of the products, manufacturing processes, and planning systems? (0 - no, 10 - our material planners understand these areas very well)

0	1	2	3	4	5	6	7	8	9	10

M-77 Do scheduling and/or material problems flow back to the planners from a variety of sources? (0 - they usually find out about something after the fact, 10 - feedback flows from anywhere whenever some problem or potential problem occurs)

0	1	2	3	4	5	6	7	8	9	10

M-78 Do planners go through edit / audit reports to check for bad planning factors so they may be corrected? (0 - they usually find out about something like that after the fact, 10 - the database is constantly being scanned for defective planning factors, bad ones are corrected quickly)

0	1	2	3	4	5	6	7	8	9	10

M-79 When it comes to data integrity of the planning factors, is it clear who is responsible for these planning factors? (0 - that stuff often does not get fixed because we thought someone else was going to do it, 10 - the moment we find a bad planning factor we know exactly who is responsible)

0	1	2	3	4	5	6	7	8	9	10

M-80 Is there an organized documented process for information exchange regarding details of the supply chain? (0 - not really, we often find out about important details after the fact, 10 - yes, and it works well for us keeping surprises to a bare minimum)

0	1	2	3	4	5	6	7	8	9	10

M-81 How many priority control systems are there? (0 - we have so many that they conflict with each other creating confusion, 10 - the priority and sequence of the schedule are very clear to everybody)

0	1	2	3	4	5	6	7	8	9	10

M-82 Does the material planning system use weekly or smaller buckets for the immediate horizon? (0 - we do not have this or we use some bucket size bigger than weeks, 10 - we use weeks or smaller for our MRP planning buckets)

0	1	2	3	4	5	6	7	8	9	10

M-83 How frequently does MRP run? (0 - we are often lacking in the information that we need because MRP has not regenerated yet, 10 - we run the MRP frequently, we even run special MRP runs if needed)

0	1	2	3	4	5	6	7	8	9	10

M-84 Does the computer system attempt to match supply with demand through the use of action messages like, expedite, defer, cancel, past due, etc...in the MRP system? (0 - we do not have this capability or do not use it, 10 - our system does this and we track and monitor these messages aggressively)

0	1	2	3	4	5	6	7	8	9	10

M-85 Are firm planned orders used where needed? (0 - we do not have this capability or do not use it, 10 - our system has this capability and we use it as needed)

0	1	2	3	4	5	6	7	8	9	10

M-86 Is pegging used to identify sources of demand? (0 - we do not have this capability or do not use it, 10 - our system has this capability and we use it as needed)

0	1	2	3	4	5	6	7	8	9	10

M-87 Can planners use the system to determine if material shortages exist before releasing orders? (0 - we do not have this capability or do not use it, 5 - we have this capability, but it is very difficult to do, 10 - our system has this capability and we use it as needed)

0	1	2	3	4	5	6	7	8	9	10

M-88 Can the parts list be modified for an individual work order that is different from the bill of material? (0 - we do not have this capability or do not use it, 5 - we have this capability, but it is very difficult to do, 10 - our system has this capability and we use as needed)

0	1	2	3	4	5	6	7	8	9	10

M-89 Are MPS/MRP planning messages reviewed and processed on a timely basis? (0 - we do not have messages or only look at them when we get around to it, 10 - we have clear concise documented deadlines for getting our messages reviewed and processed)

0	1	2	3	4	5	6	7	8	9	10

M-90 Are MPS/MRP planning messages monitored and tracked for each planner? (0 - we do not track or if we do we group it all together, 10 - all planning messages are monitored and tracked for each planner, results flow back to some decision making centralized resource)

0	1	2	3	4	5	6	7	8	9	10

M-91 Are work orders released without shortages and adequate leadtime 95% of the time or greater? (0 - we are constantly experiencing part shortages and past due work orders, 10 - on rare occasion we have a past due work order or part shortage)

0	1	2	3	4	5	6	7	8	9	10

M-92 Is the shop floor control dispatch list the primary tool for determining what comes next for production? (0 - we do not have this or do not use it, 10 - this is the primary tool that production uses)

0	1	2	3	4	5	6	7	8	9	10

M-93 Does production work in synchronization with the MPS meeting work order due dates? (0 - production arranges schedules and work orders independently of the MPS, 10 - production works on the orders in the order that is specified in the MPS meeting due dates)

0	1	2	3	4	5	6	7	8	9	10

M-94 Does the system provide routing start and stop information at the work order level? (0 - our system does not have this or we do not use it, 10 - our system does this and we use it as needed)

0	1	2	3	4	5	6	7	8	9	10

M-95 Does the system provide routing start and stop information at the work order level that can be overridden? (0 - our system does not have this or we do not use it, 10 - our system does this and we use it as needed)

0	1	2	3	4	5	6	7	8	9	10

M-96 Is production reported by operation step? (0 - our system does not have this or we do not use it, 10 - our system does this and we use it as needed)

0	1	2	3	4	5	6	7	8	9	10

M-97 Are dispatch lists organized by work centers showing basic work order information? (0 - our system does not have this or we do not use it, 10 - our system does this and we use it as needed)

0	1	2	3	4	5	6	7	8	9	10

M-98 Have over 85% of the suppliers received training in concepts such as JIT and MRP so that supplier scheduling concepts are understood? (0 - they do not understand these concepts or we are not really sure what our suppliers know in this area, 10 - our suppliers understand these concepts well and practice them continuously)

0	1	2	3	4	5	6	7	8	9	10

M-99 Are suppliers good about organizing their raw material and internal capacity to meet the needs of the company? (0 - we seem to always have problems getting parts from our suppliers, 10 - we seldom have a problem getter our parts and raw materials from our suppliers)

0	1	2	3	4	5	6	7	8	9	10

M-100 Are there clear responsibilities that have been documented between the supplier, schedulers, and buyers? (0 - we are not really sure who is responsible for what, 10 - we have clear concise documentation that explains the roles and responsibilities for each function listed)

0	1	2	3	4	5	6	7	8	9	10

M-101 Do suppliers provide schedules or provide feedback for what they are actually going to do vs what was requested by the company? (0 - we usually do not find out about changes from suppliers until after the fact, 10 - our suppliers make every effort to alert us if something is going to wander off plan)

0	1	2	3	4	5	6	7	8	9	10

M-102 Is there a frozen period for supplier schedules that starts today and extends out forward to some future point? (0 - nothing is frozen, we always get surprised by our supplier deliveries, 10 - our suppliers understand the need to keep delivery schedules on time and the follow them closely)

0	1	2	3	4	5	6	7	8	9	10

M-103 Are the supplier schedules expressed in weekly buckets or smaller for the immediate future? (0 - we do not have this or we use larger buckets, 10 - buckets are expressed as weeks or smaller)

0	1	2	3	4	5	6	7	8	9	10

M-104 Does the purchasing function frequently communicate with the planning function so that the schedules will be verified? (0 - these two functions do not talk to each other, 10 - these two functions communicate with each other extensively through written and verbal communication)

0	1	2	3	4	5	6	7	8	9	10

M-105 Do the suppliers take a proactive role in communicating any past due deliveries? (0 - it seems like we are always finding out about missed deliveries after the fact, 10 - we always know well in advance if there is going to be a missed delivery)

0	1	2	3	4	5	6	7	8	9	10

M-106 How often are supplier schedules communicated to the supplier? (0 - not often enough, they don't get the critical information that they need, 10 - more frequently then they probably need)

0	1	2	3	4	5	6	7	8	9	10

M-107 What percentage of purchase orders are released with adequate lead time? (0 - we have a lot of trouble in this area and are constantly paying surcharges to rush material in, 10 - over 95% of our purchase orders have adequate lead time, we seldom pay expedite shipping charges)

0	1	2	3	4	5	6	7	8	9	10

M-108 Is there a documented procedure for defining supplier chain management for key materials or parts needed to support the business strategy? (0 - we have no documented procedure for handling critical items and often get into trouble with those items, 10 - we have defined and documented our supplier chain management for all critical items)

0	1	2	3	4	5	6	7	8	9	10

M-109 Is capacity planning utilized as a tool in planning labor and machines? (0 - no, 10 - yes)

0	1	2	3	4	5	6	7	8	9	10

M-110 Is there confusion and/or duplication of effort when it comes to capacity planning? (0 - it seems like we have many different people with different ideas on how much capacity we have, this often creates confusion, 10 - we have clear universal agreement on how much capacity we actually have)

0	1	2	3	4	5	6	7	8	9	10

M-111 How long does it take for an MRP regeneration? (0 - 24 hours or more, 5 - 24 to 12 hours, 10 - 1 hour or less)

0	1	2	3	4	5	6	7	8	9	10

M-112 Does the MRP replanning process tend to cause earthquakes? (0 - surprises are constantly popping up, 10 - the results of the MRP output is almost always as expected)

0	1	2	3	4	5	6	7	8	9	10

M-113 Are there general meetings that occur weekly or more frequently to resolve/reveiw capacity issues? (0 - we are always having capacity problems but seldom meet to resolve them, 5 - we meet and resolve problems, 10 - because of good planning we seldom meet to resolve capacity problems)

0	1	2	3	4	5	6	7	8	9	10

M-114 Are capacities other than machine and labors hours considered in capacity planning? (0 - only these two are considered or we do not have capacity planning, 10 - we consider other capacities such as maintenance and design engineering in our planning)

0	1	2	3	4	5	6	7	8	9	10

M-115 Are work centers clearly defined so that priorities and capacities can be established? (0 - no, 10 - yes)

0	1	2	3	4	5	6	7	8	9	10

M-116 Are factors that will reduce capacity (such as utilization, efficiency, maintenance, etc.) factored into planning? (0 - no, 5 - sometimes, 10 - yes)

0	1	2	3	4	5	6	7	8	9	10

M-117 Is a corrective action process initiated for past due orders so they will not happen again? (0 - we are always experiencing past due orders, often for the same problem, 10 - we can not remember the last time we had a past due order)

0	1	2	3	4	5	6	7	8	9	10

M-118 Are both material and capacity related standards reviewed on a regular basis for verification? (0 - we only review the standards when we have a problem, 10 - we review our standards on a regular basis, this process is documented)

0	1	2	3	4	5	6	7	8	9	10

M-119 Does the capacity planning process produce requirements by work center? (0 - no, 5 - it can, but we never use it, 10 - yes, and we use it on a regular basis)

0	1	2	3	4	5	6	7	8	9	10

M-120 Is there capability to see input / output reports by work center in capacity units? (0 - no, 5 - yes, but it is difficult to get, 10 - yes, and we use it on a regular basis)

0	1	2	3	4	5	6	7	8	9	10

M-121 Is there a written procedure that explains who is responsible for creating and maintaining bills of materials? (0 - we have no written procedure, 10 - yes, and we follow it closely)

0	1	2	3	4	5	6	7	8	9	10

M-122 Do all the functions that are affected by the bill participate in its creation? (0 - other functions find out about a new bill long after it has been created, 10 - all critical stakeholders participate in the creation of bills of materials)

0	1	2	3	4	5	6	7	8	9	10

M-123 Are bills of material structured to match the manufacturing process and reflect the way that the products are built? (0 - our bills are structured completely independent of the way the products are built, 10 - the bill of material structure closely matches the way that the product is built)

0	1	2	3	4	5	6	7	8	9	10

M-124 Is there a written bill of material auditing procedure? (0 - we only worry about bill of material problems when we come across them, 10 - we have a written bill of material auditing procedure that measures the accuracy of bills and the procedure is followed closely)

0	1	2	3	4	5	6	7	8	9	10

M-125 Does the finance function use the bill of materials for costing the product? (0 - finance does not use the bill of material, 10 - finance does use the bill of material for product costing)

0	1	2	3	4	5	6	7	8	9	10

M-126 Is there a written procedure explaining how item master records are created, maintained and who is responsible for fields that are used? (0 - we do not have this, 10 - we have written procedures and follow them closely)

0	1	2	3	4	5	6	7	8	9	10

M-127 Is there clear accountability for inventory record accuracy through all stages of inventory from raw materials through finished goods? (0 - accountability does not exist, 10 - whenever there is a problem we know the person to go to)

0	1	2	3	4	5	6	7	8	9	10

M-128 Does the cycle counting process identify root causes of inventory inaccuracies? (0 - we do not have a cycle counting process or we do not use it for identifying root causes, 10 - we are constantly searching for root causes through our cycle counting program)

0	1	2	3	4	5	6	7	8	9	10

M-129 What role does the physical inventory process play? (0 - our physical inventory is critical in getting our inventory accuracy within acceptable limits, 10 - we do not have a physical inventory process)

0	1	2	3	4	5	6	7	8	9	10

M-130 Are category codes used to classify item numbers? (0 - we do not use category codes, 10 - category codes are used for every single part number and is considered critical for sorting and identifying part numbers or groups of items)

0	1	2	3	4	5	6	7	8	9	10

M-131 Do all the functions that are affected by the routing participate in its creation? (0 - other functions find out about a new routing long after its been created, 10 - all critical stakeholders participate in the creation of routings)

0	1	2	3	4	5	6	7	8	9	10

M-132 Are routings structured to match the manufacturing process and reflect the way the products are built? (0 - our routings are structured completely independent of the way the products are built, 10 - the routing structure closely matches the way the product is built)

0	1	2	3	4	5	6	7	8	9	10

M-133 Is there a written procedure that explains how to calculate routing accuracy and what to check for including things like run times and operation sequence numbers? (0 - we have no documented or written procedures, 10 - we have a written procedure and follow it closely)

0	1	2	3	4	5	6	7	8	9	10

M-134 Does the finance function use the routings for costing the product? (0 - finance does not use the routings for costing the product, 10 - finance does use the bill of material for product costing)

0	1	2	3	4	5	6	7	8	9	10

M-135 Is there a documented distribution resource planning procedure? (0 - no, 10 - we have one and follow it closely)

0	1	2	3	4	5	6	7	8	9	10

M-136 Does the distribution resource planning process interface with the sales and operation plan and the master production schedule? (0 - our DRP acts independently of these two, 10 - our DRP function performs in an integrated fashion with both MPS and sales and operation planning)

0	1	2	3	4	5	6	7	8	9	10

M-137 Have all DRP items been identified along with associated planning factors? (0 - our DRP system is chaotic; it seems like we always have the wrong part in the wrong place at the wrong time, 10 - our DRP function performs smoothly with few disruptions)

0	1	2	3	4	5	6	7	8	9	10

M-138 Are forecasts kept by part number at the distribution center? (0 - we do not have a forecast or we do not keep one at the distribution center, 10 - we have a forecast by part number at the distribution center)

0	1	2	3	4	5	6	7	8	9	10

M-139 Are weekly or smaller buckets used for the immediate horizon in DRP planning? (0 - we use buckets larger than weeks, 10 - our planning buckets are weekly or smaller)

0	1	2	3	4	5	6	7	8	9	10

M-140 How frequently does DRP run? (0 - we are often lacking in the information that we need because DRP has not regenerated yet, 10 - we run the DRP frequently, we even run special DRP runs if needed)

0	1	2	3	4	5	6	7	8	9	10

M-141 Does the computer system attempt to match supply with demand through the use of action messages like, expedite, defer, cancel, past due, etc...in the DRP system? (0 - we do not have this capability or do not use it, 10 - our system does this and we track and monitor these messages aggressively)

0	1	2	3	4	5	6	7	8	9	10

M-142 Does the DRP planning process provides consolidated shipments to reduce transportation costs? (0 - we do not have this capability or do not use it, 10 - our system does this and we use it as needed)

0	1	2	3	4	5	6	7	8	9	10

M-143 Are Kanban systems used in the DRP systems where appropriate? (0 - we do not use Kanban, 10 - we use Kanban as needed)

0	1	2	3	4	5	6	7	8	9	10

18.16

SIC Industry Codes

Agriculture, Forestry and Fishing

01 Agricultural Production-Crops
02 Agricultural Production-Livestock And Animal Specialties
07 Agricultural Services
08 Forestry
09 Fishing, Hunting, and Trapping

Mining

10 Metal Mining
12 Coal Mining
13 Oil And Gas Extraction
14 Mining and Quarrying On Nonmetallic Minerals, Except Fuels

Construction

15 Building Construction-General Contractors And Operative Builders
16 Heavy Construction Other Than Building Construction-Contractors
17 Construction-Special Trade Contractors

Manufacturing

20 Food and Kindred Products
21 Tobacco Products
22 Textile Mill Products

23 Apparel And Other Finished Products Made From Fabrics And Similar Material
24 Lumber And Wood Products (Except Furniture)
25 Furniture And Fixtures
26 Paper And Allied Products
27 Printing, Publishing And Allied Industries
28 Chemicals and Allied Products
29 Petroleum Refining And Related Industries
30 Rubber And Miscellaneous Plastics Products
31 Leather And Leather Products
32 Stone, Clay, Glass And Concrete Products
33 Primary Metal Industries
34 Fabricated Metal Products (Except Machinery And Transportation Equipment)
35 Industrial And Commercial Machinery And Computer Equipment
36 Electronic And Other Electrical Equipment And Components (Except Computer Equipment)
37 Transportation Equipment
38 Measuring, Analyzing, And Controlling Instruments; Photographic, Medical And Optical Goods; Watches And Clocks
39 Miscellaneous Manufacturing Industries

Transportation And Public Utilities

40 Railroad Transportation
41 Local And Suburban Transit And Interurban Highway Passenger Transportation
42 Motor Freight Transportation And Warehousing
43 United State Postal Service
44 Water Transportation
45 Transportation By Air
46 Pipelines (Except Natural Gas)
47 Transportation Services
48 Communications
49 Electric, Gas and Sanitary Services

Wholesale Trade

50 Wholesale Trade-Durable Goods
51 Wholesale Trade-Nondurable Goods

Retail Trade

52 Building Materials, Hardware, Garden Supply and Mobile Home Dealers
53 General Merchandise Stores
54 Food Stores
55 Automotive Dealers and Gasoline Service Stations
56 Apparel And Accessory Stores
57 Home Furniture, Furnishing, And Equipment Stores
58 Eating And Drinking Places
59 Miscellaneous Retail

Finance, Insurance and Real Estate

60 Depository Institutions
61 Nondepository Credit Institutions
62 Security And Commodity Brokers, Dealers, Exchanges And Services
63 Insurance Carriers
64 Insurance Agents, Broker And Service
65 Real Estate
67 Holding And Other Investment Offices

Services

70 Hotels, Rooming Houses, Camps And Other Lodging Places
72 Personal Services
73 Business Services
75 Automotive Repair, Services And Parking
76 Miscellaneous Repair Services
78 Motion Pictures
79 Amusement And Recreation Services
80 Health Services

81 Legal Services
82 Educational Services
83 Social Services
84 Museums, Art Galleries, and Botanical And Zoological Gardens
86 Membership Organizations
87 Engineering, Accounting, Research, Management and Related Services
88 Services, Not Elsewhere Classified

Public Administration

91 Executive, Legislative And General Government (Except Finance)
95 Administration Of Environmental Quality And Housing Programs
96 Administration Of Economic Programs
97 National Security And International Affairs

Our ERP system can do a lot but we are not sure if it can do what you are asking....

19

Common ERP Venders

This section lists a variety of common ERP vendors and related products. Included are the basic contact information, and more helpfully, their Website addresses. The process of exploring ERP vendors' websites can be highly educational. One may learn a great deal of about the ERP industry by browsing through the various sections of all the different ERP vendors' websites. Some ERP vendors will even demonstrate their software through the Internet.

At the time of this writing, approximately 1500 different ERP solutions was available from a variety of vendors. All various degrees of sophistication, functionality, pricing, and scalability can be found. The ERP industry is highly unpredictable. Sudden changes in marketing strategies, technology, and business relationships create for a dynamic environment. The careful review of this chapter by using the Internet and the given URL addresses will provide the reader the latest in ERP functionality, technology, and strategies.

Name: ***ABB Automation Inc.***
Revenue: $140
OS: NT, Unix, Windows 95/98
Database: MS SQL Server, Oracle
Functions: Chemicals, Food & Beverage, Pharmaceuticals, Process Manufacturing Industries, Batch Processing, Continuous Flow, Contract, Hybrid Process, Make to Order, Process
Website: http://www.abb.com/

Name: ***Adonix Transcomm***
Revenue: $29
OS:
Database:
Functions: Discrete Manufacturing Industries, Process Manufacturing Industries Discrete, Process
Website: http://www.adonix.com/

Name: ***American Software***
Revenue: $78
OS:
Database:
Functions: Automotive, Consumer Packaged Goods, Discrete Manufacturing Industries, Electrical Equipment, Electronics, Food & Beverage, Industrial Goods, Pharmaceuticals, Assemble to Order, Configure to Order, Continuous Flow, Discrete, Make to Stock, Mixed Mode, Repetitive
Website: http://www.amsoftware.com/

Name: ***AremisSoft Corp.***
Revenue: $18
OS: NT, Unix
Database: Informix, Oracle
Functions: Discrete Manufacturing Industries, Assemble to Order, Configure to Order, Discrete, Make to Order

Website: http://www.aremissoft.com/

Name: ***Aspect Development***
Revenue: $86
OS: NT, Unix
Database: Oracle
Functions:
Website: http://www.aspectdv.com/

Name: ***Aspen Technology***
Revenue: $251
OS: NT, Unix
Database: MS SQL Server, Oracle,
Functions: Chemicals, Food & Beverage, Pharmaceuticals, Process Manufacturing Industries
Website: http://www.aspentech.com/

Name: ***AutoSimulations***
Revenue: $12
OS: NT, Unix
Database: IBM DB2, Informix, Ingres, MS Access, MS SQL Server, Oracle, Sybase
Functions: Aerospace, Automotive, Discrete Manufacturing Industries, Electronics, Food & Beverage, Industrial Goods, Machining Operations, Metal Fabrications, Pharmaceuticals, Semiconductors, Batch Processing, Configure to Order, Contract, Discrete, Highly Engineered Products, Make to Order, Make to Stock, Mixed Mode, Process
Website: http://www.autosim.com/

Name: ***Brain North America***
Revenue: $100
OS: OS/400
Database:
Functions: Automotive, Discrete, Process

Website: http://www.brainna.com/

Name: ***Camstar Systems***
Revenue: $20
OS: NT, OS/400.
Database: MS SQL Server, Oracle.
Functions: Aerospace, Chemicals, Consumer Packaged Goods, Discrete Manufacturing Industries, Electrical Equipment, Electronics, Food & Beverage, Industrial Goods, Metal Fabrications, Pharmaceuticals, Process Manufacturing Industries, Semiconductors, Paper, Batch Processing, Discrete, Highly Engineered Products, Hybrid Process, Mixed Mode, Process, Repetitive.
Website: http://www.camstar.com/

Name: ***Catalyst International, Inc***
Revenue: $34
OS: NT, Unix
Database: Informix, Ingres, Oracle
Functions: Automotive, Consumer Packaged Goods, Discrete Manufacturing Industries, Electronics, Food & Beverage, Pharmaceuticals, retail
Website: http://www.catalystwms.com/

Name: ***Ci Technologies***
Revenue: $28
OS: NT, Windows 95/98.
Database: IBM DB3
Functions: Discrete Manufacturing Industries, Process Manufacturing Industries, Continuous Flow, Discrete, Highly Engineered Products, Process
Website: http://www.citect.com/

Name: ***CIMLINC***
Revenue: $16

OS: NT, Unix
Database:
Aerospace
Functions: Discrete, Highly Engineered Products
Website: http://www.cimlinc.com/

Name: ***Cincom Systems, Inc***
Revenue: $70
OS: DEC Open VMS, NT, Unix, Windows 95/98, IBM S390
Database: MS Access, MS SQL Server, Oracle, DBMS
Functions: Aerospace, Consumer Packaged Goods, Discrete Manufacturing Industries, Electrical Equipment, Electronics, Industrial Goods, Machining Operations, Metal Fabrications, Process Manufacturing Industries, Semiconductors, Repair/Overhaul, Assemble to Order, Batch Processing, Configure to Order, Contract, Discrete, Highly Engineered Products, Hybrid Process, Make to Order, Make to Stock, Mixed Mode, Demand Flow Manufacturing
Website: http://www.cincom.com/

Name: ***CMI-Competitive Solutions Inc***
Revenue: $18
OS: NT, Unix
Database: MS SQL Server, Unidata
Functions: Automotive, Discrete, Mixed Mode, Repetitive
Website: http://www.trans4m.com/

Name: ***CMS Manufacturing Systems***
Revenue: $8
OS: OS/400
Database: IBM DB2
Functions: Automotive, Consumer Packaged Goods, Discrete Manufacturing Industries, Electrical Equipment,

Electronics, Metal Fabrications, plastics molding, Assemble to Order, Batch Processing, Continuous Flow, Discrete, Make to Order, Make to Stock, Mixed Mode,
Website: http://www.cms400.com/

Name: ***Cube Technology, ORSI Group Co***
Revenue: $36
OS: Windows NT
Database:
Functions: Discrete, Process
Website: http://www.orsiamerica.com/

Name: ***Datastream Systems***
Revenue: $98
OS: DEC Open VMS, Novell Netware, NT, OS/400, Unix, Windows 95/98
Database: MS Access, MS SQL Server, Oracle
Functions:
Website: http://www.dstm.com/

Name: ***Datasul***
Revenue: $62
OS: Novell Netware, NT, OS/400, Unix, Windows 95/98.
Database: Progress.
Functions:
Website: http://www.datasul.com/

Name: ***Descartes Systems Group***
Revenue: $49
OS: DEC Open VMS, NT, Unix, IBM MVS.
Database: IBM DB2, Informix, MS SQL Server, Oracle, Sybase
Functions:
Website: http://www.descartes.com/

Name: ***Epicor Software Corp***
Revenue: $200
OS: Novell Netware, Unix, Windows NT
Database:
Functions: Discrete Manufacturing Industries, Process Manufacturing Industries, Discrete, Process
Website: http://www.epicor.com/

Name: ***ESI/Technologies***
Revenue: $16
OS: Novell Netware, NT, Unix, Windows 95/98.
Database: Oracle.
Functions: Aerospace, Automotive, Consumer Packaged Goods, Discrete Manufacturing Industries, Electrical Equipment, Food & Beverage, Healthcare, Industrial Goods, Machining Operations, Metal Fabrications, Pharmaceuticals, Semiconductors, Assemble to Order, Configure to Order, Continuous Flow, Contract, Discrete, Highly Engineered Products, Hybrid Process, Make to Order, Make to Stock, Mixed Mode, Repetitive
Website: http://www.esitech.com/

Name: ***EXE Technologies***
Revenue: $93
OS: Supply Chain Execution, Warehouse Management NT, Unix
Database: IBM DB2, Informix, MS SQL Server, Oracle
Functions: Automotive, Consumer Packaged Goods, Discrete Manufacturing Industries, Food & Beverage, Healthcare, Industrial Goods, Pharmaceuticals, Assemble to Order
Website: http://www.exe.com/

Name: ***Exel Computer Systems plc***

Revenue: $16
OS: NT
Database: MS SQL Server
Functions: Aerospace, Automotive, Discrete Manufacturing Industries, Electrical Equipment, Electronics, Industrial Goods, Metal Fabrications, Assemble to Order, Batch Processing, Configure to Order, Discrete, Highly Engineered Products, Make to Order, Make to Stock, Mixed Mode, Repetitive
Website: http://www.exel.co.uk/

Name: ***Fourth Shift Corp***
Revenue: $26
OS: Novell Netware, NT, IBM AS/400.
Database: MS SQL Server, Other DBMS.
Functions: Automotive, Consumer Packaged Goods, Electronics, Food & Beverage, Computers
Website: http://www.fs.com/

Name: ***Foxboro Co***
Revenue: $300
OS: NT, Unix
Database: Informix, Oracle
Functions: Chemicals, Food & Beverage, Pharmaceuticals, Process Manufacturing Industries, Semiconductors, Batch Processing, Continuous Flow, Hybrid Process, Process
Website: http://www.foxboro.com/

Name: ***Friedman Corp***
Revenue: $24
OS: OS/400.
Database: IBM DB2, MS SQL Server
Functions: Consumer Packaged Goods, Discrete Manufacturing Industries, Metal Fabrications, Assemble to Order,

Configure to Order, Continuous Flow, Discrete, Make to Order, Mixed Mode
Website: http://www.friedmancorp.com/

Name: ***GE Fanuc Automation***
Revenue: $65
OS: NT, Unix, Windows 95/98.
Database: MS Access
Functions: Aerospace, Automotive, Chemicals, Discrete Manufacturing Industries, Electrical Equipment, Food & Beverage, Machining Operations, Metal Fabrications, Pharmaceuticals, Process Manufacturing Industries, Semiconductors, Continuous Flow, Discrete, Process, Repetitive
Website: http://www.gefanuc.com/

Name: ***Gensym Corp***
Revenue: $19
OS: DEC Open VMS, NT, Unix
Database: IBM DB2, Informix, Ingres, MS Access, MS SQL Server, Oracle, Sybase
Functions: Aerospace, Chemicals, Discrete Manufacturing Industries, Food & Beverage, Pharmaceuticals,Batch Processing, Continuous Flow, Discrete, Process
Website: http://www.gensym.com/

Name: ***Glovia International***
Revenue: $55
OS: NT, Unix
Database: MS SQL Server, Oracle
Functions: Aerospace, Automotive, Discrete Manufacturing Industries, Electrical Equipment, Electronics, Industrial Goods, Machining Operations, Metal Fabrications, Semiconductors, Assemble to Order, Configure to Order, Continuous Flow, Contract, Customer Service Industries, Discrete, Highly

Engineered Products, Hybrid Process, Make to Order, Make to Stock, Mixed Mode, Repetitive
Website: http://www.glovia.com/

Name: ***Great Plains***
Revenue: $108
OS: NT, Windows 95/98
Database: MS SQL Server
Functions: Discrete Manufacturing Industries, Electrical Equipment, Electronics, Machining Operations, Metal Fabrications, Discrete, Make to Order, Make to Stock, Mixed Mode
Website: http://www.greatplains.com/

Name: ***HarrisData***
Revenue: $28
OS: OS/400, System 36
Database: IBM DB2
Functions: Automotive, Consumer Packaged Goods, Discrete Manufacturing Industries, Industrial Goods, Machining Operations, Metal Fabrications, specialty furniture, Assemble to Order, Discrete, Make to Order, Make to Stock, Repetitive
Website: http://www.harrisdata.com/

Name: ***HK Systems***
Revenue: $90
OS: NT, Unix.
Database: Informix, MS SQL Server, Oracle, Sybase
Functions:
Website: http://www.hksystems.com/

Name: ***i2 Technologies***
Revenue: $362
OS: NT, Unix, Windows 95/98

Database: IBM DB2, Informix, Ingres, MS Access, MS SQL Server, Oracle, Sybase
Functions:
Website: http://www.i2.com/

Name: ***iBASEt***
Revenue: $10
OS:
Database:
Functions: Aerospace, Discrete, Process
Website: http://www.ibaset.com/

Name: ***ICC-GR Software***
Revenue: $17
OS: Unix
Database: Informix, Oracle
Functions:
Website: http://www.genrad.com/grs/

Name: ***IFS, Inc***
Revenue: $156
OS: NT, Unix, Windows 95/98
Database: Oracle
Functions: Aerospace, Consumer Packaged Goods, Discrete Manufacturing Industries, Electrical Equipment, Electronics, Industrial Goods, Machining Operations, Metal Fabrications, Assemble to Order, Batch Processing, Configure to Order, Contract, Customer Service Industries, Discrete, Highly Engineered Products, Hybrid Process, Make to Order, Make to Stock, Repetitive.
Website: http://www.ifsna.com/

Name: ***ILOG, Inc.***
Revenue: $50
OS: Unix

Database: Informix, Oracle, Sybase
Functions:
Website: http://www.ilog.com/

Name: ***Indus International***
Revenue: $196
OS: NT, Unix, OS/390, AIX
Database:
Functions:
Website: http://www.tswi.com/index2.html

Name: ***Industri-Matematik International***
Revenue: $96
OS: NT, Unix, Windows 95/98, IBM S390.
Database: Oracle
Functions: Consumer Packaged Goods, Electrical Equipment, Electronics, Food & Beverage, Healthcare, Industrial Goods, Pharmaceuticals, Configure to Order, Discrete, Make to Order, Make to Stock, Mixed Mode, Process.
Website: http://www.im.se/

Name: ***Infinium Software, Inc***
Revenue: $125
OS: NT, OS/400.
Database: IBM DB2, MS SQL Server, Oracle.
Functions: Chemicals, Consumer Packaged Goods, Food & Beverage, Healthcare, Pharmaceuticals, Process Manufacturing Industries, Batch Processing, Hybrid Process, Make to Order, Make to Stock, Mixed Mode, Process, Repetitive
Website: http://www.infinium.com/

Name: ***Intellution***
Revenue: $89
OS: NT

Database:
Functions:
Website: http://www.intellution.com/

Name: ***Intentia***
Revenue: $187
OS: OS/400
Database: IBM DB2
Functions: Automotive, Chemicals, Consumer Packaged Goods, Discrete Manufacturing Industries, Electrical Equipment, Electronics, Food & Beverage, Industrial Goods, Metal Fabrications, Pharmaceuticals, Process Manufacturing Industries, apparel, pulp & paper, Assemble to Order, Batch Processing, Configure to Order, Contract, Customer Service Industries, Discrete, Highly Engineered Products, Hybrid Process, Make to Order, Make to Stock, Mixed Mode, Process, Repetitive.
Website: http://www.intentia.com/

Name: ***Interbiz Supply Chain Group***
Revenue: $331
OS: NT, OS/400, Unix, Windows 95/98, MVS
Database: Ingres, MS SQL Server, Oracle, Sybase
Functions: Discrete Manufacturing Industries, Assemble to Order, Configure to Order, Discrete, Highly Engineered Products, Make to Order, Repetitive
Website: http://www.cai.com/

Name: ***Intrepa***
Revenue: $19
OS: OS/400
Database: DB400
Functions:
Website: http://www.logisticspro.com/

Name: ***J.D. Edwards***
Revenue: $934
OS: NT, OS/400, Unix, Digital VMS
Database: IBM DB2, MS SQL Server, Oracle
Functions: Automotive, Chemicals, Consumer Packaged Goods, Discrete Manufacturing Industries, Electrical Equipment, Electronics, Food & Beverage, Industrial Goods, Metal Fabrications, Pharmaceuticals, Process Manufacturing Industries, Semiconductors, Assemble to Order, Batch Processing, Configure to Order, Contract, Discrete, Make to Order, Make to Stock, Mixed Mode, Process, Repetitive
Website: http://www.jdedwards.com/

Name: ***JBA International***
Revenue: $487
OS: NT, OS/400, Unix
Database: IBM DB2, Oracle
Functions:
Website: http://www.jbaworld.com/

Name: ***Kewill ERP***
Revenue: $78
OS: Novell Netware, NT
Database: Pervasive SQL
Functions: Automotive, Consumer Packaged Goods, Discrete Manufacturing Industries, Electrical Equipment, Electronics, Healthcare, Industrial Goods, Machining Operations, Metal Fabrications, Process Manufacturing Industries, Semiconductors, Assemble to Order, Batch Processing, Configure to Order, Continuous Flow, Discrete, Make to Order, Make to Stock, Mixed Mode, Process, Repetitive
Website: http://www.micromrp.com/

Name: ***Kronos Inc***
Revenue: $96
OS: NT, Windows 95/98
Database: IBM DB2, Informix, MS SQL Server, Oracle
Functions:
Website: http://www.kronos.com/

Name: ***Lawson Software***
Revenue: $48
OS:
Database:
Functions:
Website: http://www.lawson.com/indexnf.html

Name: ***Lilly Software Associates Ltd***
Revenue: $61
OS: Novell Netware, NT, OS/400, Windows 95/98
Database: IBM DB2, MS SQL Server, Oracle, Centura SQL
Functions: Aerospace, Automotive, Discrete Manufacturing Industries, Electrical Equipment, Electronics, Industrial Goods, Machining Operations, Metal Fabrications, Semiconductors, Assemble to Order, Configure to Order, Discrete, Highly Engineered Products, Make to Order, Make to Stock, Mixed Mode, Repetitive
Website: http://www.visualmfg.com/

Name: ***LIS Warehouse Systems***
Revenue: $28
OS: Unix, Windows NT
Database:
Functions: Discrete, Process
Website: http://www.liswms.com/index

Name: ***Logility, Inc***
Revenue: $29

OS: NT, Unix
Database: Oracle
Functions: Automotive, Chemicals, Consumer Packaged Goods, Discrete Manufacturing Industries, Electrical Equipment, Electronics, Food & Beverage, Healthcare, Industrial Goods, Metal Fabrications, Pharmaceuticals, Discrete, Process
Website: http://www.logility.com/

Name: ***Macola Software***
Revenue: $21
OS: Novell Netware, NT, Windows 95/98.
Database: MS SQL Server.
Functions: Chemicals, Discrete Manufacturing Industries, Electrical Equipment, Electronics, Industrial Goods, Machining Operations, Metal Fabrications, Assemble to Order, Batch Processing, Configure to Order, Discrete, Make to Order, Make to Stock, Mixed Mode, Process.
Website: http://www.macola.com/

Name: ***Made2Manage Systems***
Revenue: $33
OS: Novell Netware, NT
Database:
Functions: Aerospace, Automotive, Discrete Manufacturing Industries, Electrical Equipment, Electronics, Industrial Goods, Machining Operations, Metal Fabrications, Semiconductors, Assemble to Order, Configure to Order, Contract, Discrete, Make to Order, Make to Stock, Mixed Mode
Website: http://www.made2manage.com/

Name: ***MAI Systems Corp***
Revenue: $22
OS: NT, OS/400, Unix, Windows 95/98.

Database: MS SQL Server, Oracle
Functions: Chemicals, Food & Beverage, Process Manufacturing Industries
Batch Processing, Hybrid Process, Process
Website: http://www.maisystems.com/

Name: ***Manhattan Associates***
Revenue: $62
OS: OS/400, Unix
Database: IBM DB2, Oracle
Functions:
Website: http://www.manhattanassociates.com/

Name: ***Manugistics***
Revenue: $198
OS: NT, Unix, MVS VME
Database:
Functions:
Website: http://www.manugistics.com/

Name: ***MAPICS***
Revenue: $139
OS: OS/400
Database: IBM DB2
Functions:
Website: http://www.mapics.com/intro.html

Name: ***McHugh Software International***
Revenue: $83
OS: NT, Unix, HP, Sun.
Database: MS SQL Server, Oracle
Functions: Chemicals, Consumer Packaged Goods, Pharmaceuticals, Assemble to Order, Continuous Flow, Make to Order, Make to Stock
Website: http://www.mchugh.com/

Name: ***Mincom***
Revenue: $120
OS: DEC Open VMS, NT, Unix, Windows 95/98, IBM S390.
Database: IBM DB2, Informix, MS SQL Server, Oracle, Sybase
Functions: Aerospace, Chemicals, Discrete Manufacturing Industries, Industrial Goods, Metal Fabrications, Process Manufacturing Industries, Transportation Mining, Discrete, Hybrid Process, Process
Website: http://www.mincom.com/

Name: ***Optum, Inc***
Revenue: $38
OS: NT, Unix
Database: Oracle
Functions: Consumer Packaged Goods, Electronics Assemble to Order, Configure to Order, Discrete.
Website: http://www.optum.com/

Name: ***Oracle Corp***
Revenue: $2140
OS: DEC Open VMS, NT, Unix, Windows 95/98.
Database: Oracle
Functions: Aerospace, Automotive, Chemicals, Consumer Packaged Goods, Discrete Manufacturing Industries, Electrical Equipment, Electronics, Food & Beverage, Industrial Goods, Process Manufacturing Industries, Assemble to Order, Batch Processing, Configure to Order, Continuous Flow, Contract, Customer Service Industries, Discrete, Highly Engineered Products, Hybrid Process, Make to Order, Make to Stock, Mixed Mode, Process, Repetitive.
Website: http://www.oracle.com/

Name: ***OSI Software***
Revenue: $40
OS: NT
Database:
Functions: Chemicals, Electronics, Food & Beverage, Pharmaceuticals, Process Manufacturing Industries Hybrid Process, Process
Website: http://www.osisoft.com/

Name: ***Paragon Management Systems***
Revenue: $21
OS: NT, Unix
Database: IBM DB2, Informix, Ingres, MS Access, MS SQL Server, Oracle, Sybase, Other DBMS
Functions:
Website: http://www.paragonms.com/

Name: ***PeopleSoft, Inc***
Revenue: $151
OS: DEC Open VMS, Novell Netware, NT, OS/400, Unix, Windows 95/98, IBM S390.
Database: IBM DB2, Informix, MS SQL Server, Oracle, Sybase.
Functions: Automotive, Consumer Packaged Goods, Discrete Manufacturing Industries, Electrical Equipment, Electronics, Industrial Goods, Semiconductors, Assemble to Order, Configure to Order, Continuous Flow, Discrete, Hybrid Process, Make to Order, Make to Stock, Mixed Mode, Repetitive.
Website: http://www.peoplesoft.com/

Name: ***Pivotpoint, Inc***
Revenue: $25
OS: NT, Unix
Database: Oracle

Functions: Discrete Manufacturing Industries, Electrical Equipment, Electronics, Semiconductors, Assemble to Order, Configure to Order, Contract, Customer Service Industries, Discrete, Highly Engineered Products, Make to Order, Make to Stock, Mixed Mode, Repetitive.
Website: http://www.pivotpoint.com/

Name: ***POMS Corp***
Revenue: $13
OS: NT, OS/400, Unix, Windows NT
Database:
Functions: Consumer Packaged Goods, Food & Beverage, Pharmaceuticals, Process Manufacturing Industries, Batch Processing, Continuous Flow, Discrete, Process
Website: http://www.poms.com/

Name: ***PowerCerv Corp***
Revenue: $30
OS: NT, Windows 2000, Unix
Database: MS SQL Server, Sybase
Functions: Discrete Manufacturing Industries, Electrical Equipment, Electronics, Industrial Goods, Machining Operations, Metal Fabrications, Configure to Order, Discrete, Make to Order, Make to Stock, Mixed Mode, Repetitive.
Website: http://www.powercerv.com/

Name: ***ProfitKey International***
Revenue: $35
OS: NT, Unix
Database: Oracle
Functions: Aerospace, Automotive, Discrete Manufacturing Industries, Electronics, Metal Fabrications,

Assemble to Order, Discrete, Make to Order, Make to Stock, Mixed Mode
Website: http://www.profitkey.com/

Name: ***Provia Software***
Revenue: $18
OS: DEC Open VMS, OS/400, Sun, HP.
Database:
Functions:
Website: http://www.haushahn.com/

Name: ***PSDI***
Revenue: $128
OS:
Database: MS SQL Server, Oracle, Sybase
Functions: Aerospace, Automotive, Chemicals, Consumer Packaged Goods, Discrete Manufacturing Industries, Electrical Equipment, Electronics, Food & Beverage, Healthcare, Metal Fabrications, Pharmaceuticals, Process Manufacturing Industries, Semiconductors, Discrete, Process
Website: http://www.maximo.com/

Name: ***Psipenta USA, Inc***
Revenue: $33
OS:
Database:
Functions:
Website: http://www.psipentausa.com/

Name: ***QAD***
Revenue: $193
OS: NT, Unix, Windows 95/98.
Database: Oracle, Progress
Functions: Automotive, Consumer Packaged Goods, Discrete Manufacturing Industries, Electrical Equipment,

Electronics, Food & Beverage, Industrial Goods, Pharmaceuticals, Process Manufacturing Industries, medical, Assemble to Order, Batch Processing, Configure to Order, Discrete, Make to Order, Make to Stock, Mixed Mode, Process, Repetitive.
Website: http://www.qad.com/

Name: ***Ramco Systems***
Revenue: $12
OS: NT
Database: MS SQL Server
Functions: Chemicals, Discrete Manufacturing Industries, Food & Beverage, Healthcare, Pharmaceuticals, Process Manufacturing Industries, Batch Processing, Continuous Flow, Discrete, Hybrid Process, Make to Stock, Process, Repetitive.
Website: http://www.ramco.com/

Name: ***Relevant Business Systems, Inc.***
Revenue: $15
OS: NT, Unix, Windows 95/98, Sun.
Database: IBM DB2, Informix, MS SQL Server, Oracle.
Functions: Aerospace, Discrete Manufacturing Industries, Electrical Equipment, Electronics, Industrial Goods, Machining Operations, Metal Fabrications, Maintenance Repair and Overhaul, Assemble to Order, Batch Processing, Configure to Order, Contract, Discrete, Highly Engineered Products, Make to Order, Make to Stock, Mixed Mode, Repair and Overhaul, Work Breakdown Structure.
Website: http://www.relevant.com/

Name: ***Renaissance Software, Inc***
Revenue: $10
OS: NT, OS/400, Unix
Database: Informix, Oracle

Functions: Automotive, Consumer Packaged Goods, Food & Beverage, Healthcare, Pharmaceuticals, Assemble to Order, Batch Processing, Customer Service Industries, Make to Order, Make to Stock
Website: http://www.rensoftllc.com/

Name: ***Rockwell Software***
Revenue: $100
OS: NT, Windows 95/98
Database:
Functions:
Website: http://www.software.rockwell.com/

Name: ***ROI Systems***
Revenue: $22
OS: NT, Unix
Database:
Functions: Consumer Packaged Goods, Discrete Manufacturing Industries, Electrical Equipment, Electronics, Industrial Goods, Metal Fabrications, Assemble to Order, Configure to Order, Continuous Flow, Contract, Discrete, Hybrid Process, Make to Order, Make to Stock, Mixed Mode, Repetitive.
Website: http://www.roisysinc.com/

Name: ***Ross Systems Inc***
Revenue: $83
OS: DEC Open VMS, NT, Unix.
Database: MS SQL Server, Oracle
Functions: Chemicals, Consumer Packaged Goods, Food & Beverage, Pharmaceuticals, Process Manufacturing Industries, Primary Metals, Pulp & Paper, Batch Processing, Hybrid Process, Make to Order, Mixed Mode, Process
Website: http://www.rossinc.com/

Name: ***Sage Tetra***
Revenue: $95
OS: Informix, MS SQL Server, Oracle
Database:
Functions: Chemicals, Discrete Manufacturing Industries, Electronics, Industrial Goods, Machining Operations, Metal Fabrications, Process Manufacturing Industries, Semiconductors, Assemble to Order, Configure to Order, Discrete, Highly Engineered Products, Make to Order, Make to Stock, Mixed Mode, Process, Repetitive.
Website: http://www.us.sage.com/mas90/default.asp

Name: ***SAP America***
Revenue: $2435
OS: NT, OS/400, Unix, Windows 95/98, Reliant, Solaris, IBM-AIX
Database: IBM DB2, Informix, MS SQL Server, Oracle
Functions: Aerospace, Automotive, Chemicals, Consumer Packaged Goods, Discrete Manufacturing Industries, Electrical Equipment, Electronics, Food & Beverage, Healthcare, Industrial Goods, Machining Operations, Metal Fabrications, Pharmaceuticals, Process Manufacturing Industries, Semiconductors, Contract, Customer Service Industries, Discrete, Highly Engineered Products, Make to Order, Make to Stock, Process, Repetitive.
Website: http://www.sap.com/

Name: ***Scala North America***
Revenue: $90
OS: Novell Netware, NT
Database:
Functions:
Website: http://www.scala-na.com/

Name: ***SCT Corp***
Revenue: $70
OS: NT, Unix
Database: Informix, Ingres, MS SQL Server, Oracle
Functions: Chemicals, Consumer Packaged Goods, Food & Beverage, Metal Fabrications, Process Manufacturing Industries, Batch Processing, Hybrid Process, Mixed Mode, Process
Website: http://www.sctcorp.com/

Name: ***SSI (Strategic Systems International)***
Revenue: $10
OS: AIX, HP-UX, UNIX, NT Oracle
Database:
Functions: Chemicals, Food & Beverage, Pharmaceuticals, Process Manufacturing Industries, Discrete, Process
Website: http://www.strategic-systems.co.uk/

Name: ***STG***
Revenue: $14
OS: DEC Open VMS, NT, Unix, Windows 95/98
Database: Oracle
Functions: Discrete Manufacturing Industries, Process Manufacturing Industries, Configure to Order, Discrete, Process
Website: http://www.stgamericas.com/

Name: ***Symix Systems, Inc***
Revenue: $116
OS: NT, Unix
Database:
Functions: Automotive, Discrete Manufacturing Industries, Electrical Equipment, Electronics, Industrial Goods, Machining Operations, Metal Fabrications, Assemble to Order, Configure to Order, Discrete,

Make to Order, Make to Stock, Mixed Mode, Repetitive.
Website: http://www.symix.com/

Name: ***SynQuest, Inc***
Revenue: $25
OS: NT, Unix, Windows 95/98.
Database: Oracle
Functions:
Website: http://www.synquest.com/

Name: ***Syspro Group***
Revenue: $39
OS: Novell Netware, NT, Unix, Windows 95/98, Microsoft SQL.
Database: MS SQL Server, Oracle.
Functions: Automotive, Chemicals, Consumer Packaged Goods, Discrete Manufacturing Industries, Electrical Equipment, Electronics, Food & Beverage, Industrial Goods, Machining Operations, Metal Fabrications, Pharmaceuticals, Assemble to Order, Batch Processing, Configure to Order, Contract, Discrete, Highly Engineered Products, Hybrid Process, Make to Order, Make to Stock, Mixed Mode, Repetitive.
Website: http://www.sysprousa.com/

Name: ***System Software Associates***
Revenue: $421
OS: OS/400, Unix
Database: Informix, Oracle
Functions: Automotive, Chemicals, Consumer Packaged Goods, Discrete Manufacturing Industries, Electrical Equipment, Electronics, Food & Beverage, Healthcare, Industrial Goods, Machining Operations, Metal Fabrications, Pharmaceuticals, Process

Manufacturing Industries, Assemble to Order, Batch Processing, Configure to Order, Continuous Flow, Discrete, Hybrid Process, Make to Order, Make to Stock, Mixed Mode, Process.
Website: http://www.ssax.com/

Name: ***TECSYS***
Revenue: $27
OS: NT, Unix, Windows 95/98
Database: Informix
Functions: Chemicals, Consumer Packaged Goods, Electrical Equipment, Electronics, Food & Beverage, Healthcare, Industrial Goods, Pharmaceuticals, Process
Website: http://www.tecsys.com/

Name: ***The Baan Company***
Revenue: $736
OS: NT, OS/400, Unix, Windows 95/98, IBM S390.
Database: IBM DB2, Informix, MS SQL Server, Oracle.
Functions: Aerospace, Automotive, Chemicals, Consumer Packaged Goods, Industrial Goods, Configure to Order, Highly Engineered Products, Make to Stock
Website: http://www.baan.com/

Name: ***Trilogy Software***
Revenue: $105
OS: NT, Windows 95/98
Database: MS SQL Server, Oracle, Sybase, Any ODBC Compliant
Functions: Automotive, Discrete Manufacturing Industries, Electronics, Healthcare, Pharmaceuticals, Assemble to Order, Discrete
Website: http://www.trilogy.com/

Name: ***USDATA Corp***

Revenue: $23
OS: NT, Unix, Windows 95/98.
Database: MS SQL Server, Oracle, Sybase
Functions: Automotive, Discrete Manufacturing Industries, Food & Beverage, Pharmaceuticals, Process Manufacturing Industries, Semiconductors, Discrete, Process
Website: http://www.usdata.com/

Name: ***Vastera***
Revenue: $12
OS:
Database:
Functions:
Website: http://www.vastera.com/

Name: ***Visibility***
Revenue: $22
OS: DEC Open VMS, NT, Unix.
Database: Oracle
Functions: Aerospace, Discrete Manufacturing Industries, Industrial Goods, Machining Operations, Metal Fabrications, Configure to Order, Contract, Discrete, Highly Engineered Products, Make to Order.
Website: http://www.visibility.com/

Name: ***Walker Interactive Systems***
Revenue: $79
OS: Novell Netware, NT, Unix
Database:
Functions: Aerospace, Automotive, Chemicals, Food & Beverage, Industrial Goods, Machining Operations, Metal Fabrications, Pharmaceuticals, Process Manufacturing Industries, Process
Website: http://www.walker.com/

Name: ***Western Data Systems***
Revenue: $32
OS: Unix, Windows 95/98.
Database: Oracle
Functions: Aerospace, Configure to Order, Contract, Discrete, Highly Engineered Products, Make to Order
Website: http://www.westdata.com/

Name: ***Wonderware Corp***
Revenue: $89
OS: NT, Windows 95/98.
Database: MS Access, MS SQL Server
Functions: Discrete Manufacturing Industries, Process Manufacturing Industries, Discrete, Mixed Mode, Process
Website: http://www.wonderware.com/

If we are in jelly we might be in a jam...
If we knew the difference between jelly and jam...

20

Glossary of Terms and Abbreviations

1099 - an income tax reporting form that is used for tracking payments made to persons and non-corporate entities. The form is required by the United States government.

ABCD ratings - a type of company rating that determines how well a company is using an ERP system. Class A is considered to be the best. ABCD ratings are administered by various consulting agencies. ABCD ratings have traditionally focused on operational modules like customer service management, work order management, capacity planning, material planning, supplier management, etc.

Access - the ability to obtain information or use functionality of the ERP system through menus, programs, or reports.

Account status - (1) the condition of a customer's accounts receivable transaction account. (2) the condition of some other financial account as it is used in the financial module.

Accounting period - a specific period of time that falls within a company's fiscal year. A fiscal year can contain a different number of periods from the true physical calendar, such as 14 periods instead of 12.

Accounts payable - amounts (usually money) owed for goods and services that have been rendered or received from a supplier. Accounts payable is also considered to be a module for an ERP system.

Accounts receivable - amounts (usually money) owed to a company for goods and services it has provided to its customers. Accounts receivable is also considered to be a module for an ERP system.

Accrued benefit - benefits that accumulate by employees to be used at a later time. Sick time and vacation time are examples of accrued benefits.

Acknowledgement - a document that acknowledges from a supplier that a purchase order has been received; or in sales, a message to the customer advising that an order has been accepted and/or shipped.

Action message - output of an ERP system that informs a user that a situation needs attention. In many cases an action message is set up so the user can execute it with preloaded variables creating a corrective action process. Action messages can halt a process flow until the action message is acknowledged or corrective action is taken.

Activity - any work or effort that is needed to achieve some result. It always consumes time and usually resources.

Aging - the organization of customer accounts owed sorted by due date. Aging is divided into schedules. The amount past due determines how aged the customer account is and to what schedule it should be assigned.

Aisle - the space inside a warehouse used for the efficient movement of people, materials, and equipment.

Algorithm - a logical sequence of steps for solving the problem, often written out as a flowchart, that can be translated into a computer program.

Allocation - a process that several different ERP modules use to assign or reserve something. For example, a customer service management module may allocate inventory to a customer before it is shipped.

Alpha - (1) represents combinations of letters A-Z. In ERP systems data fields are often defined as alpha, meaning that they can only accept values that are some combination of letters. (2) preliminary ERP software that is under development by an ERP vender. Alpha software comes before beta software.

Alpha test - refers to the process of testing a new ERP system, or function for the first time in a controlled environment outside of a customer's site. If the software passes the alpha test it may then be moved to a beta test site. See beta test.

Alphanumeric - represents combinations of letters A-Z and 0-9. In ERP systems data fields may be defined as alphanumeric, meaning that the data contained may be all alpha, all numeric, or a combination of both.

Alternate routing - a predefined movement of material, used for receiving or manufacturing operations, that serves as an alternate to the primary routing.

API - standing for application program interface, is a functional call from a program that allows it to access functionality or information from another program.

Applet - an application program that operates through the internet via the use of web browsers. Applets allow enhanced functionality of web browsers above and beyond what they normally could deliver.

Applicant - a prospective employee who has applied for a position with in a company. Applicant functionality may be found in human resource management modules.

Application program - is a certain type of program that provides specific functionality. Examples of application programs include: sales order entry, invoicing, forecasting, purchasing, inventory, accounts receivable, word processors, spreadsheets, etc.

Approval route - a component of workflow that is used to identify the sequence of people that the document must flow through in order to obtain approvals.

Architecture - is the overall design of a computer system including database, hardware, functions, language code, compatibility, etc.

Archive - the process of storing electronic data for future reference. The information is often moved to a different file or alternate storage media such as tape or microfiche.

Arrearage - an amount in a payroll system that could not be deducted from an employee's paycheck because the employee did not make enough money to pay for the deduction.

As of report - a report that can generate an output in summary or detail format that represents how something looked at a specific period in time.

Assembly - an item that consists of a group of items or subassemblies. They are usually manufactured and can require significant ERP functionality.

Audit - is the process of collecting information and comparing to some known standard. An ERP system can go through many audits during its lifecycle such as go live and post implementation. Audits may be conducted internally or by an outside consulting agency. Audits may be performed for legal, benchmarking, and to improve operational efficiency.

Audit adjustment - the adjustment that is made to general ledger accounts following an audit. Audit adjustments are often done following the close of the fiscal year.

Audit trail - is the detailed accumulation of transaction history. The transaction history will contain key pieces of information that will allow people to understand the nature of the transaction, when it was done, and who did it.

Authority - the right of a person to use power and exercise discipline for scheduling resources to meet an objective.

Available to promise - a method used to show the uncommitted, or unallocated, portion of inventory that will not be consumed by sales orders or manufacturing consumption. Available to promise capability can greatly enhance the functionality of customer service management, material requirements planning, and work order management.

Average cost - a popular method of valuing inventories. It is calculated based on the receipts of goods at actual cost for a period of time averaged with the previous period's average cost.

Back office - a somewhat vague term used by the ERP industry to describe core application and technical functionality necessary for all different types of companies using ERP systems. Back office programs may include programs such as address book and utility programs.

Backflush - the process of deducting inventory for the raw materials consumed during a manufacturing step. This is typically done when production is reported for a manufactured item through an ERP system.

Backorder - an unfulfilled customer order that will not be delivered on the date requested by the customer because of some delay caused by the supplier.

Backup - referring to the process of duplicating information for purposes of safekeeping. Often large databases will be backed up to magnetic media and stored offsite so that the system can be restored in the event of a data loss.

BACS - standing for bank automated clearing system is an electronic funds transfer technique used in the United Kingdom.

Bandwidth - is the amount of data transmitted per unit of time through some communication line. Larger bandwidths are capable of transmitting larger files in the same amount of time. Multimedia files can consume large amounts of bandwidth.

Barcode - referring to a system for tracking inventory or other barcodable objects. Barcoding systems consist of hardware and software that read barcodes (a series of vertical lines) and interprets them as a part number. Barcoding increases the speed of transactions and reduces keypunch errors. Barcoding systems usually come from third party providers.

Base - refers to the base functionality of the software. Additional functionality may be added through future software updates or the addition of software modules.

Base price - is the company's standard price for a product, given no other influencing factors.

Batch - (1) a group of records that are processed at the same time from a previous or future accumulated amount. (2) computer processing activity which operates with very little or no user interaction. It usually is temporary and may reoccur on a regular basis. (3) specific ERP functionality that is used in manufacturing operations to describe the amount that can be manufactured. This is often referred to as the "batch size". Batch size functionality can be found in bills of material and inventory masters.

Batch file - is a series of command lines that are collected into one single file. It is used at the operating system level and allows an organized sequence of events to take place. Unlike a program, batch files do not need be compiled for execution.

Batch header - is the process of electronically identifying a large group of records that have been, are currently being, or will be processed by the computer. Batch headers are often used to identify the group of inventory transactions to the general ledger.

Batch processing - is how an ERP system processes information. Batch processing works similar to people waiting in line to purchase movie tickets. The exchange of money for the tickets represents the batch processing. Under heavy loads a long line may form, delaying the batches. Batch management can become complex in sophisticated ERP environments. Sometimes information is accumulated. After a certain number of records have accumulated over a period of time, the batch process is started. The opposite of batch processing is interactive processing.

Batch status - is a coding system that identifies the current status of a batch and its relationship to batch processing. The coding system may be for the tracking and monitoring at the operating system level and/or application level.

Benchmarking - in ERP systems is the process of comparing one ERP system with another. Benchmarking is done for the purpose of becoming the "best in class". There are several different ways of benchmarking an ERP system including vendor to vendor and between different companies.

Beneficiary - a person, specified by the employee of the company, to receive proceeds or benefits from some company benefit program.

Benefits - the total sum of all compensations received by an employee from a company. It includes wages, health benefits, retirement plans, and more.

Beta testing - or beta test site, refers to the process of an ERP vendor or service provider using a customer as a test site for a new ERP system, or function, that has not been offered commercially to the open market. Customers often participate in beta programs to obtain free ERP software and/or services. Beta test sites are famous for having many problems.

Big bang - the process of going live on all functional modules of an ERP system at the same time. Also called cold turkey.

Bill of material - also called BOM, is a listing of all component parts that make up a manufactured item. In other cases bill of material functionality may be used to facilitate forecasting, sales, and purchasing functionality. The bill of material is critical in the proper functionality of many planning and manufacturing execution systems.

Bill to address - is the address for which a customer will be billed, or invoiced, for a good or service purchased by a company.

Bin - a specific storage area or device that is usually integrated with some type of shelving system.

Blanket order - (1) in sales order management, a blanket order represents a customer that has made a long-term commitment of several smaller shipments that will be released against the blanket order using the customer's future requested quantities and dates. (2) In supplier management, it represents a commitment to a company to purchase their goods or services for a length of time with individual shipments taking place against the blanket order.

BLOB field - standing for binary large object, is a special data field within a file that has no maximum size limit with the capability to hold any type of electronic data. Blob fields can be used to store objects such as videos or multimedia files.

Boilerplate - is written communication that has been time tested, stable, and can be used over and over again without change. Boilerplates are used in source code, contracts, guarantees, RFPs and documentation.

BOL - standing for bill of lading, is a carrier's contract and formal documentation for the purpose of transporting goods from one place to another. Bill of ladings contain descriptive information about the shipment and specifies the party to receive the shipment. In case of loss, damage, or delay, the bill of lading is the basis for filing freight claims.

BPR - standing for business processes reengineering, is the complete redesign of a one or more business process flows. Often a business process flow will be reengineered during the implementation of an ERP system. This can bring a closer functional fit between the business process flows and the ERP software.

Broadcast message - an electronic message that is conveyed to a large number of users via use of operating system tools and/or application tools within the ERP system.

Browser - a software program that translates information from servers through the use of Internet or Intranet. Browsers reside on clients such as a personal computer.

Bucketed system - functionality specific to time phased planning systems such as MPS/MRP/DRP. All of the planning output, such as projected on hand inventory, is accumulated into daily, weekly, or monthly buckets. In some ERP systems the ERP user can specify the type and number of buckets.

Bug - is a characteristic of the software that performs in an unexpected fashion or inconsistently with documentation provided by the ERP vendor. Excessive software bugs can be particularly disruptive to an ERP system. Sometimes bugs are referred to as "undocumented features".

Business partner - a vague term that represents the mutual cooperation between two different companies. In the context of ERP systems, it represents relationships between ERP vendors, integrators, third party providers, customers, and other organizations. The idea is that a business partnership in ERP systems brings higher value to the customer, but often the term can be misleading for ERP customers because there is no consistency in how business partnerships take place.

Business process flow - is a sequence of events, often predefined, that take place in a functional area of a business, such as sales, purchasing, finance, etc. Flexible workflow in an

ERP system allows good functional fits, allowing ERP software to better manage business process flows. Business process flows are often revised or changed during an ERP implementation.

Business unit - or sometimes known as a cost center, represents financial activity of a business, division, department, function, manufacturing work center, and capital equipment. Business units serve to track and segregate the money going into and coming out of different entities within a company. Business units are considered important functionality in ERP systems.

CAD - standing for computer aided design is software for designing products and/or geometric layouts. It has high geometric capability for designing three dimensional shapes. ERP systems generally have very limited CAD capability. CAD products are supplied by a third party provider and interfaced to the ERP systems. Bills of material, routings, and item masters are common interface points.

CAM - standing for computer aided manufacturing is software and hardware for the use in the manufacturing of goods. CAM systems often interface to CAD systems and less often to ERP systems. ERP systems have some CAM capability but generally do not provide direct control of process intensive capital equipment. Specialized CAM software provides for this function.

Candidate - a person who applies or is being considered for a job within an organization. That candidate may come from within the organization or external sources.

Canned - refers to using a highly standardized process or product to an ERP system. Software, software demos, and RFPs can all be canned. When something is canned it is not adjusted to business or industry specific functionality.

Canned demo - refers to using a highly standardized demonstration of an ERP system to a potential customer. Canned demos do not specifically address the unique problems encountered in a particular business.

Canned RFP - refers to the process of using a standardized RFP in an ERP software sales cycle. Canned RFPs are not adjusted to the specific needs of the business. The use of canned RFPs can be very misleading but are used because of their ease of preparation.

Capability study - or sometimes called feasibility study, is the thorough study of a proposal to determine its feasibility. Capability studies are performed for complex, difficult to answer questions such as: Are we ready for a new ERP system? Is barcoding right for us? Should business process flow be changed or software modified?

Carrying cost - the total cost of handling, storing, moving, etc. that a company accumulates in the storage of inventory products or materials.

CASE - standing for computer aided software engineering, is a computer program that is used to develop programs in a consistent fashion throughout an ERP system, creating consistent standards and functionality.

Category code - a coding system, usually user-defined and specific to a data element, that allows the classification of records for future inquiry and reporting.

Cause and effect diagram - a problem solving technique, also known as a fishbone diagram, using a graphical format that looks like a fishbone. As a tool, it is particularly effective during group brainstorming sessions to understand root causes for complex problems. Cause and effect diagrams are considered to be a part of TQM management.

CBT - standing for computer based testing or computer based training. Computer based training has become popular in ERP systems with the advancement of multimedia technology. More advanced ERP computer based training systems will contain extensive audio and graphic functionality with integrated testing capability. Some CBT programs can integrate directly into the ERP software provided by the ERP vendor.

Change agent - people who create the pathway from organization change and process improvement through ideals, feelings, thoughts, skill, will, trust, emotions or other. Change agents can play critical roles in the success of an ERP system and how well it interacts with the enterprise.

Change order - (1) a formal document that serves as the authorization to make some change in the scope, tasks, or resources of a project. (2) specifically, in an ERP system it represents the change to a document such as a sales order, work order, or purchase order. Some systems contain functionality to specifically monitor and track changes done by the use of change orders.

Character - a single digit of information used in combination with other characters to produce an almost infinite number of combinations of data and information that a computer can read, write, and store.

Chart of accounts - the financial chart that a company uses to organize its financial resources. The chart of accounts contains a hierarchy structure that allows child accounts to feed up to parent accounts. The child accounts contain detailed information and the parent accounts contain summary information. Fixed assets, accounts receivables, inventory, accounts payable, etc. are all examples of accounts that would appear in the chart of accounts. All complete ERP systems contain a chart of accounts that is integrated into the financial function of the ERP system.

Check digit - a number that is added to another number, example: 1587498 + 6 = 15874986, based on some predefined technique or mathematical formula. The concept of check digits applies strongly to ERP systems because they prevent data entry errors and increase the overall quality of the data. Check digits apply to any auto-generated number such as a part number, document numbers, etc. in an ERP system.

Check list - a list of desired characteristics or actions to a process flow or a set of process flows. Checklists are developed internally or supplied from an outside source. Checklists can be used at many points in an ERP life cycle from purchase to phase out.

Classification code - a characteristic that is assigned to a record to help identify that record as being part of a certain class or group. Classification codes can be part of user defined tables or they can work independently as managed by one or more ERP users.

Clearing account - a general ledger, that is used by the ERP system to offset journal entries.

Client - is a program that requests and receives information from a server in a client/server relationship. Web browsers are good examples of a client.

Client/Server - a relationship between two computer programs where one program, the client, requests information from another, the server. Client/Server technology is actively used with the networking of computers through LANs, WANs, and the Internet. ERP vendors have used the term client/server to represent distributed computer systems in contrast to older centralized computer resources. Client/Server software typically has GUI interfaces.

Closed loop MRP - is a material requirements planning system (MRP I) with additional functionality and input/output capability to different functional areas of the business. Sales, inventory, purchasing, capacity planning, and scheduling, are part of closed loop MRP. Because they communicate with each other, and input/output information to users, the systems are kept in synchronization. Modern ERP systems are based on closed loop MRP techniques.

Closed period - an accounting term used to describe a financial period's status. A closed period does not receive further financial transactions because all the transactions have been posted to the general ledger.

Closing - (1) a term used to describe the signing date of a contract for an ERP sale and/or services contract. After the sale has been made and the contract signed, the system is said to be "closed". (2) the financial processing done by an ERP financial module(s) at the end of the day/month/year.

CNC - (1) standing for computer numerical control, is a technique for high precision computer control of various types of manufacturing equipment. (2) standing for configurable network computing, is a highly configurable capability of an ERP system to operate on a network of multiple servers and databases. Sometimes the capability exists for a single ERP system to run on operating systems and databases from a large variety of software and hardware manufacturers.

COBRA - standing for consolidated omnibus budgets reconciliation act, is a law that requires employers to sponsor group health plans to employees and their dependents for continuation of health care coverage at group rates after an employee's resignation or other event.

Code - refers to the programming language an ERP system is based on and how it is constructed to give that ERP system its functionality. The code of an ERP system will determine an ERP system's functional capabilities and limitations. The code usually resides in the background, remaining invisible to the ERP user.

Cold turkey - the process of going live on all functional modules of an ERP system at the same time. Also called Big Bang.

Command - an instruction based upon words, phrases, scripts, configuration settings, function keys, or other, that is used to instruct the computer to perform a defined activity.

Commitment - a method of allocating inventory for either sales orders or work orders. Commitments represent demand placed against available inventory.

Common cause - a reason for variation in a process. Many problems in an ERP system often originate out of one and several common causes such as a lack of training, ownership, teamwork, etc. Sometimes a common cause is considered a root cause.

Competitive advantage - is the process of using a company's resources to produce goods and services more efficiently than the competition. ERP systems play a key role in developing a competitive advantage for businesses because of the deep integration with the business functions. The successful use of ERP in a ERM system can create a competitive advantage.

Component - also called child, is a raw material or subassembly that is used in a parent item.

Concurrent engineering - a participative design process that uses several different management techniques that can rapidly design high quality goods or services. Concurrent engineering techniques apply to the installation of ERP systems and can decrease the implementation times and produce higher quality results than would be possible otherwise.

Conference room pilot - is an organized planned pilot test of an ERP system. In a conference room pilot the entire ERP system will be stress tested with many different functional modules going through a variety of functional tasks at the same time. Conference room pilots are designed to test the stability and reliability of an ERP system before it goes live.

Configuration setting - or sometimes called processing options, is a feature that allows users to specify a variety of parameters for the purpose of providing instructions to programs for performing specific tasks. Some systems allow a multiple of different configuration settings to be saved for the same program allowing great flexibility.

Configurator - (1) is a functional module of an ERP system that is used to create valid combinations of different goods and sometimes services. (2) a software configuration management tool that is used to specify the appropriate configuration of an ERP system, based on inputs such as hardware type, industry type, number of users, desired functionality, etc.

Conflict of interest - is an activity of a person or party that conflicts in an unethical or illegal manner with another person or party. Conflicts of interest are common in ERP software sales cycles and implementations.

Conformance - a positive indicator of a process, product, or service that is operating within specification according to a viewpoint, contract, or other documented standard.

Consigned material - inventory material that is owned by one company and held by another.

Consolidation - usually referring to the process of combining information from several different divisions or business units for the creation of budgets, reports, or inquiries. Through the use of consolidation, several different companies or divisions may be represented on one balance sheet or income statement.

Constant - a value in an ERP system, numeric or alphanumeric, that usually stays the same.

Constraint - a factor that holds back a system from performing at a higher level. ERP systems routinely face constraining factors from a variety of sources such as management, lack of education, and technical issues.

Consulting - the processing of helping people to better understand complex processes and providing insight in different pathways to a desired objective. Consultants can play important roles in the successful implementation and use of an ERP system. Consultants provide a wide range of assistance including application, technical, project management, audits, feasibility studies, software selection, etc. Many times a consultant will become the change agent for an ERP system.

Continuous process improvement - also known as CPI, is the process of constantly improving a system. ERP systems that exhibit CPI have achieved a stable level of control.

Contract - an agreement between a company that purchased and/or uses ERP software and the ERP vendor and/or service provider. ERP contracts are often complex and subject to intense scrutiny and debate. When both parties reach an agreement on the contract, it is said to be "closed". Contracts specify selling price, terms and conditions, and warranties.

Conversion programs - convert data from a legacy ERP computer system to a new ERP system. They are custom software programs developed specifically for each situation. Conversion programs are used for either a split period in time during the go live or on a continuous basis to help legacy ERP systems communicate with the new ERP system. In these situations they are also sometimes referred to as interface programs.

Corrective action - the process of correcting a process that is operating out of specification. ERP systems can require extensive corrective actions.

Correlation - a relationship that shows a connection between two different sets of data, often an input and output. Correlations range from -1 to +1. +1 is a positive correlation. Specific mathematical calculations are used to calculate the correlations between two sets of data. Correlations are useful tools in troubleshooting complex ERP problems. Correlations that approach -1 or +1 may be direct causes to ERP problems.

Cost accounting - the process of performing, identifying, and communicating the cost of products and/or processes.

Cost allocation - the technique for the distribution of expenses, adjustments, or other financials among different business units.

Cost center - or sometimes known as a business unit, represents financial activity of a business, division, department, function, manufacturing work center, and capital equipment. Cost centers track the money going into and coming out and are considered important functionality in ERP systems.

Cost component - any portion of an item's cost such as material, labor, overhead, or other.

Cost drivers - any event that incurs costs.

Cost of goods sold - an accounting technique that measures the amount of cost accumulated through materials, labor, and overhead that is associated with the products or services provided for a given period of time. The cost of goods sold allows a company to determine its costs so profits may be calculated.

Cost plus contract - a pricing technique where the ERP buyer agrees to pay the seller all the acceptable costs of the ERP system, plus implementation costs, plus a fixed dollar amount for the ERP vendor and/or service provider to cover profit. Because of the extreme unpredictability of ERP systems, cost plus contracts are rarely used.

Cost rollup - the process of accumulating the costs of an inventory item, costs such as material or labor, and assigning them to that item.

Costed bill - the equivalent of the bill of material that extends the quantity per relationship of every component by the cost of those same components. The cost of bill allows ERP users to see the total cost of the product and where those costs are coming from.

Counseling - the process of providing psychological support systems for personal or work related problems. Despite the extreme psychological pressure placed on ERP team members during an ERP implementation, companies seldomly increase their psychological support systems.

CPI - standing for continuous process improvement is the process of showing continuous improvement in a system. In ERP systems evidence of CPI represents a major milestone in the stability and control of an ERP system.

CPU - standing for central processing unit, is the centralized calculation and processing unit of a computer. CPU's determine the speed (combined with other factors) in which an ERP system can operate. Historically, CPU's have shown tremendous improvement. Having the correctly sized CPU for an ERP system is important in balancing cost with adequate performance.

Crashing - an attempt to reach a milestone of an ERP project by adding an abnormal amount of resources.

Credit checking - a process a company goes through to identify the credit capability of their customers. Credit checking is functionality specific to ERP systems usually found in sales order management or accounts receivable. Approval to release an order may require intervention from a company's credit department or manager.

Credit memo - a document that is issued to a customer and used to correct the situation where the customer was overcharged, for returned goods, claim for damaged product, or good will.

Credit order - a document, often a sales order that is entered with negative quantities and amounts, used to identify products that have been or will be received from the customer for a variety of reasons.

Critical characteristics - the core requirements for an ERP system to meet a company's expectations in performing critical business process flows. ERP software sales cycles will often focus on whether the software can meet the critical requirements for the business.

Critical failure - a key characteristic or function of an ERP system that causes major disruption in the ERM system's process flows. A hard drive failure can be considered a critical failure to an ERP and ERM system.

Critical mass - a certain momentum that an organization builds up for or during an ERP implementation. It involves user participation, support, and buy-in of the critical stakeholders. After reaching a certain amount, the organization has enough to "break through" their historic beliefs and embrace the new system. Critical mass may also be used to describe the rate at which an organization can change. An organization that changes more rapidly than management and users of the ERP system can accept is said to have exceeded its critical mass.

Critical path - the sequence of activities in a project where the total duration equals the sum of individual activities in that sequence. Alternation of activities in the critical path will affect the completion date of the entire project. Critical path is used in PERT planning. (See PERT)

Critical path method - a planning technique that charts the activities of a project into sequences and paths. By the construction of the chart, the critical path can be found allowing planners to locate and find the constraining activities of an ERP project.

Critical process parameters - are the variables that affect numerous other variables. By focusing on and controlling the critical process parameters, many other process parameters will automatically fall into tolerance. An example is leadership in an ERP system. By having proper leadership in an ERP system, many complex side effects of poor leadership can be avoided.

Cross training - the capability to perform many different functional operations by one person. By training each person to do many different functional tasks, ERM systems can continue uninterrupted when one person becomes unavailable. It is wise to perform cross training in all critical positions of an ERP and ERM system.

CRT - standing for cathode ray tube is also known as a monitor. It is the primary output device of an ERP system.

Culture - the values, beliefs, and actions that make up a company. The type of culture a company has can determine its success with an ERP system.

Cumulative leadtime - a value that is determined by the analysis of individual component lead times in a bill of material that is one or more layers deep. The path that yields the highest accumulated total of individual lead-time will become the longest cumulative lead-time.

Cumulative update - is the latest released version of the software from an ERP vendor that includes the latest software bug fixes and enhancements.

Cursor - the point at which data appears upon a key press from a keyboard. The cursor may appear as a flashing vertical line or rectangle.

Cut-off - (1) refers to cycle counting characteristic in inventory management. (2) refers to batch programs that act as interfaces between two systems, such as two ERP systems, when an ending period becomes current not allowing further activity. (3)

during an ERP implementation, a period of time that a legacy system transfers to the new ERP system. During this period certain process flows and data entries must be completed.

Cyberspace - a term that refers to the total world wide internet, all of its users, communication links, and computers.

Cycle billing - a technique where a customer receives a consolidated invoice, at predefined intervals, for all the goods and services that have been provided to that company for the defined period of time.

Cycle counting - functionality that is specific to inventory management. Cycle counting verifies and adjusts the accuracy of inventory records on a continuous basis. Certain part numbers are counted on a predetermined frequency so the causes for errors can be identified. By identifying the cause for inventory errors, companies can obtain a higher level of control over their ERP and ERM systems.

Dampener - functionality associated with the concept of workflow. Dampeners have historically been used in modifying the output of action messages in MRP/DRP/MPS. To "damper" means to suppress the action message, usually based on some predefined logic.

DASD - pronounced as DAZ-dee, is the hard drive of a computer. It is a general term that can represent hard drives from mainframes to personal computers. DASD is a type of computer memory.

Data - combinations of characters and numbers that reside in humans, computers, or on paper. Data is often confused with information. Data and information are different in that data can be meaningless.

Data array - also called a matrix, is a multidimensional array; similar to an office building having length, width, and height; for the purpose of storing data. Programs use data arrays to temporarily store information until it can be processed or permanently stored.

Data collection - the process of inputting information into an ERP system through a variety of input devices such as keyboards, scanners, interfaces, etc.

Data conversions - the process of converting data from a legacy ERP system to a new ERP system. Data conversions may be done through the use of conversion programs and clerical techniques.

Data dictionary - is an application and file storage system that defines the data element characteristics of an ERP system. The data dictionary can define a field as alpha, numeric, alphanumeric, required length, default constants, etc. In addition, it may define certain objects, such as programs, and their relationship with other objects.

Data element - also called data field or field, data elements represent the most discrete unit of data in a database. Data elements are arranged in a predetermined way to create records.

Data mining - the analysis of information to find associations, sequences, classifications, clustering, and forecasting that have been previously undetected.

Data totaling - a technique that uses mathematical operators, logical functions, and comparison operators to create summary records that contain the mathematical total of the detail records that make it up. Data totaling is used in creating reports and online inquires.

Data warehouse - is the total centralized repository for all data of an enterprise. Data warehousing captures the data from many sources for access and analysis by the users.

Database - the central repository that stores information to be used by an ERP system. A database contains files, records, and fields. The concept is similar to a physical warehouse where the warehouse equals the database, the files equal a section within the warehouse, records equal a rack, and fields equal a bin.

Database administrator - also known as DBA, is a position within a company who monitors and maintains the integrity of data for the ERP system. A database administrator works with functional areas of a business to develop and insure consistent standards of data for a company. Sometimes a database administrator is referred to as "gate keeper" because requests for new standards or important records need to flow through this position for approval.

Database management system - is software and management techniques for the management and upkeep of databases. Database management software is separate from application software. Database management software deals more with raw data and does not associate application specific functionality with the data.

Database noise - data in an ERP database that is inconsistent with expectations. ERP systems are difficult to troubleshoot when they produce noise. Excessive noise is very undesirable in that it constrains integration in an ERP system. (Syn. Noise.)

Date stamp - a form of traceability. Date stamps contain basic information such as: date, time, terminal, program, user, etc. It is usually attached to the corresponding record in a file or table.

Debit memo - a formal document issued by a customer requesting a change to the amount owed to the supplier.

Debugging - a technique used by programmers for identifying software problems. Debugging systems may run interactively, showing the program executing each step of the code, or in a batch mode that generates reports. Debugging tools are helpful tools in improving the quality of code in ERP systems.

Decision matrix - is a matrix showing solution criteria relationships. Solutions are charted on one axis and criteria on another. People then evaluate each combination assigning values. Those that earn the most points are given the strongest consideration as a solution.

Deduction - the process in which a payment is reduced for a customer, employee, or supplier. Special logic is needed for the effective management of making deductions.

Default - an action or a value that will be used by a program or database unless overridden by a user.

Delinquency policy - the policy which a company uses for processing payments from customers with late payments. Late fees and delinquencies may be predefined and applied as necessary.

Delivery date - is the date on which a customer receives the product at their facility or establishment.

Delivery notes - notes that are attached to a sales order, or printed as a separate document, for the purpose of providing instructions to the delivery personnel.

Dependency - an instruction capability to do something based on some rule or predefined condition. Dependencies help to organize the logic of an ERP system. If values compared to the rule or predefined condition are false, then action is not conducted. Its successful execution is "dependent" upon the comparison to the rule or predefined condition being true.

Detail line - also called order detail line and order line, usually refers to detail order line for the goods or services in a sales or purchase order. Detail order lines contain information such as part number, prices, dates, etc.

Detail records - are the raw data records of a database. Detail records can be displayed directly on a video monitor or through a report. Detail is the opposite of aggregate or summary. (See summary.)

Deviation - (1) the process of wandering off the initial project plan in terms of activity, costs or time. Deviations are a part of scope creep. (2) refers to ERP module specific functionality such as forecasting or work order management, indicating that a process is not tracking as expected or projected.

Diagnostic study - a troubleshooting process that examines problems and root causes. A diagnostic study reveals the scope and magnitude of the problem so options for corrective action can be considered.

Direct ship order - also called drop ship, is (1) a sales order that is shipped directly to another location, such as a customer's supplier. (2) a purchase order that is shipped directly from a supplier to a specified location, bypassing the purchasing company's facilities.

Dispatch list - a sequenced list of work orders that are assigned to a work center.

Disposition - (1) the process of rejecting an item upon receiving/inspection for purposes of quality, price, or delivery date. (2) an inventory location where disposition processes, such as inspection, take place.

Distributed computing - a number of computers working together, that split the data processing tasks. Operating systems and ERP software work as integrating mechanisms to bind all the computers together as a single system.

Distribution list - is a predefined list of people for the purpose of receiving electronic or paper based messages. Distribution lists are most often, but not limited to, email programs.

DLL - standing for dynamic link library, is a program module that it is activated through an executable program. DLLs contain functions for enhancing the executable program that is calling.

Document - also referred to as a form, is the paper or electronic output, input, or storage of an ERP system specific to certain functions such as a sales order, purchase order, invoice, shipping acknowledgement, work order, etc. Documents usually represent a record(s) in a database.

Document number - a number that is used to identify and track a system document. Document numbers are used throughout an ERP system. Sometimes they are assigned manually.

Document type - (1) refers to a major class of document such as sales orders, work orders, or purchase orders. (2) refers to one of several different document types that exist within the same major classification type, such as sales orders. For example one document may be used for regular sales orders while another is used for credit orders.

Documentation - paper or electronic format that records the business process flows and how they use and interact with ERP software. Documentation is used for training, measurement standards, and certifications.

Download - is the movement of data from a centralized computer resource to a user specific computer system. Downloads are performed by using a variety of file transfer technologies. Downloads are useful in obtaining offline analysis of data.

Drill down - an important capability of integration that allows users to navigate to detail information that is related to aggregate information. Generally a user will start with aggregate information, and upon requiring more detailed information, will "drill down" to the detail records through the use of mouse clicks or function keys.

DSL - standing for digital subscriber lines, is a technology that uses conventional copper based telephone lines to bring high bandwidth information to businesses. DSL can achieve up to a theoretical 8.448 megabits per second.

Dumb terminal - a CRT display device that allows users to receive, view, and send information. Dumb terminals have little to no software to install or maintain. Their display capabilities are usually limited to text based non-GUI format. Dumb terminals, despite their limitations, have remained in active use because of their low cost, ease of maintenance, and industrial ruggedness.

EAP Program - standing for employee assistance program, is generally a professional counseling service that is conducted through a variety of methods. EAP programs provide employees an opportunity to understand specific stressors leading to dysfunctional behavior. Despite the extreme psychological pressures that ERP team members encounter during an ERP implementation, few companies recognize the need for EAP programs.

E-business - can be thought of as the complete process of marketing and promoting your company's product or service through the use of the Internet and websites. E-business includes functions such as online catalogs, product reviews, product information, performance characteristics, etc. E-business also represents the exchange of business information through the use of the Internet.

ECO - standing for engineering change order, is a document that is used to track and implement changes to products or processes, that are usually manufactured.

E-commerce - is the process of doing commercial transactions through the use of Internet and websites or electronic data interchange (EDI). Commercial transactions includes such things as quantities, credit card numbers, dates, part numbers, etc. E-commerce may be considered a function of e-business.

EDI - standing for electronic data interchange, is an electronic communication system for the exchange of documents between two companies. The documents consist of invoices, shipping notices, purchase orders, and ship authorizations. EDI uses one of several different types of standard formats. The standardization of EDI formats help computers to communicate with one another.

Edit/audit report - a report, or on screen query, that generates defective records in a database by using predetermined combinations of data selection. Through the use of edit/audit reports, defective records can quickly be located without the labor-intensive process of inspecting each record in a database.

Education - is the process of knowledge expansion. Education can be thought of as the process of "know why". Education is often confused for training. Education in an ERP system is the process of learning the features and functions and how they can be of benefit. (See Training.)

Effectivity date - also called an expiration date, is a date attached to a record in an ERP database that signifies the valid date. Effectivity data can have starting and ending effective dates. Many times the records are unavailable for use when they are outside the effectivity date. Customer pricing and bills of material use effectivity dates.

EFT - standing for electronic funds transfer, is a method of transferring funds from one bank account to another bank account of a different company.

Eighty / twenty rule - is based on the Pareto principle implying that most problems with a system come from relatively few reasons.

EIN - standing for employer identification number, is a tax identification number assigned to companies by the internal revenue service of the United States government.

E-mail - is the exchange of computer stored information through various telecommunication techniques. The Internet is actively used for e-mail messages. E-mail systems become increasingly more important in ERP systems as they integrate more deeply with functions of ERP systems. E-mail systems may be integrated with functional modules of an ERP system through the use of workflow.

Employee involvement - is the direct active involvement of employees in business process flows. It uses employee experience, creativity, and knowledge base for incorporation into the organization's efforts, bringing about quality and productivity improvements. Employee involvement in an ERP system is highly desirable because it promotes the overall heath of an ERM system.

Emulator - is a hardware device or software program that pretends to be another device. For example, a personal computer may use emulation software to mimic an outdated display terminal allowing a mainframe to communicate directly with the personal computer.

End user - a person who actively uses the software on a day-to-day basis.

Enterprise - refers to the entire entity of a company. An enterprise represents its systems, people, software, products, facilities, etc.

Entity diagram - is a visual schematic that shows the representation and relationships of functional programs, modules, and files interacting in an ERP system.

Environment - (1) or sometimes called library, represents a database file structure dedicated for one specific task. These specific tasks include: holding the go live data, testing area, post live production area, and conference room pilot. The use of environments greatly increases an ERP system's capability to test and prototype business process flows within the software. (2) refers to the industry specific characteristics a company has. (3) refers to the characteristics a company exhibits in their use and control of an ERP system: horse, cow, monkey, eagle, etc.

ERM - standing for Enterprise Resource Management, is a complete enterprise wide business solution that consists of an ERP system and functional activities occurring within each module of, and around, the ERP system. The ERP system consists of software support modules such as: marketing and sales, field service, product design and development, production and inventory control, procurement, distribution, industrial facilities management, process design and development, manufacturing, quality, human resources, finance and accounting, and information services. The functional activities occurring within each module consists of: management, decisions, training, documentation, communication, people, etc. The ERP modules and functional activities must exist in harmony to become an ERM solution. The integration/interface points of the ERP system bind the entire ERM solution together.

ERP - Enterprise Resource Planning, is a complete enterprise wide software solution. The ERP system consists of software support modules such as: marketing and sales, field service, product design and development, production and inventory control, procurement, distribution, industrial facilities management, process design and development, manufacturing, quality, human resources, finance and accounting, and information services. Integration between the modules is stressed without the duplication of information. ERP systems are an outgrowth of MRP II systems.

ERP Implementation - is the process of installing an ERP system in a company. Tremendous variations in time and cost can be found in the installations of ERP systems. Organizations must often go through significant organizational change during and after the implementation.

Ethernet - is a widely used technology for connecting computers or other devices together as a local area network (LAN). Ethernet may use coaxial cables, twisted pair wires, or 10Base T, 100Base T, or others to connect computers together through the use of networking hubs.

Event - any action or situation that occurs within an organization or computer system.

Exception report - output of an ERP system, usually paper based, that shows an out of balance situation. Exception reports are commonly used in DRP/MRP/MPS modules to alert users to perform an action for inventory items and documents that manage inventory items.

Executable - is a certain kind of a file that can be executed by a computer to run as a program.

Exit - the process and capability of a user exiting one program to go to another program. Exits may be performed through function keys or drop down menus. Sometimes an exit will pass key data to the next program to prepare it for a function, such as another inquiry. The difference between a menu option and an exit is that an exit is performed within a program.

Expedite - an intense concentrated effort to deliver or obtain materials or services in less time than it would normally take. Situations that require expediting are usually past due.

Fail safe - also known as poka-yoke or mistake proofing, is the process of making a process flow mistake proof. Well designed ERP systems provide a variety of poka-yoke tools while still allowing flexibility.

Failure mode analysis - the process of investigating a failure of a critical product or process flow. After the reasons for failure are determined, the process or product is redesigned to prevent future failures.

Family - also called groups, is a grouping of records that share some common characteristic. Families are often created based on user defined tables and used in many different functional modules of an ERP system. Families can help facilitate the viewing of information in aggregate.

Feature - (1) is descriptive of the functional capabilities of an ERP system. ERP systems that contain many features are said to be "feature rich". (2) characteristic of the goods or services that an organization offers. ERP software may provide specific functions to sell and configure feature rich products.

Feedback loop - is the part of an ERP system that records input after some type of output. By comparing the input with the output, certain business process flow measurements and adjustments can be made to keep the process in control. Feedback loops are essential for more advanced forms of control in an ERP system.

Field - (1) is a area on a computer display video that represents a certain type of information. Both input and display fields are a certain type of field. (2) a specific area within a record that is dedicated to the storage of a certain type of information such as customer number, dollar amount, document numbers, etc.

FIFO - standing for first in first out, is an inventory allocation method for the picking of inventory for sales or work orders. The assumption is that the oldest inventory is the first to be used. It is also a method for determining the value of inventory.

File - also called data file, is a section of the database that represents a collection of records. Files are carefully designed in their structure to support the functionality of an ERP system.

File structure - is the design and layout of a file system. A certain type of file structure by design will provide the functional characteristic for which it is needed. The makeup of the file structure includes how information is stored, the data elements, and how the data elements are arranged.

Finished goods - are the end products that a company offers to their customers.

Firewall - is software programs and hardware systems that protect a private network from other networking systems or outside sources such as the Internet.

Fiscal year - a company's financial calendar as it relates to their tax-reporting year. The starting and ending periods can be different from the true physical calendar.

Five whys - is the process of asking "why" five times in an attempt to understand the fundamental cause to a problem.

Fixed budget - a fixed projected use of money covering a predetermined period of time based on an expected activity.

Fixed contract - or sometimes referred to as bonding, is a contractual agreement between a company (customer) and an ERP vendor or service provider. The contractual agreement holds the ERP vendors or service provider accountable for the performance and implementation of an ERP system. Because of the high failure rates of ERP systems, a company often seeks a fixed contract hoping that it will ensure that the ERP system will be installed on time and on budget. Fixed contracts are thought to keep vendors honest when communicating with a company on performance characteristics of an ERP system. Fixed contracts often cost much more than variable contracts because of unknown variability. Fixed contacts can be a source of intense political and legal dispute between companies and ERP service providers.

Flash message - a message that pops up in a program to alert the user of some unusual characteristic information. Flash messages may be program, functionality, or data specific. For example: a flash message may be used upon sales order entry to alert the user that the customer is over their credit limit.

Flexibility - is the capability of an ERP system to use softcoding to adapt to a wide variety of business process flows and situations. Highly flexible ERP systems reduce the need for unnecessary software modifications.

Flexible budget - projected expenditures based on different levels of activity over a predetermined period of time.

Float days - the amount of time between the issue of the payment and the deduction of the dollar amount from a bank account.

Flowchart - a series of lines and geometric shapes such as squares, triangles, diamonds, etc. that represent business and ERP process flows. Flowcharts may be created before an implementation of an ERP system to better understand the business process flows. Flow charts are often a part of functional mapping.

Fold - the part of a data display screen that upon depressing a function key or menu option can display more detailed or additional information for a record.

Forecast - specific ERP functionality that examines a customer's past demand to create future projections through the use of various mathematical formulas.

Form - a specific combination of data fields and text descriptions arranged for a specific function. A form may be referred to as a video, screen, or panel.

Format - the arrangement of data as it is stored, moved, or processed. ASCII is considered a method of formatting data.

Formatting rules come from a variety of sources including; international standards, ERP vendors, and from within companies.

Fourth-generation language - also known as 4GL, is an object oriented programming language. The use of fourth generation programming language can greatly reduce the code and program size of an ERP system. Fourth-generation languages tend to be more intuitive, avoiding complex syntax found in other programming techniques.

Freeze - or freeze period, (1) refers to ERP specific functionality that prevents records from changing for a certain period of time or until a certain event occurs. (2) represents a defined stable business process flow in a period of time after an organization goes through change.

Frozen cost - a cost that is "frozen" in place for an inventory item. Frozen costs help an ERP system to calculate variances for work orders and purchase orders.

FTE - standing for full time equivalent, represents the manpower equivalents that can be dedicated to a project. For example 1.0 FTE may be composed of two different people dedicated to the project 50% of the time or one person dedicated to the project 100% of the time.

FTP - standing for file transfer protocol, is a method for the exchange of information between computers using the Internet or networking hardware. It provides simple file functions such as copy, rename, transfer, and delete.

Function - is a feature or characteristic in an ERM system that enables it for some purpose. The concept of function exists at many different levels in an ERM system. Programs achieve function by processing, moving and storing data. Several different programs working together in a specific area of business creates a functional module of an ERP system. Several different functional modules working together using integration through software creates an ERP system. Several different functions such as management, documentation, training, measurements, etc. interacting with functional modules of an ERP system creates an ERM system. All the function characteristics of a business system contribute to an overall ERM system.

Functional - also known as functional systems design, is the process of interviewing and working together as a team in understanding and documenting business process flows. Functional maps are often created on a visual aid, such as a white board or projector, so groups of people can interact creating the best possible business process flow that matches the capabilities of the ERP software. ERP team functional members and outside consultants are active participants.

Gantt chart - also called a job progress chart, is a graphical display method for showing the steps and sequence of a project. In ERP systems, Gantt charts are often used in the early phases of an ERP implementation to project the completion time and resource consumption.

Garbage in, garbage out - a phrase that explains the relationship and importance to enter in quality information in an ERP system so the system can generate valid output. This phrase is based on the concept that the data going out can be no better than the data that comes into a system.

Gateway - is the entrance point to a network. A computer server that acts as a gateway and may also act as a firewall server. Gateways often use routers and switches.

General ledger - a repository for all the company's accounts necessary to prepare income statements, balance sheets, and process financial transactions.

Gigabyte - is a measurement of computer storage capacity that equals about one billion bytes.

Go Live - also known as cut over, is a specific point in time when a company switches from their legacy system to the new ERP system.

Grade - a method of identifying the quality of the product that a company sells. Different grades of product may receive different prices and have different handling and packaging requirements. Some companies need specific ERP functionality to handle grade processing.

Grid - a display output technique that divides data into spreadsheet format through the use of rows and columns. Columns usually represent the data elements from the file and a row represents the record from that same file. Grid displays can assist in helping the user to view many records at one time interactively.

Guarantee - an obligation from a supplier to a customer to answer for some characteristic of their product or service should it not perform as noted or expected. (See warrantee.)

GUI - standing for graphical user interface, is a graphic user interface to a computer. Graphical user interfaces are usually capable of showing pictures and have good flexibility in formatting the video interface based on the needs of the user. GUI interfaces are characterized by the use of mousses and menus.

Hard coded - or sometimes known as hard coding, refers to software that can not change functionality to a desired kind. Hard coded software has no capability to adapt to specific situations. Hard coded software can be thought of as the opposite of soft coded software.

Hard copy - is a printout of a report from a computer system.

Hard drive - the main long-term storage area of a computer where the data and source code of an ERP system reside. Hard drives usually consist of rotating magnetic media. The proper sizing of a hard drive is important in balancing cost with performance in an ERP system. Hard drives are a form of computer memory.

Hard error - an error that occurs within a program that halts the data entry process or further processing. Hard errors are either fatal, causing the program to end, or are paused to require corrective action. If they are fatal then the data must be corrected and the program restarted. If they are paused the data must be corrected before the program can continue.

Hardware - a term to represent the "hard" parts of a computer system as opposed to the "soft" parts such as software. Hardware consists of the computer, computer components, and a variety of hardware peripherals. Devices not directly connected to an ERP system, such as barcoders or RF devices, are also considered to be hardware.

Head count - the number of people providing resources to a company or functional area, usually employees.

Header - or header record, is the master record that represents and ties together many smaller detailed records. Header/detail relationships are similar to parent/child relationships; however, header/detail is more often used for document type data such as sales orders, purchase orders, and work orders.

Heads down - used to describe a data entry process that is optimized for data input. A heads down data entry process consists of a keyboard and video that is optimized for the efficient data entry through the use of a keyboard. Heads down data entry does not require the use of a mouse or direct contact of vision with the monitor by the data entry person.

Help desk - a service provided internally to a company, and/or externally through a service provider, that provides assistance and help in the use of ERP systems and related products. Help desk personnel may help with application programs and setting up new users on the system.

Heuristic - an approach for learning and a method for solving problems based upon experience or intuition. Chess players use a heuristic approach.

Hierarchical database - is a database design containing parent and child records. Each child record can have only one parent record. A child record can not be added until a parent record is added. A hierarchical database is representative of a tree upside down with its trunk at the top and branches underneath.

High-level language - computer programming language, with advanced capabilities, that uses a commonly understood syntax to reduce the learning curve and programming time.

History logging - also known as journal, is a methodology that records all additions, deletions, and changes to the records in a file or database. History logging can be particularly more informative than date stamps because it gives a complete history of all the activity that has been happening to a particular record in a table or file. Some systems allow every single field in the record to be duplicated, allowing ERP users to see the exact changes occurring within the record over its entire life history.

Host - a large centralized computer that provides data processing services to a variety of terminals that connect directly to the host computer.

HTML - standing for hypertext markup language, is the premier language code used on the Internet. HTML code can be viewed by any computer containing a Web browser with an Internet connection.

HTTP - standing for hypertext transfer protocol is a communication protocol used on the Internet for the exchange of data between computers. Data such as text, graphics, sound videos, application programs, and general files can be transferred through the use of HTTP.

I/O - standing for input/output is descriptive of a device, program, or operation that transfers data. I/O devices include printers, mousses, hard disks, monitors, and communication devices.

Implementation - is the process of installing an ERP system. It covers a range of time from the initial software installation to the go live date.

Implementation plan - is the plan of how an ERP system will be installed. It can be very formal with many detailed steps, or informal, lacking any documentation. It may be provided by an ERP vendor, service provider, or it may come internally from the company.

Information - something, such as data, that has meaning. ERP system can provide information directly from databases or by output calculated from databases or input.

Input - the process of transferring data to an ERP system, or more specifically, a program in that ERP system. Input is data collection. ERP systems typically contain ways to connect to a variety of input sources. Common input devices include keyboards and mousses.

Install - the process of loading software onto a computer system either for the first time or as an upgrade to the existing system.

Integrating mechanism - any object, device, characteristic, protocol, system, etc. that uses communication to achieve a beneficial function.

Integration - an important foundation characteristic of an ERP system. Through the use of integration, ERP systems achieve communication by bringing functionality to an ERP system. Integration is achieved through a variety of interfacing techniques including, communication protocols, software, Internet, workflows, etc. Integration can be thought of as bringing together two different systems so that they act as one.

Integrity analysis - specifically designed programs, within an ERP system, that test for valid data or combinations of valid data. They may be run on a regular basis to check for data errors or after a data conversion in an ERP implementation. Integrity analysis programs can be helpful in improving the overall quality of a database.

Interactive processing - is how an ERP system processes data or information. Using interactive processing, information is submitted for processing automatically. Several interactive processes can occur at the same time. The opposite of interactive is batch processing. Interactive processing is associated with the term 'real time'. A computer program outputting and collecting information through a computer terminal is an interactive session. Interactive processing generally has little or no delay to an ERP user.

Inter-company purchase order - a purchase order that is used to facilitate the sale, picking, and movement of material from one geographic company location to another. An inter-company purchase order is often connected to an inter-company sales order.

Inter-company sales order - a sales order that is used to facilitate the sale, picking, and movement of material from one geographic company location to another. An inter-company sales order is often connected to an inter-company purchase order.

Interface - the communication process between two different points. Interfaces exist at multiple levels, between functional modules of an ERP system, computer platforms, and different software packages. Interfaces use a variety of communication technologies to exchange information between two points. Interfaces directly support integration of an ERP system. An interface can be thought of as two devices with a connector between them.

Interface program - (1) converts data from a legacy ERP system to a newer ERP system and vice versa. Each interface program is usually custom developed for the specific situation. After the go live in the new ERP system, the interface programs are discarded. (2) is a program that helps two ERP systems, or products related to ERP systems, communicate with ERP systems. These interface programs may be custom developed for specific situations or sold by software vendors as part of a commercial product.

Internal - a term referring to a process, action or characteristic that originates inside a company vs. coming from outside of a company like ERP vendors or service providers.

Interrupt - the disruption of the normal processing logic of a computer process from an outside source. Interrupts are designed to interrupt processing so the outside request can be processed.

Intranet - is a private networking system that is contained within an organization. It may consist of several local and wide area networks with access to the Internet through the use of gateways.

Inventory Accuracy - a fundamental characteristic that measures the accuracy of inventory records. Inventory accuracy plays a critical role in the successful use and implementation of an ERP system that uses distribution and manufacturing functionality. Inventory accuracy should be 95% or higher at the location level for the successful use of an ERP system.

Invoice - a document that records a list of goods and services shipped or provided to a customer. Invoices contain specific information for the sale such as prices, taxes, quantities, etc.

IS department - standing for information systems department, is also know as IT department for information technology, both represent the centralized computer support function or department for a company. The IS department will be responsible for tasks such as: system backup, performing upgrades, user security, user signon, etc.

ISDN - standing for integrated services digital network is a communication technique that uses ordinary copper based phone lines to transmit information up to 128 Kbps

ISO - is a federation of national standards from countries around the world known as the International Organization for Standards. Many different types of standards are set from methods of conducting business to communication protocols.

ISO 9000 - is a series of standards and methodologies established by the International Organization for Standardization. ISO 9000 helps a company to effectively document their standards and procedures. It helps ensure the consistent quality of goods and services that a company provides.

Issue - (1) refers to an outstanding problem waiting for resolution. (2) refers to ERP functionality for removing inventory quantities from on-hand balance.

Issue resolution policy - a documented technique that originates internally or externally for the purpose of resolving issues in ERP systems. Due to many problems that occur with ERP systems, some ERP vendors will adopt standard issue resolution policies for their ERP systems. Some ERP customers create and implement their own issue resolution policies independently of the ERP vendors' issue resolution policies.

Item availability - is the uncommitted portion of inventory available for future customer orders or work orders. It's similar to available to promise except that it is based in real time and does not contain phasing.

Item master - is considered core functionality for any ERP system using distribution or manufacturing type functions. The item master serves as a central repository to define the characteristics of a company's inventory items. The item master contains a variety of data elements including: part number, description, stocking codes, and much more.

Job description - is a documented statement of roles, responsibilities, and qualifications found in a job. ERP systems can have a great impact on job descriptions and vice versa. Job descriptions should be consistent with the capabilities and limitations of an ERP system.

Job rotation - is the process of rotating employees through different job responsibilities. Job rotation in ERP systems can minimize disruptions and protect company/ERP specific knowledge.

Journal entries - financial transactions that are based on debits and credits to accounts in the general ledger, or more specifically, the chart of accounts. Journal entries come from a variety of sources throughout an ERP system.

Justification strategy - a process that weighs the resources needed to make and maintain a modification to an ERP system against the benefits that the modification will achieve. Justification strategies can be a useful technique for eliminating many unnecessary system modifications. Many justification strategies can be used for and are similar to ROI calculations and cost/benefit analysis.

Kanban - is a visual signal to deliver or manufacture more materials. It can operate completely autonomously outside the control of an ERP system. Kanbans are usually represented by Kanban cards, which serve as the authorization to purchase, deliver, or manufacture more materials.

Key - a data field in a file that allows the contents of the file to establish a relationship with another file. Through the use of keys, databases become much more efficient in the storage of data, requiring less disk space. Keys affect the functionality of report writers.

Key punch - is the process of entering data and information into a computer system through the use of a keyboard as opposed to some other automated technique.

Key stroke - represents a single digit that is entered into a computer system through the pressing of a single key on a keyboard.

Kickback - a payment to an individual or organization from a supplier (often illegally) for obtaining new or more business. Often kickbacks will be paid through some form of bartering.

Knowledge management - the process an organization uses for gathering, organizing, refining, and disseminating data and information to aid in the fulfillment of an organization's vision and mission.

Knowledge worker - an employee who creates, analyzes, processes, moves, and collects information and data.

Leading edge - the process of a company adapting to and using management and technology to its fullest capability.

Learning curve - the capability of an organization or individual to learn through experience, making future obstacles and situations less challenging. Organizations can go through long learning curves before realizing the full benefits of an ERP system.

Legacy system - an aging ERP system that has been or is going to be replaced by a newer more robust ERP system.

Life cycle - all the phases that an ERP system goes through from conception through phase out.

Life cycle testing - the testing of a product or process in a controlled environment to reveal the durability and stability as it might appear in real life conditions.

Life support - the process of installing the bare functional essentials of an ERP system. Some companies, eager for the rapid implementation, will first install the bare essentials needed to run their business and at a later date, will implement less critical functions.

LIFO - standing for last in first out, is an inventory allocation method for the picking of inventory for sales or work orders. It is also a method for determining the value of inventory.

Local area network - also known as LAN, is a method for connecting computers and other devices, such as printers, all together in a single system. Local area networks allow computers and users to share information and data. Local area networks work as integrating mechanisms for businesses.

Location - is a storage place for an inventory item in a warehouse or stockroom bearing a unique identity in the ERP system.

Lock box processing - the process of making payments directly from a customer's bank account through the use of customer supplied tapes.

Log files - are files that are set up specifically for the purpose of tracking activity within an ERP system or other computer application. Log files provide traceability of events, allowing enhanced capability to troubleshoot problems.

Loss leader pricing - pricing goods and services below cost to gain market share and attract customers. ERP vendors use loss leader pricing techniques to aggressively promote their product.

Lot - a group of inventory items, usually having the same part number, that have a common characteristic, such as the manufacture date.

Lot control - a technique for assigning specific numbers to identifiable "lots" of materials for purposes of costing, tracing, or tracking.

Macro - software functionality that allows users to record a series of keystrokes and save it to a given name to be recalled again for future use. Macros can increase the speed and quality of data entry and help to speed the reformatting or updating of large number of records.

Mainframe - is a large computer and is usually used in large-scale requirements such as large companies. Mainframes are a type of centralized computing resource.

Management information system - also called MIS, is a broad term for the method of managing information. Generally, but not required, management information systems use computer resources to move, store, and process information. An ERP system can be one part to a total management information system.

Manufacturing execution system - also called MES, software and hardware system that provides functionality specific to manufacturing execution and control systems. MES systems contain planning, status, execution, and feedback functions that integrate to other functional areas of the business. Many ERP systems contain manufacturing execution and control systems

MAPI - standing for messaging application programming interface, a communication protocol that allows application programs such as spreadsheets, word processors, and ERP programs, to use email functionality.

Margin - the difference between the cost and the selling price of goods or services sold to the customer. Margin is the equivalent of profit.

Market penetration - how well a particular market has accepted a product or service. ERP vendors compete aggressively for market share. Companies often select an ERP system with wide market penetration.

Masking - the ability to use soft coding to hide particular features and functions such as menu options, icons, or data entry fields. The feature may be hidden system wide, to a group of specified users, or to a specific user.

Master file - a file that is the main source for information. Sub files or other files cannot be created until the information is first created in the master file. Customer, supplier, and part numbers can all have master files.

Matrix master - an individual who has a conglomerate of advanced capabilities in understanding ERP systems and their interrelationships with ERM systems. A matrix master is much more highly skilled than a power user in that they understand all functional areas of a business and the ERP systems that support those business processes. They can float in and out of different functional areas of the business creating change with little disruption. They have an intimate understanding of technology and seem to have ability to program the future using a variety of techniques and tools.

Megabyte - is a form of computer storage capacity that equals about one million bytes.

Memory - the electronic holding area of a computer that allows the microprocessor quick access. Memory represents RAM, random access memory, and hard disk drives, which are much slower but have higher capacities.

Menu - is a list of options that an ERP user may select. Each option, represented by an icon or text description, allows access to specific programs or additional menus.

Middleware - a broad term refers to all the software needed to support communications between clients and servers.

Milestone - an important event representing the completion of a major work task or group of work tasks. Reviews are often conducted upon the completion of a milestone.

MIS department - is the centralized function of a business that provides support and services of an organization. In ERP systems MIS departments often provide helpdesk, security setup, new users, backup, technical, and application assistance to the organization.

Mission statement - is a statement declaring the direction and objectives of a company, department, or a project. In ERP systems mission statements serve to define the scope, sequence, and completion dates of one or more major milestones. Mission statements are more effective in their administration, use, and measurement when completion dates are assigned. Mission statements are confused with vision statements. (See Vision statements.)

Mod - or modification, is the process of modifying the source code of an ERP system. Generally it is undesirable to make these modifications because of the deep integration between the functional modules of an ERP system. The more modifications that are made to an ERP system, the more costly and complex it becomes to maintain. Eventually some ERP systems must be replaced or reinstalled because they have an excessive amount of modifications done to them. A modification is any action performed in an ERP system that restricts the capability to upgrade the software or perform routine maintenance.

Model - is a representation of a product or process that provides conceptual insight in how well something might work in the real world. Models are often used in ERP systems as a method of testing new ideas or process flows for compatibility with the business process flows.

Modular system - an ERP system that can be broken down by functional area such as sales, accounting, purchasing, inventory, etc. Modular systems allow training, education, and implementation to occur in smaller chunks. Modular systems give ERP vendors more flexibility in how they can sell their systems and do licensing.

Module - is the equivalent of an ERP software function. Sometimes module is used for short instead of "functional module". Sales, purchasing, inventory, address book, etc. are all examples of modules.

MPS - standing for master production schedule, is a detailed statement containing dates and quantities for items an organization plans to manufacture. MPS is a direct input into MRP - materials requirements planning.

MRP - standing for material requirements planning, is a methodology that uses bills of material, on hand inventory, and various planning parameters in order to establish a replenishment system for manufactured and purchased items. MPS is direct input to MRP.

MRP II - Manufacturing Resource planning. The definition of MRP II as defined by the 9th edition of the APICS dictionary is: A method for the effective planning of all resources of a manufacturing company. Ideally, it addresses operational planning in units, financial planning in dollars, and has a simulation capability to answer "what if" questions. It is made up of a variety of functions, each linked together: business planning, sales and operations planning, production planning, master production scheduling, material requirements planning, capacity requirements planning, and the execution support systems for capacity and material. Output from these systems is integrated with financial reports such as the business plan, purchase commitment report, shipping budget, and inventory projection in dollars. Manufacturing resource planning is a direct outgrowth and extension of closed loop MRP.

Multicurrency - the capability of an ERP system to handle financial processing of multiple currencies of different countries. Multicurency must have special program logic and database design.

Network - or networking, refers to the process of connecting computers together. A local area network is a form of networking.

Next status - the next event that occurs in a workflow process. The next status may be hidden in the background as defined in the initial workflow setup or it may be attached to a document in forming users of the next step that will take place

Noise - data or processes in an ERP system that are inconsistent with expectations in an ERP system. ERP systems are difficult to troubleshoot when they produce noise. Excessive noise is very undesirable in that it constrains integration in an ERP system. Syn. Database noise.

Nonsignificant digits - the process of not assigning meaning to the key field used to identify an entire record in a file. When nonsignificant digits are used, the ERP system often automatically assigns the next available number to the record. The use of significant digits can help ERP users to identify characteristics of the product; however, their use can present awkward problems for ERP systems and management techniques. User-defined codes help provide the same functionality as significant digits when nonsignificant digits are used.

Numeric - representing combinations of numbers 0-9. In ERP systems, data fields are often defined as numeric, meaning that they can only accept values that are a number.

Object - are base components such as programs, subprograms, display techniques, processing techniques, and files that can be used for object oriented programming.

Object oriented programming - a method of programming that contains one or more objects combined to achieve the desired functionality. Each object represents a portion of the functionality. By combining objects, an almost infinite number of different combinations are possible, providing great flexibility. Each object may work as an independent compiled program, representing many lines of code.

Offline - performing some functional activity outside the capabilities of an ERP system. It may be done manually or by using some type of computer resource. It may be the processing of data or storage. Many times activities are performed offline to bypass the ERP system because of political, technical, resource, etc. reasons.

OLE - standing for object linking and embedding, is a technique for integrating various electronic objects from diverse applications.

Online - the process of using the functional capabilities of an ERP system. Generally it is better to perform activities on line than offline to achieve the benefits of integration and communication.

Operating system - foundation software that serves as a communication device between the hardware of the computer and the software applications that operate on that computer. Operating systems provide many important functions including input/output control, job management, file management, security, etc.

Operation sequence - sequential steps that are part of a routing that describe the flow or steps that should take place. Operation sequencing is used in workflows system wide and for specific functions within modules such as as engineering change order management, receipt routing, and manufacturing routings.

Optimization - the processing of configuring a system to achieve the best possible performance. Some ERP programs contain optimization functionality that, if set up correctly, can achieve the best theoretical performance.

Option - the choices that ERP users have available to them. It may be a menu option or a configuration setting in a program. The ability to have options is greatly extended in an ERP system through the use of softcoding.

Organizational development - the process of changing and reorganizing an organization's resources for purposes of process improvement. Positive organizational development is performed through the use of leadership performed by people known as change agents.

OSI - standing for open systems interconnection, is a communication protocol standards methodology developed by the International Standards Organization (ISO). It allows for the standardized interconnection of computers in networking equipment.

Output - the process of transferring data out of an ERP system, or more specifically, out of a program in that ERP system. ERP systems typically contain various ways to connect to a variety of output devices. Common output devices include monitors and printers.

Outsourcing - using outside suppliers to provide goods and services. Some companies outsource their MIS function, including hardware and software, to an outside service provider.

Override - the capability of a software system to bypass the default value or instruction. This can be done on a one-time exception basis or as a matter of routine. Overrides apply widely to an ERP system for vocabulary and configuration settings found in programs and databases.

Ownership - the way an ERP user or ERP team member feels about an ERP system. ERP team members with high ownership feel responsible for the performance and quality of the output of an ERP system. ERP team members with low ownership do not feel responsible for the performance or quality of an ERP system. Users with high ownership participate actively in the implementation and day-to-day activities of an ERP system.

Paperless system - a term used to describe the capability of an ERP system to operate completely without the use of paper. Although many modern ERP systems can operate without the use of paper, most companies still choose to include part of their output in paper format.

Parallel technique - a method of converting from a legacy ERP system to a new one. Using the parallel technique, the legacy system and the new ERP system are operated in parallel at the same time. When the performance of the new ERP system is considered adequate, the legacy system is then discontinued. The parallel technique can consume many resources, but provides good recovery options, lowering the risk.

Parameter - information that an ERP user provides that is used as an instruction for a command or program. The parameter is then used by a program as an instruction for a specific action.

Parent/child relationship - a hierarchical relationship that exists between records within a file, or between different files, within the same database. Parent/child relationships usually have the capability to have multiple children associated with one parent. Parent/child relationships are used throughout an ERP system.

Pareto law - a principle that states that 80% of the problems come from just 20% of the causes, indicating that many of the problems are created by a limited number of causes. Pareto charts are displayed in a graphical format that can be applied to ERP systems.

Password - a set of characters consisting of numbers or letters or some combination of both, that allow the use of a computer resource.

Payment - the reimbursement that is made to a supplier for goods or services.

Payment stub - the printed record of a payment, often attached or included with the payment, used for record keeping.

Payment terms - the technique in which the payment will be made. It may include the number of days to make the payment and specific discounts.

Personal computer - also known as PC, is a computer consisting of a keyboard, monitor, mouse, storage, CPU, multimedia capabilities, and graphical user interfaces. Personal computers are often used as "gateways" or terminals to ERP systems.

PERT - standing for program evaluation and review technique is a project planning technique that uses networks and mathematical formulas to determine a project's completion time and critical path. The critical path is of particular interest for it will determine the project's completion time. PERT planning is based on least, probable, most time for each activity. The use of PERT probabilities can estimate the completion date of an ERP implementation.

Phantom - is a part or subassembly that is manufactured but usually not stocked. Phantom logic allows bills of material to show depth and structure while still allowing an organization to take advantage of a multilevel bill of material and having the functionality and advantages of a flat bill of material.

Phased Implementation - the process of implementing or going live on, for a small number of functional modules over time rather than all at once.

Pick slip - a document, usually based upon a sales order or work order, that gives instructions to employees on where and how parts can be selected for shipment or use in manufacturing operations.

Pilot test - the process of testing a process flow in an ERP system. The pilot test represents a specific function, a module, or an entire ERP system. Pilot tests are performed before the go live of an ERP system or module to test the functional capability of the ERP system before going live. Pilot tests are part of conference room pilots.

Plan - a developed strategy for a predetermined period of time that represents an effort to create or develop characteristics for a specific environment.

Plan-do-check-action - also known as the Shewhart cycle or Deming cycle, is a quality management technique that is used for the quality improvement of products and processes. The plan-do-check-action is a four-step process that: plans an improvement, implements the plan, observes the effects, and studies the results to learn more about the process or product and how it can be improved.

Planning bill - a bill of material with parent/child relationships that works independently of bills of material for the purposes of facilitating MPS/MRP and forecasting.

Platform - is the basic computer system on which program applications can run. It consists of an operating system, coordinating programs, and a microprocessor.

Point of sale - also known as a POS, is a sales and inventory system that provides transaction capability at the point of sale. Barcoding or magnetic media recording equipment, interfacing with ERP software, is often used to increase the speed and efficiency at the point of sale. Point of sale capability is often used at retail outlets.

Policies - a documented or undocumented declaration designed to control a business process flow.

Population - represents a collection of records, data, or information in which sample information is taken for analysis.

Position - a functional job that exists within a team, department, or company.

Power - the capability of a person to schedule resources to meet an objective and exercise discipline.

Power user - or sometimes called super user, is a functional user of an ERP system who possesses considerably more knowledge about an ERP module, or the entire ERP system, than the average ERP user. Power users are usually capable of understanding the advanced features of the software, can troubleshoot complex problems, help other users, create customer reports, etc.

Preventive maintenance - ERP specific functionality that provides for the planning and execution of maintenance functions for plant and equipment. Preventive maintenance modules include schedules, work orders, and reporting systems.

Price discrimination - the process of selling the same products to different customers for different prices. The price for an ERP system can vary widely from customer to customer because of the wide variety of ways that ERP systems can be sold.

Pristine - is an untouched configured ERP system provided by the vendor for purposes of training or troubleshooting. Pristine environments allow analysts to determine if problems are related to source code, database corruption, configuration settings, or other.

Procedure manual - documented procedures that are arranged in some organized order for review and training of business process flows. In ERP systems, procedure manuals may be custom developed specifically for the company that uses the software by internal or external resources.

Process improvement - is identification and elimination of variability in processes, quality problems, and unnecessary tasks.

Product life cycle - the development stages that a product goes through from conception to end of life. The concept of product life cycles applies well to ERP systems in that it represents how ERP systems are defined, implemented, and eventually phased out.

Profile - a variety of characteristic data elements that have been assigned to a key field such as a user ID. Profiles are used throughout an ERP system. Some examples include: user profile, pricing profile, customer profile, supplier profile, etc. Profiles are different from parent/child relationships in that they are generally not hierarchical in nature.

Program - a series of computer statements that instruct the computer to do something based on some kind of compiled computer language. Programs may be interactive or batch. A program displayed through a CRT is an example of an interactive session and a print job is an example of a batch program.

Project - an organized effort to achieve a certain goal using a projected amount of resources and amount of time. Time, scope, and resources determine how an ERP project will be implemented and how long it will take. For an ERP project to be completed by a given date, all three of these should be in balance. A project is a one time job that has defined starting and ending dates, a clearly specified scope of work to be performed, a pre-defined budget, and usually a temporary team that is dissipated once the project is completed.

Project duration - the amount of time from the beginning of the project to the end of a project. Time, scope, and resources all have a direct input in determining the project duration.

Project management - the process of controlling, planning, instructing, observing, scheduling, evaluating, and organizing through the use of specific skill sets for the purpose of achieving a desired outcome. Project management is important for the successful implementation and maintenance of an ERP system.

Prompt - an action taken by a computer program for the purpose of creating a reminder or asking for additional information. The user will generally respond to the prompt and the execution of the program will continue.

Proof of concept - in an ERP system, refers to the process of testing an idea to make sure that it is realistic and feasible. Proof of concepts are used when the capabilities or limitations of the ERP software are not fully known.

Proprietary - software or hardware that is specific to a supplier or manufacturer. Proprietary systems will not work with other software or hardware systems.

Protocol - a set of formalized standards that specify how hardware and software should communicate with each other through the use of networking resources.

Prototype - a model of a product or process that is used for testing and evaluation prior to the use or implementation of that product.

Prototyping - the process of creating and testing a sample product or process for the purposes of evaluation. Through the use of adequate prototyping, considerable time and money can be saved and higher quality implementations can take place in ERP systems.

Pseudo company - a fictitious company that is used as a collection point to consolidate financial or other information.

PSW - standing for project strategy workshop; also known as IPS – implementation planning session, PPS - Project Planning Session, PPW – project planning workshop; is an early planning session between a company that has purchased an ERP system and the service provider. The PSW is designed to gain detailed understanding of how the software is going to be installed and the resources it will take. A PSW can occur before the installation of an ERP system or afterwards, during a re-implementation.

PTF - standing for program temporary fix, is a temporary modification to the source code, usually supplied by the ERP vendor or service provider, that corrects mis-functioning software.

Purchase order - a document that represents a commitment to buy from a supplier. Purchase orders serve as a centralized point for recording and performing transactions for all activity related to that purchase order.

Purge - the process of removing records or files from a database. Many ERP systems contain purging utilities within the application software to help keep the database at a manageable size.

Quantity break - the capability for the system to change prices on a sales or purchase order once a certain quantity or dollar amount has been reached. Software capable of quantity breaks can usually have several "layers" of quantity breaks for different quantities or dollar amounts.

Query - a method of obtaining data as a report or on screen display. Report writers are often based upon query tools or query principles. Queries are helpful tools in displaying information not provided for in the functionality of an ERP system.

Queue - or queuing, is the process of managing jobs on a computer. Queuing can determine how often something arrives, how it can jump ahead, and how multiple queues are managed. Queuing serves to effectively manage the critical resources of a computer.

Quotation - a response by a vendor that gives the price and conditions of sale to a potential customer for goods or services. Quotations can be documented or undocumented.

RAD - standing for rapid application development, is the process of developing products and business process flows by gathering requirements, prototyping, scheduling, and open communications within team environments. Some ERP vendors include RAD products or methodologies in their systems and services.

Random access - a method of storing records in a computer database. Random access records allow the computer to directly access the record without sorting through the file or loading it to memory.

Real time - refers to processing, updating records, and displaying information in a non-delayed fashion. Real time is associated with interactive processing.

Receipt routing - a series of steps that represents the process of a purchased part being shipped from the supplier all the way through receiving at the customer's site. Receipt routing processes allow users to view where incoming supplies are located for incorporation into the overall planning process.

Record - data fields arranged in a predetermined order that the computer can treat as one grouping of information. All the data fields connected together through a record are related because they are all part of that record.

Record lock - a situation that occurs when two or more people are competing for the right to update a record in a database. Usually the first person who accesses the record will have the authority to update the record (presuming that security allows update capability to that person). The other person or persons will be unable to update the records until the first person has completed processing it. Some ERP systems will notify the user of a record lock and others will not.

Recurring invoice - capability of an ERP system to handle the processing of invoices that become due for payment at predetermined intervals. Recurring invoices may be used for insurance, rents, payments, etc.

Redundancy - an extra resource that serves as a backup for the primary resource. Backup systems for databases and cross training for users are forms of redundancy. Redundancy in ERP systems help to improve the overall reliability.

Refresh - the process of updating a video display with the most current information. This is often done through the use of a function key. A database can also be refreshed with original data.

Relational database - a file structure system that allows programs to obtain information from more than one source. Relational databases can join together and access multiple databases, files, or tables through the use of keys.

Release level - is an identification method by a software vendor for their software system. For example, a software version may be called 6.0 and its release levels to follow would be called 6.1, 6.2, 6.3, etc.

Reliability - the likelihood that a product or service will perform as documented or expected. Reliability in ERP systems can be increased through thorough prototyping and testing.

Relieve - the process of deducting inventory from on-hand quantity after it has been consumed from one of several different methods.

Requirements definition - specification of the functional characteristics of an ERP system. It is usually done prior to the purchase of a new ERP system to help the company and ERP vendor better understand the requirements of the new system and provide functionality that matches the company's business process flows.

Requisition - an electronic document in an ERP system that serves as a notice to request a function, goods, services, employees, machine repairs, etc. Requisitions are used throughout an ERP system and are usually incorporated with workflow.

Reset - the process of transforming a program configuration setting, record, file, or database back to its original settings.

Some ERP programs contain "reset" options to change configurations back to the original supplier configurations.

Retainer - an amount of payment that is asked for in advance before the goods or services are provided. Some ERP vendors, service providers, or consultants ask for retainers before providing services or products.

Return on investment - also called ROI, is a technique for measuring the return on an investment. It is calculated by the earnings produced by the assets compared to the money invested in the asset. ROI calculations are often used in the justification of new ERP systems, and also to measure how well an ERP system has been implemented, or for implementing new or additional functionality.

Revision level - indicates the number of times that a document or record has gone through a significant change. Examples include, sales order, purchase orders, bills of materials, and part numbers.

RF device - is hardware that can communicate with an ERP system through the use of radio frequencies. RF device can provide great mobility, bringing data entry and data display capabilities directly to the place where it is needed. RF devices are often used in warehouses for inventory management.

RFI - standing for request for information, is less involving than an RFP. It is a high level questionnaire containing general questions about the ERP vendor, service provider, products, and general capabilities.

RFP - standing for request for proposal, is a series of questions given to a sales function representing an ERP system. The questions are designed to determine if the ERP system contains the necessary business functionality desired by the company.

RFPs often go by the name of RFQ standing for request for quotation.

Risk factors - anything that increases the possibility of something going wrong and interfering with the completion of milestones for the ERP project.

Routing number - number that is assigned by the United States federal reserve board to uniquely identify United States banks. It consists of two parts: a routing number and a transit number.

Safety stock - the amount of inventory kept on hand covering for any unforeseen demand.

Sales order - a document that represents a commitment to purchase from the customer. Sales orders serve as a centralized point for recording and performing transactions for all activity related to that sales order.

Same as except logic - is the capability of the software to copy and existing data structure and make changes to it at the same time. This ability can greatly reduce clerical data entry as well as reduce mistakes. Same as except logic is used in bills of material, routings, workflow, configuration management, documents, accounting structures and more.

SAR - standing for supplier action request, or more specifically in ERP vendors, software action request, is an outstanding documented issue that a software vendor or service provider is examining for purposes of finding a resolution. After filing the complaint, an ERP vendor may issue an SAR number, which will provide the means to track the issue within their communication systems.

Scalability - is the capability of software and hardware to expand for additional users, software functionality, database support, and hardware systems.

Scope - generally refers to the amount of work to be done in a project. It may define what modules and what types of functionality will be implemented in an ERP system.

Scope creep - refers to how an ERP project increases over original estimates. Scope creep can increase the implementation time if needed resources are not added accordingly. Scope creep can greatly add to the cost of an ERP implementation. Scope creep can happen because management makes a conscious decision to do so or because management is disconnected from the implementation allowing it to wander off course.

Script - (1) is a series of instruction statements for a computer program. (2) a paper or electronic document used to guide a certain process flow in an ERP system. Scripts are used in ERP software demos and developed internally by the companies or obtained through a consulting agency.

Search - the process of using special computer programs and functions to find information. For example, an ERP user may use a search window to locate a customer phone number by typing in the customer names. By searching on the customer name, the computer locates the customer record, allowing the user to obtain the customer phone number.

Server - hardware and software systems that provide computer services through the use of networking for the clients requesting them. Servers provide functions such as: database, application programs, backup, and processing capability. Servers will often contain the database for an ERP system.

Service provider - service providers focus on providing products and services directly related to ERP systems. Some services they provide include business consultation, application consulting and technical services.

Ship confirm - the process of recording a shipment of goods or services to the customer. It is a significant step in the sales cycle because it sets up accounts receivable for payment and deducts inventory.

Ship to - is the address of where shipments are sent as specified in the sales or purchase orders.

SIC - standing for standard industry classification, is a United States government classification system to identify the business environment to which a company belongs. Certain ERP vendors will target specific SIC codes in their marketing efforts.

Significant digits - the process of assigning meaning to the key field used to identify an entire record in a file. For example, a part number in an inventory item master may be created as 500-100-200. The segment 500 indicates that the product is red, 100 indicates that it is shaped like a square, and 200 indicates its weight in pounds. The use of significant digits can help ERP users to identify characteristics of the product. However, their use can present awkward problems for ERP systems and management techniques.

Simulation - the capability of the software to perform "what-if" analysis. Simulation capability can greatly extend the usefulness and functionality of an ERP system by optimizing business process flows.

Soft coded - refers to the capability of an ERP system to be flexible, which allows the ERP system to greatly increase its functionality, avoiding hard coded changes to the software. Soft coding is the opposite of hard coding.

Soft error - an error that occurs within a program that halts the data entry process or further processing. Soft errors are generally warning messages that seek the user's approval. Upon a key press, the process can be set in motion again.

Software - the operating systems and programs that instruct the computer in how to perform certain tasks.

Sold to - is the address of where the invoice is sent for the sale of goods or services indicated on a sales order.

Source code - the instructions of an ERP system that determine the functionality of the system. Source code usually consists of logical operators, conditional functions, comparison operators, and values all working together to create a specific function. Source code is usually programmed by people with specific skill sets in that programming language.

Spool file - is a job management system for print jobs that are going to be, or are in the process of being printed. Through the use of spool files, users can hold print jobs, change printers, adjust output, and set priorities.

Stakeholder - or sometimes called critical stakeholder, is a person who has a concerning interest in the successful use of an ERP system.

Standard cost - is an inventory valuation method. Standard cost can be calculated manually or through use of tools provided with the ERP system. It is based on the accumulation of costs from purchase price, labor, overhead, etc.

Standard industrial classification - also called SIC code, is a standardized classification coding system for the types of products and services that an organization provides. ERP vendors often develop and market systems specifically for targeted SIC codes.

Standardization - is a basic display and functional characteristics common throughout an ERP system. For example: the use of the F1 key will bring up a help dialog box anywhere on the system. Standardization is an important concept that greatly helps users to learn how to use different modules of an ERP system, which makes cross training more effective.

Structured query language - also called SQL, is a standardized methodology for interacting with databases. Through the use of SQL, information may be extracted and updated. Basic functions include, select, insert, update, record information, etc.

Subassembly - is usually a manufactured component that becomes a child for another parent assembly.

Subcontracted - referring to an ERP vendor, integrator, service provider, or company that uses resources outside their company to implement or maintain an ERP system.

Subfile - additional information that exists for a record on which an ERP user is inquiring. The additional information can usually be displayed upon a mouse click or a depressed function key.

Substitute - a part number or item that can be replaced with another on documents such as sales orders, purchase orders, and work orders.

Subsystem - a separate electronic operating system that can operate independently or in synchronization with the primary system.

Summary - or summary record is the total of detail records. Summary records can be viewed through video monitors or reports. Summary records are the opposite of detail records. (See Detail records.)

Super backflush - the ability to relieve inventory and labor (consume it) at specific points as defined by a routing.

Superflush - the ability to relieve inventory and labor through all levels in the bill of material down to the bill's lowest level.

Supplier - also known as a vendor, is an organization that provides goods and services to its customers.

Supplier scheduling - ERP specific functionality that defines a delivery schedule for each supplier. Suppliers receive advanced shipping notices and demand forecasts so that just in time production and delivery can take place. The ERP system can generate a supplier schedule, based on MRP output, using supplier profiles and predefined rules.

Supply chain - a general term used to describe the relationships, planning, and execution of materials from purchased components to finished goods. Supply chain management includes sales, purchasing, warehousing, distribution, and manufacturing.

Swapping - a term used specifically in equipment maintenance to describe the process of quickly exchanging a machine component for another equivalent. The process of swapping minimizes machine down time thus increasing productivity.

System - a collection of functional modules that operate together within one operating system to create the functionality of an ERP system. The word "system" is often used to describe the group of programs.

System administrator - is a person, or group of people, responsible for the administration of a system. The system administrator may be responsible for setting up security and issuing user IDs and passwords to new employees.

System integrator - a system integrator's functions are similar to a service provider between the ERP vendor(s) and the end customer. They differ slightly from service providers in that they have more of a focus on consolidating multiple software products related to ERP systems for one customer.

T1 - is known as the t-carrier system. It is a communication line used for connecting computer resources together. It is commonly used for the connection of computers on the Internet. Capacity of a t-carrier system varies depending on the level and number of channels used.

Tab stop - the next data element the cursor moves to in a data entry screen upon pressing the tab key. User definable tab stops allow the user to control the sequence of data elements to where the cursor will go when pressing the tab key.

Table - (1) represents a series of user defined codes and text descriptions that work with program functionality in validating and insuring consistent standardized data entry. These user defined codes usually represent some characteristic type of information that relates to the record to which it is attached. (2) the equivalent of a file. For some databases that combine all ERP data into one super file, it will often be broken apart into several sections called tables.

Tag count - or sometimes called physical inventory, is the process of counting all the items for a given location, such as a manufacturing plant or stockroom. Paper tags are printed from the system and each and every location is counted and verified for accuracy. Sometimes cycle counting is used in place of tag counts.

TCO - standing for total cost of ownership, is the complete consideration of how much a system will cost to implement and maintain over its entire life.

TCP/IP - is a communication protocol used to connect computers together on private networks and through the Internet. TCP/IP is used with client/server software.

Tension mechanism - a statement, person, event, or other that creates a feeling within a person that causes that person to become motivated in a positive or negative manner. Natural tension mechanisms can come from vision and mission statements.

Terabyte - is a form of computer storage capacity that equals about one thousand billion bytes.

Terminal - a device consisting of a CRT and keyboard that allows users to view, send, and receive information to a centralized computing resource. A terminal may be a PC using emulation software or it may be a dumb terminal.

Terminal identification - is the identification of a computer terminal, or other input device in an ERP system. Some ERP systems track and stamp terminal identifications to date stamps on records to provide higher levels of traceability.

Thin client - are low cost personal computers that are configured with only the essential features needed to communicate in a client/server relationship. They are designed to be managed by a centralized resource and may work off of applications stored on the server with which they communicate. Thin clients also represent low cost computers designed to hook directly to the Internet through Internet service providers.

Third party provider - is a company that provides software (and sometimes hardware) to enhance the performance or functionality of an ERP system through the use of interfaces. Third party providers supply software products such as finite scheduling, barcoding, point of sale, e-business, e-commerce, etc.

Tier - a method for rating ERP vendors in regards to their size. The classifications are tier I, tier II, tier III, and tier IIII. Different sources classify ERP vendors by different methods. Sales dollars and market share are common. Sometimes companies select ERP software by choosing one of a number of different vendors that exist in that tier.

Timecard - a record tracking system that tracks an employee's hours or the amount of time that a company spends on a particular job. Timecards are used to calculate employees' pay.

Total employee involvement - a participative process that summons employees to share responsibility in areas normally done by the management of the company.

TQM - standing for total quality management, is a series of management techniques such as teamwork, process improvement, leadership, and documentation for the purpose of creating higher quality and better performing systems. Companies and ERP vendors have traditionally been weak in applying the concepts of TQM to ERP systems.

Traceability - a characteristic that allows users of an ERP system to identify who, what, when, where, and why something happens on the system. Traceability in an ERP system is provided through the use of date stamps on the records and transaction logging. It can be a system wide characteristic or apply to a specific function such as inventory items.

Training - the process of learning the "know how". Training programs in an ERP system are tailored specifically for process flow of that company and ERP system. Training is specific and detailed. Users well trained in an ERP system will understand how to do something, but may lack the "know why". Detailed training programs often occur before go live of an ERP system to prepare for the go live. (See Education.)

Transaction - is any activity or event on an ERP system that causes a record to be created or updated in an ERP database. Some systems provide the capability to view transaction history, which provides traceability information.

Transaction history - is the electronic accumulation of transaction activity on an ERP system. Transaction history allows users to better understand activity leading up to an event. Through the use of transaction history, users can better troubleshoot and understand ERP systems. Transaction history files can take up considerable disk space.

Transfer - usually refers to the process of moving inventory from one location to another.

Turn key - when an ERP vendor or service provider takes complete responsibility for setting up and installing an ERP system for a company.

UDT - standing for user-defined table, is a table consisting of a series of user-defined codes and text descriptions. User-defined tables extend the functionality of an ERP system by creating a flexible database that can be connected to the integrity checking process of data entry programs. User-defined tables are supplied by the ERP vendor or created specifically for a particular business environment. User-defined tables are considered a form of soft coding.

Unapplied receipt - a document that is applied to the customer's account balance that has not been matched to an invoice.

Unit of measure - the method for expressing the quantity of an inventory item, such as each, boxes, pounds, etc.

Upgrade - is the process of bringing a software and/or hardware system up-to-date. Upgrades of ERP software and hardware can be complex, requiring several days to perform.

Upload - is the movement of data from a user-specific computer system to a centralized computer resource. Uploads are performed by using a variety of file transfer technologies.

UPS - standing for uninterruptible power supply, is a device that allows a computer to continue in its operations during a power failure, preventing potential data loss.

URL - standing for uniform resource locator is the address of a resource that is accessible through the Internet. An example of an URL is http://www.cibres.com

User - a user is generally a person who uses an ERP system. The total number of users is often a factor in determining the appropriate hardware configuration and size for an ERP system. ERP vendors use the total number of users for pricing ERP systems. The total number of users on a system is sometimes measured as concurrent users. Concurrent users are the number of users signed on to the system at any particular point in time.

User friendly - a descriptive term that describes the ease of use in a software package. User friendly systems are intuitive in nature and require less training and documentation. Software systems that are difficult to use are often referred to as being user-unfriendly.

User group - is a group of ERP users that, generally, function independently of ERP vendors. They are specific to an ERP system. User groups promote the successful implementation and use of a particular ERP system. They meet together on a regular basis to see presentations and share ideas and expertise. Many user groups function as non-profit organizations.

User identification - is the unique system identifier that an ERP system uses to track a user who signs onto the system. User identifications are usually predefined by the information systems administration function of a company. User identifications are most useful in tracking transactions that occur within an ERP system.

Validation - is the process a program goes through to verify the integrity of the data as it is being entered by a user through a terminal or other method. When the computer program recognizes that the input is out of specification it will halt the input process until the data is corrected or it will allow the user or process to continue after it generates an error message. Hard errors and soft errors are closely connected to the process of validation.

Value added reseller - is a business that takes an OEM product, such as a mainframe, adds an additional product, such as an ERP system and sells the complete package to the end customer.

Vanilla - (1) referring to an unfeatured product in its most basic form. (2) refers to using an ERP package without making any modifications to it.

Variable - a value that changes based on situations and conditions. Variables are used by programs to increase their functionality and flexibility. A variable can also represent something that is unknown, in an ERP system, to a user or management group.

Variable allocation - the ability to allocate and distribute expenses, adjustments, or other, to several different business units based on a variable

Variance - the difference between some known standard and another figure. Variances are used for detecting unusual cost fluctuations in purchase orders and manufacturing work orders or budgets in ERP projects.

VAT - standing for the value added tax, is a recoverable tax assessed in some countries.

Vision statement - is the statement or statements that provides the overall viewpoint and direction of an organization, department, function, or project. Vision statements are continuous and ongoing in nature. They are supported by mission statements. Vision statements are often confused with mission statements. (See Mission statements.)

Vocabulary overrides - a form of soft coding that allows specific terminology in the system to be overridden and replaced with something more appropriate, often something specific to the company using the ERP system.

Voucher - a document that is used by a company to verify that certain goods or services were received and that payment may be made.

Voucher match - the process of matching and applying payment to specific vouchers.

War room - is a physical location for the day-to-day activities of implementing an ERP system. The war room is capable of holding meetings, computer terminals, projection equipment, visual aids, and small training classes. The war room is usually dedicated to the ERP system and sometimes remains active after the implementation.

Warranty - a commitment on the part of the vendor that a certain characteristic is or will be true in the future, lasting a certain time, and providing terms and conditions for replacement of faulty products or services. (See Guarantee.)

What if analysis - the process of performing simulations to determine different outcomes based on different inputs. The process of conducting a 'what if' analysis allows companies to select one of several different business strategies that best meets their needs.

White paper - is an article, usually written by a service provider or ERP vendor, on an issue or certain product functionality. White papers differ from documentation in that they are not usually subject to the same strict formalities of formal documentation. White papers can give useful unbiased insight into product functionality and can show how to fix software bugs.

Wide area network - also called WAN, is a computer networking system that connects many computers together over a large geographic area. Sometimes wide area networks will be made up of several smaller local area networks.

Wildcard - (1) represented by the symbol (*) is a form of softcoding that allows programs to access data in specific ways. For example, using the wildcard in the phone number as 708-* in a search window could bring all the telephone codes in area code 708 exchange. (2) represents an uncertain manager or user position in an ERP project. A functional manager or critical stakeholder that shows uncertainty in supporting an ERP implementation might be considered a wildcard, meaning that the manager's support for the project could go either way and affect the outcome.

Work breakdown schedule - is a method of subdividing work into smaller increments to permit estimates of duration, resource requirements, and costs.

Work day calendar - is an electronic calendar that is used by the ERP system to determine if the organization is open on certain days so that the system can properly plan sales orders, work orders, and purchase orders.

Work in process - also known as WIP, (1) represents that some activity is being performed and awaiting completion. (2) is an inventory holding location for items awaiting alteration or assembly into a parent item.

Workbench - an exploratory summary program that allows ERP users to sort, filter, and drill down into detailed records. Workbenches are often used for the management of documents such as sales orders, purchase orders, work orders, customer invoices, etc.

Workflow - represents process flows found within an ERP system. Workflow is broken into two parts, application specific and cross functional. Workflow helps functional modules adapt to specific situations, making an ERP system more flexible. Workflow may be fully integrated into the software carrying no clear identity, or it may exist as another functional module, or both. The concept of workflow helps to build consistent stable business process flows.

Workstation - is the working area that contains workspace and a computer terminal, personal computer, or other input/output devices that interact with the ERP system.

XML - standing for extensible markup language, is a method, conceptually similar to EDI, for sharing information between computers and companies in a predefined format easily understood by computers. XML is used on the Internet.

Y2K - standing for year 2000, was a significant event in the history of ERP systems. Because many systems used source code that was created in 2 digit format (00), programs could not tell if year 00 represented 1900 or year 2000. Realizing the threat to time sensitive functions such as payroll, invoices, orders, accounting, etc. companies raced to install new ERP systems by the turn of the century.

Other CIBRES Publications (www.cibres.com)

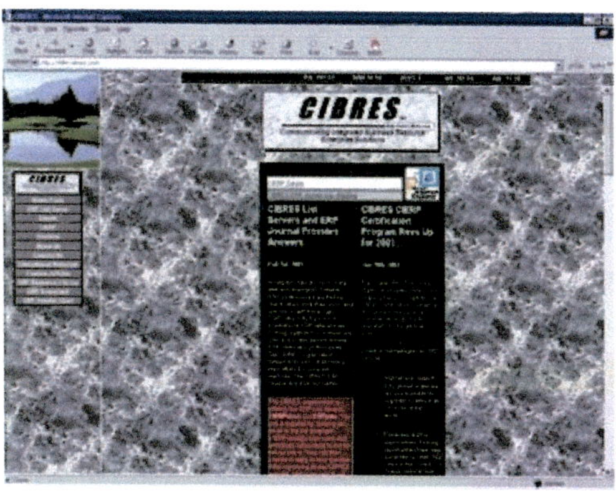

Visit the CIBRES Website for the latest publications and services of the CIBRES organization. Same day shipment on almost all educational materials, certification exam registrations, interesting articles on ERP, list servers, diagnostic tools, seminar registrations, and the latest news!

1. ERP: A-Z Implementer's Guide For Success (CIERP preparation text book). In Stock (Usually ships in 12 hours)

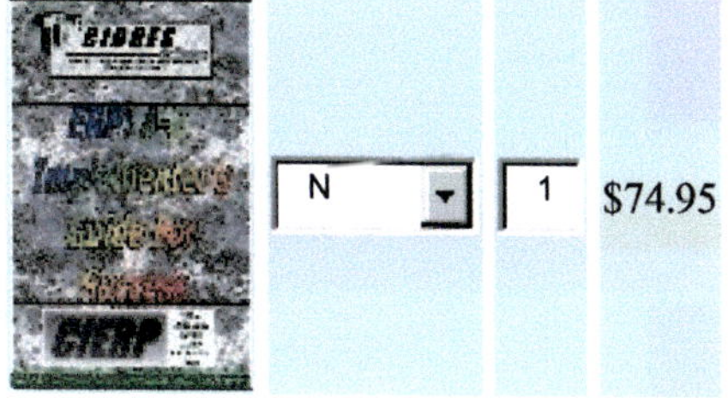

2. Basic Concepts of ERP Systems In Stock (Usually ships in 24 hours)

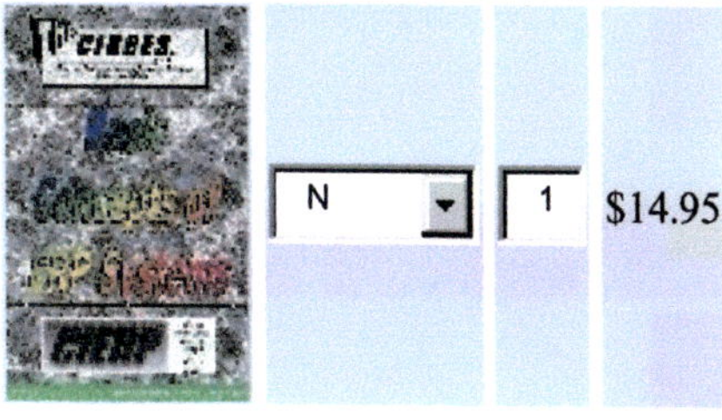

3. Life Cycles and Sequences of ERP Implementations In Stock (Usually ships in 24 hours)

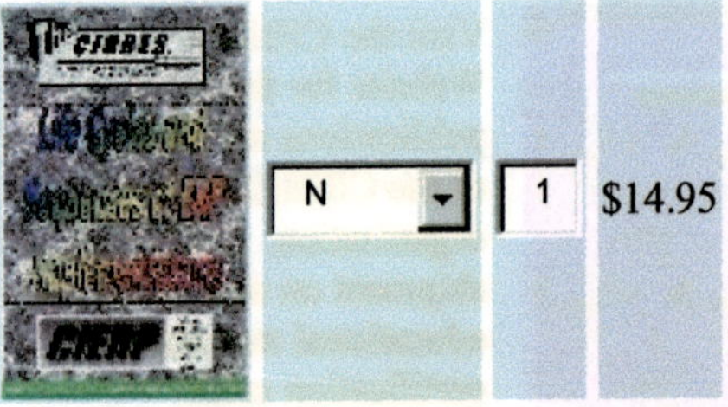

4. Teams Structures for ERP Systems In Stock (Usually ships in 24 hours)

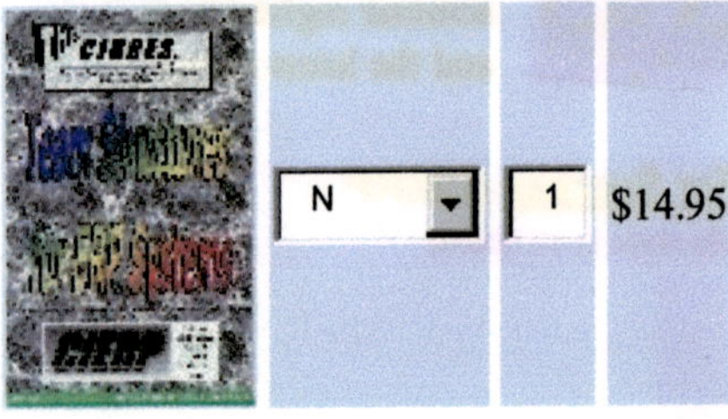

5. Transition Strategies for ERP Systems In Stock (Usually ships in 24 hours)

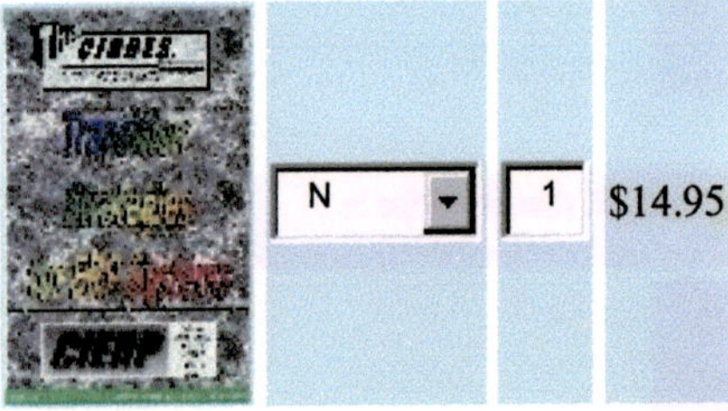

6. Data Conversions in ERP Systems In Stock (Usually ships in 24 hours)

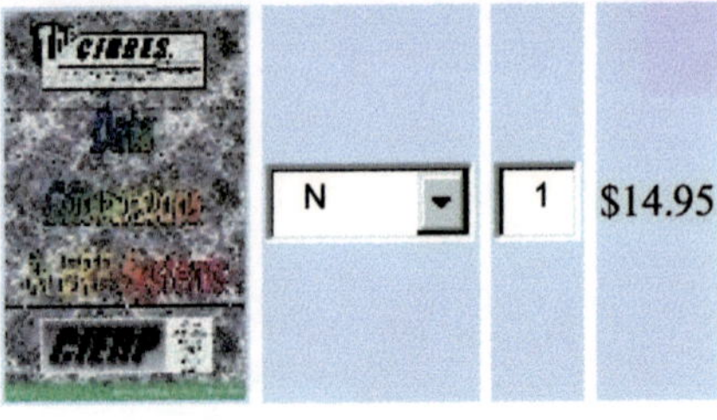

7. Prototyping and Testing for ERP Systems In Stock (Usually ships in 24 hours)

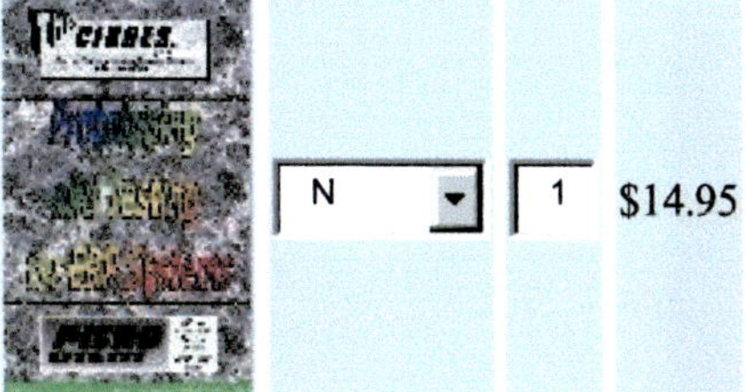

N 1 $14.95

8. Environment and Control Systems In ERP Systems In Stock (Usually ships in 24 hours)

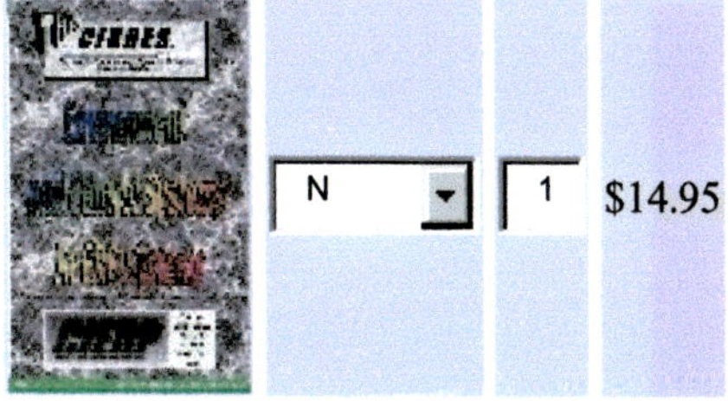

N 1 $14.95

9. Change Management Techniques for ERP Systems In Stock (Usually ships in 24 hours)

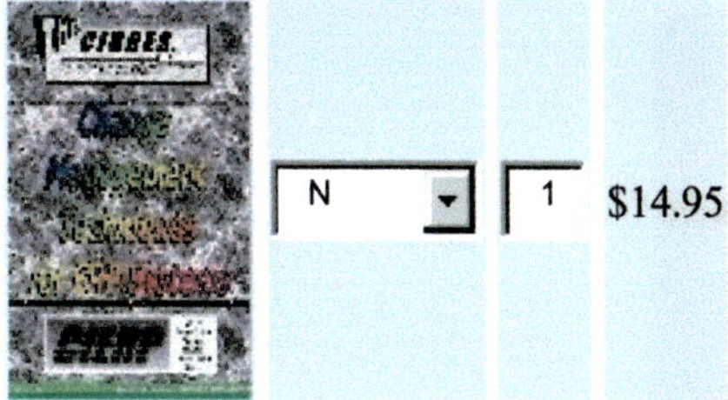

N 1 $14.95

10. How to Manage ERP Consultants In Stock (Usually ships in 24 hours)

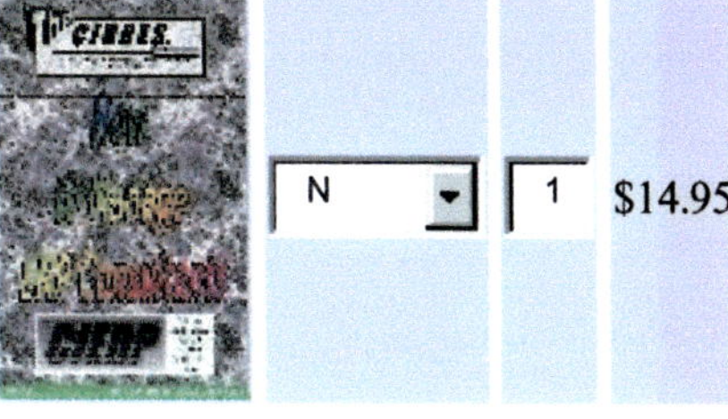

N 1 $14.95

11. How to Conduct a Project Planning Session for ERP Systems In Stock (Usually ships in 24 hours)

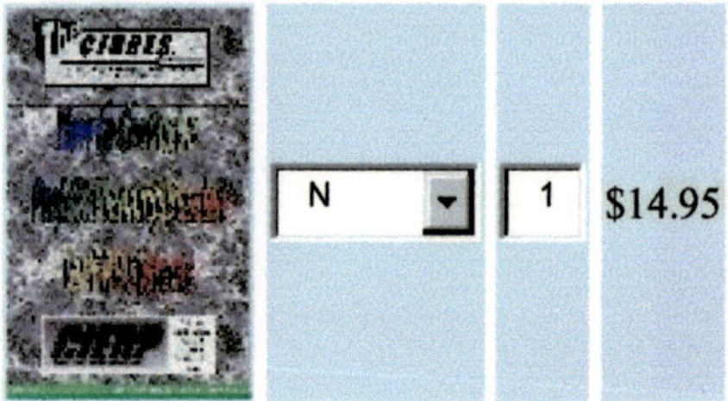

12. RFP for ERP Software Selection In Stock (Usually ships in 24 hours)

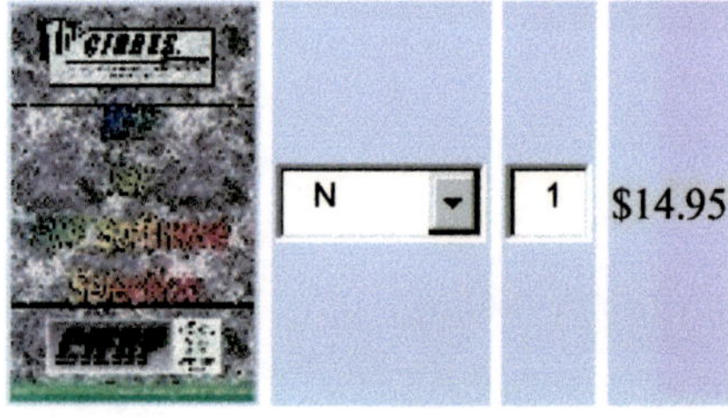

13. TQM for Successful ERP Systems In Stock (Usually ships in 24 hours)

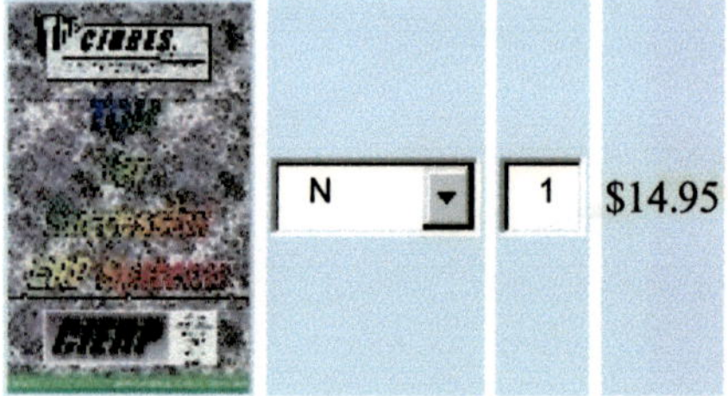

14. ROI Techniques for ERP Systems In Stock (Usually ships in 24 hours)

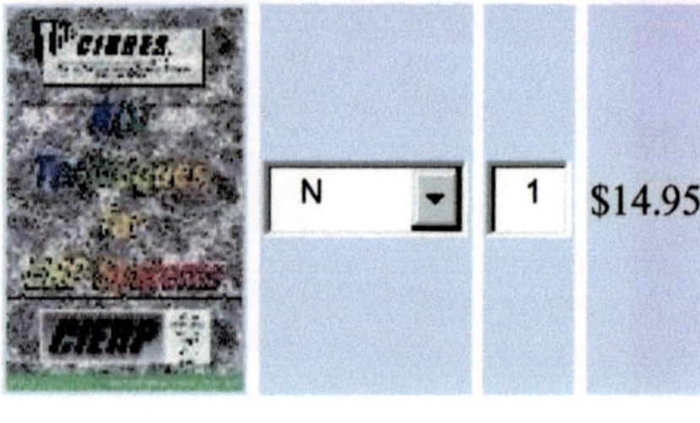

15. Integration and Relationships for ERP Systems In Stock (Usually ships in 24 hours)

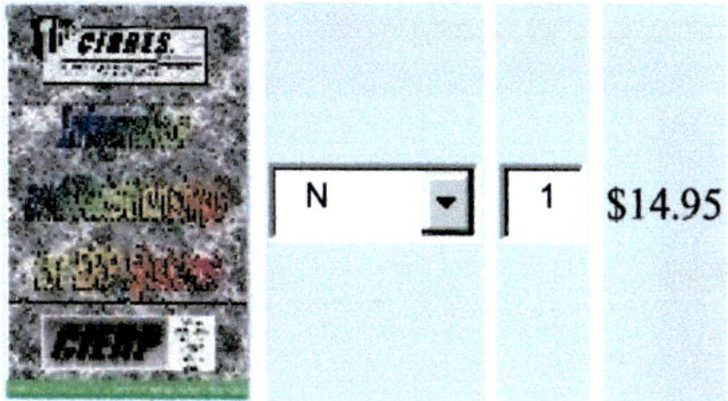

	N	1	$14.95

16. Scorecard System For World Class Enterprise Resource Management In Stock (Usually ships in 24 hours)

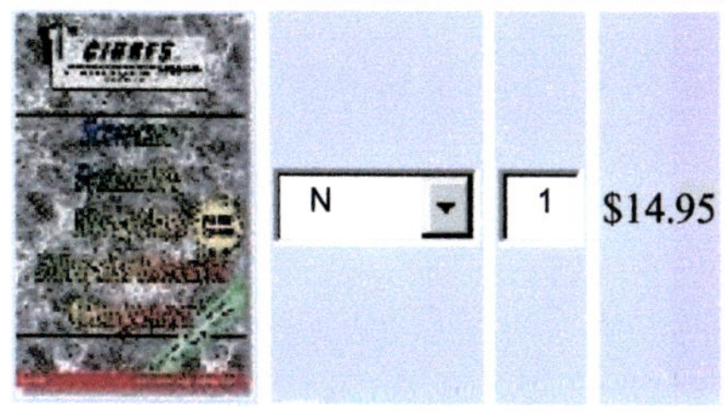

	N	1	$14.95

17. The ERP Dictionary In Stock (Usually ships in 24 hours)

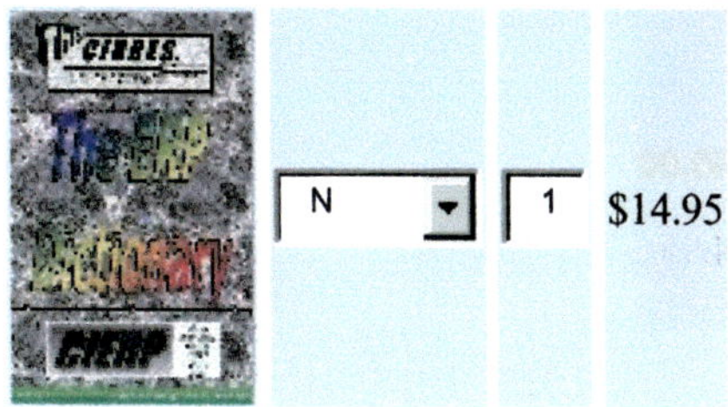

	N	1	$14.95

18. Journal Of Research Findings Of ERP Systems And Enterprise Resource Management. (Ships biannually)

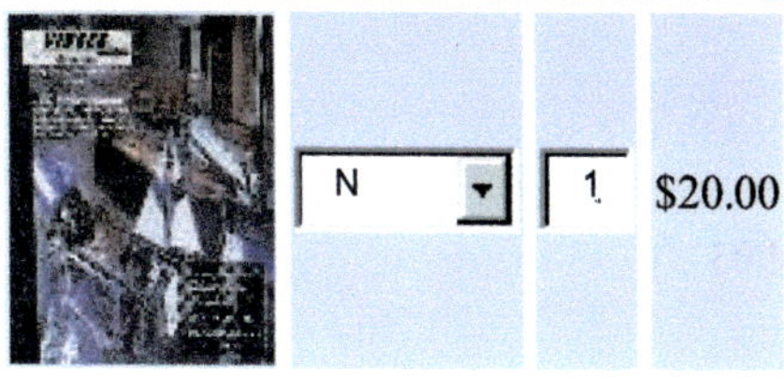

	N	1	$20.00

19. CIERP Certification Preparation Study Guide Used in CIERP certification preparation seminars and classes. In Stock (Usually ships in 24 hours)

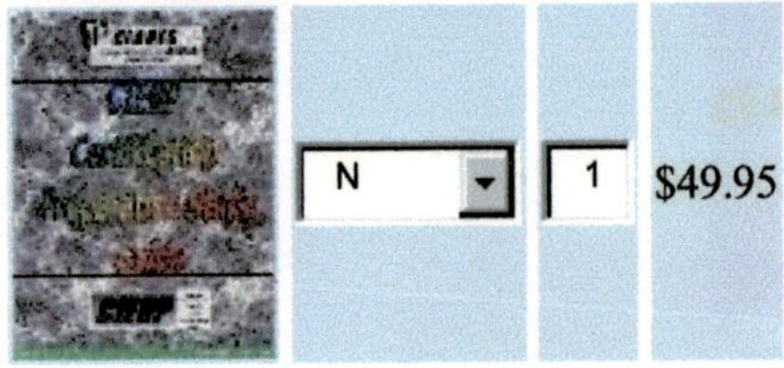

20. CIERP Sample Exam In Stock (Usually ships in 24 hours)

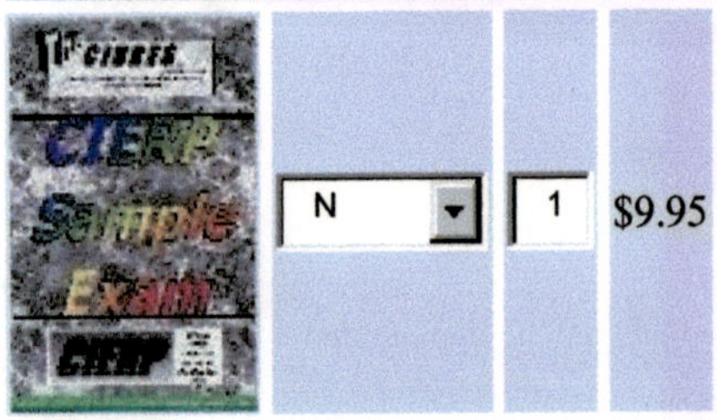

20. CIERP Certification Exam

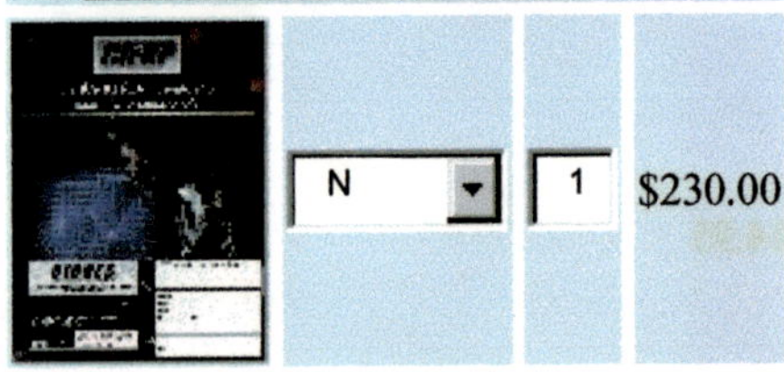